African American History
Volume II

First Edition

Edited by Robin Dearmon Muhammad
Ohio University

University Readers™
San Diego, CA

Bassim Hamadeh, CEO and Publisher
Christopher Foster, General Vice President
Michael Simpson, Vice President of Acquisitions
Jessica Knott, Managing Editor
Kevin Fahey, Cognella Marketing Manager
Jess Busch, Senior Graphic Designer
Melissa Barcomb, Acquisitions Editor
Sarah Wheeler, Senior Project Editor
Stephanie Sandler, Licensing Associate

First published in the United States of America in 2012 by University Readers, Inc.

16 15 14 13 12   1 2 3 4 5

Printed in the United States of America

ISBN: 978-1-62131-023-5 (ppk)

University Readers™
800.200.3908 | www.universityreaders.com

CONTENTS

CHAPTER 7

CHAPTER 8

CHAPTER 9

CHAPTER 10

CHAPTER 11

CHAPTER 12

INTRODUCTION

By Robin Dearmon Muhammad

During the long twentieth century, African Americans embarked on a new journey to shape the culture, politics, and economics of the United States. *African American History*, Volume II continues the story of African American creativity and industrial output. From 1880 to 1930, the black community transformed itself from a largely rural Southern community to an increasingly urban population. These fifty years represented the movement from Reconstruction to the eve of the Great Depression, and the myriad strategies employed by African Americans to challenge white backlash and to galvanize community-centered artistic, industrial, entrepreneurial, and political efforts. The period following World War II represented a dramatic series of changes: the decline of segregation laws, the rise of the civil rights movement, and the entering of black artists into the mainstream.

This volume extends the analyses initiated in *African American History*, Volume I. We will continue to focus on the historiography, methodology, and sources that cross the discipline of African American studies and related fields. This textbook can be used in one of two ways: first, the chapters are arranged in roughly chronological order, enabling the class to move through each historical period and capture related themes and topics. In the alternative, the chapter can be grouped in clusters of related themes centering on certain questions. Four broad areas of study will guide our work: (1) socio-economic class, government, and social movements; (2) art, literature, and identity; (3) education, research methodology, and politics; (4) media and critical theories.

Each chapter presents a facet of African American life during the long twentieth century, from the Gilded Age through the Age of Obama. During this period black workers underwent fundamental changes in their relation to the economy and the state. Joseph Abel's work looks at the challenges of entering the aircraft industry despite the assistance of the first federal agency in history to intervene on behalf of workers discriminated against on the basis of race, creed, religion, or national origin. Black aircraft workers forged a coalition between the locals and the FEPC against racist employers.

Krochmal expands our understanding of how African American workers in the heart of the civil rights movement—Birmingham, Alabama—forged the bulwark of civil rights unionism of the 1950s and 1960s. Using segregated locals of railroad and sanitation workers, black workers organized other workers, students, and religious leaders to raise funds and generally organized protests and protection throughout the movement.

Through our black labor studies we will focus on the point of production and the way labor struggles radiated back and forth between the factory and the neighborhood. Leisure—how and why workers use their hours and days away from work—has long been a significant theme in black labor history. Resistance through direct action and political organization is no less potent in the realm of the creation of community institutions and cultural production in the games, festivals, and public events in the black community. Scholars Richmond and Johnson take us into the leisure activity of a growing population of working-class blacks; however, this is a rarely studied group of workers—incarcerated African American, Asian, white and Latino men in the prison industrial complex. For prisoners the arena of race and politics extends to their own regulation of leisure—not limited to physical exercise—and to their attempts to define the rules of game behind bars.

A reading audience, wherever it is found, appreciates how Black novelists have historically provided an important window to the African American experience. Experimenting with new forms and reinventing folklore, Bergman finds new interpretations of the Black Mother in Pauline Hopkins' turn of the century novel, *Of One Blood*. Psychoanalysis and literary criticism allow Bergman to shed new light on the motherless child motif.

The black experience in the late nineteenth century rendered the slave-master relationship obsolete as successive generations of African Americans born in freedom struggled to reconcile the slave past with the free present. Heritage, whether found in the identity of a U.S. citizen or an African compatriot, is a key element of the diaspora.

Jackson picks up on these twin themes of universality and black distinctive in his treatment of the blues and the jazz in the African diaspora. The relationship between musicians and audience is a key frame through which to analyze the jazz and blues aesthetic.

Reflecting on how African Americans shape and make use of multiple cultural forms, scholars Inniss and Feagin delve into the impact *The Cosby Show* on black and white viewers. Middle-class aspirations for the black community are held up against an almost unobtainable image of the perfect TV family.

Religious and pedagogical practices within the black community allow us to explore how community and public institutions from the Black church to universities have been transformative in how African Americans engage social movements and how those same social movements are remembered by subsequent generations.

Since the role of the media has exploded into everyday life, is fitting to give exceptional attention with three penetrating readings. Chapters 4, 6 and 10 unravel some of the issues involving black representations in the media through film, sports and political discourses. Diawara catalogues the rites of passage and ancestral guidance in the New Black Realism in film. Sports, its history and the role African Americans played in excelling in as participants, is not a new theme, but in the hands of Hylton's application of critical race theory, the fields of competition and fair play are challenged.

Finally, this textbook intends to provide an introduction to the social policies which most affect African Americans today. Through the prism historical research and interdisciplinary methodology, we will engage a usable past for contemporary issues.

THE MOTHERLESS CHILD

IN PAULINE HOPKINS'S *OF ONE BLOOD*

By Jill A. Bergman

[T]he desire of the mother is the origin of everything (283).

> Jacques Lacan, "Antigone Between Two Deaths," 1960.

Sometimes I feel like a motherless child,
Sometimes I feel like a motherless child,
Sometimes I feel like a motherless child,
A long ways from home;
A long ways from home. (581)

> —*African American spiritual*
> *As quoted in Eric J. Sundquist,* To Wake the Nations:
> Race in the Making of American Literature

In Pauline Hopkins's final novel, *Of One Blood,* her protagonist, Reuel Briggs, is a mixed-race man passing for white. When confronted with the racial identity he has inherited from his slave mother, Reuel responds emotionally: "[A]pparently struggling for words ... [he] ... fell on his knees in a passion of sobs agonizing to witness. 'You know then ... that I am Mira's son?'" (593). By acknowledging his racial heritage and family history, Briggs reclaims his biological and national mother. This scene highlights a central theme in Hopkins's work: the restoration of the mother as a means of personal and national redemption. Hopkins anticipates Stuart Hall's delineation of a text's ability to impose "an imaginary coherence on the experience of dispersal and fragmentation, which is the history of all enforced diasporas." As Hall explains, "[B]y representing or 'figuring' Africa as the mother of these different civilizations," texts seek to "restore an imaginary fullness or plentitude, to set against the broken rubric of our past" (224–25). In *Of One Blood,* Hopkins imagines just such a restorative as she casts the African American community as motherless and counters the "broken rubric" of the African American past and present with a story of proud racial heritage and national entitlement made possible by the restoration of the national mother.

We can understand Hopkins's focus on the community's relationship to the mother more fully through the lens of psychoanalytic theory. Treating the post-Reconstruction African American community—the community to which Pauline Hopkins belonged and for whom she primarily wrote—as the subject in

Sigmund Freud's Oedipal model clarifies the position occupied by that group. In Hopkins's work, the rejected or absent mother figures as the cause of African Americans' alienation in the post-Reconstruction United States, but also, as we shall see, as a potential source of power. In what follows, I outline the trope of motherlessness as Hopkins appropriated and extended it, exploring its resonance via psychoanalytic models. I then read *Of One Blood* using these models, examining the motherlessness that signified national alienation and powerlessness and identifying how the mother is able to restore national identity and unity.

THE MOTHERLESS CHILD

Numerous scholars have detailed the nineteenth-century domestic ideology that placed mothers in an exalted position in both home and society.[1] The popular domestic novel typically placed the mother at the center of its protagonist's development, often paradoxically highlighting the importance of her presence with her absence. Motherlessness posed a significant obstacle to overcome and constituted a lack that would prompt a powerful emotional response from readers. In *Uncle Tom's Cabin,* for example, Harriet Beecher Stowe made some of her most poignant appeals to readers through characters such as young Harry, about to be torn from his adoring mother, Topsy, raised by a speculator and thus bereft of motherly guidance and love, and Eva, who learns to care for others despite the selfish neglect of her anti-mother, satirically named Marie. Stowe's strategy was far from idiosyncratic: Susan Warner's Ellen, Maria Susanna Cummins's Gerty, E. D. E. N. Southworth's Capitola, Elizabeth Stuart Phelps's Avis, and even Edith Wharton's Lily all experience the effects of motherlessness.

If this trope appealed to a white, middle-class readership in the nineteenth century United States, it may have resonated still more powerfully for African Americans, who had extensive experience with motherlessness. Slavery systematically undermined women's reproductive rights and their relationships with their children. Frederick Douglass characterizes his early separation from his mother as "a common custom," a strategy designed "to hinder the development of the child's affection toward its mother, and to blunt and destroy the natural affection of the mother for the child" (242). Harriet Jacobs depicts the mother's viewpoint, describing her excruciating separation from her children as her only route to freedom. Spirituals bemoan the loss of the mother—"Sometimes I feel like a motherless child, / A long ways from home"—and long for the comfort of her restoration—*"Oh, mother, don't you love your darling child, / Oh, rock me in the cra-dle all the day"* (Sundquist 581, 509). Nor did the end of slavery remedy pervasive motherlessness. Families separated under slavery did not easily reunite; Eric Foner notes that as late as the turn of the twentieth century, black newspapers advertised searches for missing family members (84). And, according to Kate McCullough, rape, an act of "racial terrorism" in the post-Reconstruction United States, robbed African American women of their "right to 'motherhood'" (39). In her work, then, Hopkins transforms the powerful experience of motherlessness into an image metonymically representing the pain and alienation suffered by African Americans in a racist nation.

Freud's Oedipal model of individual development does much to explain the psychological relevance of the absent mother trope. To develop properly, Freud claimed, the individual must reject its infantile attachment to and desire for the mother, choosing instead to identify with the father. Whereas in the domestic novel, the mother's absence signals an obstacle to be overcome, Freud's model makes the mother's absence (or at least her diminishment) crucial to order and harmony.[2] Building on Freud's theories, Jacques Lacan argues that during the pre-Oedipal stage, marked by the symbiotic relationship with the mother, the child perceives a unified self and a sense of plenitude deriving from it—although, Lacan insists, this sense of unity is imaginary. The father's intrusion into and prohibition of this relationship ushers the child into the social world, the Symbolic Order, which assigns social roles and dictates proper behavior in society, including the repression of both the original incestuous desire for the mother and the plenitude that the child believed to derive from that relationship. This loss elevates the mother as "the prehistoric Other that it is impossible to forget" ("On the moral law" 71). In short, "the desire of the mother," says Lacan, "is the origin of everything" ("Antigone Between Two Deaths" 283), and that desire is inextricable from loss.

As numerous scholars have recognized, psychoanalytic models do not apply exclusively to white culture. Indeed, as Hortense J. Spillers argues in her analysis of Jacobs's *Incidents in the Life of a Slave Girl,* narratives depicting "an incestuous, interracial genealogy uncover slavery in the United States as one of the richest displays of the psychoanalytic dimensions of culture before the science of European psychoanalysis takes hold" (77). I am persuaded by Claudia Tate's assertion, developed in her important study *Psychoanalysis and Black Novels,* that "psychoanalysis can tell us much about the complicated social workings of race in the United States and the representations of these workings in the literature of African Americans" (5). Following Tate's lead, then, we can recast Freud's family romance as a description of African American experience in a predominantly white, turn-of-the-century society, with the African American community as the subject, African heritage and an imagined, idealized Africa as the mother, and dominant white US culture as the father. Since, under slavery, children followed the condition of the mother, she came to represent the source of African lineage and African American culture. Writing of Jacobs, Lauren Berlant explains, "The slave mother was the 'country' into which the slave child was born, a realm unto herself whose foundational rules constituted a parody of the birthright properties of national citizenship" (559). Parody indeed. In the post-Reconstruction United States, this mother deviated profoundly from the domestically empowered antebellum ideal, and African heritage deriving from her resulted in marginalization and disempowerment. This lack of power facilitates the Oedipal crisis: Just as the child comes to understand that, lacking the phallus, the mother lacks power—an understanding that turns the child's interest to the father—the collective African American subject recognizes its disadvantaged place in American society by virtue of its connection to the mother, who stands in a marginalized position in relation to the white father. According to Freud's formulation, this recognition causes the child more readily to identify with the powerful father.

Ironically, however, identification with the father for this community is prohibited even as it is expected. The imperative to follow the condition of the mother extended well beyond emancipation: The 1896 *Plessy v. Ferguson* decision required persons with African heritage to continue identifying with the mother, an identification that barred them from full participation in white society. Vijay Mishra and Bob Hodge describe this paradox as the effect of a typical maneuver under colonialism:

> [T]here is always, in the colonial regime, a tantalizing offer of subjectivity and its withdrawal which, for the colonized, momentarily confirms their entry into the world of the colonizer only to be rejected by it. The colonized never know when the colonizers consider them for what they are, humans in full possession of a self, or merely objects. (278)

If the African American "colonized" experience a troubled relationship with the colonizer, or father, their relationship with the mother, Africa, is complicated as well. While Africa may represent a place of belonging, civic entitlement, and freedom, as a mother, Spillers argues, she is largely—or solely—metaphorical for late nineteenth-century African Americans who have inherited the systematic erasure "of the African name, of kin, of linguistic, and ritual connections" (73). Thus, the concept of mother Africa becomes an idealized, fictional image—in Freud's term, an imago, and for Lacan, the pre-Oedipal or prehistoric Other, impossible to forget. The persistent recurrence of motherlessness in the cultural productions of the African American community—and in the work of Hopkins—can be understood as the original desire for the mother. Alienated from the rights and privileges of the father of white society and unable to reclaim a mother that exists only as an ideal, the African American becomes an always motherless child, longing for the mother—Africa, African heritage—as the source of restored plenitude, a plenitude believed to have existed in an African home never seen but imagined as a place of belonging unthinkable in the United States.

HOPKINS'S PROJECT

This powerful notion of motherlessness surfaces repeatedly in Pauline Hopkins's politically charged work, where she envisions motherhood, mothers, and a feminized form of racial uplift as a means of healing her community's fragmentation and loss. Like Hall, who credits texts with the ability to address the wrongs of the past by "restor[ing] an imaginary ... plentitude" (225), Hopkins believed fiction could "raise the stigma of degradation from [her] race" by "dwell[ing] upon the history of the past, seeking there a solution" (*Contending Forces* 13,14). So it should come as no surprise that *Of One Blood* is haunted by the profound sense of loss that Lacan attributed to the Oedipal rejection of the mother and that, in answer to this loss, the novel centers around the search for and recovery of a missing mother and a proud history.

Set in the 1880s, *Of One Blood* tells the story of medical student Reuel Briggs. Although Reuel rejects his mother—a former slave—by passing for white, he is haunted by her appearance in visions and dreams, which sustain his longing for her. He has inherited his mother's mystical powers, so when Dianthe Lusk, a soprano touring with a choir of former slaves, becomes seriously injured in a train wreck, Reuel uses mesmerism to restore her to consciousness. She suffers from amnesia, however, forgetting her past as a slave and believing herself to be white. Reuel falls in love with Dianthe and, keeping her identity a secret, marries her and then joins an archeological expedition to Africa as a moneymaking venture. There, he discovers the thriving lost city of Meroe, along with evidence that Ethiopia is the true source of civilization. In Reuel's absence, his duplicitous friend, Aubrey Livingston, blackmails Dianthe into becoming his mistress. Hearing of Aubrey's betrayal and learning that he, Dianthe, and Aubrey are all siblings, Reuel returns to the United States to save Dianthe, but too late. Aubrey poisons Dianthe and takes his own life. Reuel returns to Meroe to fulfill his destiny as king.

The ethos of motherlessness marks *Of One Blood*, starting with the introduction of Reuel Briggs. A morose character, Reuel remains isolated from his fellow medical students, who find him mysterious with "apparently no relatives" (444). The key missing relative, of course, is his mother; by passing, Reuel has followed the Oedipal directive of denying his mother, Mira, along with the African heritage he inherited from her. He distances himself from his racial identity, expressing to Aubrey his "horror of discussing the woes of unfortunates, tramps, stray dogs and cats and Negroes" (449). He strives instead for identification with the father of white patriarchal society, longing for the approval of the medical men at Harvard. Upon Dianthe's arrival at the hospital, Reuel wishes to help her, but he also relishes the opportunity to impress his colleagues and superiors with his ability to "reanimat[e]" the patient whom all doctors agree is beyond hope. He brings Dianthe back to consciousness, much to the amazement of his audience. His performance has the desired effect, and word of his success spreads quickly through the white medical community. Scientific journals celebrate the "re-animation after seeming death," and "[c]lassmates who had once ignored him now sought familiar association, or else gazed upon him with awe and reverence" (472).

Aubrey undermines Reuel's success, however, by informing prospective employers of his racial identity. Thus barred from full identification with the father of white society, Reuel can find a post as doctor only on an archeological expedition to Africa. His denial of the mother, however, continues. He shares the goal of the other "capitalists" on the expedition of looting "ancient Meroe and the pyramids of Ethiopia" (507, 496), adopting the imperialistic leanings of the father evidenced in such turn-of-the-century escapades as the annexation of Hawaii, the war in Cuba, and the seizing of the Philippines from Spain. One member of the expedition speculates on the possibility of turning the African setting into a circus: "Arabs, camels, stray lions, panthers, scorpions, serpents, explorers, etc., with a few remarks by yours truly, to the accompaniment of the band … a sort of combination of Barnum and Kiralfy. … There's money in it" (514).

Reuel's Oedipal quest for the father brings about a distinct sense of loss as he persistently desires the plenitude associated with the pre-Oedipal mother, the "Other that it is impossible to forget" (Lacan, "On the Moral Law" 71). When he meets Dianthe, he feels drawn to her as that which "he had vaguely sought and yearned for all his forlorn life" (464). He misinterprets this longing as romantic love, but since Dianthe, as we later learn, is his sister, we can read his attraction to her as the desire for his mother projected onto the family he lacks. The fact that he never consummates his relationship with Dianthe, postponing their marriage until minutes before he departs for Africa, further suggests affection based not on passion but rather on familial camaraderie. Dianthe, also motherless, experiences similar feelings for Reuel. Rather than a romantic or passionate attraction for this man who has, in effect, given her life, she feels a familial attraction, like a child looking for its mother. At Reuel's declaration of love, she responds "with the sigh of a tired child [and creeps] into his arms" (492).

Reuel experiences relief from this loss only when his mother—whom we assume to be dead, although the novel remains unclear on this point—appears to him. He feels no alarm or fear at her ghostly presence. Rather, "it was as if a familiar and welcome visitor had called upon him." Indeed, her presence brings about a "dreamy ecstasy of a past time" (522). Dianthe has a similar experience. Separated from her mother at an early age, she has no memory of her and only vaguely recalls a shadowy time of close attachment. She tells Reuel, "Do you know, I sometimes dream or have waking visions of a past time in my life? But when I try to grasp the fleeting memories they leave me groping in darkness" (499). Both characters experience their mother's memory or appearance as momentary, albeit unrecognized, apprehensions of pre-Oedipal plenitude.

Mira's ghostly appearances point to the powerful potential of the pre-Oedipal mother, a figure crucial to the political agenda in this novel. A number of feminist scholars have critiqued Freud's theory, specifically his twinned assumptions that a culture must be sufficiently masculine and that this masculine culture requires rejection of the mother.[3] For scholars such as Madelon Sprengnether, "the preoedipal [sic] mother ... emerges as a figure of subversion, a threat to masculine identity as well as to patriarchal culture. Never a major figure in Freud's theory ... she has a ghostlike function, creating a presence out of absence" (5).[4] Thus, restoring the pre-Oedipal mother becomes an answer to the "father" of patriarchal society that delegitimized her and made association with her a cause for marginalization. Similarly, Hopkins's work valorizes the pre-Oedipal mother, imagining her restoration as a means to cultural healing.

In *Of One Blood,* Mira's mystical abilities effect this healing; such powers are described by the narrator of *Contending Forces* as "once the glory of the freshly imported African" (199). Mira heals her children through reestablishing their connection to her, a connection that leads to the African American community's recovery of a proud history. With Dianthe, she recalls what Hall identifies as the "broken rubric" of the horrific recent past (224–25). Dianthe's forced relationship with Aubrey replicates her slave mother's relationship with her master, uncovering what the narrator describes as "the accumulation of years of foulest wrongs heaped upon the innocent and defenceless women of a race" (594). The incestuous relationship between Aubrey and Dianthe underlines the devastating destruction of both family and community caused by motherlessness, ironically precipitating the very taboo that the Freudian prohibition of the mother seeks to avoid. As the pre-Oedipal mother, Mira ministers to Dianthe, first by telling her story and uncovering the crimes against her. Shortly after Aubrey blackmails Dianthe into a relationship with him, Mira appears to her. Like Reuel, Dianthe feels no fear at the specter, "recognizing instantly the hand of mysticism in this strange occurrence" (506). Mira points Dianthe to a biblical text as her promise: "For there is nothing covered that shall not be revealed" (506).[5]

This bleak history is, in some measure, countered by Dianthe's reestablished connection to her mother. Poisoned by Aubrey and nearing death, Dianthe sits with her maternal grandmother—an extension of her mother—who holds her and makes real the wish expressed in the spiritual "Bright Sparkles": "Mother, rock me in the cra-dle all day" (Sundquist 509). To this personal comfort, the novel adds national reparation, highlighting the grandmother's privileged position in the nation of Ethiopia. Music plays, offering "the welcome of ancient Ethiopia to her dying daughter of the royal line" (615). Dianthe's death recalls Uncle Tom's violent murder, a tragedy qualified, according to the terms of that novel, by his deliverance to heaven, the destination toward which he has been traveling throughout the story. Hopkins secularizes Stowe's vision, changing Dianthe's redemption from spiritual to national. Dianthe's death transports her not to heaven, but to the imago of Africa.

Mira restores Reuel, as well, delivering him from the despair of motherlessness and installing him as the king of Meroe. He recalls his childhood relationship with his mother and its national implications:

> The nature of the mystic within him was, then [in childhood], but a dreamlike devotion to the spirit that had swayed his ancestors; it was the shadow of Ethiopia's power. The lotus [mark] upon his breast he knew to be a birthmark [indicating his royal lineage]. Many a night he had been aroused from childhood's slumbers, to find his mother bending above him, candle in hand, muttering broken sentences of prayer to Almighty God as she examined his bosom by the candle's rays. (558)

As a child, Reuel had begun the process of suppressing his national identity to a shadowy, "dream-like" state. Nevertheless, Mira's double function—as a personal mother who watches while he sleeps and as a national mother from whom he inherits his royal lineage—remains clear to him in memory. And it is in this shadowy, pre-Oedipal realm that he most readily rediscovers his mother.

Reuel's journey to Africa and his discovery of the hidden city of Telassar—a figuration of Reuel's repressed mother—can be read as a psychically charged journey (Luciano 170–75; Rohy 220–21). His experience in the dreamlike city replicates the pre-Oedipal time in which the mother reigns. Reuel experiences a distinct sense of déjà vu as he tours the city, where "[s]hadowy images of past scenes and happenings flitted across his brain like transient reflection[s] of a past perfectly familiar to him." He explains to the prime minister, "I am surprised to find that it all seems familiar to me, as if somewhere in the past I had known just such a city as this" (551). The novel emphasizes the pre-Oedipal character of Telassar; Ethiopia having been referred to repeatedly as a mother country, Telassar exhibits a maternal quality, as demonstrated by the current reign of Queen Candace, who holds the place for the future king. Dana Luciano observes that although Meroe is ostensibly a masculine place to be ruled by a king, Candace wields considerable power. She "claim[s]" Reuel and—exhibiting a trait that has come to signify African heritage in the novel—exercises "magic influence" over him (*Of One Blood* 571, 570). Thus, as Luciano points out, "the affective and maternal power that has maintained African American survival seems to continue, as it were, undercover" (180). Significantly, Luciano also recognizes that Candace closely resembles Dianthe (178), who, we have seen, metonymically represents the mother, Mira, for Reuel and so "continues the matriarchal tradition established by" Mira and her mother, Hannah (180). Thus, this collection of women—queen, sister, mother, nation—merge in the city of Telassar.

Reuel's journey to redemption through the recovery of the mother occurs primarily in two important moments. First, in a series of conversations, the party of archaeological adventurers debate and discuss the history of the African diaspora. Here, the novel shares Frantz Fanon's condemnation of the colonial project to devalue, distort, disfigure, and destroy pre-colonial history. In response, says Fanon, colonized people rediscover and retell the history of "a beautiful and splendid era" (210). *Of One Blood* pursues this project, joining the contemporary discourse of Ethiopianism that posited Ethiopia as the source of western civilization. As Hopkins had put it in the *Colored American Magazine* just a few months before publishing the first installment of *Of One Blood*, "[W]e trace the light of civilization from Ethiopia to Egypt, to Greece, to Rome, and thence diffusing its radiance over the entire world" ("Famous Women" 130). As Reuel discusses this history with the professor leading the expedition, his interest in and loyalty to his racial community increase. Whereas earlier in the novel he had expressed his "horror of discussing the woes of unfortunates," including "Negroes" (449), here he enthusiastically participates in the discussion, speaking passionately and loyally of Ethiopia as the source of civilization (520–21). Later, as the residents of Meroe explain their history, Reuel's pride in his connection to this history swells. Still not entirely persuaded, however, Reuel continues his quest for identification with the father: While conversing with Meroe's prime minister, he wonders, "What would the professors of Harvard have said[?]" (576).

Reuel's identification with the mother is complete only when he reclaims his biological mother and owns his identity as an African American. When the secret of his identity finally comes out, Reuel has a powerful emotional reaction. The scene recalls the sentimentally charged domestic novel that made the trope of motherlessness so popular, as Reuel "[falls] on his knees in a passion of sobs agonizing to witness" (593). Everything in the novel—his sense of loss and isolation, the racism that forced him to join the African expedition, his new understanding of his maternal heritage, and his exalted role in the mother country—has prepared him for this moment. Personal and national redemption merge as Reuel's acknowledgement of his mother leads to his inauguration as king of Meroe, a tide for which he has been destined since birth. Thus, his Oedipal cycle has been completed: Having earlier sought identification with the father, by the end of the novel he "curse[s] with a mighty curse the bond that bound him to the white race of his native land" (594).

Through this story of the Ethiopian "mother country" (529), the novel enacts the project outlined by Hall of "'figuring' Africa as the mother" to counter the "broken rubric" of the past (224–25). Far from remaining a cause of marginalization, by the end of the novel, following the condition of the mother becomes a source of power and prestige. At the opening of the novel, Reuel suffers from poverty, which keeps him from his intellectual pursuits. Now, he has jewels and wealth beyond his wildest dreams. Whereas earlier he had hidden his family heritage and dreaded his expedition to "that dark and un-known country to which Fate has doomed [him]" (496), now, thanks to that same family heritage, he finds himself king of a great civilization with a proud history. By telling the story of the true source of civilization, the novel offers a glorious heritage for the African American community. The power of the pre-Oedipal mother—Africa—becomes the remedy to the motherlessness of the African American's contemporary reality.

CONCLUSION

Of One Blood does not end with unqualified optimism. The horrific past recalled by Dianthe's story points to the rape and lynching of African Americans in Hopkins's own day, issues she had taken up in her previous work. In this context, the sexually coded language used to describe Reuel's fear of "the advance of mighty nations *penetrating* the dark, mysterious forests of his native land" becomes particu-larly ominous (621; emphasis added), pointing to the persistent threat posed by the father. Nevertheless, Hopkins's keen awareness of the challenges facing the African American community did not quell her commitment to what Berlant has called the pursuit of "a post-diasporic national fantasy" (558).[6] Two years after publishing *Of One Blood*, Hanna Wallinger points out, Hopkins published *A Primer of Facts Pertaining to the Early Greatness of the African Race and the Possibility of Restoration by Its Descendants—with Epilogue*, a "treatise" that revisited the Ethiopianist theories of an exalted precolonial and pre-Oedipal history for the African race (112).[7] With this publication, she continued to tout a proj-ect that had found a voice in varying degrees throughout her oeuvre, perhaps most strongly in *Of One Blood*: the restoration of the national mother and the recovery of the glorious African past as the best remedy to the motherlessness of the African American community.

NOTES

1. See Baym 22–50; Ryan 75–117; and Tompkins 165–72.
2. See Freud, *Three Essays on the Theory of Sexuality and Civilization and Its Discontents.*

3. See *Civilization and its Discontents*, chapter 4, for Freud's assumptions about masculine culture. For some feminist responses, see Homans 12–13 and Kristeva.

4. Similarly, Julia Kristeva identifies the disruptive power of the remnants of the pre-Oedipal phase in "semiotic" language play (62), attributing to such play the possibility of undermining the symbolic order, associated with the Law of the Father (62–67).

5. See Wallinger 218–19 for a discussion of Hopkins's treatment of Christianity in this novel.

6. Berlant uses this phrase to describe the efforts of Frances E. W. Harper to "[re-imagine] … social value and civic decorum in a radically reconstructed America" (558).

7. Wallinger reprints Hopkins's *Primer of Facts* as an Appendix to her biography of Hopkins (291–314).

Works Cited

Baym, Nina. *Woman's Fiction: A Guide to Novels by and about Women in America, 1820–70*. 1978. Chicago: U of Illinois P, 1993.

Berlant, Lauren. "The Queen of America Goes to Washington City: Harriet Jacobs, Frances Harper, Anita Hill." *American Literature* 65 (1993): 549–74.

Douglass, Frederick. *Narrative of the Life of Frederick Douglass*. 1845. *Classic American Autobiographies*. Ed. William L. Andrews. New York: Mentor, 1992. 229–327.

Fanon, Frantz. *The Wretched of the Earth*. Trans. Constance Farrington. New York: Grove, 1963.

Foner, Eric. *Reconstruction: America's Unfinished Revolution, 1863–1877*. New York: Harper, 1988.

Freud, Sigmund. *Civilization and Its Discontents*. 1930. Trans. James Strachey. New York: Norton, 1961.

———. *Three Essays on the Theory of Sexuality*. 1905. *The Standard Edition of the Complete Psychological Works of Sigmund Freud*. Trans. James Strachey. Vol. 7. London: Hogarth, 1953. 24 vols.

Hall, Stuart. "Cultural Identity and Diaspora." *Identity: Community, Culture, Difference*. Ed. Jonathan Rutherford. London: Lawrence & Wishart, 1990. 222–37.

Homans, Margaret. *Bearing the Word: Language and Female Experience in Nineteenth Century Women's Writing*. Chicago: U of Chicago P, 1986.

Hopkins, Pauline. *Of One Blood. Or, the Hidden Self*. 1902–1903. *The Magazine Novels of Pauline Hopkins*. New York: Oxford UP, 1988. 439–621.

Hopkins, Pauline E. *Contending Forces: A Romance Illustrative of Negro Life North and South*. 1900. New York: Oxford UP, 1988.

———. "Famous Women of the Negro Race: Educators." *Colored American Magazine* 5 (1902): 125–30.

———. *A Primer of Facts Pertaining to the Early Greatness of the African Race and the Possibility of Restoration by Its Descendants—with Epilogue*. 1905. Wallinger 291–314.

Kristeva, Julia. *Revolution in Poetic Language*. Trans. Margaret Waller. New York: Columbia UP, 1984.

Lacan, Jacques. "Antigone Between Two Deaths." 1960. Lacan, *The Seminar* 270–83.

———. "On the Moral Law." 1959. Lacan, *The Seminar* 71–84.

———. *The Seminar of Jacques Lacan, Book VII: The Ethics of Psychoanalysis, 1959–1960*. Ed. Jacques-Alain Miller. Trans. Dennis Porter. New York: Norton, 1992.

Luciano, Dana. "Passing Shadows: Melancholic Nationality and Black Critical Publicity in Pauline E. Hopkins's *Of One Blood*." *Loss: The Politics of Mourning*. Ed. David L. Eng and David Kazanjian. Berkeley: U of California P, 2002. 148–87.

McCullough, Kate. "Slavery, Sexuality, and Genre: Pauline Hopkins and the Representation of Female Desire." *The Unruly Voice: Rediscovering Pauline Elizabeth Hopkins*. Ed. John Cullen Gruesser. Chicago: U of Illinois P, 1996. 21–49.

Mishra, Vijay, and Bob Hodge. "What is Post(-)colonialism?" *Colonial Discourse and Post-colonial Theory: A Reader*. Ed. Patrick Williams and Laura Chrisman. New York: Columbia UP, 1994. 276–90.

Rohy, Valerie. "Time Lines: Pauline Hopkins' Literary History." *American Literary Realism* 35 (2003): 212–32.

Ryan, Mary P. *Womanhood in America: From Colonial Times to the Present*. 1975. New York: New Viewpoints, 1979.

Spillers, Hortense J. "Mama's Baby, Papa's Maybe: An American Grammar Book." *Diacritics* 17.2 (1987): 65–81.

Sprengnether, Madelon. *The Spectral Mother: Freud, Feminism, and Psychoanalysis*. Ithaca: Cornell UP, 1990.

Sundquist, Eric J. *To Wake the Nations: Race in the Making of American Literature*. Cambridge: Harvard UP, 1993.

Tate, Claudia. *Psychoanalysis and Black Novels: Desire and the Protocols of Race*. New York: Oxford UP, 1998.

Tompkins, Jane. *Sensational Designs: The Cultural Work of American Fiction, 1790–1860*. New York: Oxford UP, 1985.

Wallinger, Hanna. *Pauline E. Hopkins: A Literary Biography*. Athens: U of Georgia P, 2005.

JAZZ PERFORMANCE AS RITUAL

THE BLUES AESTHETIC AND THE AFRICAN DIASPORA

By Travis A. Jackson

The African American music known as jazz generally merits little mention in discussions of the musics of the African diaspora. One could perhaps account for its absence by examining the contexts in which it has been discussed and researched. Those who have written about jazz have typically understood Western concert music—if indeed they understood any music—better than they did jazz (Gennari 1991; Gabbard 1995). Moreover, they have frequently tried to fit jazz into modernist discourses on art and aesthetics (Gioia 1988 furnishes a good example; for a critique, see Johnson 1993). Jazz's relation to other forms of African American music is minimal in their analyses (Starks 1981, 1993), surfacing only in cursory mentions of jazz's seemingly passive "mixture" of European and African elements (Gridley 1997). Indeed, jazz is separated from other African American musics to emphasize its status as art and its expansive "Americanness" at the expense of its ritual functions and seemingly less expansive *African*-Americanness. Thus, alongside musics associated with *santería, candomblé,* and *vodou,* as well as *samba, salsa,* and *konpa,* it might be seen as one of the most "European" and least "African" of all African-derived musics in the Americas.[1]

In this regard, its low level of "Africanness" is a function of the surface features of musical sound—discernible Africanisms in musical form or melodic or rhythmic patterning. As a number of commentators have argued, such an evaluative framework, freighted as it is with assumptions about what "sounds African" and what "sounds European," fails to distinguish between the expressive medium of musical sound and the conceptual bases that inform its production (Olly Wilson 1974, 1985, 1992; Reyes Schramm 1986; Logan 1984; Monson 1990; Floyd 1995). In other words, such evaluation privileges form over concept in determining the cultural meaning of a particular performance for its participants.

Still, a diaspora perspective is not without its difficulties. Gilroy (1994) pointedly raises some of the questions that complicate this view:

> How are we to think critically about artistic products and aesthetic codes which, though they may be traceable back to one distinct location, have somehow been changed either by the passage of time or by their displacement, relocation or dissemination through wider networks of communication and cultural exchange? (94)

Indeed, the scholar conducting work that tries to link the cultural practices of those in diaspora with one another or with Africans risks having her/his work dismissed as "essentialism or idealism or both"

(94). Gilroy suggests that scholars think critically about the relationships between cultural identity and performative acts:

> If ... a style, genre, or performance of music is identified as expressing the absolute essence of the group that produced it, what special analytical problems arise? What contradictions appear in the transmission and adaptation of this cultural expression by other diaspora populations and how will they be resolved? How does the hemispheric displacement and global dissemination of Black music get reflected in localised traditions of critical writing and, once the music is perceived as a world phenomenon, what value is placed upon its origins in opposition to its contingent loops and fractal trajectories? (96)

Gilroy, unfortunately, does a better job of raising such questions than he does answering them. Perhaps the strength of his writing is its theoretical suggestiveness. More than suggestive is the ethnomusicological literature that shows how these questions are being answered among diaspora populations (Mensah 1971–72; Coplan 1985; Collins 1987; Waterman 1990; Erlmann 1991; Guilbault et al. 1993).

But taking up Gilroy's challenge and focusing on practices shared by Black Atlantic populations opens up interesting avenues of inquiry, particularly the relationship of musical performance to ritual and the meanings that obtain in ritual settings. As he observes, in black diaspora cultures, records (or songs) lose privileged status as objects, becoming instead tools for creative improvisation. Thus recast, these objects become "central to the regulation of collective memory, perception and experience in the present, to the construction of community by symbolic and ritual means in dances, clubs, parties, and discos" (Gilroy 1991b: 211).

In this essay, I will explore jazz's performance rituals and the aesthetic that informs them, later posing connections to ritual and aesthetic in other Black Atlantic musics. I will begin by comparing a number of works by selected scholars interested in accounting for meanings in African American musics (Baraka 1963; Ellison 1964; Murray 1970, 1976; Levine 1977; Small 1987; Floyd 1995). The conclusions of that survey will be placed in relief against the ideas and attitudes of the individuals interviewed during fieldwork conducted in New York City in the mid-1990s. Through such a juxtaposition, I will show that one of the primary forces driving the creation and making possible the interpretation of African American musics and, in particular, jazz is concern both with the blues as an aesthetic or sensibility and with performance as a sacred, ritual act.

SCHOLARLY VIEWS OF MEANING IN AFRICAN AMERICAN MUSIC

Much of the writing and criticism of jazz prior to the early 1960s was predicated on conceptions of musical style and performance that had very little to do with how practitioners of the music thought and acted (Starks 1993:150–56). The hobbyists, discographers, critics, and historians who devoted themselves to jazz wrote from vantage points that saw it and jazz performers primarily as primitive, libidinal, rebellious, or "artistic" (for overviews, see Welburn 1987; Gioia 1988; Gennari 1991). Those writers expressing the artistic view typically concerned themselves with the culture and attitudes of musicians, but their work had its clearest analogues in the work of text-based music scholars (Gennari 1991).

Amiri Baraka's *Blues People* (1963)[2] was perhaps the first book-length study to attempt sustained theoretical argument about the relations between African American culture and African American musical forms.[3] In the book's introduction, Baraka presents his main premise: "If the music of the Negro in America, in all its permutations, is subjected to socio-anthropological as well as musical scrutiny, something about the essential nature of the Negro's existence in this country ought to be revealed, as well as something about the essential nature of this country, *i.e.*, society as a whole" (x, see also 137 and 153).[4] His concern throughout is examining the progression of social and historical forces that brought the first African captives to the colonies of North America and, through the experiences of slavery and the years following emancipation, helped transform them into African Americans with distinct worldviews and attendant cultural forms. The theoretical underpinning for Baraka's tracing of this progression is Melville Herskovits's theory of acculturation and its companion concept syncretism (Herskovits 1990).[5] In his discussion of the differing forms and styles of African American music (32–94), Baraka's view of meaning in African American music is one that sees it as purely derived from or expressive of social conditions.

He believes that one must understand the blues in order to understand jazz: "Blues is the parent of all legitimate jazz" (17). He is not merely attempting to police the boundaries of "legitimate" jazz, to see the presence or absence of the blues, however defined, as a sort of litmus test. He is asserting, additionally, that all music that would be called jazz has to negotiate and maintain a close relationship with the blues, that it must somehow trace its lineage through the blues. In that sense, he sees the development of jazz performance in terms of what Charles Keil has called an "appropriation-revitalization" process (Keil 1991:43–48)[6]: in successive waves, blues-based jazz forms are appropriated and have their blues content diluted by whites and the recording industry. In response, black musicians in each generation—such as bebop pioneers like Charlie Parker and Dizzy Gillespie or musicians from the early 1960s like John Coltrane and Ornette Coleman—find ways to revitalize the music by reaffirming the centrality of blues-based practices (225).

He intensifies his view of the relationship between blues and jazz when he glosses "jazz" as "purely instrumental blues" (71) and explains that "although jazz developed out of a kind of blues, blues in its later popular connotation came to mean *a way of playing jazz*" (71; emphasis in original). Blues, in relation to jazz, then, functions not only as a noun denoting a musical progenitor and a higher level of musical categorization, but also as one describing modifiable musical forms (8-, 12-, and 16-bar I-IV-V progressions: see Koch 1982) and an approach to playing derived from performance on such forms. One major facet of that approach was a way of adapting sounds, techniques, and concepts to the playing of jazz: "In order for the jazz musician to utilize most expressively any formal classical techniques, it is certainly necessary that these techniques be subjected to the emotional and philosophical attitudes of Afro-American music—that these techniques be used not canonized" (230, cf. Levine 1977:195–96).

While writers like Ralph Ellison would not quarrel with Baraka's insistence on the importance of the blues, they would disagree about the way in which Baraka arrived at his conclusions. In a now famous review of *Blues People,* Ellison takes issue with the statement previously quoted from Baraka's introduction: "The tremendous burden of sociology which [Baraka] would place upon this body of music is enough to give even the blues the blues" (1964:249). He is also highly critical of Baraka's facile linking of social status and racial purity with forms of musical expression, explaining that from Baraka's account,

"One would get the impression that there was a rigid correlation between color, education, income and the Negro's preference in music."

Beyond his critique of Baraka, Ellison's comments on the importance of the blues are instructive. Near the end of his review, he writes eloquently about the role that the blues and the sensibility that informs them have played in African American culture:

> The blues speak to us simultaneously of the tragic and the comic aspects of the human condition[,] and they express a profound sense of life shared by many Negro Americans precisely because their lives have combined these modes. This has been the heritage of a people who for hundreds of years could not celebrate birth or dignify death and whose need to live despite the dehumanizing pressures of slavery developed an endless capacity for laughing at their painful experiences. This is a group experience shared by many Negroes, and *any effective study of the blues would treat them first as poetry and ritual* … There are levels of time and function involved here, and the blues which might be used in one place as entertainment might be put to a ritual use in another. Bessie Smith might have been a "blues queen" to the society at large, but within the tighter Negro community where the blues were part of a total way of life, and a major expression of an attitude toward life, she was a priestess, a celebrant who affirmed the values of the group and man's ability to deal with chaos. [The] blues are not concerned with civil rights or obvious political protest; they are an art form and thus a transcendence of those conditions created within the Negro community by the denial of social justice. As such they are one of the techniques through which Negroes have survived and kept their courage. (256–57, emphasis added; cf. Ellison 1964:78–79)

What Ellison adds to Baraka's view is the notion that the blues function not only as individual expression but as part of a ritual involving words, music, and trappings of spirituality. The ritual itself crystallizes some of the most essential values of African Americans with regard to survival and daily living. Ellison is also careful to divorce his explication of the functions of the blues from one that simply equates them with protest. For him, they and the music they inspire constitute, in Albert Murray's borrowed phrase, "equipment for living."[7]

More than Baraka, Ellison delves into the nature of that ritual by exploring its larger implications. In short, each performance helps each individual performer to negotiate his or her identity vis-à-vis other musicians, the larger community, and the history of the music:

> [T]rue jazz is an art of individual assertion within and against the group. Each true jazz moment (as distinct from the uninspired commercial performance) springs from a contest in which each artist challenges all the rest; each solo flight, or improvisation, represents (like the successive canvases of a painter) a definition of his identity: as individual, as member of a collectivity and as a link in the chain of tradition. Thus because jazz finds its very life in an endless improvisation upon traditional materials, the jazzman must lose his identity even as he finds it. (1964:234)

He elaborates in another essay: "The delicate balance struck between strong individual personality and the group during those early jam sessions was a marvel of social organization. I had learned too that the end of all this discipline and technical mastery was the desire to express an affirmative way of life through [a] musical tradition and that this tradition insisted that each artist achieve his creativity within its frame. He must learn the best of the past, and add to it his personal vision" (1964:189). In this sense, each jazz performance takes on meaning through the interactions of the performers with one another and with the music's history. For Ellison, even the non-performing participant in a musical event also partakes of those interactions with history (1964:197).

Ellison's ideas about the nature of jazz performance have been extended, elaborated, and refined[8] by his younger classmate from Tuskegee Institute, Albert Murray. In a series of essays and fictional works since 1970, Murray has continually returned to the blues, using it not only as the basis for aesthetic theorization but also as a way of characterizing the nature of the American experience. For him, Ellison's writing about ritual, affirmation, and interaction with tradition are subsumed under the rubric of the blues.

In his first collection, *The Omni-Americans* (1970), Murray borrows from Constance Rourke the notion that American culture is hybrid, choosing himself to see it as a "mulatto culture" (3, 13–22, 78–85). The blues is a particular response to adversity within that mulatto culture, the response of African American people. He echoes something of Baraka's relating of sound structure to social structure when he says,

> [W]hat is represented in the music, dance, painting, sculpture, literature and architecture of a given group of people in a particular time, place, and circumstance is a conception of the essential nature and purpose of human existence itself. More specifically, an art style is the assimilation in terms of which a given community, folk, or communion of faith embodies its basic attitudes toward experience. (55)

What is different, however, is his emphasis on expression, rather than determination. Social and cultural circumstances do not so much predict or shape the forms that artistic expressions will take as they provide raw materials that might be transformed according to individual and group proclivities (cf. Gilroy 1991a:154).

For African Americans, working primarily within what he refers to as the "blues idiom," the element of "play" (cf. Hall 1992) and its potential for making existence meaningful are paramount. The blues come to constitute equipment for living through their modeling of the way in which individuals confront the difficulties they face in daily life; the most successful individuals will see the necessity of playing with the materials and situations before them as essential:

> The definitive statement of the epistemological assumptions that underlie the blues idiom may well be the colloquial title and opening declaration of one of Duke Ellington's best-known dance tunes from the mid-thirties: "It Don't Mean a Thing if It Ain't Got That Swing." In any case, when the Negro musician or dancer swings the blues, he is fulfilling the same existential requirement that determines the mission of the poet, the priest, and the medicine man. … Extemporizing in response to the exigencies of the situation in which he finds himself, he is confronting, acknowledging, and contending with the infernal absurdities and ever-impending frustrations inherent in the nature of existence *by playing with the possibilities that*

are also there. Thus does man the player become man the stylizer and by the same token the humanizer of chaos; and thus does play become ritual, ceremony, and art; and thus also does the dance-beat improvisation of experience in the blues idiom become survival technique, aesthetic equipment for living, and a central element in the dynamics of U.S. Negro lifestyle. (58; emphasis in original)

Like Baraka and Ellison, Murray is concerned with the multivalence of the blues. They work not only on the level of musical form, technique, or style, but also on the level of prevailing ethos, as an approach to dealing with the exigencies of daily life. Or put more simply, what works in the context of musical performance is extensible to the performances that are our daily interactions with other people, institutions, and situations (cf. Goffman 1959).

Murray also delves into the specific kinds of dynamics that characterize the blues-based ritual of performance. He carries out this work most exhaustively in *Stomping the Blues* (1976), a book that some individuals have referred to as one the best books ever written about jazz.[9] Blues and jazz for him are synonymous both in style and function: "[T]he fundamental function of the blues musician (also known as the jazz musician) … is not only to drive the blues away and hold them at bay at least for the time being, but also to evoke an ambiance of Dionysian revelry in the process. … [E]ven as [a performer and entertainer, he was] at the same time fulfilling a central role in a ceremony that was at once a purification rite and a celebration, the festive earthiness of which was tantamount to a fertility ritual" (17).

Murray foregrounds the amount of skill and preparation that go into performing effectively and creatively in the blues idiom:

After all, no matter how deeply moved a musician may be, whether by personal, social, or even aesthetic circumstances, he must always play notes that fulfill the requirements of the context, a feat which presupposes far more skill and taste than raw emotion. … [Such skill and taste] represent … not natural impulse but the refinement of habit, custom, and tradition become second nature, so to speak. Indeed on close inspection what was assumed to have been unpremeditated art is likely to be largely a matter of conditioned reflex, which is nothing other than the end product of discipline, or in a word, training. … That musicians whose sense of incantation and percussion was conditioned by the blues idiom in the first place are likely to handle its peculiarities with greater ease and assurance than outsiders of comparable or even superior conventional skill should surprise no one. (98; cf. Berliner 1994)

Such training is deployed in a ritual all of whose musical and performative parameters can be "refined, elaborated, extended, abstracted, and otherwise played with" (106). And the techniques through which musicians extend, elaborate, and refine those parameters can be described as "intermusical" (Monson 1994:303–7) in that their most immediate references are other musical events: "[M]uch goes to show that what musicians are always most likely to be mimicking (and sometimes extending and refining and sometimes counterstating) are the sounds of other musicians who have performed the same or similar compositions" (Murray 1976:125). Blues playing, therefore, "is not a matter of having the blues and giving direct personal release to the raw emotion brought on by suffering. It is a matter of mastering the elements of craft required by the idiom. It is a matter of idiomatic orientation and of the refinement of auditory sensibility in terms of idiomatic nuance. It is a far greater matter of convention, and hence tradition, than of impulse. It is not so much what blues musicians bring out of themselves as what they do with existing conventions" (126).

Writers following Murray in writing about African American musics have also recognized the centrality of blues in the interpretation of musical meaning. In *Black Culture and Black Consciousness* (1977), Lawrence Levine focuses on the constant interaction between the forms of music making that have been called gospel, blues, and jazz (179–85), noting that social function may be the only criterion that could definitively distinguish them from one another (186). And he sees the importance of African American music in its ability to affirm and reaffirm the values of African Americans and to reinforce their most basic conceptions of themselves (189). Drawing on the work of Charles Keil and John Szwed, he argues that African American musical performances typically have ritual significance and that, in them, musicians serve a shamanistic function—blending elements of the sacred and the secular (234–37). He contends as well that jazz partakes of the same impulses and can be described in the same terms as blues: "It is clear that for both its partisans and its detractors, jazz came to symbolize many of the very qualities we have found central to the blues" (293, cf. 238).

Christopher Small sees all of African American music as having ritual significance. The subtitle of *Music of the Common Tongue* (1987a)—*Survival and Celebration in Afro-American Music*—makes clear what the function of that ritual is for him. Understanding the role of music in ritual requires an explanation first of what music means to him. He writes that music

> *is not primarily a thing or a collection of things, but an activity in which we engage.* One might say that it is not properly a noun at all, but a verb. I define the word to include not only performing and composing, but also listening and even dancing to music; all those involved in any way in a musical performance can be thought of as musicking. (50, emphasis in original)

And by extension African American music is "an approach to the act of music making, a way of playing and responding to music" (14). The most expressive moments in or performances of music, he argues, will be those that "most subtly, comprehensively and powerfully [articulate] the relationships of our ideal society—which may or may not have any real, or even possible, existence beyond the duration of the performance" (70). It is in its capacity to articulate ideal relationships that music—from any society—has a ritual significance informed by performance practice, performance context, and the relationships between the participants in a musical event. African American music is thus configured as a ritual concerned with survival under hostile, changing conditions and with the celebration of triumphs and occasional good fortune.

Small accords a high place to the blues sensibility in these rituals: "The blues style of performance, which pervades almost the whole of the Afro-American tradition as a colour, an emotional tinge, has also given rise to a poetic and musical form, which is to say a definitive way of organizing a performance, of simplicity, clarity and seemingly infinite adaptability" (198). And through developing a blues-based sensibility, through learning to play with form, pitch, rhythm, timbre, and any of a number of other musical, interactive, and performative parameters, the performer becomes a model for how one can "play" with living, within the constraints of culture:

But while the players are free to engage in dialogue with one another, to explore, affirm and celebrate their various identities and their relationship ... they are still bound by the requirements of the idiom; there are ways in which they may respond to one another and ways in which they may not. They are caught in the ancient and creative paradox of all human social life: that relationships can be established between people only through the acceptance of some kind of common language. (302)

Moreover, he does not draw the lines between black and white performance styles so strictly within the jazz idiom. For any musician playing jazz, he suggests, the act of performance is an exploration of African American identities.

Samuel A. Floyd Jr.'s *The Power of Black Music* (1995) is an expansive attempt to mine the insights of Sterling Stuckey's *Slave Culture* (1987) and Henry Louis Gates Jr.'s *The Signifying Monkey* (1988) for African American musical scholarship. Floyd says that his book "is based on the assumption that African musical traits and cultural practices not only survived but played a major role in the development and elaboration of African American music" (5). He also asserts that he will demonstrate that

African survivals exist not merely in the sense that African-American music has the same characteristics as its African counterparts, but also that the musical *tendencies,* the mythological beliefs, assumptions, and the interpretive strategies of African Americans are the same as those that underlie the music of the African homeland, that these tendencies and beliefs continue to exist as African cultural memory, and that they continue to inform the continuity and elaboration of African-American music. (5)

He focuses much of his attention on applying Gates's concept of signifyin(g) to African American music, pointing out the ways in which African American musics signify on one another as well as other forms.

Within the world of signifyin(g) African American musical practices, he accords great importance to the blues, suggesting that "[s]ince the blues appears to be basic to most forms of black music, and since it seems to be the most prominent factor in maintaining continuity between most of them, we might think of it as the Urtrope of the tradition" (79). For jazz performance practice, he explains the importance of the blues as bedrock for bebop's experimentation and expanded harmonic conception; its more "highly syncopated, linear rhythmic complexity" and "melodic angularity"; its reemphasis on percussiveness and "ring-centered" values; and its extension of the improvising vocabulary beyond paraphrase to melodic invention based on "running changes" (138). And through performance practice, jazz becomes linked to cultural memory, signifyin(g) and ritual:

The technique, knowledge of structure and theory, and the external ideas that facilitate and support improvisation, then, must be called on to convey, in coherent and effective presentation, what emerges from cultural memory. It is this dialogical effectiveness that jazz musicians strive for as they create and recreate, state and revise, in the spontaneous manner known as improvisation; it is this Signifyin(g) revision that is at the heart of the jazz player's art; and it is this Signifyin(g) revision that debunks the notion that jazz is merely a style, not a genre, for in meeting the substantive demands of Signifyin(g) revision, it is not merely the *manner* in which attacks, releases, sustainings, tempi, and other technical-musical requirements are rendered that makes jazz. On the contrary, it is the dialogical *substance,* the content *brought to* and *created in* the experience that determines a genre. Style is a given. But as with any genre, it is the substance and its structures that make the difference—the Signifyin(g) difference—in jazz. … The similarity of the jazz improvisation event to the African dance-possession event [is] too striking and provocative to dismiss, but in the absence of a provable connection, it can only be viewed as the realization of an aspect of ritual and of cultural memory. (140–141)

Like the other writers, then, Floyd shares a preoccupation with the importance of the blues for African American music making. Moreover, he posits performance as the central arena in which the blues and African American musics make their impact. Those performances, however, cannot be interpreted solely on the basis of sound: one must be attentive to what is brought to each musical encounter and its relationship to African American culture.

The writers just surveyed can be broadly characterized as being concerned with jazz performance as a blues-based, ritual activity. In different ways, they emphasize the roles of cultural background, skill, and training, and individual and group expression. Moreover, they see the power of jazz in its ability to communicate through the practices of performers and listeners African American views of the world and ways of organizing and responding to experience. The musical performance has meaning because it assumes a metaphoric or synecdochic relationship to other aspects of African American culture: it comments on, reflects, and articulates actual and idealized visions of existence.[10] A survey of the interviews I conducted with various musicians for this project shows that similar concerns have been verbalized by musicians active on the New York scene.

Musicians' Normative Views of Jazz Performance

In their normative statements about jazz performance and jazz audiences, the musicians I interviewed reveal a number of concerns that, taken cumulatively, express a considered vision of how one has to approach the varied facets of "musicking." Those concerns can be characterized as the importance of having an individual voice; developing the ability to balance and play with a number of different musical parameters in performance; understanding the cultural foundations of the music; being able oneself to "bring something to the music"; creating music that is "open enough" to allow other musicians to bring something despite or because of what has been provided structurally or contextually; and being open for transcendence to "the next level" of performance, the spiritual level. All are important for the ability of the musician to communicate with listeners and other performers, individually and collectively. Below, I discuss each of those concerns and how they have been explained by the musicians consulted.

Perhaps the chief concern of every musician I interviewed is having an immediately distinguishable, individual sound. The word *sound* refers not only to the timbre of one's playing but also to particular usages of harmonic, rhythmic, and textural resources in performance and composition. The way in which such individual sounds are achieved varies from instrument to instrument, musician to musician, but a number of variables as well as motivated and unmotivated decisions enter into the process. For players of wind instruments, for example, the embouchure (the way in which the mouth touches the instrument), the type of mouthpiece, the manufacturer of the instrument, and the amount of air blown into it are among the factors that determine the timbral aspects of an individual's sound. Players of string instruments like the guitar write their timbral signatures through their methods of producing sound (plucking with fingers or plectra made of various materials), the size and type of strings they use, the manufacturer and materials of one's guitar of choice, as well as through one's preferred amplifier(s) and settings for equalization and electronic effects (like reverb and chorus).

Players interested in achieving such distinctive sounds play and practice diligently to determine what type of sound pleases them or expresses their particular attitude(s) toward music. Pianist Bruce Barth says that he is constantly listening to and absorbing ideas and techniques from the playing of other musicians. When he sits down to practice, however, he focuses on those ideas and techniques that seem "unique to him"—that is, most appealing to him—and tries to "amplify them and develop them" (Barth 1994). Similarly, the saxophonists interviewed tend to start their practice routines with "long tones," playing each note in a scale or in the instrument's range as long and as evenly as possible, paying attention to the way the sound exits the horn and the way the vibrations feel in their mouths.[11]

Steve Wilson (1995) explains the importance of working on individual sound in discussing his teaching methods. He notes that many students come to him wanting to know how to play "the hippest stuff on the changes"—that is, the most sophisticated material in terms of harmony and rhythm. He redirects their energies toward sound production, asking whether they could play a particular whole note in a tune the way alto saxophonist Johnny Hodges might have and hoping they will understand the skill required to produce such a sound:

> That's the litmus test. That's how you can identify Lester Young, Johnny Hodges, Coleman Hawkins, Sonny Rollins, Coltrane: *by one note.* Because they knew how to play a whole note. And, um, I remember being in college and hearing cats, some of the older cats, saying, you know, "Baby, a whole note is sure the hardest thing in the world to play." And for years I didn't understand that. Like, "Man, what are they talking about?!" And I understand that now, you know. If I can play one good note, that's it. And that's the way I try to approach my teaching. It's to really have your own sound, after all is said and done, after studying everybody. *Have your own identity,* you know.

Or as saxophonist Antonio Hart (1995) says, "If cats want to be identified, they need [their own] identities."

Having an individual sound also includes the use that a player makes of other musical resources expressed through preferences for certain kinds of harmonies, harmonic substitutions, or voicings; regular use of certain melodic phrases (sometimes formulaically); methods of constructing a solo or writing a composition; along with approaches to rhythm, texture, and interaction. A musician like Thelonious Monk, therefore, is recognizable not only for the way in which he produces each individual sound, but also for the way in which he chains those sounds together in performance or composition. Sam Newsome (1995) believes that playing in the quintet of trumpeter Terence Blanchard for three years was quite important in his own development because

[Blanchard] kinda went against like the whole trend that was, I think, that was happening around New York [in the late 1980s and early 1990s], this kind of "retrospective" approach to playing. 'Cause his whole thing was just like getting in, you know, getting in touch with yourself and just, uh, just trying to develop your *own personality* on the instrument. You know, still remaining true to the tradition, just as far as like keeping the, the, the swing element and the blues element in the playing, but not really, just not really taking everything so verbatim. 'Cause I always kinda looked at it as like, it's like I would treat, I try to treat music like a, as like I would treat a proverb [laughs]. You know, it's like you don't, you don't take it—if someone says "Don't put all of your eggs in one basket"—you don't take that literally. I mean, you kind of look at it that way musically, too. It's like if I hear someone play, like if I were to take Trane [John Coltrane], it's like if I just took, uh, the way, the *three-tonic*[12] system of Trane, it's like I, I wouldn't, I wouldn't think of playing it the way he would play it. It's like I would just use it as, um, as a *harmonic* device that he introduced. [I]t's up to the, it's up to the individual to *interpret* it any way that they want to.[13]

Newsome, like Barth in a previously cited comment, underscores the importance of taking whatever resources one gets from elsewhere and giving them a personal spin, an individual interpretation. He later amplifies his point and Wilson's previous one by asserting that one's sound should be consistent regardless of the tune serving as a vehicle for improvisation. Musicians without distinctive sounds tend to place the emphasis in the wrong place, having the attitude that

You know, if you play, I don't know, if you play "Impressions," [you should] play like Trane [John Coltrane]. And if you're playing a ballad, try to play like Ben Webster. And if you're playing "Confirmation," you know, try to play like Bird [Charlie Parker], rather than just have *one approach* which is you and just keep that.[14]

Musicians who do not possess their own sounds, who seemingly mimic the sound of other musicians, are singled out for particularly harsh criticism, sometimes referred to as "clones" who sound "just like" Miles Davis, John Coltrane, Herbie Hancock, Betty Carter, or other well-known musicians. The point of the criticism is not so much that one should be "innovative" or do something *novel* in terms of sound or approach, but that one should strive for something *different* and *distinctive*. Bruce Barth (1995), for example, stresses the importance of

saying something that's *original*. I'm not saying necessarily *ground-breaking* or *revolutionary*, but something that isn't just … like a, like a generic *rehashing* of things that you've heard before. Where you put that record on and you say, "That sounds exactly like *this*. This piano player sounds like such-and-such a player. This tune sounds like such-and-such a tune," you know.[15]

The ability to balance and deal with a number of different musical parameters in the course of performance follows from having an individual sound, for the possession of an identifiable musical persona is the product of having considered a number of approaches and synthesized them into a "concept."

Steve Wilson praised alto saxophonist Kenny Garrett precisely for his ability to play well in and adapt to the demands of a variety of contexts—from his work in traveling shows like *Sophisticated Ladies* in the early 1980s to that in groups led by Freddie Hubbard, Woody Shaw, and Miles Davis. Garrett's concept, according to Wilson, works precisely because it balances a number of different elements and approaches, but it does so in a way that identifies their usage as "Kenny Garrett's." While a student at the Berklee School of Music, Sam Newsome learned about the need for balance from pianist Donald Brown. Brown told Newsome that most musicians know more harmony than they actually need for performing. According to Newsome (1995), Brown asserted that

> "If you use *too much* [harmony], it's going to sound mechanical." 'Cause he, 'cause he always, he told me, he felt [there] wasn't enough *room* … if he wanted to be *musical* … to have too much harmony 'cause that doesn't leave much room for *melody* or, or dealing with rhythmic ideas. It doesn't leave room for, for maybe if you wanted to *develop* ideas, you know, that doesn't leave room for, for dealing with *blues,* the *blues aspect* of harmony. So I mean … there are so many *elements* that, that go into producing like a, a good, a good *solo,* that if you were to incorporate too much of *one* thing, it's, you know, it's gonna sound mechanical and unmusical.

These musicians work on being balanced in their practice routines, which, according to their performance, recording, and touring schedules, can vary considerably. Because their time is often limited—as little as a couple of hours per day, and sometimes less—they frequently apply themselves to practical problems, focusing attention on the technical demands of their instruments, on improving their abilities to hear and respond to harmonies, substitutions, and chord scales, on playing well at different tempos, and on ways of developing melodic, harmonic, or rhythmic ideas. Sometimes, those sessions involve listening to recordings of their own performances or going over difficulties they have encountered in performing. Joshua Redman (1995) says that his focus at such times is on "trying to learn tunes I don't know, play through the melodies, play them in different keys. As a general rule, I try to work on things that don't come naturally. The general concept is to stretch and grow." Both Antonio Hart (1994) and Sam Newsome (1995) speak of having notebooks full of harmonic concepts that they have not fully incorporated into their playing, concepts that will require extensive practice to internalize and make effective in performing contexts. Newsome, for example, has been interested in applying John Coltrane's three-tonic system to improvising over minor chords, while Hart, inspired by the music of Eric Dolphy, has been working out ways to apply "incorrect" harmonic substitutes and scales to harmonic progressions in improvisation—for example, superimposing a B-major scale over an F dominant-seventh chord.[16] Guitarist Peter Bernstein stressed the importance of using practice time to internalize standard forms and harmonic schemes in the jazz repertoire. But those specific materials and activities are only part of practice routines that vary depending on what a musician feels she or he has neglected, has failed to do well, or needs to improve. Those lacunae are revealed when a player feels the elements of individual style to be improperly balanced.

Mention has to be made here of another issue raised in one of Newsome's previously cited statements—where he refers to the "blues aspect of harmony." He partially defines traditional jazz playing with reference to "the blues" and rhythmic swing. In that way, he summarizes many conversations I have had with musicians and fans, most of whom considered developing the ability to play the blues or to play with blues feeling essential skills for playing jazz. The integration and mastery of such skills is precisely what allows performers such as pianist Wynton Kelly, tenor saxophonist Hank Mobley, and guitarist Grant Green to be considered important figures in the music's history from the standpoint of knowledgeable players and listeners (Rosenthal 1992; Starks 1993:149). While historians rarely mention them because they were not decidedly "innovative" in terms of their technical or harmonic conceptions, their playing is suffused with the blues sensibility via phrasing, rhythms, and pitch choices.[17] Pianist Bruce Barth (1995), for example, took Wynton Kelly and Herbie Hancock as models for learning how to "comp," partially because of their occasional and compelling use of "blues licks" and melodic phrases in place of chords.[18] And, as Newsome asserted, playing with "blues feeling" is also an essential component in performance on tunes not using one of the variants of blues form. Indeed, in the field of rhythmic, harmonic, melodic, and timbral conceptions, the blues-based conception is thought to be of integral importance in "making a connection" with audiences, in expressing a type of "soulfulness."

Joshua Redman (1995) credits his study of the playing of saxophonist Stanley Turrentine with having taught him about that soulfulness and its roots in the blues:

> I think any kind of music has its own soul, and you can have, you know, you can play from the soul in any style of music. I mean, I think that *Pat Metheny* is a very soulful player. That['s one] definition of soul. There's another definition of soul which is more of a specific kind of, has more specific stylistic connotations, you know. A certain kind of emoting. Soulfulness which is associated with the blues, you know, the blues idiom and blues expression. And under that definition, Pat Metheny wouldn't, doesn't play with that, you know, that type of soul. … That's not pejorative. Whereas someone like Stanley Turrentine to me is exemplary of that. I mean, he is just an incredibly bluesy, soulful player. … And, um, I think the thing I've gotten from him more than anything else is, you know, by listening to him I really learned a lot about playing the blues, and, and … that kind of "soul" style of tenor playing. Um, I've learned, I've learned a lot about, you know, how important the *strength* of your sound is, you know. Before you even worry about what notes, or what combination of notes, just the *power* you put into your sound and the *strength* of each attack, you know, and the way you play a note, whatever the note is. What you can do with that note, the kind of passion you can put into that note. Because, you know, if you broke down and ana … , if you broke down Stanley Turrentine's improvisations and analyzed them, you know, from a harmonic standpoint, they wouldn't be what you would call particularly complex, you know. Even some of the combinations of notes that he plays, some of the licks that he plays, are in some ways very standard. I mean, you can get those combinations out of any, you know, book on bebop. Bebop textbook. But the *way* in which he plays them, the way in which he phrases them, is *so unique* that there's no one who's, I mean, he has *such* an identifiable style. I can literally from two notes [snaps fingers] [know that it's] Stanley Turrentine.

Blues-derived playing and expression, then, become not a function of harmonic or rhythmic complexity. Neither, however, are they merely a function of simplicity. Rather, they are concerned with the projection of "strength" and "power" through the way in which one approaches whatever rhythmic,

harmonic, or timbral resources are being utilized.[19] Implicit in Redman's statement is the assumption that other participants in a musical event know such "strength" and "power" when they hear it.

To some degree, Redman's assertions are borne out by the evaluative commentary of audience members at musical events. On numerous occasions, I heard musicians, critics, and other participants disparage musicians whose playing was marked by an inability to play compellingly on blues-based compositions or with convincing blues feeling. The major criticism was that these players weren't "saying anything," that their playing was cold or mechanical. Peter Bernstein informed me in July 1994 that saxophonist Lou Donaldson, an elder musician with whom he performs frequently, refers to such musicians as "sad mother-fuckers." What is implied in Donaldson's criticism is that the blues feeling is a sine qua non in jazz performance. The balance that Donald Brown advocates, therefore, includes a blues sensibility among the parameters to be balanced. The importance of blues feeling for the evaluations made by differing participants will be illustrated later in this essay, where I note how often positive responses to performances come at those moments that are expressive via blues-derived performance practices.

To a large degree, the necessity of having an individual sound, the notion of balance, and the importance of the blues are seen as products of a larger *African American* musical or performative sensibility. Interestingly, none of the questions in my interview schedule specifically addressed issues of race or culture. Each African American musician brought issues of race into the interviews at many points,[20] and I infer the importance of African American sensibilities from non-African American musicians' frequent references to African American musics and musicians as influential and inspirational.

Peter Bernstein did so, for example, by citing as his early, nonjazz influences folk and rock singer Bob Dylan, rock and blues guitarists Jimi Hendrix and Eric Clapton, blues guitarists B.B. King and Freddie King, and the heavy rock group Led Zeppelin. With Bob Dylan as a notable exception, almost all of the musicians he named—African American or not—were heavily involved in playing blues and blues-derived musics. In discussing his jazz influences, he constructed a list consisting largely of African American musicians. His list included guitarists Wes Montgomery, Grant Green, Kenny Burrell, Joe Pass, John Abercrombie, and Pat Metheny; trumpeter Miles Davis; pianists Duke Ellington, Wynton Kelly, and Keith Jarrett; saxophonists John Coltrane, Cannonball Adderley, Wayne Shorter, and David Murray; and bassist Paul Chambers.[21]

Some musicians and some scholars argue that it is impossible to understand the music without understanding African American culture.[22] Older musicians such as Duke Ellington and Dizzy Gillespie articulated such ideas in published writings and interviews (Ellington 1939; for Gillespie's statements, see Taylor 1993:126–27), the latter lamenting the "whitewashing" of writing about jazz.[23] In stating their belief in similar principles, younger musicians frequently cite a specific historical vision that is not always put forward in educational settings. They see African American musicians as those whose contributions have been picked up and studied most extensively by other musicians.[24] That particular vision, however, is not the one they see educational institutions promulgating. As Sam Newsome (1995) says:

> I feel a lot of times with the, when you institutionalize jazz, it takes it, in a way, it takes it from the culture. And a lot of institutions don't like to deal with that. It's like I, I heard very little about jazz coming from the black culture when I was at, at Berklee. ... A lot of times you end up getting like a watered-down version of jazz, where it's like, you know, you're gonna talk some about, you know, they're like, "Well, here's Louis Armstrong and *also Bix Beiderbecke*"

And then it just goes, you know, it's like … "Here's [Charlie Parker]." Then, "Oh, okay. We also have, uh, *Lee Konitz and Paul Desmond.*" You know, it's always you have, they have to always put that, put that other like perspective on it, which in a lot of cases isn't really that necessary. I mean, it's like these, all of those players, they, they could play, but if you just really want to deal with like the, the *definitive* sound and the people who, who made like the, the real contributions to jazz, you know, I think you, you have to give credit where it's due.

Similarly, saxophonist Donald Harrison expressed disappointment when I told him of a debate that took place in a New York University classroom where I had lectured. The students passionately questioned whether jazz was "African American music" or "American music." Harrison invoked the wisdom of drummer Art Blakey, who said he did not care what the music was called as long as everyone "gave credit to the music's creators and innovators" (Fieldnotes, 12 October 1994), thus keeping the relationship between the music and African American culture in the foreground.

In the formal interviews I conducted, issues of race and culture were most frequently mentioned in response to a question about the effectiveness of jazz education.[25] Unanimously, musicians felt that jazz education was good for teaching technique and specific ways to use harmony, but noted a gap between what could be taught in a conservatory setting and what one needed to know to play the music well (cf. Ellison 1964:209). Donald Harrison, Antonio Hart, Gregory Hutchinson, Sam Newsome, James Williams, and Steve Wilson all suggested that young musicians had to engage with African American culture and be apprenticed to master musicians—the majority of whom in their estimation are African American—to be effective performers of the music. Hart (1995), for example, sought and was sought by older musicians on his arrival in New York. He has performed extensively with Nat Adderley, Slide Hampton, and Jimmy Heath. Those experiences, he believes, allowed him to tap "some of that spirit, some of that fire, of what the music is really about." Hutchinson feels that he has grown enormously as a musician through working with Betty Carter and Ray Brown, while Donald Harrison and James Williams say the same of their time with Art Blakey.[26] Even musicians from outside the United States who want to be good players on the New York scene—like pianist Jacky Terrasson—were encouraged to work with seasoned African American performers like Betty Carter and Arthur Taylor in order understand the concepts that underlie the technical demands of jazz performance.

In that sense, African Americans who have been socialized in communities that transmit values similar to those that have nurtured some of the most influential musicians have an advantage over others of whatever ethnicity or cultural background. They conceivably have less distance to travel to tap into "what the music is really about." Both Barth and Newsome expound on this idea in describing different audience responses to jazz performance. Each of them relates anecdotes comparing gigs in other countries with those in United States African American communities. Barth (1995) feels jazz has a certain "romantic appeal" for European (and some American) audiences. He contrasts their responses to performance with those of African Americans in North Philadelphia: "[Europeans] love the idea of jazz; they respect the tradition, that it's an American music, that it's a black music. And sometimes I feel that … especially like a younger audience in Europe, you won't necessarily have the kind of audience that knows the music the way [they do in Philadelphia]. Like you'll find, like you go to an audience, you play a club in Philly, and you'll … , there are a lot of people in the audience who knew McCoy [Tyner], you know. People who knew Lee Morgan and McCoy [and John Coltrane] when he lived there.

Who know the music … who have just a very close, *personal* connection with the music." And, more pointedly, Sam Newsome (1995) asserts ("N" designates Newsome's words, while "J" designates mine):

> N: I think … a black person that's … , you know, familiar with the music can relate to something that comes from the black culture on a much deeper level than someone who doesn't. I mean, it's, um, I mean, even if it's someone that's [not familiar] maybe … they can hear like the *soulful* side of soloing. It's like, uh, I don't know, I think someone black can relate to *that* on a deeper level … than someone who doesn't, doesn't really come from the culture.
> J: And, um, how can you tell?
> N: They … respond in the right places. 'Cause I remember I did this thing in Japan, and it's like they would start clapping at the most bizarre places during a solo. It's like places that were not meant to excite them [laughing]. Whereas like the, the experiences I've had with black audiences, it's like, you know, it's like where you may peak your solo at a certain place, and it's like you're … exuding like a certain amount of emotions, and it's like you can feel like you're connected. Where with someone else, you … may *not* be able to, it's more … maybe more intellectual. *Not to say that other people can't connect spiritually,* but it's, I don't think, on the same … deeper level.

Note here that Newsome is emphasizing certain forms of learned cultural knowledge that are deployed in responding to music, particularly those related to soulfulness and blues feeling that Joshua Redman described previously.

The cultural component of performing, along with having an individual identity and balancing a number of musical elements in performance, is linked to what Steve Wilson referred to as "bringing something to the music" (cf. Floyd 1995:140–41). Wilson (1995) connects the depth and variety of one's nonmusical experiences to that capacity when he explains: "The music is only what you bring to it, you know. And if your life condition is not … set, or if it, if it's not, if your life condition doesn't have a solid foundation, um, more often than not, your music won't." He continues by noting that what made a musician like Duke Ellington so important was his connection to tradition and his understanding of African American culture:

> I mean, let's take a look at tradition. What is tradition, you know? I mean, you cannot discard, uh, you cannot take out or pick and choose out of our experience what you want, you know. It's just like if you look at, if you look at the emancipation of black people in America, you can't, you can't, uh, say, "Okay, well I'll take Frederick Douglass, but I'll delete the Emancipation Proclamation," you know. That's all a part of our experience, too, you know. So, it's just … hey, man, all that comes into the music, you know. All of our experiences, music or any artistic endeavor or expression, you know, be it by word of mouth or painting or dance or whatever. All of it is there. And, and, uh, I think that that's what they were doing in the Harlem Renaissance, man. … [T]hey were taking a look at all of our experiences, and that's why Duke Ellington was such a, such a master, man. He took … all of our experiences and put 'em into his art form.[27]

Other musicians expressed similar sentiments, though all were largely silent on the processes whereby the experiences of daily life are translated into or expressed in musical performance. The silence, however, is an indicator not of the illegitimacy of the concept, but of the difficulty of verbalizing experiential and musical concepts (Feld 1994b) that are deeply felt.

The complexity of "bringing something" as a metaphor was underscored near the end of my interview with Wilson. I routinely concluded sessions with an invitation for the interviewee to raise questions that had occurred to him or her during the course of the interview but had not been asked. Wilson pointedly asked what I, as a young African American listener, brought to the music. What emerged from that question was a lengthy discussion about modes of listening, musical preferences, performing experiences, and criteria for evaluating music. I explained that I brought a set of experiences from listening to various forms of African American and African-derived musics beginning in my childhood, feeling the most contact with the work of musicians like Stevie Wonder, Marvin Gaye, Al Green, Bobby Womack, and Bob Marley. In addition, I brought a specific knowledge of jazz history and current jazz practice to each performance as well as a desire to *listen* to the kinds of interactions taking place in a performance. In the ensuing dialogue, Wilson stressed the interconnectedness of forms of African American music, the necessity of understanding tradition (see the previous quotation), and the importance of communicating with audiences. All of the other musicians felt as well that one had to bring something to the music to be able to communicate, to say something to audiences. The "something" that one brings to the music is the sum of his or her experiences—musical and nonmusical—as well as his or her individuality, musical skill, taste, and ability to empathize with other musicians.

The necessity of bringing something to the music has implications as well for the way that jazz musicians structure their compositions and performances. By necessity, jazz's musical structures have to be somewhat "open." In addition to allowing room for improvisation, they have to be the kinds of vehicles that facilitate interaction among the participants in a musical event. Guitarist Peter Bernstein (1995) discussed the alternatives he considered in preparing for the recording session for his CD *Signs of Life:*

> with *jazz,* the thing that's been hard is to, like, 'cause really when you write a jazz kind of thing, it's really about letting people bring something to it. And that's what I learned, especially doing this last record, like, keeping the tunes so, you know, someone could just look at [them and play them], and you have to have enough of yourself in the tune, but you don't want to restrict the player, the individuality of the player from coming out. 'Cause that's when … when you get a good bass player [Christian McBride] and good drummer [Gregory Hutchinson], you know, it's not about telling them what to play, having them read eighteen pages of written music because … why have them? Why not have the guy from the, from the, you know, you know, Philharmonic, you know. I mean, it's like jazz is, is individual music. It's really about, you know, it's about egos and, like, making the egos work together, but you need the ego[s], you know.

So while one of his tunes ("Minor Changes") may require that the musicians stick with notated harmonies and accents during the head, the structure on which they improvise, a minor blues progression,

is a more open structure with only the key and tempo of the performance dictated.[28] The musicians are free, after the head, to play harmonic substitutes[29] and to blur the boundaries of the form.

The ways in which bandleaders interact with sidemen are equally subject to the requirement that there be a certain amount of "space" for each musician to make a contribution. When asked about the leadership styles of bandleaders with whom they had worked, each musician said that openness and adaptability were marks of great leaders. Steve Wilson (1995) noted that individuals like Miles Davis and Duke Ellington were great precisely because they "let the personalities shape the music." About leading his own groups, Wilson says, "I have a concept about what I want to do, but I realize it's the personalities of the other players that are really going to bring it to fruition." In a sense, then, such openness is a way of dealing with the materials at hand (structure, sound, skill, personalities, performing context) and fashioning them into viable and meaningful expression. They are also a direct outgrowth of the other factors discussed thus far. Flexible frameworks for improvisation and flexible leadership strategies have the potential to work well precisely because it is expected that each musician is knowledgeable and skillful enough to fill in what is not explicitly arranged.

All of these criteria ultimately work in the service of reaching a state of transcendence, of getting to "the next level."[30] This next level has been described as being the "spiritual" level of the music, the level during which participants in the musical event are in a state akin to what psychologist Mihaly Csikszentmihaly (1982, 1988) refers to as "flow"[31] or what others might refer to as trance or possession. In those situations performance takes place seemingly on its own. Musicians speak of their being outside of themselves, of their being completely in tune with all that is going on around them musically, of instruments playing themselves. While their descriptions of being in such a state could only approximate the experience, they are clear about what conditions are necessary for them to reach that level.

Steve Wilson notes that each musician must bring to the performance all that he or she can. In other words, each musician must come to a gig or recording session prepared to play, prepared to listen, and prepared to respond to other musicians and participants. Wilson describes the drummer Ralph Peterson, very much influenced by Art Blakey, as someone who puts all of his energy into making every performance—whether it is a live gig, a recording session, or even a rehearsal—the best it possibly can be. For Peterson, the aim is putting the maximum into the music, knowing what he wants from it, and always pushing it to the edge, for that is the only way to get the maximum out of it, to tap into the music's spiritual side. Peter Bernstein (1995) learned from his study with guitarist Kevin Eubanks that one has to "be serious about music[, for e]very thing you play counts." Bernstein explained that such a feeling could equally be applied to practice and performance. Part of reaching that spiritual level, then, is coming to each musical situation prepared and ready to engage and be engaged by the process of performing with others.

Audiences are also responsible for whether the music reaches the next level. They, too, have to bring something to the performance. In addition to knowledge of the music's history and the work of individual performers, Wilson (1995) feels that they must be willing to listen attentively and to respond to musical events:

> It's kinda like ... in a sense going to church, you know, as they say, "You have to be ready to receive," you know. ... I don't even go to hear music if I'm not in the frame of mind to listen to it. I don't go just to be hanging, you know. If I'm really not in the frame of mind to go and

support my peers and really listen to what they have to say musically, I don't go because that's a disservice to them. So, uh, when I do go to hang out, I really not only go to hang out for the social part, but for that too. And I think it should be the same for the audience.

He continues by specifying the conditions necessary for musicians to get to that next level:

Once each musician can focus on the purpose at hand, and when you get the sense that each musician is focused on the purpose at hand, that will, uh, that will allow or facilitate that to happen, you know, that, that spiritual level to happen. I know particularly with bassist Buster [Smith]'s band, it was the use of space that everybody allowed, you know, and that, uh, you knew that you didn't have to, you weren't just *boxed in,* musically speaking, you know.. Once you get the sense that you are allowed to use, um, your imagination and, um, to tune in with all of the other, uh, players, then *really* that sets the stage … for, for it to really, you know, to go to another level spiritually. And we had a few of those nights when it was just., you know, it really went *beyond* what, you know, at least what I felt, um, [was] just a musical performance, you know. … Because everyone has to be in tune. Yeah. Everyone has to be *subservient* to that.

And when a musician or group of musicians reach that level, they sometimes make inexplicable strides in their playing, feel themselves carried by the flow of the music, and transported by the varied sounds and activities constituting a musical event. They frequently find themselves unable to recall exactly what happened immediately after a performance. (It is also interesting to observe the spiritually tinged language employed by Wilson, particularly his references to "receiving" and "subservience.")

As an example of what happens in such moments, I include here an excerpt from my fieldnotes for 5 September 1994. The excerpt describes a performance by saxophonist Antonio Hart, pianist Benny Green, and bassist Ed Howard at Bradley's on the night of 4 September 1994, 12:00 A.M. set:

During the second tune ["91st Miracle"], Hart … initiated some stimulating metric and rhythmic activity, most notably the superimposition of patterns in 3/8 over a 4/4 metric framework. He really got hot in this solo, getting lots of good, encouraging, sympathetic audience response. At one point, after playing some particularly intricate and long phrases that kept building in intensity, he stopped playing. What was most interesting about his stopping was that previously he had started to rock back and forth with the peaks and accents in his phrases. When he stopped playing, he continued to rock back and forth with the horn out of his mouth and with a look of intense concentration or absorption or pain or intensity (almost a pain-filled frown) on his face. After about eight seconds of rocking back and forth [without playing a note], he put the horn back into his mouth and resumed playing. I wonder what was running through his head at that moment. Did he have too much to say? Nothing to say? No way to say what he wanted to?

When I asked him about this performance in an interview in December 1994, he said the following:

I do that all the time, man. I, you know, I'm gone. When I'm playing, when the situation's right, I'm usually gone. I'm not even on Earth anymore, you know. I'm really not here. So, um, a couple of … People tell me I do that all the time. I'll stomp my feet or I'll scream, you know. 'Cause I'm like in a trance, man. I'm, I'm not there. I remember doing stuff like that probably because [there's] something saying, "Stop. Breathe. Leave some space, leave some air." So um, that's what I do. And you, you pretty much hit it on the nose, man, I just. I didn't know what to do, so I just stopped and cleared my head and tried to get my thoughts back together and tr[ied] to come back and say something 'cause I am trying to talk. You know, I'm *trying* to. It doesn't always work, man.

It's a blessing just to *play* music. … It's just a blessing, and I try to take it that way. Every day, I try to think of it that way. … It's not me that's playing. I'm just a tool that the music's coming through, the compositions are coming through, that's why when you see me going off and I'm rocking and shit, it's not me. At that particular point, I'm there, but I'm not there. The more spiritual I become—I've been laying low on that—but the more spiritual I become, the further my music is gonna go. I know that already.

Not every transcendent moment is as intense as this one, nor is every response the same. But the connection between stimulating jazz performance and feelings that are best described as spiritual becomes more apparent through this example. Hart's mention of being a tool—along with Wilson's use of the words *receive* and *subservient*—suggests that at those and similar moments, the individual's sense of self is temporarily suspended, and he or she becomes part of something else. What happens at those moments is the core of what is meaningful about jazz performance for performers and other knowledgeable participants. It is one of the major shared understandings of what jazz performance is supposed to be "about." Those shared understandings emerge from performance and the importance in it of having an individual voice, balancing a number of musical and performative parameters, understanding the cultural foundations of the music, bringing something to each performance, allowing other musicians and participants to bring something, and, in the end, being open toward moving to the next level.

TOWARD A BLUES AESTHETIC

On the basis of my survey of scholarly literature and of musicians' normative views of jazz performance—from which one can infer ways of evaluating it as well—I want to posit the existence of an integrating and encompassing aesthetic. Because of the emphasis that musicians place on blues feeling, particularly as something that must guide the use of other resources,[32] this aesthetic might be called the blues aesthetic. I use the term *aesthetic* to denote a set of shared normative and evaluative criteria. It is also used as a label for a certain "iconicity of style." As Steven Feld (1994a:131–32) writes, when a style term (in musical performance, for example) becomes a "cross-modal homology" connecting differing modes of interpersonal expression, its metaphoric force leads us to view it as "naturally real, obvious, complete, and thorough." That is, because of its versatility and applicability across modes, it takes on a force that makes it seemingly part of everything in the world. As a result, what could be considered a metaphor—like the blues[33]—becomes iconic, a symbol that stands for itself and is experienced "as feelingfully synonymous from one domain or level of image and experience to another" (Feld 1994a:132). Surveying the comments of scholars and musicians makes it clear that blues-based performance, as synonym for jazz performance, is metaphorically linked to other realms of experience: It is an ethos that informs African American visual art (Powell 1989:19–35), literature (Baker 1984; Gates 1988), and daily living (Ellison 1964; Murray 1970, 1976; Small 1987; Floyd 1995; Steve Wilson 1995), in addition to music. And in the popular imagination, blues are associated with "realness," soulfulness, honesty, and sincerity.

Other scholars have proposed the existence of a "Black Aesthetic," undergirded by analyses of African American art, literature, and music. Their concept of blackness is, as the term indicates, intimately tied to phenotypic and socially constructed notions of race.[34] Many of their pronouncements started as description but quickly became programmatic, connecting expression by genetically or visibly "black" artists and writers to a unique essence possessed by all black people and dictating the kinds of expression that would qualify existing and future works as "black" (Fuller 1971; Welburn 1971; for critiques, see Baker 1984:72–91; Jarab 1985). More recent writers have sought to maintain the spirit that originally motivated work on the black aesthetic, choosing, however, to privilege culture, learning, and practice over race. They have focused on describing an "African American aesthetic" (Starks 1993), in some ways synonymous with a blues aesthetic (Andrews 1989; Powell 1989, 1994; Baraka 1991 conflates the two). Each of these writers, however, stops short of describing a blues aesthetic. They restrict their arguments to characteristics of the blues and what must precede the formulation of that aesthetic, such as consideration of the views of African American musicians as well as poets, novelists, and painters (Starks 1993:152).

The blues aesthetic, as such, is the sum of the reflective and normative assertions that musicians have made regarding processes of performance, interaction, and evaluation. In the simplest terms, it is constituted by (learned) practices derived from and continually fed by African American musics and culture. It is not, however, racially based, nor is it "coded" in the genes of any group of individuals. Rather, it is learned through the engagement of individuals with those musics and that culture—to the degree that one could view them as separable entities—through their close attention to the practices of African Americans and those in African American musics (cf. Olly Wilson 1985, 1992).[35] Participants in musical events, using the blues aesthetic as a performative and evaluative framework (cf. Marshall 1982), place a premium on individual expression within established frames for performance (Hymes 1964; Bauman 1975; Bauman and Briggs 1990) and on equally patterned interaction with other performers and participants. Such events are oriented toward each performer "saying something" (cf. Barth 1995; Monson 1996) about how to take the materials at hand (e.g., instruments, compositions, forms, harmony, venues, musicians, listeners) and spontaneously exploit their expressive potential. This aesthetic is another manifestation of a diasporic musical trace or awareness, what composer Olly Wilson has described as an African-derived "conceptual approach" to music making (1974, 1992). Novelty is not among the primary concerns of the participant motivated by the blues aesthetic; creativity, distinctiveness, and interactivity are. These concerns manifest themselves in the ways in which performers sometimes reinforce and sometimes push against the frames that surround jazz performance.[36] Even more, the blues aesthetic is a statement of the egalitarian, enabling myth of jazz performance, a myth that says that any musician who understands and actualizes the normative criteria can be seen as a good performer. The aesthetic is the shared conceptual underpinning for

what musicians do when they perform and what performing and non-performing participants call on in evaluating performance.

There are, of course, other discourses and evaluative frameworks that can be brought to bear in the analysis of jazz. In this extended world of discourse, the blues aesthetic has a related but alternate function. While it grows out of African American culture and the interaction between participants on the jazz scene, it also uses terms and concepts derived from the discourses on Western concert music.[37] Jazz scene participants, like many other people, are aware of the ways in which the discourses surrounding classical music have historically been used by educators and critics to denigrate other musical styles, to deny their specificity and cultural significance. The musicians' knowledge of Western classical music, for example, encouraged by training at institutions like the New England Conservatory or the Berklee School of Music, surely contributes to a desire to see the music they perform recognized as being on par with classical music in terms of artistry and complexity. Indeed, their knowledge of and engagement with discourses on European "art music" help them strategically to call on those same discourses to "elevate" jazz in the eyes of its detractors. Moreover, they can strategically employ those discourses to attract audiences whose understandings of music and strivings for social and cultural capital (Bourdieu 1984) lead them to evaluate and choose music on its "artistic merit."

When musicians like Donald Harrison describe jazz by analogy to classical music, therefore, they frequently do so with a specific intent that does not contradict their belief that blues aesthetic criteria are paramount in evaluating musical performance. Harrison ended a performance at Iridium in May 1995 by thanking the audience for coming to hear his group and encouraging them to continue supporting "America's classical music" by buying recordings and going to live shows. The use of the label "America's classical music" can appeal to any of a number of social actors, regardless of their racial, ethnic, or cultural backgrounds. Those who respond to it as a positive label constitute a self-selected group, perhaps allying themselves with an "American" version of classical music that is distinct from the European one. To the degree that musicians like Harrison believe that jazz is a music on par with Western classical music, they do not see as a corollary that the music must be analyzed or understood in the same way as classical music. At other times—as in Harrison's previously related anecdote about giving credit to the music's African American "creators and innovators"—they foreground the African Americanness of the music. The choice to describe jazz as American or African American is frequently a strategic one. African American musicians, for example, can describe jazz as "American" when it is to their advantage, that is, when it serves to include the widest possible number of potential audience members or attract potential listeners. Alternately, they can emphasize its African Americanness when a focus on its supposedly universal characteristics threatens to erase what they see as its cultural roots. Non-African Americans, likewise, can use the term *America's classical music* to escape the feeling that a term like *African American music* questions their participation in or erases their contributions to jazz (cf. Monson 1996: 200–203).

Like some of their "classical" counterparts, however, either group can describe jazz in nontechnical, nonacademic terms without mentioning (African American) culture for other strategic reasons. In such situations, they are arguing for separating jazz from an overly cold and analytical paradigm that seems concerned only with harmony, melody, rhythm, and other notable aspects of performance. In that case, they are moving closer to a classical notion of "transcendence." Joshua Redman's liner notes from his 1994 recording *Mood Swing* are instructive here:

Jazz is music. And great jazz, like all great music, attains its value not through intellectual complexity, but through emotional expressivity. True, jazz is a particularly intricate, refined, and rigorous art form. Jazz musicians must amass a vast body of idiomatic knowledge and cultivate an acute artistic imagination if they wish to become accomplished creative improvisers. Moreover, a familiarity with jazz history and theory will undoubtedly enhance a listener's appreciation of the actual aesthetics. Yes, jazz *is* intelligent music. Nevertheless, extensive as they might seem, the intellectual aspects of jazz are ultimately only means to its emotional ends. Technique, theory, and analysis are not, and should never be considered, ends in themselves.

Jazz is not about flat fives or sharp nines, or metric subdivisions, or substitute chord changes. Jazz is about feeling, communication, honesty, and soul. Jazz is not supposed to boggle the mind. Jazz is meant to enrich the spirit.

All the key words are there: "all great music," "refined," "art." Redman is at great pains to indicate the ways in which those descriptors apply to jazz, even as he wants to distinguish their use with regard to jazz from that with classical music. Classical music aficionados may make similar claims about the disservice analysis does to music, but Redman's assertions proceed differently from those that see the musical experience as communicative or expressive in and of itself (see Kivy 1990). His attempt to de-emphasize the intellectualism of musical response foregrounds notions of communication, soulfulness, and expressivity. But those terms are to be understood via their connection with the blues aesthetic and the way in which notions like soulfulness and communication are configured within it. Redman *learned* about that soulfulness from listening to Stanley Turrentine (as well as Stevie Wonder, Otis Redding, and Aretha Franklin) and from working with master musicians.

The foundations of the blues aesthetic are found in various domains of activity: in African American musical practices, in African American religious worship, and in other aspects of African American culture. Musicians and other scene participants become acquainted with the aesthetic through their engagement with and understanding of African American musics and African American culture as well their interactions with parallel and competing discourses. Through verbal and performative communication, record listening, and reading, participants tap into different aspects of the aesthetic, learning how to make, interpret, and respond to the sounds and other stimuli in musical events.

JAZZ AS RITUALIZED PERFORMANCE

The scene and the blues aesthetic constitute two related ways of framing musical events as jazz and as performance. The scene can be said to provide space and place for jazz performance, while the blues aesthetic provides a way to negotiate space and place. Other forms of music or performance can be framed or understood via their positioning in other scenes and/or via the normative and evaluative criteria of other aesthetics. Within the scene and working within the blues aesthetic, the emphasis placed by musicians on "taking it to another level," their many mentions of spirituality, and participants' church-derived responses to jazz performance suggest a ritualized view of jazz performance.

Anthropologists, scholars of comparative religion, and even literary scholars have long emphasized the importance of ritual in structuring human experience (e.g., van Gennep 1960; Kluckhohn 1942; Eliade 1959; Turner 1969; Asad 1983; Comaroff 1985; Combs-Schilling 1989; Seremetakis 1991).[38] Explicit attempts have been made as well to apply insights from the study of ritual to African American musics including jazz (Marks 1974; Burnim 1985, 1988; Leonard 1987; Small 1987b; Salamone 1988). The meanings of *ritual* have been debated, with one view tending to dominate: "The definitions of ritual that have been offered have tended to share a presupposition about their object ... indigenously represented as 'ancient' and unchanging, [connected] to 'tradition,' the sacred, to structures that have generally been represented in stasis" (Kelly and Kaplan 1990:120). In this view, rituals are essentially conservative and devoted to maintaining the status quo. They have an established, unchanging structure from which deviations can be dangerous.

This view of ritual has been challenged in anthropological theory since the late 1970s, particularly on the grounds that not all rituals are seasonal, calendrical, or concerned with healing rites. Just as researchers studying identity and ethnicity have come to see those concepts as plastic and negotiable—concerned more with policing boundaries than with specifying content (Barth 1969)—so have anthropologists begun to view ritual in ways that see it as possessing varying degrees of and responses to formalization (Irvine 1979; Schieffelin 1985; Kelly and Kaplan 1990), characterized less by rote repetition than by performative negotiations with structure. Indeed, even the seminal work of Victor Turner (1969) allowed room for the performative in the study of ritual, though later scholars seem to have ignored that dimension of his work.[39]

Regardless of whether one sees ritual as conservative or performative, there are still common themes regarding ritual's role in individual and social transformation and its power to organize experience. Jean Comaroff (1985), for example, sees the power of ritual in its ability to play "most directly upon the signifying capacity of symbols, using them as the means through which to grasp, condense, and act upon qualities otherwise diffused in the social and material world" (78). African Zionists in South Africa, she notes, "construct rituals so as to reform the world in the image they have created, to reestablish a dynamic correspondence between the self and the structures that contain it" (198). In this sense, ritual escapes the everyday association it has with meaningless routine. It not only informs the interactions that one has with the surrounding world, but provides a forum in which one can intervene directly in that world to change its structures or, at least, one's relation to them.

Similarly, in her book *Sacred Performances: Islam, Sexuality, and Sacrifice* (1989), M. E. Combs-Schilling stresses ritual's ability to combine images or ideas metaphorically in such a way that participants must search for "their points of likeness and opposition" (248). But such use of metaphor does not allow for free association. Rather, it "demands imagination and creativity and yet ... is highly constraining in the kinds of understandings it allows to be built, for it defines the parameters of comparison" (248), linking present actors with the past and other ritual practitioners. Ritual at once makes possible the perception of meaning but constrains the operations whereby one comes to apprehend it. In the process, ritually constructed meanings become iconic representations, "truths" that are not easily destroyed:

> Ritual's fullness, independence, and capacity to orchestrate experience [enable] it to build definitions that impact upon all others. ... Other definitions and experiences exist, definitions that can be quite oppositional to the ones that are ritually built.. Yet, when effective, the ritual

definitions come to dominate, for they are experienced as essential definitions—definitions in purest form. Their cultural worth enables them to overshadow all others. (253)

Issues of selfhood and cultural identity thus find perhaps their strongest articulation in rituals, for such events provide definitions that not only extend into daily life but help to determine its very fabric.

What a ritual framework allows the scholar of jazz is a way to integrate the flux and mutability of the scene with the attitudes toward performance, participation, and evaluation that achieve iconicity in blues-based performance. It becomes a single figure that contains the structure provided by the scene and musical style and the negotiations of that structure via blues aesthetic criteria, at once making possible the interpretation of meaning, but constraining its possible forms. Scholars of music and history have proposed that African American musical forms, including jazz, are ritualistic or ritualized.[40] Though each of them states the purpose of ritualized musics differently, they agree that their focus is stomping out the blues and giving participants metaphoric "equipment for living," different ways of seeing and reacting to the world around them. The parallel with anthropological literature on ritual is too strong here to be missed. Understanding the ritual nature of performance, particularly as it is suggested by statements and actions of scene participants, allows one to see more clearly that, in addition to its function as entertainment, jazz can have expressive and transformative potential (cf. Burnim 1985:160).

Christopher Small's commonsense notion of ritual (1987a) provides a point of departure for discussion of the ways in which jazz performance is ritualized activity. In noting several aspects of Western art music performance that can be characterized as "ritualistic," Small explicitly details the following: (1) that performance takes place in a space specifically set aside for that purpose; (2) that the space is constructed in such a way as to focus attention on the performers; (3) that there are workers charged with maintaining and ensuring the sacredness of the space; (4) that there are conventions regarding the dress of performers and other participants; and (5) that there are strict behavioral expectations for both performers and participants (8–11). He goes on to note that "most concerts consist mainly of a limited number of works which get played over and over again, with minute variations in interpretation, and that audiences become extremely skilled in perceiving these variations and comparing them" (13–14).

It is quite apparent that jazz as performed in bars, nightclubs, festivals, and concert halls shares many of the previously mentioned ritual characteristics: There are spaces in New York City that are set aside for jazz performance. The performers are central in those spaces, often being the reason why non-performers are present. The layout of many venues, as noted previously, focuses the attention of other participants on performers, who typically are in an area raised above floor level. To varying degrees, those spaces are maintained for the presentation of music with images of jazz musicians, instruments, and other memorabilia adorning the walls and sound systems amplifying and projecting the sound(s) of the performers. Owners and managers make more or less committed efforts to maintain performance spaces, keeping pianos in tune and even improving or modifying the appearance of a space over time.

There are, moreover, conventionalized, though variable, expectations regarding the dress and behavior of performers and other participants alike. The "quiet policies" of various venues seem intended, for example, not to prohibit all verbal activity, only that which is not in response to the music. Shouts of encouragement are prohibited only to the degree that their excessiveness interferes with the ability of others to hear or see what the performers are doing (cf. Racy 1991:15–16). Finally, there is a more or less unvarying repertoire of compositions known as "standards" that will often be performed or that can

serve as models or springboards for new compositions (cf. Monson 1991; Jackson 1992). All of these elements and behaviors link jazz performance in such venues to ritual activity.

Whereas Small is attentive to details of context, Frank Salamone focuses on the negotiation of structure within the context described by Small. In his essay "The Ritual of Jazz Performance" (1988), Salamone treats jazz as a sacred form that creates and renews itself through ritual. Like Small, he pays considerable attention to the conventions of jazz performance that make it similar to repeated ritual activity. He sees preperformance agreements about solo order, chord progressions, and so on, as part of the repeated ritual of performance. And like Neil Leonard (1987), he recognizes the degree to which conventions of song form and interaction make possible "spontaneous performance": "Only when a musician thoroughly understands musical structure is exceptional improvisation possible. The individual's seemingly featured status, therefore, is based only on the strength of the group's internal cohesiveness" (Salamone 1988:96). In that sense, the openness of musical structure previously discussed by Peter Bernstein and Steve Wilson can be conceived as an "enabler" (Jackson 1992) or frame that allows interactions to take place, for it allows musicians to bring something to a performance. While each individual must say something, each does so with the explicit support of other participants in the musical event.

Within ritualized scene- and blues-aesthetic-based performances, there is a specific governing structure, a ritual structure, if you will. There are, of course, variations depending on whether the performance takes place "live" in front of an audience or in a recording studio before a more limited set of participants (just as a wedding or funerary ritual might have contextual differences). In either event, musicians must come into a space having prepared themselves through rehearsals specifically geared toward that event or through cumulative preparation and study from their engagement with musical performance over time. They must also bring a willingness to listen to and interact with other performers and participants. Nonperformers are also expected to come to the performance with specific kinds of knowledge of how performance normatively proceeds and how to listen to and evaluate performance as it is occurring. As Steve Wilson put it, all must be "ready to receive." When listeners come with other expectations—such as to have conversation or conduct an informal meeting—a critical mass of other participants, musicians or even management can censure them through polite requests for silence or less polite calls for their immediate departure.[41] Similarly, at recording sessions observers are required to be quiet and unobtrusive, literally speaking only when addressed by someone with a more central role in the recording process.

The contours of the ritualized structure of jazz performance can be sketched by reference to a musical event in a nightclub. Its beginning is framed by lights being dimmed and/or by the introduction of the performers. Depending on their own personal preferences, the performers or the bandleader may further frame the performance by addressing the audience with talk about the occasion or the tunes they are going to play. If the order of tunes has not been set prior to the performers' entrance into the performance space, the leader will quickly communicate verbally to the other musicians what tune will be played, perhaps also indicating the key, dynamics, and other information. She or he then indicates the tempo through visual and aural means: with motions like finger snapping or foot tapping combined with *sotto voce* counting. This framing of the performance is extremely important. While a particular tune can be played at any of a number of tempos, finding one that will ensure that the musicians fall into a groove is considered an art unto itself. For that reason, a leader may clap or snap several pulses before cueing the band to start to ensure that the right pulse will be used.

Figure 2-1. Typical progression of events in a tune.

Once the tune has begun (and this scheme applies for recording sessions as well), a group will tend to follow a scheme used by small jazz groups since at least since the mid-1940s. The progression of events is generally similar to that presented in Figure 2-1. The scheme presented is merely a guide. While the italicized items can generally be omitted, any of the others can be removed or modified in some way.

The head consists of all musical material prior to the beginning or after the end of improvised solos. At the beginning of a tune, it can be referred to as the "head in." Correspondingly, it would be the head-out at the end, though the term *out-chorus* is used more frequently. The head can include a prearranged introduction or an improvised one. In some cases, the material for the introduction comes from the coda or from the statement of the theme, particularly the last portion of a sectional form—for example, the last "A" of an AABA form, the "C" of an ABAC form, or the last four measures of a twelve-bar blues progression. Likewise, the introduction can consist of a vamp on a two or four-measure harmonic progression. (Some bandleaders, like saxophonist Lou Donaldson, frequently dispense with this aspect of framing. In such situations, Donaldson simply begins to play, expecting the other members of his ensemble—like organist Dr. Lonnie Smith, guitarist Peter Bernstein, and drummer Fukushi Tanaka—to know the tune and to infer tempo and key from what and how he plays.) The statement of the theme follows the introduction (or begins the tune when the introduction has been omitted). This portion of the head most clearly allows other participants in the musical event (or record listeners) to identify the tune if it is one already known to them. Otherwise, it provides them the opportunity to hear and grasp the form of an unfamiliar composition.

Forms are harmonic/rhythmic structures that serve as a basis for improvisation. Sections within them are generally four, eight, or sixteen measures in length. Such designations as "AABA" or "blues" mark the organization of a particular form. An AABA form has two sections at its beginning and one at its end that are of equal lengths and have identical or nearly identical harmonic progressions. The B section of such a form generally modulates to a contrasting key area or through a series of contrasting keys that eventually lead back to the key area that begins the A section. George and Ira Gershwin's "I Got Rhythm" is a popular and frequently used example of an AABA form, in which each section is eight measures in length.[42] A blues form is typically twelve measures in length, though there are numerous variants (as Koch 1982 indicates). Short forms, like blues forms or sixteen-bar ones, tend to be played twice during the head, while longer forms are played only once. Indeed, while such forms may seem structurally simple, they can contain enormous variety in terms of harmonic, melodic, rhythmic, and textural activity. From section to section, there may be changes of feel,[43] meter, or any other musical parameter. In composing and improvising on tunes, jazz musicians can treat form in a highly elastic manner, taking well-known tunes or forms and extending or truncating sections to make the listening and performing experience more challenging. In some cases, the statement of the theme is so intricate that the performers choose a less complicated form for solos.[44]

For participants, recognizing and understanding form is essential to comprehending the musical event. Visual/spatial metaphors (from written notation) help them to describe some portions of the form. The top of a form or of a section, for example, is its beginning. The B section in an AABA tune is known as a bridge or a channel because it connects the A sections to one another. Performers who frequently lose their way in a form[45] are harshly criticized, for understanding and being able to perform effectively on a number of forms is a basic skill that precedes the ability to improvise effectively.

Once the statement of the theme is complete, the performers may move into the next frame—solos on the form—or delay its arrival with transitional material or a coda. As with the introduction, such material may be precomposed or improvised, for example, on a vamp. In some cases, the material for the coda and the introduction may be identical. The head-in and head-out, in any event, frame the group improvisational activity of the solo sections in the same way that verbal introductions and setting the tempo frame the performance of a tune.

The harmonies, feels, textures, meter, and tempo of the form furnish the given material that the performers work with during the solo sections of the performance (Tirro 1967; Byrnside 1975).[46] Each cycle through the form is referred to as a chorus.[47] As Figure 2-1 indicates, the order of solos generally proceeds from the solos of "horns" (brass and reed instruments), to those of chording instruments (e.g., piano, organ, guitar), then to bass, and drums. Individual ensembles or band leaders may modify those parameters from tune to tune for contrast, omitting bass and drum solos, for example, or changing the order of solo slots. Composed interludes[48] or improvised vamps may fill the space between individual solos.

In some cases, a leader or a group of soloists may "trade eights" or "fours" with one another or with the drummer (in lieu of or prior to a drum solo). Each performer solos for the specified number of measures, generally completing a phrase on the first beat of the measure after the designated grouping, and is followed by the next performer who observes the same procedure. In trading fours with a drummer, for example, a saxophonist will solo for four measures accompanied by the entire ensemble (including the drummer), finishing his or her first section of trading on the first beat of the fifth measure. The drummer will begin a four-measure solo passage at that same moment and, on the first beat of the ninth measure, will resume an accompanying role as the saxophonist begins soloing again. This procedure continues until a visual, verbal, or musical cue at the end of a chorus signals that the drummer will take an extended solo on the form or that the ensemble should play the head-out.[49] Trading passages can often generate considerable excitement, particularly when performers turn them into competition (which musician can play the fastest or most registrally extreme phrases) or manipulate the terms of trading in process (starting by trading eights, cutting down to fours, then twos, single measures, half measures, and finally beats, for example).

When the solos are finished, the leader of the group cues the band to play the head again. Introductory materials from the head-in may be reused to signal the head's return. Or the band may simply play the theme statement without introductory material and then use what was the introduction as a coda. In some cases, the final statement of the theme is followed by more solos (on a vamp) or a cadenza played by the leader of the group. When the tune is done, and typically before the last sounds have decayed, the performers frame the end of the performance by slightly bowing their heads and acknowledging audience applause. In a studio setting, the performers maintain silence for several seconds until the recording engineer or producer informs them that they have stopped rolling tape.

This scheme characterizes the playing on most tunes in a nightclub set, in a concert hall, or on a festival stage. When one tune ends, the performers begin framing the next tune, agreeing to follow a preset arrangement or to depart from it, perhaps taking time to introduce the band members to the audience, to acknowledge other musicians or important people in the audience, to remind listeners about currently available recordings of theirs, or to announce the previous tune or the next one. Afterwards, the leader again sets the tempo, and the performers enter the tune frame. The pre- and post-tune framing differs in the context of rehearsals or recording sessions, but what happens within the tune frame is typically the same, with the important exception that the performers have the option of stopping a tune in rehearsals or in a recording session if they are not satisfied with it.

After four or five tunes, a typical nightclub set ends. The performers leave one temporal frame (see Figure 2-2). If there is another set to be played that evening, they remain within a spatial frame and may invite the participants to attend later sets. The performers might also seek ways to relax and dissipate the energy amassed during the previous set and to prepare themselves for the next one through conversation with other participants, concentration, or practice (cf. Berliner 1994:453). Or they may remove themselves from the venue, only to reenter the spatial frame before the next set begins. If they have finished an evening's final set, the performers or venue personnel invite the other participants to come again for an engagement later in the week. And if the performers have finished the last set of a week-long

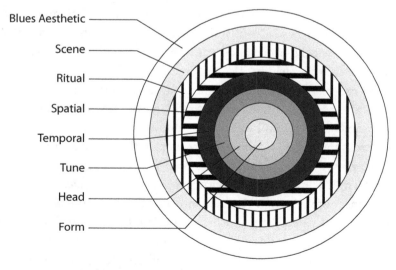

Figure 2–2. Frames around jazz performance.

engagement, then they leave that frame as well. Venue personnel focus their energies on informing other participants of other engagements. Likewise, in a recording session or rehearsal, the studio or apartment is the spatial frame within which musical performance takes place.

These different frames, graphically represented in Figure 2-2,[50] are different areas in which participants in musical events can creatively manipulate and respond to the materials they have.[51] These frames also furnish the differing arenas into which all participants are expected to bring something. They adapt themselves to the performance space, taking into account the "vibe"—the "general atmosphere" (Berliner 1994:449)—of a particular venue, studio, or rehearsal space. They adjust themselves to the temporal demands placed on them by the space within which they perform—set lengths, engagement lengths, allotted studio time, and so on. Once those adjustments are made—and they are all subject to renegotiation—the performers enter the frames in which they most specifically grapple with the performative and evaluative criteria of the blues aesthetic. Here, they find creative ways to play the head of a tune, through the way they introduce it, the ways in which they play the materials presented to them as the head of a tune (harmonies, rhythms, melodies, timbres, dynamics), and the ways in which they adhere to or obscure the form. Likewise, in the solo passages, each performer ideally plays with all the musical parameters that make up a composition and its form.

When performers successfully synthesize and work with all of the materials of a performance (space, time, tune, form, other performers, and other participants), that is when a performance is likely to proceed to the next level. Performers and other participants experience sensations or series of feelings that they describe, like Antonio Hart, as being literally "out of this world." Every element of a performance seems to fit, and each individual appears to be making a contribution to what is occurring. Some of the feelings associated with possession or ecstasy lead to an apparent nullification of time outside of the performance and of space outside the venue. In process, the musical event is said to be "swinging," "burning," "on," or some similar phrase that indicates positive motion, activity, and good feeling (cf. Monson 1990:35).

The responses of participants attending such events are variable and sometimes virtually indistinguishable from those that might accompany stirring sermons in African American Baptist and Pentecostal churches. At a performance by trumpeter Nicholas Payton, pianist Mulgrew Miller, bassist Peter Washington, and drummer Lewis Nash at the Village Vanguard in March 1995, the shared nature of response to impressive musical performance was foregrounded via silent, visually perceived actions. In the middle of the tune "Maria's Melody," Washington and Nash played an intense groove over which Miller soloed—playing riff-based figures alternating with long, intricate single-line passages with his right hand. One of my table companions, Bess Weatherman, was moving her head up and down in time with the groove in the same fashion that I was. As the interaction between the rhythm section members intensified, I looked across the room and made eye contact with Sharon Blynn, who opened her mouth as if silently to say, "Wow," nodded her head in the direction of the stage, and looked back at me in awe. I nodded in agreement, smiled, and turned my gaze back toward the stage.

In some cases, responses are clearly verbalized and spur the performers on to greater performative heights. One could assert that when the performers have "said something" to nonperforming participants, those nonperformers feel free literally to say something in response (cf. Burnim and Maultsby 1987:132–33). This kind of interactive response, not generally encouraged in some performance venues, is essential to jazz performance and connects it, again, to other forms of African American music. The way in which Keil (1991) describes the reactions of African American audiences to blues performances in Chicago, or in which Haralambos (1970) and Ward (1998) describe reactions to soul and rhythm and blues are strikingly similar to what sometimes happens in jazz performances. A clear example comes from a performance by pianist James Williams, singer Kevin Mahogany, and bassist Curtis Lundy at Bradley's in October 1994. It also highlights the degree to which blues-inflected performance can generate positive audience response. Near the end of a set, the musicians performed the song "Since I Fell for You." Some of the participants seated at the bar were urging Mahogany on as he sang the melody and lyrics at the beginning of the tune. They shouted encouragement to him at every bluesy turn of phrase and every decoration of the tune's standard melody. Most interestingly, one shouted, "Go on, Kevin! Sing the blues!" right before the word "blues" came up in the text. Perhaps in response, but definitely on cue, Mahogany caressed the word by descending pentatonically from the initial pitch on that syllable. He also mirrored the pitch descent by gradually decreasing dynamics. One could argue here that performance is truly participatory and dialogic with performers and non-performing participants contributing to and influencing the emergent shape of a musical event.

Jazz performers ideally take the materials at their disposal, what is provided and what they bring, and attempt to "say something" with them, to become like one (Jackson 1992) with one another and with other participants in the musical event. The blues aesthetic shapes the way they approach those materials, and the materials themselves—framed by space, time, tune, and form—are part of ritualized jazz performances. The scene and the aesthetic provide conditions that allow the participants in the musical event to go to the next level, to remove them temporarily from all concerns beyond those of the performance, and to give them metaphoric tools for seeing and relating the world differently once the performance has ended. Each musician who shows him or herself capable of responding creatively, distinctively, and interactively at the same time shows other musicians and participants ways of seeing what is possible within the structures of musical performance and the varied structures within which individuals live their lives.

It is in this sense that jazz performance is a kind of social action that intervenes in the daily lives of those who listen to and perform it. It does not merely reflect the events and circumstances that frame it. Rather, within those frames, musical items or other sound terms (Meyer 1956)—phrases, rhythms, voicings, approaches, compositions, and techniques—become symbols, associatively and connotatively linked via the shared "interpretive moves" (Feld 1994b) of performers and other participants with other performances, performers, and musics. They are not so much symbols *of* something that can be categorized and classified, but symbols that can be *linked* to something. Meanings emerge from the linkages and oppositions between juxtaposed musical sounds and their interpretations by listeners.

Each musical item and its creative use becomes a way of connecting with some of the most deeply held values of African Americans toward performance, toward living, and toward who they are as people, values that stress tolerance of individual variation and group cooperation in the service of survival (see the introduction of Gwaltney 1993; see also Roberts 1989). It is not merely a music of resistance—a term closely associated with social action; it is a music of survival as well for those, regardless of racial, cultural, or ethnic background who understand the ways in which various conventions are or can be manipulated in performance. Jazz performance therefore assumes a synecdochic relationship to African American culture: one brings to the musical event those ideals that should motivate daily living—as in music, so in life. As Joshua Redman noted in discussing playing with older musicians, one hopes that from playing with them, he or she will internalize something of their spirit and wisdom in order to become not just a better musician but a more mature person.

Similar processes can be observed in a number of other musics created and performed by Black Atlantic populations. In a much-overlooked article, Morton Marks (1974) makes similar claims regarding a number of different African-derived performance traditions in the African diaspora. Noting that performance itself models social behavior and reflects adaptive strategies (cf. Whitten and Szwed 1970: 220), his aim is to show how "the patterned use of sounds, both linguistic and musical ... reflect and/ or actually bring about changes from one social or psychological state to another" (67). He examines, in turn, Afro-Brazilian Carnival, Latin popular music in New York performed by *santeros,* and African American gospel performance. In the second of those examinations, he details how a commercially released song performed by Justi Barretto, "El Santo en Nueva York," is framed as sacred through the use of verbal and musical elements from a *toque* for Yemaya, one of the *santos* for practitioners of *santería,* when it begins. Immediately afterwards, the performance switches to a dance-band format with words in Spanish and a standard harmonic progression that one might find in a typical jazz composition. As it unfolds, however, the performers "switch" musical and linguistic codes: changes of harmony are simplified, alternating only between a tonic and dominant-seventh chord every two measures; call and response patterning becomes the dominant mode of presentation; and the singer gradually shifts from singing in Spanish to singing in Lucumí, the Yoruba language in Cuba. The importance of such switching, he argues, lies in its preservation of essential group values:

> What this shift signifies is that even though drastic changes have taken place in the *natural* setting which render the practices of *santería* difficult, the *cultural* forms which pay homage to the deities are still intact. ... The opening dance-band format might be seen as a masking device which hides the real content of the song. The code-switching near the end is a type of de-masking, which symbolically reaffirms the ritual by moving away from the "acculturated" format and[,] symbolically, from the problems created in the transplant of the religion to the United States. (86–87)

In a sense, therefore, changes in performance and the specific content of performance (in terms of structures and what happens within those structures) support a normative vision of the relationship that one must have with the *santos.* They communicate how one is to live under new circumstances: through mastering several musical and linguistic codes and using them creatively and expressively in performance. Marks's discussions of Afro-Brazilian and African American practices come to similar conclusions.[52]

Similarly, in his writings about tradition and cultural identity in modern-day Nigeria, Christopher Waterman (1990) shows that one can find clear correspondences between musical and social orders despite Western analytical frameworks that separate reified musical structures from music's more expressive, qualitative parameters. The relational processes that build individual and group identity among the Yoruba in Nigeria are mirrored in ritualized transactions—involving money, status, and the management of meaning—and uses of metaphor in musical performance (217–19). These processes become understandable when he describes the composition and performance of larger ensemble:

The larger bands in Ibadan, based on the Sunny Ade and Ebenezer Obey paradigms ... are comprised of three semi-autonomous units. The guitar section includes a lead or solo player (generally not the band captain) supported by interlocking tenor guitars, Hawaiian guitar, and bass guitar. The senior talking drummer improvises on a rhythmic base created by the cumulative interaction of supporting drums. The praise singer is flanked and supported by his chorus. Thus, the fundamental relationship between *elé* (lead part, call, "that which drives ahead of or into something") and *ègbè* (subordinate part, choral response, "supporters" or "protectors") is reproduced in each section of the band. The aural gestalt generated by the intersection of these micro-hierarchies metaphorically predicates an idealized social order: a congeries of localized networks focused on big men. (219)

"An effective performance of jùjú," he continues, "predicates not only the structure of the ideal society, but also its interactive ethos or 'feel': intensive, vibrant, buzzing, and fluid" (220). Such performance "externalizes, comments upon, metaphorically grounds, and helps to reproduce the hegemonic values that guide behavior at secular urban secular rituals. ... Put simply, juju performances advance the following arguments concerning the relationship of the individual to culture and community: (1) 'We're all Yoruba'; (2) 'Our values are intact'; and (3) 'Keep working'" (227). Indeed, jùjú performance achieves its power and impact precisely through its "metaphoric correlation of social-structural, ideological, and aural patterns" (227), through its ability to communicate in the ritual context the kinds of behaviors and interactions that will be most effective in daily life.

There are numerous other examples that could be marshaled to underscore the importance and ritual nature of music making in the African diaspora outside those already mentioned. Paul Gilroy's writing about black music in Britain in the 1980s (1991a); Stephen Stuempfle's (1995) work on music in Trinidad; various writings concerning reggae and politics (Bones 1986; Waters 1985; Hebdige 1979); Karen McCarthy Brown's study of Haitian *vodou* (1991); Jocelyne Guilbault's book on zouk (1993); and Veit Erlmann's (1991) and David Coplan's (1985) writings on the history and meanings of South African music are just a few examples of works that concern themselves with musical performance by African diaspora populations and the ways in which those performances and their attendant rituals can become, as Gilroy (1991a:211) has observed, central to the regulation of collective memory and experience, as well as the construction of community. Each of those works notes how important the elasticity and flexibility of musical performance is, the kinds of negotiations with structure and setting that make performance meaningful. The meaning is never solely in the sound; rather, it is in the interactions that make the sound possible and the ongoing adjustments of the sound to the context.

It is in this sense that jazz performance, conceived as ritual and motivated by the blues aesthetic, is connected to other musics in the African diaspora. Just like the other musics of the diaspora, and in many similar ways, it privileges interaction, participation, and formal flexibility in the service of transcendence and communication of normative values and cultural identity. Musical performance does not merely serve to reproduce or express the hierarchies or frames that surround it. It is also concerned with transcending them through metaphoric encodings of deeply held values and strategies for survival.

NOTES

1. Describing jazz in such a fashion recalls the scale of intensities that was part of Herskovits's syncretic paradigm. See Herskovits (1990). For critiques, see Apter (1991) and Scott (1991).

2. See also Gilroy (1991a, b, 1993, 1994, 1995).

3. Gilroy, however, is not the first to propose such a perspective for viewing and understanding African-derived musics. Indeed, the "black-music cultural sphere" described by Olly Wilson (1974) has boundaries that mark it as coterminous with Gilroy's area. More will be said about Wilson's work later.

4. Baraka was known as Leroi Jones at the time of the book's release.

5. Some aspects of Herskovits's ideas and methods have come under criticism in recent years. See Harrison (1988), Apter (1991), and Scott (1991).

6. Keil's notion is drawn at least partially from his reading of *Blues People*.

7. See Burke (1964).

8. In *Stomping the Blues* (1976), Murray repeatedly encapsulates the spirit of what bluesmen do with the words "extension, elaboration, and refinement."

9. See, for example, Crouch (1990:47). During the course of my fieldwork, critic Peter Watrous and pianist Eric Reed, among others, expressed similar views.

10. Note that the use of the term *African American culture* does not presuppose homogeneity in that culture. Indeed, what defines the culture are its ways of looking at and adapting to changing situations rather than the specific responses to them. Culture, in this sense, is conceived as a number of strategies or practices for responding to and making sense of experience.

11. A good sound has not only to sound good but also to feel good.

12. Coltrane's three-tonic system, reportedly influenced by his practicing with Nicolas Slonimsky's *Thesaurus of Scales and Melodic Patterns* (1947), was a system that allowed the substitution of chord scales a major third away from a dominant chord's root in improvisation or composition. On a G-dominant chord, for example, one could typically use pitches from a Mixolydian scale starting on G. In the three-tonic system, Mixolydian scales starting on E♭ and B are permissible substitutes for the G-based scale (though each may require some chromatic alteration to "fit"). This system is employed most famously on "Giant Steps" from *Giant Steps* (compact disc, Atlantic 1311–2, recorded 4 May 1959).

13. One way in which Blanchard forced his musicians to break old habits was to write compositions relying heavily on nonfunctional tonal progressions, particularly using the sonority of the minor-seventh chord with a flattened sixth. With C as root, the pitches contained in a closed position voicing of the chord would be C-E♭-G-A♭-B♭

14. "Impressions" can be found on John Coltrane's *Impressions* (MCA/ Impulse MCA-5887, recorded 26 November 1961). An example of a late Ben Webster ballad is his recording of "How Long Has This Been Going On?" from Ben Webster and "Sweets" Edison, *Ben and "Sweets"* (Columbia CJ 40853, recorded 7 June 1962). "Confirmation" can be found on Charlie Parker's *Bird's Best Bop on Verve* (Verve 314 527 452–2, recorded 30 July 1953).

15. This statement has interesting correspondences with ideas developed by Mikhail Bakhtin (1981). The meaning of a particular word or utterance, for him, is not static but is intimately tied to previous meanings and emerging from the social and material circumstances of its use: "The word in language is half someone else's. It becomes 'one's own' only when the speaker populates it with his own intention, his own accent, when he appropriates the word, adapting it to his own semantic and expressive intention" (293–94). As with Barth and Newsome's statements, the emphasis is not on novelty or revolutionary usage, but on making the word (sound) "one's own" through deploying it in specific contexts with specific, personal intentions.

16. The substitution is "incorrect" because the E natural in the B-major scale creates a clash with E♭ the seventh of the F dominant chord. Jazz harmonic theory generally forbids chord extensions or embellishments that create minor-ninth intervals with respect to lower-voiced chord tones (except with the root of a dominant chord).

17. William Tallmadge (1984) discusses the definitions and applicability of the terms *blue note* and *blue tonality,* particularly as they relate to harmonic progressions, whether categorized as "blues progressions" or not. In short, blue tonality is characterized by certain kinds of pitch play in specific harmonic contexts. So that a blue note on a C dominant seventh chord, such as E♭, might not be a blue note in another harmonic context, such as over an F dominant-seventh chord (an E♭ is part of the dominant chord).

18. To comp is to provide rhythmic/harmonic/textural accompaniment for instruments playing melodies.

19. This line of argument has continuity with Gates's understanding of "signifyin(g)": one does not signify *something,* one signifies *in some way.* The centrality of the blues is confirmed as well by the staggering number of compositions based on its 8-, 12-, and 16-bar forms throughout the history of the music. For a discussion of those forms and their various transformations, see Koch (1982). Wynton Marsalis paid tribute to the music with his 1989 recording *The Majesty of the Blues* (Columbia CK 45091, recorded 27–28 October 1988, New York, New York).

20. Compare those responses with the negation of the importance of race when the researcher is non-African American (Monson 1990: 38–39).

21. Burrell, Pass, Abercrombie, Metheny, and Jarrett are non-African Americans on the list. Wynton Kelly (1931–71) was black and born in Jamaica, but his family moved to New York when he was four years old.

22. Reyes Schramm (1986) notes that analysts frequently confuse a music's "content system"—that is, its meaning to culture bearers—with its expressive system, sound. The latter is a way of getting to the former, with innovations in the expressive system usually helping to preserve the traditions that constitute the content system. Traditional musicological analysis focuses attention on the expressive system but tends to ignore (or take for granted) the context system. See also Higgins (1991).

23. The Ellington essay is reprinted in Mark Tucker's *The Duke Ellington Reader* (1993: 132–35). A number of African American musicians with whom I talked expressed dismay over the place accorded African American musicians and culture in the writing of history and criticism, fearing that too much concentration on the artistic complexity of the music would eclipse its role as a form of African American cultural expression/communication.

24. For example, musicians like Louis Armstrong, Duke Ellington, Lester Young, Billie Holiday, Charlie Parker, Dizzy Gillespie, Miles Davis, John Coltrane, Wayne Shorter, Herbie Hancock, Woody Shaw, Kenny Garrett, and Mulgrew Miller are more frequently cited as influential by musicians of differing backgrounds than are non-African American musicians like Bix Beiderbecke, Gil Evans, Bill Evans, Scott LaFaro, Dave Holland, Joe Zawinul, or Michael Brecker. Those in the latter group are most often cited only by European American musicians. Based on what African American musicians and audience members say, it would seem that the reason for the continued importance of African American musicians might be located in the connections between wider African American cultural practices and musical performance. This argument is often thought to be essentialist, when, in fact, it stresses learning and enculturation.

25. Antonio Hart saw as problematic the segregation of different groups of musicians at the Berklee School of Music in Boston in the late 1980s, observing that racial and cultural differences mapped onto stylistic ones. Sam Newsome confirmed the same for his experiences there, starting a few years prior to Hart's arrival. Newsome asserted that the majority of white—European and European American—students were interested in musicians like Gary Burton, while many of the African American musicians were interested in learning "how to swing."

26. So pervasive is Blakey's influence that a number of musicians who had played with him spent nearly an hour discussing his wisdom and his foibles during and after a break at the second evening of recording for James Williams's CD *Truth, Justice, and the Blues* (Fieldnotes, 12 December 1994).

27. Note here an apparent difference between Wilson's understanding of tradition and that usually espoused by scholars. Whereas scholars have recently viewed traditions as selective constructions and "inventions" (Hobsbawm and Ranger 1983), Wilson seems to be contradicting that view. He is saying, in effect, that one does not "invent" tradition; rather, it is already "there," and one must negotiate a relationship to it. Obviously, this view of tradition is still one that is constructed and invented, though his emphasis is on selecting a whole corpus of materials from the cultural matrix rather than valorizing some and passing over others.

28. Herbie Hancock's composition "Eye of the Hurricane" (Maiden Voyage, compact disc, Blue Note CDP 7 46339 2, recorded 17 May 1965) is a similar but more complicated example. Hancock's tune has a difficult head with abrupt metric and harmonic shifts, but the form for solos is blues in F minor.

29. For a discussion of substitute harmonies, see Steven Strunk's entry on harmony in the New Grove Dictionary of Jazz (1988).

30. Note that this next level is not so much a transcendence of place or circumstance, but a form of communion in which participants share aspects of their identities and understandings in the context of musical performance. In other words, it is less a form of escape than it is a form of deep involvement.

31. In a flow situation, the individual does not feel or recognize the passage of time or other items that normally register in his or her consciousness. Moments of flow are most likely to occur when the challenge of a particular activity and the skills possessed by an individual are nearly matched. When the challenge outweighs one's skill, anxiety about one's skill is the result. When one's skills exceed what is required by a certain challenge, then boredom is highly likely.

32. Scholars writing about African American musics have often seen the blues as musical form and/or as ethos as pivotal to an understanding of all African American musics.

33. Its metaphoric quality is immediately apparent through its description of the aural via the visual.

34. See Fields (1982) for a discussion of race as a social and ideological construct.

35. Indeed, I prefer blues aesthetic to African American aesthetic because the term African American has a tendency to be equated with biological and ideological constructions of race, even though its meaning has more to do with cultural practice (cf. Powell 1989:20–21).

36. This argument has some continuity with studies of hegemony and resistance that note that any act that resists hegemony also serves in some ways to reinforce it. Likewise, there is a suggestive relationship to Pierre Bourdieu's notion of habitus, defined as "a system of lasting, transposable dispositions which, integrating past experiences, functions at every moment as a matrix of perceptions, appreciations, and actions, and makes possible the achievement of infinitely diversified tasks" (Bourdieu 1977:82–83).

37. For a more extensive discussion of the epistemological foundations of this aesthetic, see Jackson (1998:122–30).

38. Van Gennep's book was originally published in 1908 as Les rites de passage. Some of the literary scholars who have focused on ritual include Gilbert Murray, Jane Ellen Harrison, and Lord Raglan. I thank Robert O'Meally for bringing them to my attention, particularly because they were influential for Ralph Ellison.

39. Turner writes in his introduction: "In order to live, to breathe, and to generate novelty, human beings have had to create—by structural means—spaces and times in the calendar or in the cultural cycles of their most cherished groups[,] which cannot be captured in the classificatory nets of their quotidian routinized spheres of action. These liminal areas of time and space—rituals, carnivals, dramas, and latterly films—are open to the play of thought, feeling, and will; in them are generated new models, often fantastic, some which may have sufficient power and plausibility to replace eventually the force-backed political and jural models that control the centers of society's ongoing life" (vii, emphasis added). Turner's turn toward the performative became more pronounced as he came to view ritual as dramaturgical and to focus on the theatrical aspects of daily living. See Turner (1974a, b; 1982).

40. See, for example, Ellison (1964:256–57), Keil (1991:164), Murray (1970: 58; 1976:17), Levine (1977:234–37), Leonard (1987:23, 53–55, 61–64, 71–75), Small (1987a:70, 302), Salamone (1988), and Floyd (1995:14041).

41. The responses to such requests are highly variable. The privileges that some individuals ascribe to having paid admission fees complicate such situations when they assert their "right" to do whatever they want because they are "paying customers." The disdain reserved for such audience members is quite similar to that engendered by the increasing number of European tourists visiting Harlem churches in recent years. As tourists, they disrupt services by taking photographs, for example, as times that are disrespectful. See Lii (1995), Bruni (1996), and Gomes (1996).

42. That is, as the tune is frequently performed by jazz musicians. Gershwin's published version of the tune is a thirty-four bar structure with the last section comprising ten measures. Indeed, in the same way that one can say "Blues in F minor" and count off a tempo and have other musicians play along, one can also say "Rhythm changes in F" indicating the harmonic progression from the Gershwin tune and a key—and get a similar result.

43. *Feel* refers to the rhythmic/accentual/textural patterning of or approach to playing a tune or section thereof based on conventional understanding. Several different feels exist; among the most common named ones are Latin, bossa, samba, ballad, two-beat, and swing, each of which carries with it expectations about how rhythm section members (piano, bass, and drums, in particular) are supposed to play.

44. Herbie Hancock's previously cited "Eye of the Hurricane" is a good example. The form for the solos is a blues progression. David Sanchez's composition "Ebony" (1994, *The Departure*, compact disc, Columbia CK 57848, recorded 23–24 November and 7 December 1993, New York, New York) is a thirty-two-bar form divided into eight-, six-, eight-, and ten-bar sections, respectively. There are also marked changes of feel, as when the ensemble switches to a Latin feel in the second eight-bar section.

45. For example, in an AABA tune, one plays three A sections in succession between each B section. Some performers unwittingly drop one of the A sections from time to time. The resultant harmonic and rhythmic clashes can be embarrassing for the performer and other participants in the musical event (cf. Monson 1991:245–52).

46. In a sense, the term *solo* is misleading, for multiple performers are improvising during the "solo" sections of a performance. The term *feature* might be more appropriate.

47. If a soloist plays through the form four times, she or he has taken a four-chorus solo.

48. Under different circumstances, these interludes might be called "sendoffs" or "shout choruses."

49. See Jackson (1992) for more discussion of communication and cueing.

50. By nesting the scene frame within the blues aesthetic frame, I am leaving open the possibility of examining other African American music scenes through the prism of a blues aesthetic.

51. Performances not framed by blues aesthetic criteria, such as "pit bands" for Broadway shows, will of course proceed in different ways.

52. One might also favorably compare some of the conclusions Frances Aparicio (1998) makes regarding salsa for modern-day Puerto Ricans in the United States and elsewhere.

REFERENCES

Andrews, Dwight D. 1989. "From Black to Blues." In *The Blues Aesthetic: Black Culture and Modernism,* edited by Richard J.Powell, 37–41. Washington, DC: Washington Project for the Arts.

Aparicio, Frances R. 1998. *Listening to Salsa: Gender, Latin Popular Music, and Puerto Rican Cultures.* Hanover, NH: Wesleyan University Press.

Apter, Andrew. 1991. "Herskovits's Heritage: Rethinking Syncretism in the African Diaspora." *Diaspora* 1:235–60.

Asad, Talal. 1983. "Notes on Body Pain and Truth in Medieval Christian Ritual." *Economy and Society* 12:287–327.

Baker, Houston A., Jr. 1984. *Blues, Ideology, and Afro-American Literature: A Vernacular Theory.* Chicago: University of Chicago Press.

Bakhtin, M. M. 1981. *The Dialogic Imagination: Four Essays.* Edited by Michael Holquist. Austin: University of Texas Press.

Baraka, Amiri (LeRoi Jones). 1963. *Blues People: Negro Music in White America.* New York: Morrow.

———. 1991. "The 'Blues Aesthetic' and the 'Black Aesthetic': Aesthetics As the Continuing Political History of a Culture." *Black Music Research Journal* 11(2): 101–9.

Barth, Bruce. 1994. Interview by author. Brooklyn, NY. 14 December.

———. 1995. Interview by author. New York, NY. 22 February.

Barth, Fredrik. 1969. "Introduction." In *Ethnic Groups and Boundaries: The Social Organization of Culture Difference,* edited by Fredrik Barth, 9–38. Boston: Little, Brown.

Bauman, Richard. 1975. "Verbal Art As Performance" *American Anthropologist* 77: 290–311.

Bauman, Richard, and Charles L. Briggs. 1990. "Poetics and Performance As Critical Perspectives on Language and Social Life." *Annual Review of Anthropology* 19:59–88.

Berliner, Paul F. 1994. *Thinking in Jazz: The Infinite Art of Improvisation.* Chicago: University of Chicago Press.

Bernstein, Peter. 1995. Interview by author. New York, NY. 31 January.

Bones, Jah. 1986. "Reggae Deejaying and Jamaican Afro-Lingua." In *The Language of the Black Experience: Cultural Expression through Word and Sound in the Caribbean and Black Britain,* edited by David Sutcliffe and Ansel Wong, 52–68. Oxford: Basil Blackwell.

Bourdieu, Pierre. 1977. *Outline of a Theory of Practice.* Cambridge: Cambridge University Press.

———. 1984. *Distinction: A Social Critique of the Judgement of Taste.* Cambridge: Harvard University Press.

Brown, Karen McCarthy. 1991. *Mama Lola: A Vodou Priestess in Brooklyn.* Berkeley: University of California Press.

Bruni, Frank. 1996. "Drawn to Gospel, If Not Gospels, Foreigners Arrive by Busload." *New York Times,* 24 Nov.: 37.

Burke, Kenneth. 1964. "Literature As Equipment for Living." In *Perspectives by Incongruity,* edited by Stanley Edgar Hyman, 100–109. Bloomington: Indiana University Press.

Burnim, Mellonee V. 1985. "The Black Gospel Music Tradition: A Complex of Ideology, Aesthetic, and Behavior." In *More Than Dancing: Essays on Afro-American Music and Musicians,* edited by Irene V. Jackson, 147–67. Westport, CT: Greenwood Press.

———. 1988. "Functional Dimensions of Gospel Music Performance." *Western Journal of Black Studies* 12(2):112–21.

Burnim, Mellonee V., and Portia Maultsby. 1987. "From Backwoods to City Streets: The Afro-American Musical Journey." In *Expressively Black: The Cultural Basis of Ethnic Identity,* edited by Geneva Gay and Willie L. Baber, 109–36. New York: Praeger.

Byrnside, Ronald. 1975. "The Performer As Creator: Jazz Improvisation." In *Contemporary Music and Music Cultures,* edited by Bruno Nettl, Charles Hamm, and Ronald Brynside, 233–51. Englewood Cliffs, NJ: Prentice-Hall.

Collins, Edmund John. 1987. "Jazz Feedback to Africa." *American Music* 5: 176–93.

Comaroff, Jean. 1985. *Body of Power, Spirit of Resistance: The Culture and History of South African People*. Chicago: University of Chicago Press.

Combs-Schilling, M. E. 1989. *Sacred Performances: Islam, Sexuality, and Sacrifice*. New York: Columbia University Press.

Coplan, David. 1985. *In Township Tonight! South Africa's Black City Music and Theatre*. London: Longman.

Crouch, Stanley. 1990. "Chitlins at the Waldorf: The Work of Albert Murray." In *Notes of a Hanging Judge: Essays and Reviews, 1979–89*, 42–48. New York: Oxford University Press.

Csikszentmihalyi, Mihaly. 1982. "Toward a Psychology of Optimal Experience." *Review of Personality and Social Psychology* 3:13–36.

———. 1988. "The Flow Experience and Its Significance for Human Psychology." In *Optimal Experience: Psychological Studies of Flow in Consciousness*, edited by Mihaly Csikszentmihalyi and Isabella Selega Csikszentmihalyi. Cambridge: Cambridge University Press, 15–35.

Eliade, Mircea. 1959. *The Sacred and the Profane: The Nature of Religion*. New York: Harcourt Brace.

Ellington, Duke. 1939. "Duke Says Swing Is Stagnant!" *Down Beat*, February: 2, 16–17.

Ellison, Ralph. 1964. *Shadow and Act*. New York: Random House.

Erlmann, Veit. 1991. *African Stars: Studies in Black South African Performance*. Chicago: University of Chicago Press.

Feld, Steven. 1984. "Sound Structure As Social Structure." *Ethnomusicology* 28: 383–409.

———. 1994a. "Aesthetics As Iconicity of Style (Uptown Title); or, (Downtown Title) 'Lift-Up-Over Sounding': Getting into the Kaluli Groove." In *Music Grooves: Essays and Dialogues*, edited by Charles Keil and Steven Feld, 109–50. Chicago: University of Chicago Press.

———. 1994b. "Communication, Music, and Speech about Music." In *Music Grooves: Essays and Dialogues*, edited by Charles Keil and Steven Feld, 77–95. Chicago: University of Chicago Press.

Fields, Barbara J. 1982. "Ideology and Race in America." In *Region, Race, and Reconstruction: Essays in Honor of C. Vann Woodward*, edited by J. Morgan Kousser and James M. McPherson, 143–77. New York: Oxford University Press.

Floyd, Samuel A., Jr. 1995. *The Power of Black Music: Interpreting Its History from Africa to the United States*. New York: Oxford University Press.

Fuller, Hoyt W. 1971. "Towards a Black Aesthetic." In *The Black Aesthetic*, edited by Addison Gayle Jr., 3–12. Garden City, NY: Doubleday.

Gabbard, Krin. 1995. "Introduction: The Jazz Canon and Its Consequences." In *Jazz Among the Discourses*, edited by Krin Gabbard, 1–28. Durham, NC: Duke University Press.

Gates, Henry Louis, Jr. 1988. *The Signifying Monkey: A Theory of African-American Literary Criticism*. New York: Oxford University Press.

Gennari, John. 1991. "Jazz Criticism: Its Development and Ideologies." *Black American Literature Forum* 25:449–523.

Gilroy, Paul. 1991a. *"There Ain't No Black in the Union Jack": The Cultural Politics of Race and Nation*. Chicago: University of Chicago Press.

———. 1991b. "It Ain't Where You're From, It's Where You're At: The Dialectics of Diasporic Identification." *Third Text* 13:3–16.

———. 1993. *The Black Atlantic: Modernity and Double Consciousness*. Cambridge: Harvard University Press.

———. 1994. "Sounds Authentic: Black Music, Ethnicity, and the Challenge of a *Changing* Same." In *Imagining Home: Class, Culture and Nationalism in the African Diaspora,* edited by Sidney J. Lemelle and Robin D. G. Kelley, 93–117. London: Verso.

———. 1995. "Roots and Routes: Black Identity As an Outernational Project." In *Racial and Ethnic Identity: Psychological Development and Creative Expression,* edited by Herbert W. Harris, Howard C. Blue, and Ezra E. H. Griffith, 15–30. New York: Routledge.

Gioia, Ted. 1988. *The Imperfect Art: Reflections on Jazz and Modern Culture.* Oxford University Press.

Goffman, Erving. 1959. *The Presentation of Self in Everyday Life.* New York: Doubleday.

Gomes, Peter J. 1996. "Religion As Spectator Sport." *New York Times,* 28 Nov.: 29.

Gridley, Mark C. 1997. *Jazz Styles: History and Analysis.* 6th ed. Upper Saddle River, NJ: Prentice-Hall.

Guilbault, Jocelyne, et al. 1993. *Zouk: World Music in the West Indies.* Chicago: University of Chicago Press.

Gwaltney, John Langston. 1993. *Drylongso: A Self-Portrait of Black America.* New York: New Press.

Hall, Edward T. 1992. "Improvisation as an Acquired, Multilevel Process." *Ethnomusicology* 26:223–35.

Haralambos, Michael. 1970. "Soul Music and Blues: Their Meaning and Relevance in Northern United States Black Ghettos." In *Afro-American Anthropology: Contemporary Perspectives,* edited by Norman E. Whitten Jr. and John F. Szwed, 367–84. New York: Free Press.

Harrison, Faye V. 1998. "Introduction: An African Diaspora Perspective for Urban Anthropology." *Urban Anthropology* 17:111–41.

Hart, Antonio. 1994. Interview by author. Brooklyn, NY. 22 December.

———. 1995. Interview by author. Brooklyn, NY. 17 February.

Hebdige, Dick. 1979. *Subculture: The Meaning of Style.* London: Routledge.

Herskovits, Melville J. 1990. *The Myth of the Negro Past.* Boston: Beacon Press.

Higgins, Kathleen Marie. 1991. *The Music of Our Lives.* Philadelphia: Temple University Press.

Hobsbawm, Eric, and Terence Ranger, eds. 1983. *The Invention of Tradition.* Cambridge: Cambridge University Press.

Hymes, Dell. 1964. "Introduction: Toward Ethnographies of Communication." *American Anthropologist* 66(6):1–34.

Irvine, Judith T. 1979. "Formality and Informality in Communicative Events." *American Anthropologist* 81:773–90.

Jackson, Travis A. 1992. "Become Like One: Communication, Interaction, and the Development of Group Sound in Jazz Performance." Master's thesis, Columbia University.

———. 1998. "Performance and Musical Meaning: Analyzing 'Jazz' on the New York Scene." Ph.D. diss., Columbia University.

Jarab, Josef. 1985. "Black Aesthetic: A Cultural or Political Concept." *Callaloo* 8(3): 587–93.

Johnson, Bruce. 1993. "Hear Me Talkin' to Ya: Problems of Jazz Discourse." *Popular Music* 12(1):1–12.

Keil, Charles. 1991. *Urban Blues.* Chicago: University of Chicago Press.

Kelly, John D., and Martha Kaplan. 1990. "History, Structure, and Ritual." *Annual Review of Anthropology* 19:119–50.

Kivy, Peter. 1990. *Music Alone: Philosophical Reflections on the Purely Musical Experience.* Ithaca, NY: Cornell University Press.

Kluckhohn, Clyde. 1942. "Myths and Rituals: A General Theory." *Harvard Theological Review* 35:45–79.

Koch, Lawrence O. 1982. "Harmonic Approaches to the Twelve-Bar Blues Form." *Annual Review of Jazz Studies* 1:59–71.

Leonard, Neil. 1987. *Jazz: Myth and Religion.* New York: Oxford University Press.

Levine, Lawrence W. 1977. *Black Culture and Black Consciousness: Afro-American Folk Thought from Slavery to Freedom.* New York: Oxford University Press.

Lewis, Alan. 1987. "The Social Interpretation of Modern Jazz." In *Lost in Music: Culture, Style and the Musical Event,* edited by Avron Levine White, 33–55. London: Routledge & Kegan Paul.

Lii, Jane H. 1995. "God, Gospel and the Camcorder." *New York Times,* 26 Mar.:3.

Logan, Wendell. 1984. "The Ostinato Idea in Black Improvised Music: A Preliminary Investigation." *Black Perspective in Music* 12:193–215.

Lomax, Alan. 1959. "Folk Song Style." *American Anthropologist* 61:927–54.

———. 1976. *Cantometrics: An Approach to the Anthropology of Music.* Berkeley: University of California Extension Media Center.

Marks, Morton. 1974. "Uncovering Ritual Structures in Afro-American Music." In *Religious Movements in Contemporary America,* edited by Irving I. Zaretsky and Mark P. Leone, 60–134. Princeton: Princeton University Press.

Marshall, Christopher. 1982. "Towards a Comparative Aesthetics of Music." In *Cross-Cultural Perspectives on Music,* edited by Robert Falck and Tim Rice, 162–73. Toronto: University of Toronto Press.

Mensah, Atta Annan. 1971–72. "Jazz—The Round Trip." *Jazzforschung* 3–4: 124–37.

Meyer, Leonard B. 1956. *Emotion and Meaning in Music.* Chicago: University of Chicago Press.

Monson, Ingrid. 1990. "Forced Migration, Asymmetrical Power Relations and African-American Music: Reformulation of Cultural Meaning and Musical Form." *World of Music* 32(3):22–45.

———. 1991. "Musical Interaction in Modern Jazz: An Ethnomusicological Perspective." Ph.D. diss., New York University.

———. 1994. "Doubleness and Jazz Improvisation: Irony, Parody, and Ethnomusicology." *Critical Inquiry* 20:283–313.

———. 1996. *Saying Something: Jazz Improvisation and Interaction.* Chicago: University of Chicago Press.

Murray, Albert. 1970. *The Omni-Americans: Some Alternatives to the Folklore of White Supremacy.* New York: Da Capo.

———. 1976. *Stomping the Blues.* New York: Da Capo.

Newsome, Sam. 1995. Interview by author. Brooklyn, NY. 5 February.

Pareles, Jon. 1996. "Jelly Roll and the Duke Join Wolfgang and Ludwig." *New York Times,* 2 July: C11, 15.

Powell, Richard J. 1989. "The Blues Aesthetic: Black Culture and Modernism." In *The Blues Aesthetic: Black Culture and Modernism,* edited by Richard J. Powell. Washington, DC: Washington Project for the Arts, 19–35.

———. 1994. "Art History and Black Memory: Toward a 'Blues Aesthetic.'" In *History and Memory in African-American Culture,* edited by Robert G. O'Meally and Genevieve Fabre, 228–43. New York: Oxford University Press.

Racy, Ali Jihad. 1991. "Creativity and Ambience: An Ecstatic Feedback Model from Arab Music." *World of Music* 33(3):7–27.

Redman, Joshua. 1994. *Mood Swing.* Compact disc. Recorded New York, NY, 8–10 March 1994: Warner Brothers 9 45643–2.

———. 1995. Interview by author. New York, NY. 27 February.

Reyes Schramm, Adelaida. 1986. "Tradition in the Guise of Innovation: Music among a Refugee Population." *Yearbook for Traditional Music* 18:91–101.

Roberts, John W. 1989. *From Trickster to Badman: The Black Folk Hero in Slavery and Freedom*. Philadelphia: University of Pennsylvania Press.

Rosenthal, David H. 1992. *Hard Bop: Jazz and Black Music, 1955–1965*. New York: Oxford University Press.

Salamone, Frank A. 1988. "The Ritual of Jazz Performance." *Play and Culture* 1: 85–104.

Schieffelin, Edward L. 1985. "Performance and the Cultural Construction of Reality." *American Ethnologist* 12:707–24.

Scott, David. 1991. "This Event, That Memory: Notes on the Anthropology of African Diasporas in the New World." *Diaspora* 1:261–84.

Seeger, Charles. 1977. "The Musicological Juncture: 1976." *Ethnomusicology* 21: 179–88.

Seremetakis, C. Nadia. 1991. *The Last Word: Women, Death, Divination in Inner Mani*. Chicago: University of Chicago Press.

Slonimsky, Nicolas. 1947. *Thesaurus of Scales and Melodic Patterns*. New York: Scribner's.

Small, Christopher. 1987a. *Music of the Common Tongue: Survival and Celebration in Afro-American Music*. New York: Riverrun Press.

———. 1987b. "Performance As Ritual: Sketch for an Enquiry into the True Nature of a Symphony Concert." In *Lost in Music: Culture, Style and the Musical Event*, edited by Avron Levine White, 6–32. London: Routledge & Kegan Paul.

Starks, George L., Jr. 1981. "The Performance Context and Sociocultural Perspective: Avenues to the Understanding of African American Music." *Proceedings of NAJE Research* 1:100–105.

———. 1993. "Jazz Literature and the African American Aesthetic." In *The African Aesthetic: Keeper of the Traditions*, edited by Kariamu Welsh-Asante, 143–57. Westport, CT: Greenwood Press.

Strunk, Steven. 1988. "Harmony (i)." In *New Grove Dictionary of Jazz*, edited by Barry Kernfeld. New York: Macmillan.

Stuckey, Sterling. 1987. *Slave Culture: Nationalist Theory and the Foundations of Black America*. New York: Oxford University Press, 1987.

Stuempfle, Stephen. 1995. *The Steelband Movement: The Forging of a National Art in Trinidad and Tobago*. Philadelphia: University of Pennsylvania Press.

Tallmadge, William. 1984. "Blue Notes and Blue Tonality." *Black Perspective in Music* 12:155–65.

Taylor, Arthur. 1993. *Notes and Tones: Musician-to-Musician Interviews*. New York: Da Capo.

Tirro, Frank. 1967. "The Silent Theme Tradition in Jazz." *Musical Quarterly* 53: 313–34.

Tucker, Mark, ed. 1993. *The Duke Ellington Reader*. New York: Oxford University Press.

Turner, Victor. 1969. *The Ritual Process: Structure and Anti-Structure*. Ithaca, NY: Cornell University Press.

———. 1974a. *Dramas, Fields, and Metaphors: Symbolic Action in Human Society*. Ithaca, NY: Cornell University Press.

———. 1974b. "Liminal to Liminoid, in Play, Flow, and Ritual: An Essay in Comparative Symbology." *Rice University Studies* 60(3): 53–92.

———. 1982. *From Ritual to Theatre: The Human Seriousness of Play*. New York: PAJ Publications.

van Gennep, Arnold. 1960. *The Rites of Passage*. Chicago: University of Chicago Press.

Ward, Brian. 1998. *Just My Soul Responding: Rhythm and Blues, Black Consciousness, and Race Relations*. Berkeley: University of California Press.

Waterman, Christopher Alan. 1990. *Jùjú: A Social History and Ethnography of an African Popular Music.* Chicago: University of Chicago Press.

Waters, Anita M. 1985. *Race, Class, and Political Symbols: Rastafari and Reggae in Jamaican Elections.* New Brunswick, NJ: Transaction Books.

Welburn, Ron. 1971. "The Black Aesthetic Imperative." In *The Black Aesthetic,* edited by Addison Gayle Jr., 132–49. Garden City, NY: Doubleday.

———. 1987. "Jazz Magazines of the 1930s: An Overview of Their Provocative Journalism." *American Music* 5:255–70.

Whitten, Norman E., and John F. Szwed., eds. 1970. *Afro-American Anthropology: Contemporary Perspectives.* New York: Free Press.

Wilson, Olly. 1974. "The Significance of the Relationship between Afro-American Music and West African Music." *Black Perspective in Music* 2: 3–22.

———. 1985. "The Association of Movement and Music As a Manifestation of a Black Conceptual Approach to Music Making." In *More Than Dancing: Essays on Afro-American Music and Musicians,* edited by Irene V. Jackson, 9–23. Westport, CT: Greenwood Press.

———. 1992. "The Heterogeneous Sound Ideal in African-American Music." In *New Perspectives on Music: Essays in Honor of Eileen Southern,* edited by Josephine Wright and Samuel A. Floyd Jr., 327–38. Warren, MI: Harmonie Park Press.

Wilson, Steve. 1995. Interview by author. New York, NY. 2 March.

PEDAGOGY OF SELF-DEVELOPMENT

THE ROLE THE BLACK CHURCH CAN HAVE
ON AFRICAN AMERICAN STUDENTS

By Carlos R. McCray, Cosette M. Grant, and Floyd D. Beachum

Historically, the Black Church has been an institutional stronghold in the Black community and has thereby sustained a cultural ethos that has enabled African Americans to combat racial prejudice and hostility for generations. Therefore, this article will unearth Yosso's notion of alternative capital that students of color have at their disposal and the Black church's role in its nourishment. Alas, educators and administrators who are charged with educating African American students have, in many cases, been negligent in their efforts to recognize such contrarian capital. This has been mainly due to the fact that schools are undergirded by precepts of implicit and explicit racial biases. The authors will attempt to add to the notion of pedagogy of self-development as we elucidate that such a cogent standard to traditional capital is doing increasing harm and contributing to the on-going academic decline of many African American students in U. S. schools.

The slogan black is beautiful ... is not an expression of reverse racial chauvinism; rather it registers the fact that black is a tremendous spiritual condition, one of the greatest challenges anyone alive can face. (Glaude, 2007, p. 13)

Today, African American students seem to be the recipients of disproportionate disciplinary procedures and educational practices that are ushering them out of the entire educational process (Day-Vines & Day-Hairston, 2005; Ferguson, 2001; Peterson, 2003; Skiba & Peterson, 1999). African American students in the United States make-up 16.9% of the student population, yet account for 33.4% of all school suspensions (Day-Vines & Day-Hairston, 2005). Even for the many African American students who manage to not find themselves subjected to impartial disciplinary practices, they are frequently misinstructed, miscategorized, or underserved (Beachum, Dentith, McCray, & Boyle, 2008; Jackson, 2008; Ferguson, 2001; Obiakor, 2007; Obiakor, Harris-Obiakor, Garza-Nelson, & Randall, 2005). Young Black males, for example, represent 9% of the student population; however they make up 20% of all students enrolled in special education classes. An unfortunate corollary is that they only represent 4% of those in the gifted and talented programs (Thomas & Stevenson, 2009). This unfortunate reality calls attention to the drastic need of colleges, educators, and school leaders, as well as community institutions and organizations to critically review and intervene in these issues in order to eliminate the deprived conditions many African American students are facing in the educational system. Such intervention represents a holistic perspective as to what is needed in order to address the

Carlos McCray, Cosette Grant, and Floyd Beachum, "Pedagogy of Self-Development: The Role the Black Church Can Have on African American Students," *The Journal of Negro Education*, vol. 79, no. 3, pp. 233–248, 438–439. Copyright © 2010 by Howard University Press. Reprinted with permission. Provided by ProQuest LLC. All rights reserved.

dire circumstances in which many African American students find themselves. More specifically, the Black Church is an appropriate institution within this holistic intervention to help improve some of the said conditions many African American students regularly confront in their matriculation through the educational system. The opening quote by Glaude (2007) reveals the continued need to focus on the self-efficacy of African American students in order to prepare them for the potential racial and class-based hostility they may encounter within their schools (Dantley, 2009; Feagin & Feagin, 1978; Foster, 2009; Perry, 2003; Tatum, 2007).

As such, racial and class-based hostility are part of the calculus of the continued lack of success many African American students are experiencing. Additionally, the aforementioned discrepancy in academic achievement can be partially addressed with an increasing emphasis on African American students' self-efficacy. These authors assert that the Black Church has had a significant role in African American's finding solace in the midst of racial discrimination that is endemic throughout this country's history (Quarles, 1987). From a *post hoc* perspective, this same comfort that African Americans have historically found via the Black Church can also be part of the solution in helping to reduce the number of African American students dropping out of school. It also can be a cogent factor in reducing the academic achievement gap. Therefore, the purpose of this article is to illuminate the critical role that the Black Church can have in the education of many African American children who have seemingly fallen through the cracks.

Historically, the Black Church has also been an institutional stronghold in the African American community and has thereby sustained a cultural ethos that has enabled African Americans to combat racial prejudice and hostility for generations (Foster, 2009; Quarles, 1987; Randolph, 2009). Foster (2009) offered a compelling description of how the Black Church has served and should continue to serve the African American community and African American students. According to Foster, the Black Church has a crucial role in providing:

> … consistent and continuous support and structures that provide strong racial socialization for African American students. Then, these students will be able to envision and actualize themselves as … psychosocially competent, capable, and achieving individuals of a main-stream culture who possess and use cultural capital to understand and navigate the ambiguity and pitfalls of continuing prejudice and discrimination. … (p. 167)

Accordingly, this role consists of the purported notion of self-efficacy (Tatum, 2007), which is under-girded by the *pedagogy of self-development* (i.e., self-realization and self-assertion).

In addition to the pedagogy of self-development, this article will also explicate Yosso's (2005) notion of alternative capital that students of color bring with them from within their own communities. Yosso suggested that African American students and students of color have six forms of alternative capital that are not readily recognized by educators and school leaders. The forms of capital Yosso identified were *aspirational capital, linguistic capital, familial capital, social capital, navigational capital, and resistant capital*. School teachers and administrators who are charged with educating African American students and other students of color potentially have been negligent in their efforts to recognize such contrarian capital. This has been mainly due to the fact that schools, and other organizations and institutions in the United States are undergirded by precepts of implicit and explicit racial biases (Feagin & Feagin,

1978). The authors therefore assert that a stringent standard to traditional forms of capital, led by racist and classist policies, is doing increasing harm and causing a rapid decline in the positive educational outcomes (i.e., good grades, high test scores, high graduation rates, etc.) of many African American students in U. S. schools (Tatum, 2007). In order for such narratives to change, the Black Church must play a more active role in helping to parlay the alternative forms of capital African American students have at their disposal into academic success.

THE BLACK CHURCH OF YESTERDAY AND TODAY

The historical role of the Black Church with regard to assisting African Americans in the struggles for integration, educational access, economic parity with Whites, and social justice in general has never been an ostensible one. The Black Church has always been at the forefront in intimating the need for racial justice. According to Shelby (2005), the concept of racial justice is that "... in a just society each [individual] has a chance to carry out his or her own plan of life without being unfairly inhibited in this pursuit by other's racial prejudice or racial biases" (p. 131). Throughout this article, the authors intend to illuminate the role the Black Church has played and can continue to play to ensure that racial justice is prevalent within the schools that are educating the most disadvantaged students. The venerable historian Benjamin Quarles (1987) noted that this amalgamation between the Black Church and its role in fighting for racial justice began to take shape around the Reconstruction era. Quarles stated:

> The fading of the great expectations of Reconstruction days led the Negro to look anew to the church as an agency of uplift and inspiration. And has it happened, the Negro church in the South was able to assume an even larger role than in the antebellum days, for the Civil War had freed the Negro church ... The white preacher and the white observer was no longer on the scene. (p. 159)

This sense of uplift and inspiration that African Americans began to receive from the Black Church during and after Reconstruction would play a pivotal role in their fight for racial justice in the years to come.

At the epicenter of the conflation of the Black Church and its support for racial justice was the voluble Black clergyman. The Black clergyman was vivacious as well as a bonhomie, but he was also obstinate with regard to ensuring that his church and congregation were actively involved in those issues that impacted the community the most. Quarles (1987) attributed these characteristics of the "Negro clergyman" to the fact that the he had a position that did not require him to be accountable to forces outside of the community. With regard to the active involvement of the Black Church and its clergyman, Quarles also proffered:

> The role of the Negro church, like that of its pastor, did not stop with Sunday service. The Negro's church was a highly socialized one, performing many functions. The church served as a community center, where one could find relaxation and recreation. It was a welfare agency, dispensing help to the sicker and poorer members. It was a training school in self-government,

in the handling of money, and in the management of business. The church was the Negro's very own, giving him the opportunity to make decisions for himself, which was seldom available elsewhere. (p. 162)

This function of the Black Church and its clergymen would continue in the South and the North well into the Civil Rights Movement, roughly another 100 years (Douglas & Hopson, 2001). The role of the Black Church in the mid-twentieth century, in relation to African Americans fighting for a better way of life, is well documented. Therefore, no attempt to give a comprehensive account is provided of how the Black Church immersed itself into the struggles of African Americans' fight for better way of life in the United States. What will be conveyed; however, is that the Black Church's responsibility in many instances was the vortex of planning and strategizing for the procurement of social justice from Reconstruction up to the Civil Rights Movement (Anderson, 1988; Brown & Hopson, 2001; Dyson, 2009; Glaude, 2007; Quarles, 1987; Tillman, 2004). Dyson (2009) has noted that "When the civil rights movement was drenched with the foul spray of white supremacy and Jim Crow, it took cover in sanctuaries [Black churches] across the land" (p. 25).

The crucial question today given the dire predicament that many African American students, especially those in urban areas, find themselves on educational attainment is what role should the Black Church plays in helping to ameliorate the academic achievement gap and reducing the number of African American students who are dropping out of school. Dyson (2009) has conveyed that the Black Church does have a role today in continuing to fight for social justice just as it did in the past. Nevertheless, Dyson added the caveat that Black churches must not continue to succumb to the notion of prosperity gospel if they are to continue the legacy of its predecessors as champions of social justice. Dyson intimated that the notions of prosperity gospel started in the 1920s, and continued in the 1930s and 1940s which had a major influence on White and Black preachers. Furthermore, Dyson continued, prosperity gospel has made a tremendous resurgence back into the pulpits of Black churches. And according to Dyson, this particular type of gospel is undergirded by two precepts, (a) health and (b) wealth. Dyson readily admits that inspiring congregants to achieve better health and position themselves to achieve economically is not in of itself problematic. However, he strongly condemns Black preachers who capitulate completely to the edicts of the prosperity gospel over a material religion that emphasizes social justice. According to Dyson, "I think one explanation for its revival is the attempt of new members of the upper Black middle class to offer theological grounds for their success without feeling guilty, or responsible for those left behind" (p. 26). Therefore, it is without contestation that more than 47 years after Dr. Martin Luther King, Jr. gave his "I Have a Dream Speech" in Washington DC that there are a plethora of African Americans who have been left behind, largely by the educational system (McCray, 2008).

The aforementioned material religion is tantamount to the notions and principles of social justice. Dyson (2009) stated, "The former archbishop of Canterbury, William Temple, said that Christianity is the most material religion there is because we address the flesh, we deal with the body. A material religion takes seriously the issues of disease, suffering, pain, death, and so on" (p. 26). According to Dyson, not only does a material religion focus on these serious issues that humans are susceptible to, but a material religion is also drastically concerned with the "forces that causes economic [and other] inequality" (p. 26). Similarly, Shelby (2005) intimated that the essence of social justice is the notion of acknowledging and dealing with those structural issues that are the impetus for social injustice (Bogotch, Beachum,

Blount, Brooks, & English, 2008). In lieu of the current predicament that many African American students are facing in their schools, can the Black church afford to forgo the edicts of a material religion in favor of solely focusing on a prosperity gospel? Do Black churches have an obligation to try to address the structural and cultural issues that are plaguing Black students' academic performance?

These pivotal questions are asked fully aware of the increasing arguments of differentiation of African Americans (Gooding-Williams, 2009). The notions of differentiation among African Americans is the acknowledgement that Blacks have become so diverse that it is impossible to ask of them to coalesce around specific or micro-goal attainments. The authors will not spend too much time on this argument. However, it is felt that a case could be made that a good majority of Black churches are in segregated Black communities. The corollary is that churches are still probably one of the most segregated institutions in the United States. And in many instances, upper middle-class Blacks, gay Blacks, Black feminists, as well as poor and destitute African Americans (McCray, 2008), are all worshiping in the same locale (Reed, 2008), in a segregated Black community.

As Reed (2008) pointed out, "It is somewhat problematic to use the term Black church as 'monolithic' concept" (p. 211). According to Reed, "Within the Black church, [there are] divergent perspectives [existing] on numerous issues" (pp. 211–212). Nevertheless, this argument is that by virtue of geographical location—namely, the worshiping in many instances in segregated and destitute communities—the notion of differentiation is probably not as cogent when it comes to issues surrounding social and cultural community uplift. Nevertheless, if the geographical location critique is not sufficient enough to usurp the differentiation argument, then perhaps the dismal graduation rate among many African American young males (Cosby & Poussaint, 2007) is satisfactory enough to make anemic the argument of differentiation. The dismal graduation rate among African American males is in many cases leading to a pipeline from the school yard to the prison yard. Such a pipeline is bound to have a detrimental impact on the African American family with everything from economic potential to the number of qualified males who are suitable for marriage (Beachum & McCray, in press; Cosby & Poussaint, 2007). So perhaps self-preservation is a rational argument to cast aside the notion of differentiation for what U. S. Secretary of Education Arne Duncan has called the civil rights issue of our generation, which is a quality education for all students. Conflating the belief that a quality education is tantamount to the Civil Rights Movement, Duncan issued the following diatribe with regard to how he thought Dr. King would view the state of education for Black and Brown students. Duncan lamented that,

> [Dr. Martin Luther King Jr.] would have been angered to see that disadvantaged students still have less effective teachers; they still have fewer opportunities to take rigorous college-prep courses in high school; that Black and Brown, and low-income children are still languishing in aging facilities and high schools that are little more than dropout factories ... and [he] would have been dismayed to learn of schools that seem to suspend and discipline only young African American boys. ("Civil Rights in Education," 2010, p. A22)

This poignant assessment by Secretary Duncan on the state of education for African American students and students of color from low-wealth communities cannot be seen simply as an impasse and therefore an excuse for capitulation to the current status quo. To the contrary, it must in the words of Dr. King create a sense of fierce urgency among educators, school administrators, and community leaders—Black church leaders and their congregants—to come together to ameliorate the seemingly draconian educational policies undergirded by racism and classism (Dantley, 2009; Foster, 2009; Shelby, 2005; Tatum, 2007).

According to Reed (2008), "Historically, the Black church has been a key social institution for the pursuit of equity [and social justice] in the Black community" (p. 212). It goes without saying that the Civil Rights Movement in the 1960s was undergirded by the principles and precepts of social justice, which is tantamount to Shelby's (2005) notion of racial justice. If education is the civil rights issue of our time as Secretary Duncan has proclaimed, and African American students are the ones who are overwhelmingly adversely impacted from high dropout rates to educational misidentification, misassessment, and misplacement (Obiakor et al., 2005), then the Black Church can ill-afford to not engage in this monumental crisis equipped with its historical meliorism perspective—the intrinsic belief that the state and condition of the community is bound to improve (Glaude, 2007).

The effective engagement by the Black church in the challenging issues faced by many African American students in schools has to be undergirded by what Dyson (2009) articulated as a material religion conflated with Shelby's (2005) notion of racial justice. Precepts of an amalgamation of a cogent material religion and earnest racial justice critique calls on Black Church leaders and their congregants to passionately deal with the structural issues within the school that protract the educative process as well as the cultural issues within the community that may also have a disadvantageous impact on learning (Beachum & McCray, in press). Black churches situated in communities where the plight of African American students is in drastic need of change should be cognizant of the need to increase Black students' sense of academic awareness while attempting to rectify the racist and classist structural academic impediments.

Tantamount to the racist and classist structural issues hindering academic success is the notion that many African American students, especially those from urban areas, are at a cultural and social deficit (Bourdieu & Passceron, 1977; Lightfoot, 2009; McKenzie, 2001; Rodriguez, 2004; Valencia, 1997; Valencia & Solorzano, 1997; Yosso, 2005). Many educators and school leaders feel it is their mission for the short duration students are at the school to provide cultural amelioration to Black and Brown students from urban communities. Such beliefs by educators and school officials can oxymoronically make matters worse due to African American students picking up on educators' and school officials' disposition toward their culture (Tatum, 2007). It can in essence create a cultural collision among African American students and those designated to teach them (Beachum & McCray, 2004). According to Beachum and McCray (2004), cultural collision among many African American students and their teachers occurs when students bring their own culture to school that often may not coincide with the school's macroculture. Such clashes of culture are usually undergirded by disparate perceptions of which forms of capital should be valued.

ALTERNATE FORMS OF CAPITAL AND THE PEDAGOGY OF SELF-DEVELOPMENT

In many of our schools serving African American students, the notion of *capital pluralism* ceases to exist. Capital pluralism is present in schools when educators not only acknowledge the existence of a macrocosm of social and cultural capital, but they also concede to the idea that African American students have their own form of capital. The corollary of educators and school officials' acceptance of the notion of capital pluralism is their capitulation to the pedagogical practices undergirded by a correspondence theory comparable to Paulo Freire's (1973) Banking Model (where teachers "deposit" knowledge into students' minds as opposed to co-creating learning spaces and opportunities) combined with racist undertones and overtones. In many instances, educators and school officials choose to ignore any potential capital students of color bring with them to the educational process. Consequently, the paramount question is how can African American students enhance their own sense of self-efficacy in lieu of the racist and classist precepts, with little room for capital pluralism, which undergirds many U.S. schools? Part of the answer entails educators and school leaders recognizing that students of color have multiple forms of capital, even if they are not readily recognizable and valued by the organization (Franklin, 2002; Yosso, 2005).

Scholars (Foster, 2009; Franklin, 2002; Perry, Steele, & Hilliard, 2003; Tillman, 2009; Venkatesh, 2006; Wilson, 2009; Yosso, 2005) have stated that cultural and social capital does exist among African American students, students of color, and the communities in which they reside. As has been asserted, when educators and school officials choose to disregard the cultural and social capital that students of color and their communities manifest, it has the potential to not only affect their academic achievement but their behavior as well. According to Yosso (2005), "Various forms of capital nurtured through cultural wealth include: *aspirational, navigational, social, linguistic, familial, and resistant capital*" (p. 69). Furthermore, "these forms of capital draw on the knowledge students of color bring with them from their home communities into the classroom" (p. 69).

Aspirational Capital

The aspirational form of capital Yosso (2005) has offered deals with students of color's meliorism—the expectation that the educative process will nurture their own ambition and goals. Although many African American students, especially those from urban areas, face daily despair within their communities and schools, they still maintain a sense of optimism and hope for a better tomorrow through the means of education (Foster, 2009). According to Foster:

> whereas the substantial numbers of African American students in K–12 schools held high expectations for attending college and other postsecondary institutions, only slightly more than half (56 percent) of them were progressing toward their goals, as compared to 89 percent of White students who had the same or similar aspirations. (p. 161)

Linguistic Capital

Yosso's (2005) second form of capital is linguistic capital. He indicated that this form of capital has "multiple language and communication skills" (p. 78). According to Yosso:

> In addition, these children most often have been engaged participants in a storytelling tradition, that include listening to and recounting oral histories, parables, stories ... and proverbs. ... This repertoire of storytelling skills may include memorization, attention to detail, dramatic pauses, comedic timing, facial affect, vocal tone, volume, rhythm and rhyme. (pp. 78–79)

Unfortunately, linguistic capital can actually work to the detriment of African American students as well as those from poorer communities (Ovando, 2001). This type of capital can easily be transformed into increased academic achievement but can also be viewed as a deficit needing to be corrected. It also can be used as a gatekeeper to other forms of capital and, perhaps, as a barrier to goals and aspirations. Such a notion was illuminated when Senator Harry Reid Spoke of then presidential candidate Obama as being attractive to voters because he was "light skinned and had no 'Negro dialect." The Negro dialect or Black English vernacular (Hymes, 1981; Ogbu, 1999; Ovando, 2001; Perry & Delpit, 1998) that Senator Reid was speaking of might be sufficient grounds to block a Black person's ascendency to the White House as far as voters are concerned. However, it is a mistake for educators and school leaders to juxtapose the Negro dialect or Black English with Standard English has a barometer for aptitude or academic achievement. Ovando (2001) has found that languages and dialects are cultivated within cultures and communities because they meet the needs of groups with regard to their customs and backgrounds. It is shortsighted at best and pedagogical malpractice at worst for educators to treat students who have not mastered Standard English as educationally deficient and not capable of high achievement (Ovando, 2001).

Familial and Social Capital

Two additional forms of capital are familial and social, which Yosso (2005) conveyed that students of color bring with them to the educational organization. These two forms of capital intersect at points. Yosso noted that familial capital "engages a commitment to community well being and expands the concept of family to include a more broad understanding of kinship" (p. 79). Likewise, social capital likewise solidifies the "commitment to the community" through well established "networks of people and community resources" (p. 79). Both familial and social capitals have also been identified as essential by African American scholars (Beachum, Obiakor, & McCray, 2007; Du Bois, 1989; Foster, 2009; Karenga, 1989; McCray, 2008; Shelby, 2005). In this lies the chance for the Black church to play an important role, by creating an environment where those within the African American community, who were fortunate enough to achieve their professional and personal aspirations, are able to reach out and form relationships of solidarity with those who are less fortunate (Gooding-William, 2009; McCray; 2008, Shelby, 2005). This notion is what buttressed much of Du Bois's lifelong research—the belief that prosperous Blacks would at some point reach back and help other African Americans who have yet to make it (Gooding-Williams, 2009; McCray, 2008; Shelby, 2005). Beachum and colleagues (2007) called this community uplift. McCray (2008) identified such an effort as an insurgency.

Fictive kinship was recognized by Cornel West (Foster, 2009) and called Black solidarity by Shelby (2005). Regardless of the terminology used, it challenges schools to not only recognize the individual efforts of African Americans' aspiration but to also embrace the collective efforts (Karenga, 1989). As Karenga explained "Individual values along with the collective principles ... are needed for the improvement of the education that many Black youth [and students of color] are experiencing" (p. 264). The Black church can play a major role in not only helping African American students understand how such individual values and collective principles undergirds notions of community uplift, insurgency, fictive kinship, and Black solidarity, but the Black church should also work with schools and increase their awareness of this form of capital that African American students have at their disposal.

Navigational Capital

Another form of capital identified by Yosso (2005) is navigational capital. This form of capital is the "… ability of [students of color] to maneuver through institutions not created with Communities of Color in mind" (p. 80). Tatum's (2007) depiction of the racial and class-based hostility that undergirds many schools that educate African American students makes clear the need for African American students and students of color to have navigational capital at their disposal in order to achieve academically. Scholars (Allen & Sol6rzano, 2001; Alva, 1991; Perry, et al., 2003) have found that students of color despite "racial hostility" (Alva, 1991, p. 19) have continuously found ways to circumvent the unaccommodating school environment and achieve at high levels. Nevertheless, it would be romanticism, if not negligent to suggest that all African American students have mastered the art of navigating the racial hostility found in many schools.

According to Wilson (2009), many African American youth, especially those within U. S. inner cities, have yielded to the structural impediments (e.g., grinding poverty, rampant crime, gangs, unemployment, etc.), resulting in an increased level of resignation (i.e., dropouts, underachievement, and acting out; Gregory & Mosely, 2004; Thomas & Stevenson, 2009). The navigational capital that African American students and students of color bring with them to the educational process depends upon a level of cultural pluralism that allows students to develop their self-efficacy that has long been established within their communities (Foster, 2009). Hersey, Blanchard, and Johnson (1996), insightfully inserted, "Resignation or apathy occurs after prolonged frustration, when people lose hope of accomplishing their goal(s) in a particular situation and withdraw from reality and the source of their frustration" (p. 31). Unfortunately, there has been far too much resignation among African American students from the within the inner city (Day-Vines & Day-Hairston, 2005; Ferguson, 2001; Peterson, 2003; Skiba & Peterson, 1999). In many urban schools, the dropout rate is increasing exponentially among these student populations. This ushering out of students is especially high among African American males, with the dropout rate approaching 50% in many urban schools (Cosby & Poussaint, 2007).

Resistant Capital

The final form of alternative capital Yosso (2005) identified was resistant capital. Resistant capital, "refers to that knowledge and those skills fostered through oppositional behavior that challenges inequality" (p. 80). The problem with resistant capital displayed by African American students is educators and school leaders often mistake such capital as deviant or insubordinate behavior in need of immediate correction. For most educators, it is difficult to conceive of resistant conduct as an affront to the racial inequity and biases that might exist within the school climate and culture (Tatum, 2007). Resistant capital has been part of the African American community from the inception of the United States via resisting slavery; resisting the indictment of inferior mental ability and inadequate aesthetic appeal; resisting poor educational facilities; and resisting unequal rights (Bell, 2004; Carruthers, 1999; Collins,

2005; Foster, 2009; Quarles, 1987). Regarding the continued legacy of racial biases within schools, Foster (2009) conveyed the following:

> Unlike the physical assault that characterized the journey of earlier African Americans seeking access and admission to public education, large numbers of African American students in public schools today are targets for psychic assaults that demean their intellectual ability and competence and make them vulnerable to educational malpractice. (p. 157)

Therefore, it would be a mistake for educators and school officials to presume that African American students and students of color from the poorest communities will suddenly cease any form of resistance in lieu of racial and class biases they are experiencing at school (Tatum, 2007). Instead, educators need to work diligently to reduce the prejudicial judgments, biased behaviors, stigmatization, and stereotyping that give rise to such resistance. Yosso (2005) discovered that when such efforts are made by educators and school officials, resistance capital can be redirected into a transformative resource that motivates students to perform academically and socially.

The Black Church's Role for the Enhancement of Capital

As indicated throughout this article, African American students are painfully aware of how educators and school officials in many instances are dismissive of the form of capital they bring with them to school. If African American students and students of color have not managed to attain what is tantamount to middle-class Whites' education-dialect and lexicon (cultural capital), and the "right" connections and networks (social capital)—they are quickly labeled at a disadvantaged (i.e., deficit thinking; Bourdieu & Passceron, 1977; Lightfoot, 2009; McKenzie, 2001). Thus, it is quite evident of the educational benefit to those students who have considerable wealth and material possessions (economic capital) at their disposal (Bourdieu & Passceron, 1977; Nesbitt, 2009).

School leadership for the 21st century requires new knowledge, a comprehensive set of skills, and more diverse dispositions than in previous years. It is apparent that the demographic trends that are taking place in U. S. schools will continue to rise, increasing the nation's ethnic and racial diversity (Villegas & Lucas, 2002). These trends should alter the way in which schools serve diverse student populations in order to enhance educational excellence and equity (Obiakor & Beachum, 2005). Unfortunately, inadequate attention to the increasing diversity can lead to a culture where African American students and students of color are implicitly and explicitly devalued, dismissed, and disregarded. School leaders must have the passion and the will to ensure the school culture and climate promotes high expectations while valuing diversity. According to Lindsey, Roberts, and Campbell-Jones (2005):

> Educational leaders who pursue the goals of pluralistic and democratic schooling act intentionally with the belief that all children and youth not only have the capacity to learn but also are learning something about themselves and others at every moment. Although these democratic educators would acknowledge that most U.S. schools are very successful in the work of educating the students for whom they were designed, they recognize that this designated

group is a narrow, unicluster of students who represent the mainstream European American individualistic values that dominate public education in the United States. (p. xix)

School leaders have a duty to efficiently and effectively serve all students who enter their doors. Unfortunately, due to the disparate perceptions with regard to which forms of capital are worthy of consideration, this charge is not always carried out in earnest. These authors assert that the Black church can play a crucial role in alleviating such disparate perceptions among educators and school leaders by working to change the structural dynamics of the school that too often impede learning and achievement. A framework called culturally relevant leadership is offered as a way for school leaders to conceptualize and carry out the task of addressing the needs of all learners. But it is also maintained that it is the Black church and its congregants that have a crucial role in helping school leaders understand and commit to the forms of capital that African American students have at their disposal.

The Black Church's role should be one of providing school leaders and educators with the necessary knowledge and information with regard to the forms of capital African American students bring with them to school (see Yosso, 2005). In order for school leaders to be committed to culturally relevant leadership, they need to have a firm grasp and understanding of the different cultures of their many students. Tatum (2007) has found that of the 3 million teachers here in the United States only 15.6% are teachers of color. Also, of that number, African American teachers only represent 7.5% of the teaching workforce. According to Tatum (2007), "Most students of color today are being taught by a teaching force that is predominantly White and female. ..." (p. 25) Tatum went on to indicate that "nowhere is the current cultural mismatch between students and teachers more visible than in urban school districts where White teachers make up 65 to 76 percent ... of the teaching population and students of color represent 76 percent of the urban student population" (pp. 25–26). It is inevitable that misunderstandings are going to take place with such drastic racial and cultural discrepancies between the student population and their teachers (Haberman, 2005; Tatum, 2007). Therefore, the culturally relevant leadership is undergirded by greater mutual understanding, which the Black church has a pivotal role in enhancing this greater mutual understanding between African American students and educators (teachers and school leaders).

Culturally relevant leadership is a conceptual approach for educators, especially in leadership that seeks to create effective and nurturing educational environments regardless of students' race/ethnicity, social class, gender, and so forth. It resembles earlier notions of culturally relevant pedagogy (Ladson-Billings, 1994) and culturally responsive pedagogy (Gay, 2000). However, culturally relevant leadership emphasizes greater leadership responsibility in schools. The three basic elements of culturally relevant leadership include: (a) liberatory consciousness, (b) pluralistic insight, and (c) reflexive practice.

These three tenants work together to assist the leader in gaining new knowledge, processing information, situational application with reflection based on experience, and continuous self-improvement. Liberatory consciousness is akin to notions of critical consciousness and seeks to raise awareness levels and increase knowledge and understanding regarding diversity and social justice (Beachum & McCray, 2010; Ryan, 2005; Tatum, 1997). Educational leaders seek out theoretical, philosophical, and intellectual development opportunities. This is where the Black church can provide crucial historical memory and context, such as information about the local community, demographic changes, and local people of interest. Pluralistic insight has to do with educators' attitudes and expectations towards

students. It encourages an affirming and positive perspective of students (especially students of color) that acknowledges the uniqueness of their experiences and their rich diversity and the alternative forms of capital they bring (Yosso, 2005). The Black church can reinforce positive values, which should undergird the practice of all educators. It should be noted that the emphasis on values should not be mistaken for proselytizing. Reflexive practice views educators (teachers and administrators) as change agents who engage in ongoing praxis (reflection and action) for overall better student outcomes. The Black church could connect to its historical role as vanguard of social justice by making sure that the reality of students' school experiences matches the lofty rhetoric. If indeed, the education of today's African American youth (and all youth), is akin to the civil rights struggle of decades past, then the Black church should fulfill its same role as a place of shared information, community organizing, and collective action.

The work of school leaders should be hands-on, dynamic, and evolutionary. What they do on a daily basis with students, especially African American students, should become moments of meaning and opportunities for unique learning that informs future diversity-related actions. This work can be significantly informed by the Black church acting as a community partner in the educative process.

The Black Church and the Pedagogy of Self-Development

The Black church—the clergyperson and his or her congregants—should work diligently with school leaders on reducing any racial or class-based hostility that might exist within the school climate or culture. Such efforts in the amelioration of racial and class bigotry or the eradication of deficit thinking fit well within the framework of culturally relevant leadership. It is disingenuous for educators and school leaders to make the assumption that African American students and students of color from low wealth communities are going to miraculously conform to their cultural ethos. And the Black church must act as a conduit in building a relationship with schools to dismantle such paradigms and to ensure that African American students are not penalized for such resistance (unless of course, the form of resistance disrupts the educational environment). Such thinking is what undergirds educational malpractice. This type thinking by educators and school leaders leave students feeling powerlessness and frustrated. The Black church can help school leaders have an impact on the culture of an organization and reduce such feelings among African American and students of color (Foster, 2009; McCray, Alston, & Beachum, 2006; Randolph, 2009) by helping to cultivate culturally relevant leadership among school leaders. Such collaboration addresses negative cultural issues within schools while also subscribing to cultural pluralism that allows for alternative forms of capital to be acknowledged and valued. The authors proffer that this acceptance of alternative capital will lead to the pedagogy of self-development. Such pedagogy is buttressed by notions of self-realization and self-assertion among those students who have been disenfranchised due to their lack of social, cultural, and economic capital. Self-realization is the way in which people make their dreams a reality, the way they feel about themselves, and how they understand the world around them. Self-assertion deals with the way in which people prepare themselves for and seize opportunities. Self-realization involves believing and self-assertion involves achieving. Educators play a critical role in this equation because they can assist or deter these efforts. Just as the Black church has a role in working with school leaders to assist them in the cultivation of culturally relevant leadership; it also has a crucial role in ensuring that African American students in the community are grounded in the notions of self-assertion and self-realization. Together, they form the pedagogy of self-development. Goodman (2008) defined pedagogy as "the practice of teaching, including methods and content. A pedagogy is based on a particular philosophy of education, which included the set of beliefs that form the basis upon which the teacher makes instructional decisions" (p. 264). The pedagogy of self-development is linked to teaching because the educators and school leaders involved must be very purposeful in making sure that self-assertion and self-realization are both being addressed within the classroom. Not only can the pedagogy of self-development be cultivated within schools, it can also be manifested within the Black church, especially one that is undergirded by the precepts of a material religion. The pedagogy of self-development has particular potential when conflated with the alternative forms of capital as suggested by Yosso (2005; see Figure 1).

Self-realization entails the elements of familial, resistant, and linguistic capital. These three forms of capital are helpful as students formulate goals, careers, and dreams for the future. Self-assertion encompasses aspirational, social, and navigational capital. These forms of capital address how students cope with others, operate in society, and develop resiliency. This framework has insightful implications for not only teachers and school leaders, the Black church and its congregants.

RECOMMENDATIONS FOR PRACTICE

What is being proposed is a collaborative endeavor that will involve dedication, commitment, and trust among all stakeholders. It, therefore, is important for to address how this relationship might look in action because this kind of scholarship can sound great in theory but lack substance in practice. The scholarship should be well-grounded in appropriate bodies of research while being terse and tangible

```
        ┌─────────────────────┐
        │  Pedagogy of Self-  │
        │    Development      │
        └─────────────────────┘



┌──────────────────────┐   ┌──────────────────────┐
│   Self-Realization   │   │    Self-Assertion    │
│   Familial Capital   │   │  Aspirational Capital│
│   Resistant Capital  │   │    Social Capital    │
│  Linguistic Capital  │   │ Navigational Capital │
└──────────────────────┘   └──────────────────────┘
```

Figure 1. Pedagogy of self-development and alternative forms of capital

enough to inform the daily work that goes on in urban schools and communities. It is with these considerations, the authors offer the following suggestions:

School-Community Committee—this committee would be made up of school personnel, parents, local business leaders, church leaders, and/or anyone who has a stake in the school. This committee would serve in an advisory capacity around mutual issues of interest (e.g., school-to-work, community safety, etc.). This committee would also serve as a two-way means of communication between the school and community members whereby school personnel could inform the group of activities and initiatives and vice versa. This approach is directly connected to culturally relevant leadership because it relies on community members who can directly provide feedback and guidance to inform liberatory consciousness, pluralistic insight, and reflexive practice.

After-School Mentoring Clubs—these clubs could meet alter school and be advised and facilitated by congregants from the local Black church and teachers or administrators. They could plan collaboratively meetings and activities. This effort would give church members who seek opportunities to work with youth an organized program sanctioned by the school. The content of the meetings could deal with issues raised by the students, as well as agreed upon ideas from the adults. The school and the Black church would work together to promote the pedagogy of self-development, thereby reinforcing alternative forms of capital.

Community Night—this event would celebrate the best of what the community has to offer. This effort could be planned collaboratively and executed by both the school and the Black church. This event could be used to highlight school accomplishments, inform the community of upcoming events, and/or spotlight community talent (e.g., choirs, singers, speakers, etc.). This event could also teach the community about historical events (local history, Black History Month, Dr. Martin Luther King's birthday, etc.). This endeavor would have to be well planned, communicated, and executed through the collective actions of the school and the Black church. Such an event could be connected directly to promoting the pedagogy of self-development and used to encourage self-realization and self-assertion. It also can inform culturally relevant leadership with regard to liberatory consciousness and pluralistic insight

Weekend School—the weekend school could take place at the local Black church (on Saturday mornings, for instance). This "school" could be used to supplement educational instruction with tutoring, emphasis on literacy and numeracy, and/or cultural information. This learning environment could be staffed by teachers from the school and church members. While at the church, the emphasis would not necessarily be on religious conversion or content (unless a specific course was added to the curriculum); rather an emphasis on collective values of respect, responsibility, unity, etc., could permeate the efforts. This approach supports the tenants of the pedagogy of self-development.

Collaborative Community Service—this would be a jointly-planned community service event(s) that involves both the school and the Black church. The school-community committee mentioned above or a designated subcommittee would be charged with the identification of an issue of concern (e.g., violence prevention, community beautification, dropouts, etc.) and then plan a community-based service activity to address the issue. This endeavor would have benefits for all involved. For educators, it informs culturally relevant leadership by working with the Black church and engaging in the service act itself. For students it encourages die pedagogy of self-development by students asserting themselves towards the service activity and working to make it a reality. The Black church benefits by the collaborative relationship forged with the school as they address an issue of mutual concern, as well as the congregants serving as mentors and models for the youth in the service activity.

Of course, these suggestions are not exhaustive, but they provide some guidance for schools and Black churches as they brainstorm and plan their collective efforts.

Conclusion

Finally, in our postmodern world of pervasive consumerism and hedonism, narcissism and cynicism, skepticism and nihilism, the Socratic love of wisdom and prophetic love of justice may appear hopeless.

Who has not felt overwhelmed by dread and despair when confronting the atrocities and barbarities of our world? And surely a cheap optimism or trite sentimentalism will not sustain us. We need a bloodstained Socratic love and tear-soaked prophetic love fueled by a hard-won tragicomic hope. (West, 2004, pp. 215–216)

In this somber yet sustaining statement, Cornel West captured the feelings of despair, disillusionment, disengagement, and disrepair in many urban communities in the United States. Instead of a "tragicomic hope" (which the authors support), we offer the phrase "tenacious hope." This form of hope is stalwart, viscid, and manifests great potential and power. It is this kind of hope that is needed to do the difficult and rewarding work of community connections and collaboration as outlined in this article. In this article, a historical background of the Black church's role has been provided, an educational rationale for engaging education as a civil rights issue has been asserted, and a theoretical framework for educational leaders (culturally relevant leadership) and students (pedagogy of self-development), including some practical applications has been proffered. Beachum and McCray (2010) described the mentality that should accompany this work when they noted it entails "hope in the midst of hopelessness, action and advocacy in the face of hegemony, and a sense of spirit, which replenishes the soul and revives the will for change" (p. 215).

Ultimately, this kind of collaborative work must engage the head, the hands, and the heart. It must make sense mentally to those who are doing the work (the head). It must be action-oriented so the efforts do not die from being "talked to death" (the hands). Finally, this work must seize our emotions giving us the political and moral will to get the job done (the heart).

REFERENCES

Allen, W., & Solórzano, D. (2001). Affirmative action, educational equity, and campus racial climate: A case study of the university of Michigan law school, *Berkeley La Raza Law Journal, 12,* 237–363.

Alva, S. (1991). Academic invulnerability among Mexican American students: The importance of protective resources and appraisal, *Hispanic Journal of Behavioral Sciences, 13,* 18–34.

Anderson, J. D. (1988). *The education of Black in the South, 1860–1935.* Chapel Hill: University of North Carolina Press.

Beachum, F. D., Dentith, A., & McCray, C. R., & Boyle, T. (2008). Havens of hope or the killing fields: The paradox of leadership, pedagogy, and relationships in an urban middle school. *Urban Education, 43,*189–215.

Beachum, F. D., & McCray, C. R. (2004). Cultural collision in urban schools. *Current Issues in Education, 7.* Retrieved from http://cie.asu.edu/volume7/number5/

Beachum, F. D., & McCray, C. R. (2010). Cracking the code: Illuminating the promises and pitfalls of social justice in educational leadership. *International Journal of Urban Educational Leadership, 4,*206–221. Retrieved from http://www.uc.edu/urbanleadership/current_issues.htm

Beachum, F. D., & McCray, C. R. (in press). *Cultural collision and collusion: Reflections on hip-hop culture, values, and schools.*

Beachum, F. D., Obiakor, F., & McCray, C. R. (2007). Community uplift theory for positive change of African Americans in urban schools. In M. C. Brown & R. D. Bartee (Eds.), *Still not equal: Expanding educational opportunities in society* (pp. 269–278). New York: Peter Lang.

Bell, D. (2004). *Silent covenants: Brown v. Board of Education and the unfilled hopes for racial reform.* Oxford: Oxford University Press.

Bogotch, I., Beachum, F. D., Blount, J., Brooks, J., & English, F. (2008). *Radicalizing educational leadership: Dimensions of social justice.* Rotterdam, NL: Sense Publishing.

Bourdieu, P., & Passeron, J. (1977). *Reproduction in education, society and culture.* London: Sage.

Carruthers, J. H. (1999). *Intellectual warfare.* Chicago: Third World Press.

"Civil rights in education." (2010, March 16). *New York Times,* A22.

Collins, P. H. (2005). *Black sexual politics: African Americans, gender, and the new racism.* New York: Routledge.

Cosby, B., & Poussaint, A. F. (2007). *Come on people: On the path from victims to victors.* Nashville: Thomas Nelson.

Dantley, M. E. (2009). African American educational leadership: Critical, purposive, and spiritual. In L. F Foster & L. C. Tillman (Eds.), *African American perspectives on leadership in schools: Building a culture of empowerment* (pp. 39–56). Lanham, MD: Rowman & Littlefield Education.

Day-Vines, N. L., & Day-Hairston, B. O. (2005). Culturally congruent strategies for addressing the behavioral needs of urban, African American male adolescents. *Professional School Counseling, 8,* 236–243.

Douglas, K. B., & Hopson, R. E. (2001). Understanding the Black church: The dynamic of change. *Journal of Religious Thought, 56–57,* 95–113.

Du Bois, W. E. B. (1989). *The soul of Black folks.* New York: Bantam. (Original work published 1903)

Dyson, M. E. (2009). *Can you hear me now? The inspiration, wisdom, and insight of Michael Eric Dyson.* New York: Basic Civitas Books.

Feagin, J. R., & Feagin, C. B. (1978). *Discrimination American style: Instructional racism and sexism.* Malabar: FL: Krieger.

Ferguson, A. A. (2001). *Bad boys: Public school in the making of Black masculinity.* Ann Arbor: The University of Michigan Press.

Foster, L. (2009). Leadership in K–12 schools for promoting educational aspirations: A mental model for school advancement. In L. Foster & L. C. Tillman (Eds.), *African American perspectives on leadership in schools: Building a culture of empowerment* (pp. 157–170). Lanham, MD: Rowman & Littlefield Education.

Franklin, V. P. (2002). Introduction: Cultural capital and African American education. The *Journal of African American History, 87,* 175–181.

Freire, P. (1973). *Pedagogy of the oppressed.* New York: The Seabury Press.

Gay, G. (2000). *Culturally responsive teaching: Theory, research, and practice.* New York: Teachers College Press.

Glaude, E. S. (2007). *In a shade of blue: Pragmatism and the politics of Black America.* Chicago: University of Chicago Press.

Gooding-Williams, R. (2009). *In the shadow of Du Bois: Afro-modern political though in America.* Cambridge, MA: Harvard University Press.

Goodman, G. (2008). *Educational psychology: An application of critical constructivism.* New York: Peter Lang.

Gregory, A., & Mosely, P. M. (2004). The discipline gap: Teachers' views on the overrepresentation of African American students in the discipline system. *Equity and Excellence in Education, 37,* 18–30.

Haberman, M. (2005). Personnel preparation and urban schools. In F. E. Obiakor & F. D. Beachum (Eds.), *Urban education for the 21st Century: Research, issues, and perspectives* (pp. 34–58). Springfield, IL: Charles C. Thomas.

Hersey, P., Blanchard, K. H., & Johnson, D. E. (1996). *Management of organizational behavior: Utilizing human resources.* Upper Saddle River, NJ: Prentice Hall.

Hymes, D. H. (1981). Foreword. In C. A. Ferguson & S. B. Heath (Eds.), *Language in the USA* (pp. v–ix). New York: Cambridge University Press.

Jackson, J. H. (2008). *Given half a chance: The Schott 50-state report on public education and African American males.* Cambridge, MA: Schott Foundation for Public Education.

Karenga, M. (1989). *The African-American holiday of Kwanzaa: A celebration of family, community, and culture.* Los Angeles: University of Sankore.

Ladson-Billings, G. (1994). *The dreamkeepers: Successful teachers of African-American students.* San Francisco: Jossey-Bass.

Lightfoot, J. (2009). Toward a praxis of antiracist school leadership preparation. In L. F. Foster & L. C. Tillman (Eds.), *African American perspectives on leadership in schools: Building a culture of empowerment* (pp. 211–236). Lanham, MD: Rowman & Littlefield Education.

Lindsey, R. B., Roberts, L. M., & Campbell Jones, F. (2005). *The culturally proficient school: An implementation guide for school leaders.* Thousand Oaks, CA: Corwin.

McCray, C. R. (2008). Constructing a positive intrasection of race and class for the 21st century. *Journal of School Leadership, 18,* 249–267.

McCray, C. R., Alston, J. A., & Beachum, F. D. (2006). Principals' perceptions of multicultural education and school climate. *Multicultural Learning and Teaching, 1,* 12–22. Retrieved from http://www.mltonline.org/current-articles/beachum2.pdf

McKenzie, K. B. (2001). *White teachers' perceptions about their students of color and themselves as White educators* (Unpublished doctoral dissertation). University of Texas at Austin.

Nesbitt, R. E. (2009). *Intelligence and how to get it: Why schools and cultures count.* New York: Norton.

Obiakor, F. E. (2007). *Multicultural special education: Culturally responsive teaching.* Upper Saddle River, NJ: Pearson Merrill/Prentice Hall.

Obiakor, F. E., & Beachum, F. D. (2005). Urban education: The quest for democracy, equity, and excellence. In F. E. Obiakor & F. D. Beachum (Eds.), *Urban education for the 21st century: Research, issues, and perspectives* (pp. 3–19). Springfield, IL: Charles C. Thomas.

Obiakor, F. E., Harris-Obiakor, P., Garza-Nelson, C., & Randall, P. (2005). Educating urban learners with and without special needs: Life after the *Brown* case. In F. E. Obiakor & F. D. Beachum (Eds.), *Urban education for the 21st century: Research, issues, and perspectives* (pp. 20–33). Springfield, IL: Charles C. Thomas.

Ogbu, J. U. (1999). Beyond language: Ebonics, Proper English, and identity in a Black-American speech community. *American Educational Research Journal, 36,* 147–184.

Ovando, C. J. (2001). Language diversity and education. In J. A. Banks & C. A. McGee Banks (Eds.), *Multicultural education: Issues and perspectives* (4th ed., pp. 268–291). New York: Wiley.

Perry, T. (2003). Up from the parched earth: Toward a theory of African-American achievement. In T. Perry, C. Steel, & A. G. Hilliard (Eds.), *Young gifted and Black: Promoting high achieving among African-American students* (pp. 1–108). Boston: Beacon.

Perry, T., & Delpit, L. (1998). *The real Ebonics debate.* Boston: Beacon.

Perry, T., Steele, C., & Hilliard, A. (2003). *Young, gifted, and Black: Promoting high achievement among African-American students.* Boston: Beacon.

Peterson, R. L. (2003). Teaching the social curriculum: School discipline as instruction. *Preventing School Failure, 47,* 66–73.

Quarles, B. (1987). *The Negro in the making of America.* London: Collier Macmillan.

Randolph, A. L. W. (2009). The historical tradition of African American leadership in African American schools: 1830–1955. In L. Foster & L. C. Tillman (Eds.), *African American perspectives on leadership in schools: Building a culture of empowerment* (pp. 17–37). Lanham, MD: Rowman & Littlefield Education.

Reed, L. C. (2008). An expansion of a scholar's social justice perspective: A meeting at the crossroads. *Journal of School Leadership, 18,* 200–223.

Rodriguez, G. M. (2004). Vertical equity in school finance and the potential for increasing school responsiveness to student and staff needs. *Peabody Journal of Education, 79,* 7–30.

Ryan, J. (2005). *Inclusive leadership.* San Francisco: Jossey-Bass.

Shelby, T. (2005). Justice, deviance, and the dark ghetto. *Philosophy & Public Affairs, 35,* 126–160.

Skiba, R. J., & Peterson, R. L. (1999). The dark side of zero tolerance: Can punishment lead to a safe school? *Phi Delta Kappan, 80,* 372–376.

Tatum, B. D. (1997). *Why are all the Black kids sitting together in the cafeteria? And other conversations about race.* New York: Basic.

Tatum, B. D. (2007). *Can we talk about race? And other conversations in an era of school resegregation.* Boston: Beacon.

Thomas, D. E., & Stevenson, H. (2009). Gender risks and education: The particular classroom challenges for urban low-income African American boys. *Review of Research in Education, 33,* 160–180.

Tillman, L. C. (2004). African American principals and the legacy of *Brown. Review of Research in Education, 28,* 101–146.

Tillman, L. C. (2009). Facilitating African American parental involvement in urban schools: Opportunities for school leadership. In L. Foster & L. C. Tillman (Eds.), *African American perspectives on leadership in schools: Building a culture of empowerment* (pp. 75–94). Lanham, MD: Rowman & Littlefield Education.

Valencia, R. R. (1997). *The evolution of deficit thinking: Educational thought and practice. Stanford series on education and public policy*. London: Falmer.

Valencia, R. R., & Solórzano, D. G. (1997). Cultural deficit model thinking. In R. R. Valencia (Ed.), *The evolution of deficit thinking: Educational thought and practice* (pp. 160–210). Stanford Series on Education and Public Policy. London: Falmer.

Venkatesh, S. A. (2006). *Off the books: The underground economy of the urban poor*. Cambridge, MA: Harvard University Press.

Villegas, A. M., & Lucas, T. (2002). *Educating culturally responsive teachers: A coherent approach*. Albany, NY: State University of New York Press.

West, C. (2004). *Democracy matters: Winning the fight against imperialism*. New York: Penguin.

Wilson, W. J. (2009). *More than just race: Being black and poor in the inner city*. New York: Norton.

Yosso, T. J. (2005). Whose culture has capital? A critical race theory discussion of community cultural wealth. *Race, Ethnicity, and Education, 8,* 69–91.

AUTHORS

CARLOS R. McCRAY is Associate Professor at Fordham University in New York at the Educational Leadership, Administration, and Policy Division where he teaches a seminar on ethics and social justice. **COSETTE M. GRANT** is Adjunct Professor in Higher Education Administration at Duquesne University in Pittsburgh. **FLOYD D. BEACHUM** is the Bennett Professor of Urban School Leadership at Lehigh University in Bethlehem, Pennsylvania. All comments and queries regarding this article should be addressed to cmccray2@fordham.edu

LIST OF CONTRIBUTORS

HUSSAIN AL-FADHLI is Associate Professor of Sociology at Jackson State University in Mississippi. Al-Fadhli has a wide range of academic and administrative experiences including his role as a department chair at Tougaloo College and Jackson State University from 1996–2007.

KENNETH ALONZO ANDERSON is Assistant Professor, Howard University School of Education, in the Department of Curriculum & Instruction. His research interest is reading achievement, and standardized test performance of African-American male PK–12 students.

BRUCE MAKOTO ARNOLD is an invited instructor at the University of Missouri-Columbia in the Department of History. Mr. Arnold is an advanced doctoral candidate of history at Louisiana State University specializing in American cultural history, Asian-American history, and African and African-American history.

BRIAN D. BARRETT is Assistant Professor in the Foundations and Social Advocacy Department, School of Education, at the State University of New York College at Cortland. His research and teaching interests include urban education, the sociology of education and knowledge, and teacher education.

FLOYD D. BEACHUM is the Bennett Professor of Urban School Leadership at Lehigh University in Bethlehem, Pennsylvania. He is also Associate Professor and program coordinator for the Educational Leadership program in the College of Education. His research interests include: leadership in urban education, moral and ethical leadership, and social justice issues in K12 schools.

LINDA M. CHATTERS is Professor of Public Health and Professor of Social Work at the University of Michigan, Ann Arbor. Her research interests encompass family and church-based social support and the relationship between religious involvement and health.

JENNIFER R. CURRY is Assistant Professor of Counselor Education in the Department of Educational Theory, Policy and Practice at Louisiana State University. She is the president of the national Association for Spiritual, Ethical and Religious Values in Counseling and Post-Secondary Vice President of the Louisiana School Counselor Association.

T. ELON DANCY II is Assistant Professor of Adult and Higher Education in Department of Educational Leadership and Policy Studies at the University of Oklahoma in Norman.

MICHAEL E. DANTLEY is Associate Provost and Associate Vice President for Academic Affairs and Professor of Educational Leadership at Miami University. He is considered a leader in the area of spirituality and education.

ROBERT W. GAINES H is a third-year doctoral student in the Department of Lifelong Education, Administration, and Policy at the University of Georgia in Athens. His research interests include the intersection of race, religion, and the history of education.

MARK S. GILES is Assistant Professor in the Department of Educational Leadership at Miami University-Ohio. Dr. Giles focuses his research on African American educational history, the intersection of leadership and spirituality, and critical race theory.

MARK A. GOODEN is Associate Professor of the University of Texas at Austin Principalship Program (UTAPP) in the Educational Administration Department. His research interests include the principalship, anti-racist leadership, issues in urban educational leadership and legal issues in education.

COSETTE M. GRANT works in Higher Education Administration at Duquesne University. Her research focuses on the challenges and opportunities offered by mentoring relationships, with a focus on how these relationships may be changing as a result of increasing diversity. Her work includes issues women and people of color face as they develop mentoring relationships.

CHRISTOPHER C. JETT is Clinical Assistant Professor of Mathematics Education in the Department of Middle-Secondary Education and Instructional Technology in the College of Education at Georgia State University. His research interests are centered on employing a critical race philosophical and theoretical perspective to mathematics education research and investigating the experiences of academically successful African American students in mathematics.

WILLIAM H. JEYNES is Professor in the Department of Teacher Education at California State University at Long Beach.

LES T. JOHNSON is a doctoral student in Urban Education at the University of Wisconsin-Milwaukee. His research interests include the intersections of race, class, and gender identities; academic achievement of transgender students; and emotional safety in online learning environments.

THOMAS MICHAEL KERSEN is Assistant Professor of Sociology at Jackson State University. His research interests are social capital, community, sociology of religion, military sociology, and intentional communities.

MUHAMMAD KHALIFA is Assistant Professor of Educational Leadership and Policy Studies at the University of Texas at San Antonio. His research interests look at how contexts influence school leadership. Specific areas include school leadership in urban, racialized, and international contexts, as well as for at-risk and refugee students.

MOOSUNG LEE is Assistant Professor of Educational Policy and Leadership at the Hong Kong Institute of Education.

NA'IM MADYUN is Assistant Professor of Postsecondary Teaching and Learning at the University of Minnesota-Twin Cities.

CARLOS R. MCCRAY is Associate Professor at Fordham University in New York. His research interests include multicultural education and building level leadership. He has also done extensive research on issues surrounding urban education.

ROLAND W. MITCHELL is Assistant Professor and Program Chair of Higher Education in the Department of Educational Theory, Policy, and Practice, Louisiana State University in Baton Rouge.

JASON NELSON is a part-time educational researcher specializing in the connections between religion and education, both as a subject to be studied and as part of the lived experience of teachers, students, and other stakeholders in education. A graduate of the University of Washington's doctoral program, he also specializes in educational leadership, social and cultural foundations, and multicultural education, with a focus on identity issues of religion, race, gender, and class.

Black American Cinema

The New Realism

By Manthia Diawara

The release of D. W. Griffith's *The Birth of a Nation* in 1915 defined for the first time the side that Hollywood was to take in the war to represent Black people in America. In *The Birth of a Nation*, D. W. Griffith, later a founding member of United Artists, created and fixed an image of Blackness that was necessary for racist America's fight against Black people. *The Birth of a Nation* constitutes the grammar book for Hollywood's representation of Black manhood and womanhood, its obsession with miscegenation, and its fixing of Black people within certain spaces, such as kitchens, and into certain supporting roles, such as criminals, on the screen. White people must occupy the center, leaving Black people with only one choice—to exist in relation to Whiteness. *The Birth of a Nation* is the master text that suppressed the real contours of Black history and culture on movie screens, screens monopolized by the major motion picture companies of America.

Griffith's film also put Black people and White liberals on the defensive, inaugurating a plethora of historical and critical writings against *The Birth of a Nation,* and overdetermining a new genre, produced exclusively for Black audiences, called race films. More insidiously, however, the racial conflict depicted in *The Birth of Nation* became Hollywood's only way of talking about Black people. In other words, whenever Black people appeared on Hollywood screens, from *The Birth of a Nation* to *Guess Who's Coming to Dinner?* to *The Color Purple,* they are represented as a problem, a thorn in America's heel. Hollywood's Blacks exist primarily for White spectators whose comfort and understanding the films must seek, whether they thematize exotic images dancing and singing on the screen, or images constructed to narrate a racial drama, or images of pimps and muggers. With *The Birth of a Nation* came the ban on Blacks participating in bourgeois humanism on Hollywood screens. In other words, there are no simple stories about Black people loving each other, hating each other, or enjoying their private possessions without reference to the White world, because the spaces of those stories are occupied by newer forms of race relation stories which have been overdetermined by Griffith's master text.

The relations between Black independent cinema and the Hollywood cinema just described above parallel those between Blackness and Americanness; the dichotomy between the so-called marked cultures and unmarked cultures; but also the relations between "high art" and "low art." The complexity of these relations is such that every independent filmmaker's dream is to make films for Hollywood where she/he will have access to the resources of the studios and the movie theaters. On the other hand, the independents often use an aesthetic and moral high ground to repudiate mainstream cinema, which is dismissed as populist, racist, sexist, and reactionary. Furthermore, a look at the relations between Oscar Micheaux and the Hollywood "race films," Melvin Van Peebles and the Blaxploitation films, Charles

Burnett *(Killer of Sheep)*, Haile Gerima *(Bush Mama)*, and Spike Lee and the rethematization of urban life in such films as *City of Hope, Grand Canyon, Boyz N the Hood,* and *Straight Out of Brooklyn* reveals that mainstream cinema constantly feeds on independent cinema and appropriates its themes and narrative forms.

Some of the most prominent Black film historians and critics, such as Albert Johnson, Donald Bogle, and Thomas Cripps, emphasize mainly mainstream cinema when discussing Black films. With the exception of a few breakthrough films, such as those by Micheaux, Van Peebles, and Lee, these historians are primarily concerned with the issues of integration and race relations in mainstream films, Black actors and actresses on the big screen, and the construction of stereotypes in Hollywood films. They rarely pay attention to independent cinema, which includes far more Black directors than Hollywood, and in which aesthetics, political concerns such as authorship and spectatorship, and the politics of representation with respect to Black cinema are more prevalent. Critics and historians such as Clyde Taylor, Toni Cade Bambara, Phyllis Klotman, and Gladstone Yearwood are the first to focus on Black independent cinema as a subject of study. More recently, the *Black Film Review* has assumed the preeminent role in Black film history and criticism.

Hollywood's block-booking system prevents independently produced films from reaching movie theaters and large audiences. This may be one reason why film historians and critics neglect independent cinema: some film magazines, such as *Cineaste,* adopt a policy of accepting only reviews of films that have been distributed and seen by their readers, it is also possible to argue that Black independent cinema has remained marginal until now because its language, not unlike the language of most independent films, is metafilmic, often nationalistic, and not "pleasurable" to consumers accustomed to mainstream Hollywood products. Black independent cinema, like most independent film practices, approaches film as a research tool. The filmmakers investigate the possibilities of representing alternative Black images on the screen; bringing to the foreground issues central to Black communities in America; criticizing sexism and homophobia in the Black community; and deploying Afrafemcentric discourses that empower Black women. The narratives of such films are not always linear; the characters represent a tapestry of voices from W. E. B. DuBois, Frantz Fanon, Toni Morrison, Malcolm X, Martin Luther King, Jr., Karl Marx, Angela Davis, Alice Walker, and Zora Neale Hurston. Even what passes as documentary in Black independent films, like *The Bombing of Osage Avenue* (Louis Massiah), is an artistic reconstruction of archival footage and "real" events.

What is, therefore, the Black independent cinema, and what constitutes its influence on mainstream cinema? The French appropriately refer to independent cinema as *cinema d'art et essai*. In France, the government sponsors such a cinema by imposing a distribution tax on commercial films. The *cinema d'art at essai* is less concerned about recouping its cost of production and making a profit; its main emphasis is toward artistic development, documenting an area of research, and delineating a certain philosophy of the world. In the late 1950s, a group of French youth, who were dissatisfied with commercial films and wanted to make their own films, mobilized private and personal funds along with government funds to produce low-budget films. The result is well known today as the French New Wave, considered by some as one of the pivotal moments in film history.

As an alternative to commercial cinema, which emphasized the well-made story, acting, and the personality of the actor, the New Wave put in the foreground the director, whom it raised to the same artistic level as the author of a painting, a novel, or a poem; the New Wave also demystified the notion of the well-made story by experimenting with different ways of telling the same story, and by deconstructing the notion of actor and acting. Jean-Luc Godard's *Breathless* (1959), for example, is famous for its reinsertion of the "jump-cut" as a valid narrative device. The jump-cut, which was avoided in Hollywood films in order not to disrupt the spectator with "unnecessary" repetitions, has today become a powerful narrative device used by directors such as Spike Lee, who redefines it and uses it to describe the repetition and the sameness in racial and sexual stereotyping. In *Do the Right Thing* (1988) Lee uses the same angle to repeat several shots of Blacks, Italians, Jews, and Koreans repeating racial stereotypes, unlike Godard, who uses the same image twice from the same angle. Lee practices the same device in *She's Gotta Have It* (1985) to construct sexual stereotypes among young Black males.

This example of the New Wave reveals that independent filmmakers come to their vocation for at least two reasons: one political, and the other artistic. Politically, they are dissatisfied with commercial cinema's lack of courage to address certain issues. They feel that they have to make their own films if they want to see those issues on the screen. Artistically, they want to explore new ways of telling stories; they want to experiment with the camera, the most powerful invention of modern times, and engage the infinite possibilities of storytelling. There are other examples of alternative or independent cinemas that occupy important places in the history of film. The Italian Neorealism, the Brazilian Cinema Novo, and the Argentinian Third Cinema have all created alternative narrative techniques that were at first unknown to commercial cinemas, but are claimed today as part of traditional narrative practices.

Similarly, the cloning of Hollywood's mind to Black history and culture, which do not revolve around White people, is the reason why most Black filmmakers since Oscar Micheaux have turned first to the Independent sector. Since Oscar Micheaux, Black independents have pioneered creating alternative images of Blacks on the screen, constructing new narrative forms derived from Black literature and folklore, and denouncing racism, sexism and homophobia in American culture.

This is not, however, to romanticize the independent practice. Micheaux made his films by selling personal property and borrowing money from friends. Still today, independent filmmaking causes many people to become poor. It takes more than six years for some filmmakers to gather the money for one film. Charles Burnett's *To Sleep With Anger,* and Julie Dash's *Daughters of the Dust* came only after arduous years of fundraising. Halle Gerima has been trying to raise funds for *Nunu* for several years now. We have not yet seen second features by talented directors such as Billy Woodberry *(Bless Their Little Hearts),* Larry Clark *(Passing Through),* Alile Sharon Larkin *(A Different Image),* and Warrington Hudlin *(Street Corner Stories).* Spike Lee sums up the harsh reality of independent production as follows:

When I went to film school I knew I did not want to have my films shown only during Black History Month in February or at libraries. I wanted them to have a wide distribution. And I did not want to spend four or five years trying to piecemeal together the money for my films. I did my first film, *She's Gotta Have It,* independently for $175,000. We had a grant from the New York State Council on the Arts and were raising money the whole time we were shooting. We shot the film in twelve days. The next stage was to get it out of the lab. Then, the most critical part was when I had to hole up in my little apartment to get it cut. I took about two months to do that. I had no money coming in, so I had to hold off the debtors because I knew if I had enough time to at least get it in good enough shape to show, we could have some

investor screenings, and that's what happened. We got it blown up to 35mm for a film festival. What you have to do is to try to get a distributor. You enter as many film festivals as you can.[1]

Black independent cinema is any Black-produced film outside the constraints of the major studios. The filmmakers' independence from Hollywood enables them to put on the screen Black lives and concerns that derive from the complexity of Black communities. Independent films provide alternative ways of knowing Black people that differ from the fixed stereotypes of Blacks in Hollywood. The ideal spectators of the films are those interested in Black people's perspectives on American culture. White people and Whiteness are marginalized in the films, while central positions are relegated to Black people, Black communities, and diasporic experiences. For example, the aesthetics of uplifting the race in a film like *The Scar of Shame* (1928, The Colored Players) concern particularly Black spectators, whom the filmmakers' stated mission is to entertain and educate. The film posits Black upper-class culture as that which should be emulated by lower class Blacks—in order to humanize themselves. Unlike Hollywood films of that time, which identified with the ideal White male, the camera in *The Scar of Shame* identifies with the position of the Black bourgeoisie. The film is precious today as a document of Black bourgeois ways of being in the 1920s and 1930s. Crucially, it constitutes, with Oscar Micheaux's films, a genre of Black independent cinema which puts Black people and their culture at the center as subjects of narrative development; in these films, Black people are neither marginalized as a problem, nor singled out as villainous stereotypes such as Hollywood constructs in its films.

Contemporary independent films continue the same effort of inquiring into Black subjectivities, the heterogeneity of Black lives, the Black family, class and gender relations, and diasporic aesthetics. Recently, independent Black women filmmakers such as Kathleen Collins *(Losing Ground),* Alile Sharon Larkin *(A Different Image),* Ayoka Chenzira *(Zajota: the Boogie Spirit),* Julie Dash *(Daughters of the Dust),* and Zeinabu Davis *(A Powerful Thang)* have explored such themes as Black womanhood and spirituality, diaspora art and music, and Afrocentric aesthetics. Black manhood, the urban landscape, unemployment and the Black family are thematized in films like *Sweet Sweetback's Baaaaadasss Song* (Van Peebles), *Killer of Sheep* (Burnett), *Bless Their Little Hearts* (Woodberry), *Serving Two Masters* (Tim Lewis), *Street Corner Stories* (Warrington Hudlin), *Chameleon Street* (Wendell Harris), and *Ashes and Embers* (Halle Gerima). The themes of sexuality and homophobia are depicted in *Tongues Untied* (Marlon Riggs), *Storme: Lady of the Jewel Box* (Michelle Parkerson), *She's Gotta Have It* (Spike Lee), *Ganja and Hess* (Bill Gunn), *Splash* (Thomas Harris), and *She Don't Fade* (Cheryl Dunye). The major Black documentary artists, such as William Greaves, Louis Massiah, Camille Billops, and Sinclair Bourne, have also enriched the documentary genre by focusing their cameras on Black people in order to reconstruct history, celebrating Black writers and activists, and giving voice to people who are overlooked by television news and mainstream documentaries.

TWO PARADIGMS OF BLACK CINEMA AESTHETICS

In her contribution to this volume, Jane Gaines defines Oscar Micheaux's editing style as follows: "Perhaps to elude any attempt to essentialize it, we could treat this style as more of an ingenious solution to the impossible demands of the conventions of classical Hollywood style, shortcuts produced by the exigencies of economics, certainly, but also modifications produced by an independent who had nothing at stake in strict adherence to Hollywood grammar." Gaines goes on to posit that Micheaux's "freewheeling cinematic grammar" constitutes both a misreading and an improvement upon Hollywood logic. Clearly, Micheaux's "imperfect" cinema (to borrow a term from Julio Garcia Espinoza), which misreads and improves upon Hollywood logic, is a powerful metaphor for the way in which African-Americans survived and continue to survive within a hostile economic and racist system, and used the elements of that survival as raw material to humanize and improve upon American modernism. Micheaux's "loose editing," like the improvisation of jazz, surprises and delights the spectator with forbidden images of America that Hollywood's America conceals from its space. In so far as the classical Hollywood narrative proceeds by concealment of space, Micheaux's "imperfect" narrative constitutes an excess which reveals the cheat cuts, the other America artificially disguised by the Hollywood logic. It is in this sense that Gaines writes of improvement of film language by Micheaux. Another contributor to the volume, Ron Green, compares Micheaux's film style to Black English, and to jazz. His cinema is one of the first to endow African-Americans with cinematic voice and subjectivity through his uncovering of new spaces at the threshold of dominant cinema.

The first step in interpreting a Black film aesthetic must therefore be directed towards an analysis of the composition of the new shots discovered by Micheaux, and their potential effects on spectators. In this volume, Micheaux's films are discussed in an in-depth manner for the first time by Jane Gaines and Ron Green. Micheaux's legacy as an independent filmmaker not only includes his entrepreneurial style in raising money and making films outside the studios. He also turned his cameras towards Black people and the Black experience in a manner that did not interest Hollywood directors of race films. Crucially, Micheaux's camera positioned Black spectators on the same side as the Black middle-class ideology, acquiring for his films an aesthetic that was primarily specific to the ways of life of that class.

Similarly, in the 1970s, Melvin Van Peebles and Bill Gunn positioned spectators with respect to different imaginaries derived from the Black experience in America. In *Sweet Sweetback's Baadasssss Song*, Van Peebles thematizes Black nationalism by casting the Black community as an internal colony, and Sweetback, a pimp, as the hero of decolonization. In her contribution to this book, Toni Cade Bambara refers to *Sweet Sweetback* as "a case of Stagolee meets Fanon or Watermelon Man plays Bigger Thomas?" *Sweet Sweetback* is about policing and surveillance of Black communities, and the existentialist straggle of the film's main character, a Black man. As Bambara notices, Bigger Thomas is not the only literary reference in the film; it also draws on the theme of the running Black man in *Invisible Man*, which is collapsed into a transformed Hollywood stereotype of the Black stud. As such, *Sweet Sweetback* is famous as the paradigmatic text for the 1970s Blaxploitation films. The theme of the Black man running from the law or from Black-on-Black crime, which links Van Peebles to such Black American writers as Richard Wright, Ralph Ellison, and Chester Himes, is also echoed in 1990s films like *Juice, Straight Out of Brooklyn,* and *Boyz N The Hood,* not to mention *New Jack City,* a film directed by Van Peebles's son, Mario Van Peebles.

Sweet Sweetback's aesthetic draws on the logic of Black nationalism as the basis of value judgment, and defines itself by positioning the spectator to identify with the Black male hero of the film. Bambara rightly criticizes the centrality of Black manhood at the expense of women in *Sweet Sweetback,* but recognizes nationalist narratives as enabling strategies for survival, empowerment, and self-determination. As Sweetback is helped to escape from the police by one Black person after another, the nationalist discourse of the film transforms the ghetto, where Black people are objects, into the community, where they affirm their subjecthood. To put it in Bambara's words, "Occupying the same geographical terrain are the *ghetto*, where we are penned up in concentration-camp horror, and the *community*, where we enact daily rituals of group validation in a liberated zone."

In *Ganja and Hess,* Bill Gunn aestheticizes the Black imaginary by placing the spectator on the same side as the Black church. The spectator draws pleasure from the film through the confrontation between the ideology of the Black church and vampirism, addiction to drugs and sex, and materialism. *Ganja and Hess* is perhaps the most beautifully shot Black film, and the most daring with respect to pushing different passions to their limits. The Black artist, Meda (played by Bill Gune himself), is a nihilist who advocates total silence because, as a Black person, his art is always already overdetermined by race in America. The love scenes in the film are commingled with vampiristic gestures that are attractive and repulsive at the same time. At the Cannes Film Festival in 1973, Gunn's daring camera angles during one of the loves scenes brought spectators to joy, applauding and screaming "Bravo! Bravo!" in the middle of the film. *Ganja and Hess* also pushes the classical narrative to the threshold by framing a frontal nude image of a Black man coming out of a swimming pool and running toward a window where a woman, Ganja (Marlene Clarke), smilingly awaits him.

What is radical about both *Ganja and Hess* and *Sweet Sweetback* is their formal positioning of Black characters and Black cultures at the center of the screen, creating a sense of defamiliarization of the classical film language. The two films also inaugurate for Black cinema two narrative tracks with regard to time and space. While *Ganja and Hess* is cyclical, going back and forth between pre-Christian time and the time after Christ, *Sweet Sweetback* is a linear recording of the progress of Black liberation struggle.

With regard to Black aesthetics, it is possible to put in the same category as *Ganja and Hess* such films as *A Powerful Thang* (Davis), *Daughters of the Dust* (Dash), *Losing Ground* (Collins), *Killer of Sheep* and *To Sleep with Anger* (Burnett), *Tongues Untied* (Riggs), and *She's Gotta Have It* (Lee). These films are concerned with the specificity of identity, the empowerment of Black people through mise-en-scène, and the rewriting of American history. Their narratives contain rhythmic and repetitious shots, going back and forth between the past and the present. Their themes involve Black folklore, religion, and the oral traditions which link Black Americans to the African diaspora. The narrative style is symbolic.

Sweet Sweetback, on the other hand, defines its aesthetics through recourse to the realistic style in film. The story line develops within the logic of continuity editing, and the characters look ordinary. The film presents itself as a mirror on a Black community under siege. The real effect is reinforced throughout the film by events which are motivated by racial and gendered causes. The sound track and the costumes link the film to a specific epoch in the Civil Rights Movement. Unlike the first category of films, which uses the symbolic style and concerns itself with the past, *Sweet Sweetback* makes the movement toward the future-present by confronting its characters with obstacles ahead of them. Other films in this category include *Cooley High* (Michael Schultz), *House Party* (Reginald Hudlin), *Chameleon Street* (Harris), *Passing Through* (Clark), *Do The Right Thing* (Lee), *Straight Out of Brooklyn* (Rich), *Juice* (Ernest Dickersoe), and *Boyz N The Hood* (Singleton). These lists are neither exhaustive nor fixed. The realist category has more in common with the classical Hollywood narrative, with its quest for the formation of the family and individual freedom, and its teleological trajectory (beginning, middle, and end). The symbolic narratives have more in common with Black expressive forms like jazz, and with novels by such writers as Toni Cade Bambara, Alice Walker, and Toni Morrison, which stop time to render audible and visible Black voices and characters that have been suppressed by centuries of Eurocentrism.

The comparison of the narrative styles deployed by *Sweet Sweetback* and *Ganja and Hess*[2] is useful in order to link the action-oriented *Sweet Sweetback* to modernism, and the reflexive style of *Ganja and Hess* to postmodernism. *Sweet Sweetback* defines its Afro-modernism through a performative critique of the exclusion of Blacks from reaping the fruits of American modernity and liberal democracy. *Ganja and Hess* is a postmodern text which weaves together a time of pre-Christian Africa, a time of Christ's Second Coming in the Black church, and a time of liberated Black women. Crucially, therefore, the repetition of history as played out on the grid of the Black diaspora is important to the definition of Gunn's film language. Through the repetition of these Black times in the film, Bill Gunn defines a Black aesthetic that puts in the same space African spirituality, European vampire stories, the Black church, addiction to drugs, and liberated feminist desires.

THE NEW BLACK FILMS

It is easy to see the symbolic, reflexive, and expressive styles in films such as *Killer of Sheep* and *Daughters of the Dust,* and the active, materially grounded, and linear styles in *Boyz N the Hood.* But before looking more closely at these films, it is important to put into some perspective the ways in which Black films posit their specificity by challenging the construction of time and space in Hollywood films. It is only in this sense that arguments can begin about whether they displace, debunk, or reinforce the formulaic verisimilitude of Hollywood.

The way in which a filmmaker selects a location and organizes that location in front of the camera is generally referred to in film studies as mise-en-scène. Spatial narration in classical cinema makes sense through a hierarchical disposition of objects on the screen. Thus space is related to power and powerlessness, in so far as those who occupy the center of the screen are usually more powerful than those situated in the background or completely absent from the screen. I have described here Black people's relation to spatially situated images in Hollywood cinema. When Black people are absent from the screen, they read it as a symbol of their absence from the America constructed by Hollywood. When they are present on the screen, they are less powerful and less virtuous than the White man who usually occupies the center. Hollywood films have regularly tried to resolve this American dilemma, either through token or symbolic representation of Blacks where they are absent—for instance, the mad Black scientist in *Terminator 2;* or through a substitution of less virtuous Blacks by positive images of Blacks—for instance, *Grand Canyon* or *The Cosby Show.* But it seems to me that neither symbolic representation nor positive images sufficiently address the specificity of Black ways of life, and how they might enter in relation to other Americans on the Hollywood screen. Symbolic representation and positive images serve the function of plotting Black people in White space and White power, keeping the real contours of the Black community outside Hollywood.

The construction of time is similarly problematic in the classical narrative. White men drive time from the East to the West, conquering wilderness and removing obstacles out of time's way. Thus the "once upon a time" which begins every story in Hollywood also posits an initial obstacle in front of a White person who has to remove it in order for the story to continue, and for the conquest ideology of

Whiteness to prevail. The concept of beginning, middle, and end, in itself, is universal to storytelling. The difference here is that Hollywood is only interested in White people's stories (White times), and Black people enter these times mostly as obstacles to their progress, or as supporting casts for the main White characters. "Once upon a time" is a traditional storytelling device which the storyteller uses to evoke the origin of a people, their ways of life, and the role of the individual in the society. The notion of *rite de passage* is a useful concept for describing the individual's separation from or incorporation into a social time. The classical narrative in cinema adheres to this basic ideological formula in order to tell White people's stories in Hollywood. It seems that White times in Hollywood have no effect on Black people and their communities: whether they play the role of a negative or positive stereotype, Black people neither grow nor change in the Hollywood stories. Because there is a dearth of Black people's stories in Hollywood that do not revolve around White times, television series such as *Roots*, and films such as *Do the Right Thing*, which situate spectators from the perspective of a Black "once upon a time," are taken out of proportion, celebrated by Blacks as authentic histories, and debunked by Whites as controversial. To return again to the comparison between *Sweet Sweetback* and *Ganja and Hess*, it is easy to see how important time and space are to defining the cinematic styles they each extol. The preponderance of space in films such as *Ganja and Hess* reveals the hierarchies of power among the characters, but it also reveals the preoccupation of this style of Black cinema with the creation of space on the screen for Black voices, Black history and Black culture. As I will show later with a discussion of space in *Daughters of the Dust*, Black films use spatial narration as a way of revealing and linking Black spaces that have been separated and suppressed by White times, and as a means of validating Black culture. In other words, spatial narration is a filmmaking of cultural restoration, a way for Black filmmakers to reconstruct Black history, and to posit specific ways of being Black Americans in the United States.

The emphasis on time, on the other hand, reveals the Black American as he/she engenders him/herself amid the material conditions of everyday life in the American society. In films like *Sweet Sweetback* and *Boyz N the Hood*, where a linear narrative time dominates, the characters are depicted in continuous activities, unlike the space-based narratives, where the past, constantly interrupts the present, and repetitions and cyclicality define narration. Crucially, whereas the space-oriented narratives can be said to center Black characters on the screen, and therefore empower them, the Black-times narratives link the progress of time to Black characters, and make times exist for the purpose of defining their needs and their desires. Whereas the space-based narratives are expressive and celebratory of Black culture, the time-based narratives are existentialist performances of Black people against policing, racism, and genocide. I would like now to turn to *Daughters of the Dust* and *Boyz N the Hood* to illustrate the point.

Space and Identity: Black Expressive Style in *Daughters of the Dust*

I am the first and the last
I am the honored one and the scorned one
I am the whore and the holy one
I am the wife and the virgin
I am the barren one and many are my daughters. ...

I am the silence that you cannot understand. …
I am the utterance of my name.

(Daughters of the Dust)

I have argued that the Hollywood classical narrative often articulates time and space through recourse to a discriminating gaze toward American Blacks. When the story is driven by time and action, it is usually White times. I'll say more about this in my discussion below of *Boyz N the Hood.* Similarly, when spatial considerations dominate the production of the story, the purpose is usually to empower White men. Common sense reveals that characters that are more often on the screen, or occupy the center of the frame, command more narrative authority than those that are in the background, on the sides, or completely absent from the frame. By presence, here, I have in mind first of all the literal presence of White characters in most of the shots that constitute the typical Hollywood film, which helps to define these characters as heroes of the story. There is also the symbolic presence through which narrative authority for the organization of space is attributed to certain characters in the story. These devices of spatial narration are effective in linking characters with spaces, and in revealing space occupancy as a form of empowerment. For example, through the character played by Robert Duval in *Apocalypse Now,* Francis Ford Coppola parodies the power associated with White male actors such as John Wayne as they are framed at the center of the screen.

There is preponderance of spatial narration in Julie Dash's *Daughters of the Dust.* Black women and men occupy every frame of the film, linking Black identity to a place called Ibo Landing in the Sea Islands of South Carolina, and, more importantly, empowering Black women and their ways of life. On a surface and literal level, the wide appeal of the film for Black women depends on the positioning of the women characters as bigger than life in the middle of the screen, which mirrors the beautiful landscape of Ibo Landing. Black women see themselves on the screen, richly adorned, with different hues of Blackness and Black hair styles, and flaunting their culture. In *Daughters of the Dust,* the screen belongs to Black women. At a deeper level, where space and time are combined into a narrative, Julie Dash emphasizes spatial narration as a conduit to Black self-expressivity, a storytelling device which interrogates identity, memory, and Black ways of life. *Daughters of the Dust* stops time at 1902, when the story was set, and uses the canvas of Ibo Landing in the Sea Islands to glance backward to slavery, the Middle Passage, African religions, Christianity, Islam, the print media, photography, moving pictures, and African-American folkways, as elements with which Black people must come to terms in order to glance forward as citizens of the United States. In other words, the film asks us to know ourselves first, know where we came from, before knowing where we are going. To put it in yet another way, Ibo Landing is a symbolic space in which African-Americans can articulate their relation to Africa, the Middle Passage, and the survival of Black people and their ways of life in America. Crucially, the themes of survival, the memories of African religions and ways of life which enter into conflict with Christianity and European ways of life, and the film's proposal of syncretism as a way out, are narrativized from Black women's points of view. I want to take more time here to show how Julie Dash uses women's voices to make these themes compatible with the space of Ibo Landing.

The conflict in the film concerns the migration of the Peazant family from Ibo Landing of the Sea Islands to the North. At first the conflict is set in binary terms. For those who support the migration North, the space of Ibo Landing is primitive, full of people who worship the sun, the moon, and the river. The North therefore promises literacy, Christianity and progress. For Grandma Nana and the Unborn Child who link their identity to the space of Ibo Landing, the North represents the destruction of the family, disconnection from the ancestors, and the loss of identity for the children. For Grandma Nana, Ibo Landing is where the ancestors watch over the living, protect them, and guide them. It is in this sense that Nana does not want the family reunion to be a farewell party between those who are leaving and those staying. She prepares herself to give them something that they "can take North with [them] along with [their] big dreams."

As filmic space, Ibo Landing is the link between Africa and America. Or, to put it another way, Ibo Landing is Africa in America. According to the film, it is where the last slaves landed. *Daughters of the Dust* also argues that it is where African-Americans remained isolated from the mainland of Georgia and South Carolina, and "created and maintained a distinct imaginative and original African-American culture." The Peazant family must therefore learn the terms of their belonging to Ibo Landing, which will be an example of African-American belonging to America, and must use the space of Ibo Landing to validate their identities as Americans of a distinctive culture. It is interesting to notice here that, unlike the Hollywood narratives which claim space only as a process of self-empowerment, *Daughters of the Dust* acknowledges through the letter that Iona receives from her Indian lover that the space belonged to the Indians first.

Weaving the voices of Grandma Nana, the Unborn Child, and Eula (the mother of the Unborn Child) through the spaces of Ibo Landing, Julie Dash creates a narrative that connects Africa to America, the past to the present. Using African ancestor figures as her narrative grid, she places Grandma Nana at the center of her story, and constructs oppositional characters around her. On the one hand we have Haagar, Viola, the bible lady, and Eli, who is Eula's husband; on the other hand we have Yellow Mary, Eula, and Iona, who is Haagar's daughter. We have characters who are alike and who constitute reincarnations of ancestor figures with similar dispositions; and characters who are contraries of one another, and therefore require the intervention of the ancestors to bring peace and harmony.

Grandma Nana is the oldest person on the island. She spends most of her time visiting the graveyard where the ancestors are buried, and by the water which is a dwelling place of the spirits of the ancestors. I do not have enough space here to discuss the significance of water in *Daughters of the Dust*. But it is crucial to point out the recurring Middle Passage theme of Africans walking on water to go back to Africa. As an intertextual religious space, the use of water by Grandma Nana to communicate with the gods echoes *Yeelen* by Souleymane Cissé, where the mother baths with milk' in the middle of the river and asks the Goddess to protect her son. *Daughters* also reminds us of *Testament* by Black Audio Film/Video Collective, in which the characters walk into the middle of the river or visit graveyards in order to unlock the secret of the past. It would also be interesting to investigate the use of water in vases and on altars as a representation of Voodoo in *Daughters* and in *Dreaming Rivers* by Sankofa Film/Video Collective.

Daughters depicts the survival of African religious practices in Ibo Landing through Grandma Nana in other ways as well. She can hear the calls of the spirits, and, therefore, works with the Unborn Child to keep the family together. She teaches Eli about the core of African ancestor worship: "It's up to the living to keep in touch with the dead, Eli. Man's power don't end with death. We just move on to another place; a place where we go and watch over our living family. Respect your elders, respect your family, respect your ancestors."

A recourse to religion is central to the understanding of *Daughters of the Dust* For Grandma Nana, ancestor worship provides the strongest stability for the Black family in America and Africa. Unlike Christianity and Islam, which are teleological and reserve the final reward for the end in Heaven, the ancestors in Grandma Nana's belief system just move to another world and watch over their living descendants. The children are the reincarnation of the ancestors, and this makes them precious to the adults whose fathers and grandfathers have joined the land of the ancestors. The Unborn Child in the film is one such reincarnation. She is doubled not only in the figure of Grandma Nana herself, but also in the young girl with tribal scars who appears with her mother in one of the flashbacks. She travels through time, and she is present at different settings in the film: we see her among the first generation of Africans working with indigo dye, and we see her in a 1902 setting among children playing in the sand. Like the ancestors, her role is one of a mediator in the family. It is in this sense that Grandma Nana states that for Africans, the ancestors and the children are the most sacred elements of society.

Julie Dash also uses the religious theme of reincarnation, and links the Unborn Child to African-American survival during slavery, genocide, and the rape of Black women. In the film, the theme of the Peazant family's disintegration entailed by the migration to the North is replayed in the subtheme of Eli's self-exile from his wife, Eula, because she's carrying a child that Eli does not consider his. Eli's first reaction to Eula's pregnancy is to become an iconoclast toward the ancestor belief system that Grandma Nana wants to maintain. He puts into question the religion and culture he has received from childhood to adulthood. In other words: How can this happen to him, who has played by the rules? How come the gods are not avenging his misfortune? Subsequently, he picks up his ax and proceeds to smash all the fetishes that he had previously revered.

Grandma Nana finds an answer to Eli's blasphemous questions in her belief system. She links Eula's pregnancy to the condition of Black women in slavery who were raped, denied motherhood rights, and treated like animals. At the same time, the power and complexity of Black people come from their ability to maintain the sacredness of the womb by restoring to the group the children of interracial rape. Grandma Nana uses ancestor worship, and the place of children in it, to appropriate the baby Eula is carrying. By doing so, she bends the filiative and patriarchal rules Eli maintains in order to disavow the Unborn Child. For Grandma Nana, Eli, too, must learn the process of cleansing rape from the child's name, and making it his own child. Grandma Nana argues that the womb is as sacred as the ancestors, and that the Unborn Child is sent by the ancestors, precisely at this critical juncture in Ibo Landing's history, to ensure survival: "You need this one, Eli, to make the family stronger like it used to be." It is interesting to note the spatial organization as Grandma Nana talks to Eli. As the oldest person in the Peazant family, her role is that of a teacher. As she speaks to Eli, the space revealed on the screen is that of children playing games on the beach. The narrative implication here is that the children are the audience of her teaching. At one point during the children's game, the film changes to a slow motion. As the children fall on top of one another, we hear screaming and groaning, which remind us of the Middle Passage during which hundreds of Africans were piled on top of each other in the cabins of slave ships. The implication of Grandma Nana's teaching is that, just as captured Africans were thrown together during that painful time of the Middle Passage, Blacks today must see themselves in the same boat, and fight together to "make the family stronger."

Eli's questions about the paternity and, therefore, the race of the Unborn Child also touch on the issues of light skin and dark skin, pure blood and mixed blood, superior and inferior; in short, we are

dealing with racism among Blacks. It is in this sense that Yellow Mary is ostracized by Haagar and Viola, who use her light complexion as a sign of betrayal and try to banish her from Ibo Landing. For Grandma Nana, Yellow Mary and the Unborn Child contribute to the survival and maintenance of Black people in America, because their presence makes Blackness diverse and complex. Black survival in America confounds and embarrasses both Whiteness and essentialist notions of pure Africans. Julie Dash puts onto stage one of the most beautiful and powerful scenes in the film to illustrate this point. Haagar and others have been chastising Yellow Mary for not being Black enough, when Eula stands up and delivers a speech worthy of an ancestor figure. The mise-en-scène of this sequence reveals Black women in all their powers, as Eula reminds Haagar that no one is Blacker or purer than anyone else, and warns her and Viola about the wrath of the gods, if they were to continue their gesture of expelling Yellow Mary out of the race. Spatial representation again becomes paramount, because Eula's speech is directed to the on-screen audience of the Peazant family, as well as the off-screen spectators.

I have discussed so far the ways in which *Daughters of the Dust* uses African belief systems as the center which enables Black women and men to articulate their identities on the space of Ibo Landing. Grandma Nana, particularly, posits the ancestor worship system as a text which holds together the world of Ibo Landing and provides answers to practical daily problems. A crucial question remains: whether the belief in ancestors can coexist with other belief systems, such as Christianity and Islam, on and off the island? At first, religious systems seem to be opposed in *Daughters of the Dust*. Bilal, who is Muslim, is opposed to the Baptists, who think that their God is better. Viola and Haagar use Christianity to elevate themselves above Grandma Nana. They see ancestor worship as an idolatry which is confined to Ibo Landing. They look to the North as a sign of enlightenment and Christian salvation.

Clearly, Julie Dash represents all these belief systems on the space of Ibo Landing not to show the fixity of different religions, and their essentialist nature, but to propose all of them as part of what makes Black people in America complex. Toward the end of the film Grandma Nana brings together the different belief systems, when she ties together the Bible and a sacred object from her own religion, and asks every one to kiss the hybridized Bible before departing from the island. This syncretic move is her way of mixing up the religions in Ibo Landing, and activating their combined power to protect those who are moving North. Earlier in the film she commands Eli to "celebrate our ways" when he goes North. The syncretic move is therefore also a survival tactic for the African ways of life up North.

Arguably, another reason for deploying ancestor worship (and casting Grandma Nana at the center in the film) is to reveal its usable power in holding the Black family together. Placing women at the center of the frame is also Julie Dash's way of creating space for Black people in modernity, and is her redefinition of Black images in their relation to such modem tools as still photography, newspapers, and moving pictures. Julie Dash's spatial narrative style inextricably combines the identities of her characters with the landscape of Ibo Landing. Her mise-en-scène of Grandma Nana, Haagar, Yellow Mary, and Eula in the center of the frame makes the space theirs, and their possession of the space makes them bigger than life. They become so associated with the space of Ibo Landing, through close-ups of various sorts, that it becomes difficult to imagine Ibo Landing now without the faces of these Black women. Analogically speaking, it is like imagining America in Western films without the faces of John Wayne, Kirk Douglas, and Gary Cooper.

The spatial narrative style of *Daughters of the Dust* enables Julie Dash to claim America' as the land of Black people, to plot Africanism in American ways of life, and to make intelligible African voices that were rendered inarticulate. To return to the thematization of religion in the film, Julie Dash has made manifest an Africanism that was repressed for centuries, but that refused to die. As Grandma Nana states, "those African ancestors sneak up on you when you least suspect them." With her revival of ancestor worship as a narrative grid, as a point of reference for different themes in the film, Julie Dash has ignited the fire of love and caring among Black people. The path between the ancestors and the womb constitutes a Black structure of feeling, a caring handed down from generation to generation, which commands us to care for our children. In an article entitled "Nihilism and Black America," Cornel West proposes "a politics of conversion" as a way out of the carelessness of Black-on-Black crime, and as a protection against "market-driven corporate enterprises, and white supremacism." For West,

> The genius of our black foremothers and forefathers was to create powerful buffers to ward off the nihilistic threat, to equip black folk with cultural armor to beat back the demons of hopelessness, meaninglessness, and lovelessness. … These traditions consist primarily of black religious and civic institutions that sustained familial and communal networks of support.[3]

Perhaps Julie Dash's theory of ancestor worship should be among those institutions that constitute Black structures of feeling; as Grandma Nana puts it, let the ancestors guide us and protect us.

Black Times, Black Stories: *Boyz N the Hood*

Either they don't know, or don't show, or don't care about what's going on in the 'Hood. *(Boyz N the Hood)*

To return now to *Boyz N the Hood,* I would like to illustrate its emphasis on time and movement as a way of defining an alternative Black film language different from the spatial and expressive language of *Daughters of the Dust.* Like *Daughters of the Dust, Boyz N the Hood* begins with a well-defined date. But unlike *Daughters of the Dust,* which is set in 1902 and looks into the past as a way of unfolding its story, *Boyz N the Hood* starts in 1984, and continues for more than seven years into the future. *Daughters of the Dust* is about Black peoples' reconstitution of the memories of the past; it is a film about identity, and the celebration of Black ways of life. *Boyz N the Hood,* on the other hand, is a rite of passage film, a film about the Black man's journey in America. The story line is linear in *Boyz N the Hood,* whereas *Daughters of the Dust* unfolds in a circular manner.

In films like *Boyz N the Hood, Juice, Straight Out of Brooklyn,* and *Deep Cover,* the narrative time coincides with the development of the lives of the characters in the films. Many of these films begin with the childhood of the main characters, who then enter into adulthood, and face many obstacles in their lives. These films produce an effect of realism by creating an overlap between the rite of passage into manhood and the narrative time of the story. The notion of rite of passage, which defines the individual's relation to time in terms of separation from or incorporation into society, helps us to understand the use of narrative time in a film like *Boyz N the Hood.* The beginning, middle, and end of *Boyz N the Hood* constitute episodes that mark the young protagonist's incorporation into the many levels of society. In fact, the structure of the film is common to African-American folktales, as well as to the classical cinema.

It is as follows: A boy has to go on a journey in order to avert an imminent danger. He travels to the home of a relative or friend (uncle, aunt, father, mother, wise man, and so on) who teaches him, or helps him to overcome the obstacle. At the end, he removes the danger, and his nation (or community, or family) gets stronger with him. This skeletal structure is common to texts as diverse as *The Epic of Sunjata* (D. T. Mane), the *Aeneid* (Virgil), and *The Narrative of the Life of Frederick Douglass* (Douglass), as well as to the Hollywood Western genre, the martial art films, and the Rocky films with Silvester Stallone. The literal journey in time and space overlaps with the symbolic journey of the rite of passage. Typically, this type of storytelling addresses moments of crisis, and the need to build a better society.

The moment of crisis is symbolized in *Boyz N the Hood* by the opening statistical information, which states that "One out of every twenty-one Black American males will be murdered in their lifetime. Most will die at the hands of another Black male." Thus, *Boyz N the Hood* is a cautionary tale about the passage into manhood, and about the development of a politics of caring for the lives of Black males. More specifically, it is about Tre Styles (Cuba Gooding Jr.), the main character, and his relation to the obstacles that he encounters on his way to manhood. Crucially, the major distractive forces in the film are the police, gang life, and the lack of supervision for the youth. To shield Tre from these obstacles, his mother sends him to live with his father, whose teaching will guide him through the many rites of passage toward manhood.[4]

The film is divided into three episodes, and each episode ends with rituals of separation and transition. In the first episode the ritual ends with Tre leaving his mother (first symbol of weaning) and friends behind. The story of this episode implies that most of the friends he leaves behind will not make it. On the way to his father's house, Tre's mother says, "I don't want you to end up dead, or in jail, or drunk standing in front of one of these liquor stores." The second episode ends with Doughboy's (Ice Cube) arrest by the police, who take him to the juvenile detention camp. The third episode ends with the death of Ricky Baker, Doughboy, and many other Black males. At the end of each episode, Tre moves to a higher understanding of life.

Let us now focus on one of the episodes in order to show its internal conflicts, and the specific elements that enter into play to prevent the passage of young Black males into manhood and caring for the community. I will choose the first episode because it introduces the spectator to most of the obstacles which are complicated and repeated in the other episodes. The film opens with a shot in which the camera zooms in on a stop sign until it fills the screen. We see a plane fly over the roofs, and the next shot reveals Tre and three other young kids walking to school. The subtitles say: "South Central LA, 1984." The children walk by a one-way street sign. This sign, too, is depicted in close-up as the camera travels above to establish the crossroad. Then the four kids take a direction facing a wrong-way sign. They travel on that road and see a crime scene that is circled by a plastic ribbon with the words: "Police Line Do Not Cross."

Inside the police line there are three posters of President Ronald Reagan with a sign saying: "Reagan/ Bush, Four More Years." The kids cross the police line, as one of them moves closer to the Reagan posters. At that moment a rhythmic and violent editing reveals each of the posters in close-up with the sound of a gunshot. There are bullet holes in the poster. In the next scene, the kids are in a classroom where the students' artworks on the wall reflect the imagery of policing: drawings of a Los Angeles Police Department helicopter looking down on people, a police car, a coffin, and a poster of wanted men. Tre disrupts a lesson on the Pilgrims, and when the teacher asks him to teach the class, he points to the map of Africa and states that: "Africa is the place where the body of the first man was found." This is a reference to the multiculturalism debate not only across the curriculum, but also in rap music, and in the press. Tre's lesson ends with a fight between himself and another boy. The following shot begins with Tre walking home. He passes a group of young Black males shooting dice. They break into a fight. As Tre crosses the street to go home, he is almost ran over by a blue car which presumably is driven by gang members. His mother is on the telephone talking to the teacher about the fight and Tre's suspension. The editing of the soundtrack is interesting in this scene. As Tre walks past the men shooting dice, their noise is placed in the back-ground, and we hear in the foreground the conversation between Tre's mother and the teacher. This editing device unites different spaces through their sharing of the same sound. For example, later in the film, the community is shown as one when people in different places listen to the same rap song. (Similarly, in *Do the Right Thing,* Spike Lee uses the DJ and his music to unite the community.) The last scene in this episode involves Tre and his mother driving to his father's house. They pass by liquor stores and junkies standing by the doors. The mother reassures Tre that she loves him, and will do anything to keep him from ending up in jail, or standing in the streets in front of liquor stores.

Signs (Stop, One Way, Wrong Way, LAPD, Liquor Store, POLICE LINE DO NOT CROSS, and so on) play an important role in limiting the movement of people in South Central Los Angeles. Showing the airplane flying over the roofs not only indicates where we are in LA, but also suggests the freedom associated with flying away from such an enclosed space. Black American literature often draws on the theme of flying to construct desire for liberated spaces: Bigger Thomas of *Native Son* (Richard Wright) sees flying as a way out of the ghetto of South Side Chicago; Milkman of *Song of Solomon* (Morrison) reenacts the myth of flying Americans in order to free himself from an unwanted situation.

The signs become control tools for the police, in the way that they limit individual freedom of movement in the "hood." They also define the hood as a ghetto by using surveillance from above and outside to take agency away from people in the community. In fact, *Boyz N the Hood* is about the dispute over agency and control of the community that pits the protagonist and his allies against gang members and the police. The drawings of helicopters, police cars, and wanted men show how the police surveillance has penetrated the imaginary even of schoolchildren in the hood. Later on in the film, helicopter noise, police sirens, and police brutality are revealed to be as menacing and distracting to people in the hood as drags and gang violence.

The dispute over the control of the hood is also a dispute over images. The police need to convince themselves and the media that every Black person is a potential gang member, armed and dangerous, in order to continue the policing of the hood in a terroristic and militaristic manner. For the Black policeman in the film, the life of a Black person is not worth much: "one less nigger out in the street and we won't have to worry about him." It is by making the gang members and other people in the hood accept this stereotype of themselves that the community is transformed into a ghetto, a place where Black life is not worth much. It seems to me that *Boyz N the Hood* blames the rise of crime and the people's feeling of being trapped in the hood on a conspiracy among the gang members, the police, the liquor stores, and Reagan. Indeed, the film raises questions of human rights violation when gang warfare and police brutality collude to prevent people from moving around freely, sleeping, or studying.

On the other hand, Tre's struggle to gain agency also coincides with his passage to manhood, and the development of a politics of caring for the community. *Boyz N the Hood,* in this respect, is one of the most didactic Black films. The other contenders are *Deep Cover,* and perhaps some rap videos which espouse a politics of identification with lawbreakers against the police.[5] The didacticism of *Boyz N the Hood* emanates from the film's attempt to teach Tre not to accept the police's and the media's stereotype of him and other young Black males as worthless; and to teach him to care for his community and reclaim it from both the gangs and the police. Didactic film language abounds in the film. We see it when the camera lingers on the liquor stores and homeless people, as Tre and his mother drive to his father's house. The mother, in one of the first instances of teaching Tre in the film, states that she loves him and that is why she is taking him out of this environment. Earlier in the same episode, we also saw the Reagan posters interpreted in a didactic manner, so as to blame him for the decay of the urban community. The posters are situated in the same environment as the murder scene.

However, Tre's father, more than the didactic camera and editing styles, is the central figure of judgment in the film. He calls the Black policeman "brother" in order to teach him, In the presence of Tre, how to care about other Black people; he delivers lessons on sex education, Black-on-Black crimes, the dumping of drugs in the Black community, gentrification, and the importance of Black-owned businesses In the Black community. He earns the nickname of preacher, and Tre's friends describe him as a sort of "Malcolm/Farrakhan" figure. Crucially, his teachings help Tre to develop a politics of caring, to stay in school, and more importantly, to stay alive. It is revealing in this sense that a didactic and slow-paced film like Boyz *N the Hood* can be entertaining and pleasurable at the same time.

THE NEW BLACK REALISM

Realism as a cinematic style is often claimed to describe films like *Boyz N the Hood, Juice,* and *Straight Out of Brooklyn*. When I taught *Boyz N the Hood,* my students talked about it in terms of realism: "What happened in the film happens everyday In America." "It is like it really is in South Central LA." "It describes policing in a realistic manner." "The characters on the screen look like the young people in the movie theater." "It captures gang life like it is." "It shows Black males as an endangered species." "I liked its depiction of liquor stores in the Black community." "I identified with Ice Cube's character because I know guys like that back home."

Clearly, there is something in the narrative of films like *Boyz N the Hood* and *Straight Out of Brooklyn* that links them, to put it in Aristotelian terms, to existent reality in Black communities. In my class, some students argued that these films use hip hop culture, which is the new Black youth culture and the most important youth culture in America today. Thus, the characters look *real* because they dress in the style of hip hop, talk the lingo of hip hop, practice its world view toward the police and women, and are played by rap stars such as Ice Cube. Furthermore, the films thematize an advocacy for Black males, whom they describe as endangered species, in the same way that rap groups such as Public Enemy sing in defense of Black males.

It seems to me, therefore, that the films are about Black males' initiation into manhood, the obstacles encountered that often result in death and separation, and the successful transition of some into manhood and responsibility toward the community. In *Juice,* for example, of the four young boys who perform the ritual of growing up, two die, one is seriously injured by a gun shot, and only one seems to have been successfully incorporated into society. Removing obstacles out of Black males' way is also the central theme of *Chameleon Street, Straight Out of Brooklyn, Deep Cover* and *Boyz N the Hood.*

In *Deep Cover*, the ritual of manhood involves the main character's exposure of a genocide plotted by drug dealers in Latin America and the highest officials in the US government against the Black community. The real "deep cover" in *Deep Cover* is the recipe for caring for the community against genocidal forces like White supremacists, drugs, and Black-on-Black crime. The removal of obstacles out of the main character's way leads to the discovery of the politics of caring to the Black community. In this film, as in many new Black realism films, to be a man is to be responsible for the Black community, and to protect it against the aforementioned dangers. John (Larry Fishburne), a cop working undercover as a drug dealer, enters in an intriguing relationship with a Black detective (Clarence Williams), who plays the born-again policeman. The religious policeman keeps reminding John of his responsibility to the community, and John laughs at him. Toward the end of the film, when the character played by Clarence Williams gets shot, John is united with him by the force of caring, and realizes that he must fight both the drug dealers and the police to protect his own.

A key difference between the new Black realism films and the Blaxploitation series of the 1970s lies in character development through rites of passage in the new films. Unlike the static characters of the Blaxploitation series, the characters of the new realism films change with the enfolding of the story line. As characters move obstacles out of their way, they grow into men, and develop a politics of caring for the community. The new realism films imitate the existent reality of urban life in America. Just as in real life the youth are pulled between hip hop life style, gang life, and education, we see in the films neighborhoods that are pulled between gang members, rappers, and education-prone kids. For the black youth, the passage into manhood is also a dangerous enterprise which leads to death both in reality, and in film.

NOTES

1. Janice Mosier Richolson, "He's Gotta Have It: An Interview with Spike Lee," in *Cineaste*, Vol. 28, No. 4, (1992), p. 14.

2. For more on the aesthetics of *Sweet Sweetback* and *Ganja and Hess*, see the important book, *Black Cinema Aesthetics: Issues in Independent Black Filmmaking*, edited by Gladstone L. Yearwood, Athens: Ohio University Center for Afro-American Studies, 1982; Tommy L. Lott "A No-Theory Theory of Contemporary Black Cinema," in *Black American Literature Forum* 25/2 (1991); and Manthia Diawara and Phyllis Klotman, "*Ganja and Hess*: Vampires, Sex, and Addictions," in *Black American Literature Forum* 25/2 (1991).

3. Cornel West, "Nihilism in Black America," in *Dissent* (Spring 1991), 223.

4. Clearly, there is a put-down of Black women in the rhetoric used to send Tre to his father's house. For an excellent critique of female-bashing in the film see Jacquie Jones, "The Ghetto Aesthetic," in *Wide Angle*, Volume 13, Nos. 3 & 4 (1991), 32–43.

5. See Regina Austin, "'The Black Community,' Its Lawbreakers and a Politics of Identification," in *Southern California Law Review* (May 1992), for a thorough discussion of Black peoples' identification with the community and its lawbreakers.

AFRICAN AMERICANS, LABOR UNIONS, AND THE STRUGGLE FOR FAIR EMPLOYMENT

IN THE AIRCRAFT MANUFACTURING INDUSTRY OF TEXAS, 1941–1945

By Joseph Abel

Don Ellinger was a frustrated man in the summer of 1944. Lead examiner for the Region X office of the Fair Employment Practice Committee (FEPC) in Dallas, Texas, Ellinger and a small staff of investigators had spent the last two years working to obtain entry for African Americans into the all-white training facilities at a bomber factory owned by Consolidated-Vultee Aircraft Corporation (Convair) in nearby Fort Worth. Neither conferences, surveys, nor appeals to management had worked; if anything, Ellinger complained, since he began his investigations Convair's discriminatory practices had grown worse, expanding into such areas as hiring, upgrades, and discharge. "The attitude of the company, which from the first has been negative, is now openly hostile," he lamented, and the only means of reaching a resolution appeared to be through costly public hearings. Despite this negative assessment, Ellinger admitted that there was at least one small bright spot in the situation. Although African Americans were prohibited from joining the International Association of Machinists (IAM), J. D. Smith, the white president of IAM District Lodge 776, had offered his union's cooperation to the FEPC, in effect challenging the racial practices of the local aircraft industry and setting himself apart from the vast majority of southern labor activists. Even more heartening to Ellinger was the length to which Smith seemed willing to go to fulfill this pledge: in a gesture that would have been considered progressive within most American unions at the time, let alone one operating in the segregated South, Smith threatened to initiate arbitration proceedings against Convair management for unjustly firing an African American janitor, a tactic that gained the man's reinstatement. Having faced similar forms of managerial intransigence himself, Ellinger was pleased to be able to report back to his superiors in Washington, D.C., that Smith and District 776 "took a strong stand and fully represented the [black] worker as if he were a member of the IAM."[1]

---

1 Don Ellinger to Will Maslow, June 29, 1944, Folder "Consolidated-Vultee Aircraft Corp., 10-BR-235," Box 2, Closed Cases, Records of the Committee on Fair Employment Practice, 1940–1946, Record Group 228, National Archives and Records Administration-Southwest Region, Fort Worth, Texas, hereinafter cited as RG 228 (first quotation); Don Ellinger to Clarence Mitchell, July 21, 1944, Folder "International Association of Machinists, 10-UR-418," Box 6, *ibid*, (second quotation). I would like to thank Alex Lichtenstein, Andrew Kersten, and the anonymous readers for the *Journal of Southern History* for their insightful comments on this article.

This brief glimpse into the inner workings of Fort Worth's largest aircraft manufacturing facility both confirms and challenges a number of interrelated historical arguments surrounding the struggle for fair employment in the South during World War II. To begin with, Ellinger's tense exchanges with Convair and his feeble recommendation for public hearings will no doubt be recognizable to those who have examined the short-lived FEPC. Since the 1970s, numerous studies have laid bare the effects of outside opposition and organizational weakness on the ability of the committee to carry out its important work. In his examination of the FEPC's administrative history, Merl E. Reed paints a picture of an embattled committee that encouraged fair employment through investigations and public hearings yet lacked the authority to issue sanctions or demand full compliance. Although he acknowledges the courage and tenacity of the FEPC's integrated staff, Reed concludes that this innately weak federal agency was barely able to dent the surface of the South's caste-bound racial system, let alone overturn it, in the face of employer opposition. In a more recent study examining the impact of wartime manpower policy on the region, historian Charles D. Chamberlain agrees with Reed's assessment and presents the FEPC as generally ineffectual in removing the barriers placed before black southern workers.[2] Local accounts of the FEPC's investigations in the southern shipbuilding, oil refining, and railroad industries have all reached similar conclusions concerning managerial resistance, the committee's institutional weaknesses, and their combined effect on job prospects for black workers.[3]

As shown by Ellinger's protracted efforts to secure even minimal compliance from Convair, the heretofore neglected Fort Worth aircraft industry fits within the historiographical consensus surrounding the FEPC's shortcomings.[4] Of course, to point out the committee's overall ineffectiveness in north Texas is in and of itself nothing new. Where this article breaks new ground is in its explanation of the ephemeral yet undeniable economic gains made by black workers during World War II. Across the nation, the portion of African Americans employed in defense production increased from just 3 percent of the industry's total workforce in 1942 to more than 8 percent by 1945. During the same period in the South, African Americans gained close to 900,000 jobs.[5] Ellinger's frustrations notwithstanding, black

---

2 Merl E. Reed, *Seedtime for the Modern Civil Rights Movement: The President's Committee on Fair Employment Practice, 1941–1946* (Baton Rouge, 1991); Charles D. Chamberlain, *Victory at Home: Manpower and Race in the American South during World War II* (Athens, Ga., 2003). For detailed studies of the committee's activity in other regions of the nation, see Andrew Edmund Kersten, *Race, Jobs, and the War: The FEPC in the Midwest, 1941–46* (Urbana, 2000); and Clete Daniel, *Chicano Workers and the Politics of Fairness: The FEPC in the Southwest, 1941–1945* (Austin, 1991).

3 Merl E. Reed, "The FEPC, the Black Worker, and the Southern Shipyards," *South Atlantic Quarterly*, 74 (Autumn 1975), 446–67; Bruce Nelson, "Organized Labor and the Struggle for Black Equality in Mobile during World War II," *Journal of American History*, 80 (December 1993), 952–88; Emilio Zamora, "The Failed Promise of Wartime Opportunity for Mexicans in the Texas Oil Industry," *Southwestern Historical Quarterly*, 95 (January 1992), 323–50; Alexa B. Henderson, "FEPC and the Southern Railway Case: An Investigation into the Discriminatory Practices of Railroads during World War II," *Journal of Negro History*, 61 (April 1976), 173–87. General histories of the FEPC include Reed, *Seedtime for the Modern Civil Rights Movement*; Louis Ruchames, *Race, Jobs, and Politics: The Story of FEPC* (New York, 1953); Herbert Garfinkel, *When Negroes March: The March on Washington Movement in the Organizational Politics for FEPC* (Glencoe, 111., 1959); and Judson MacLaury, *To Advance Their Opportunities: Federal Policies Toward African American Workers from World War I to the Civil Rights Act of 1964* (Knoxville, 2008), 89–110.

4 Although there is not yet a full treatment of the wartime struggle for fair employment in the Fort Worth aircraft factories, the industry is sporadically mentioned in Chamberlain, *Victory at Home*, 129–30, 136–37, 194–95.

5 David M. Kennedy, *Freedom from Fear: The American People in Depression and War, 1929–1945* (New York, 1999), 775; Chamberlain, *Victory at Home*, 158.

workers even made advances in the Fort Worth aircraft industry, eventually occupying several thousand positions at Convair and its rival North American Aviation in the nearby town of Grand Prairie.

In their efforts to explain this important economic moment, historians have thus far advanced two main arguments. Not surprisingly, the first of these explanations tends to minimize the importance of the FEPC and instead looks to wartime labor markets for answers. According to such scholars as William H. Chafe, Richard Polenberg, and David Brody, it was the extreme shortage of manpower during the war that necessitated the temporary opening of jobs and industries long closed to African Americans. In this equation, the FEPC was symbolically important but otherwise accomplished very little for black workers.[6] Standing against this economic interpretation is the work of a more recent group of historians who focus specifically on the FEPC. While recognizing the institutional weaknesses of the committee, these scholars tend to afford it a great deal more significance. In his study of fair employment in the Midwest, for example, Andrew Edmund Kersten argues that even in cities like Detroit where labor shortages were a chronic problem, discriminatory patterns of employment persisted throughout the war. It was only through the continuous intercession of the FEPC and such allied organizations as the National Association for the Advancement of Colored People (NAACP), the Detroit Urban League, and the United Automobile Workers (UAW) that black workers were eventually able to enjoy the fruits of wartime prosperity.[7]

While there is some truth in each of these interpretations, it is Kersten's naming of a labor union as a partner of the FEPC that is most relevant to this article. To the extent that African Americans were able to break down discriminatory barriers during the war, they were dependent on the willingness of local organizations to lend their resources and influence to the government's fair employment investigations. As Ellinger's praise for the actions of J. D. Smith and the lily-white LAM indicates, it was exactly this type of cooperation that defined the FEPC's relationship with unions in Fort Worth. Indeed, had it not been for the willingness of both IAM District 776 and its crosstown counterpart, UAW Local 645, to reject the racist excuses used by Convair and North American to justify their discriminatory practices, it is unlikely that African Americans would have secured even temporary concessions through the proceedings of the institutionally weak FEPC. The question, however, is why? Why would the local leadership of a union such as the IAM—whose whites-only membership ritual was held up as a prime example of institutionalized working-class racism even in its own time—challenge the culture of its own organization by helping African Americans? More broadly, what could compel the recallable officers of either aircraft union to flout the racial mores of their membership in order to assist a government agency whose sole purpose was perceived by many as limiting the rights of white southerners?

The voluminous scholarship on working-class race relations during the 1940s provides few answers to these questions. On one side of the debate are those like Kersten who see the potential for interracial cooperation residing most prominently within the UAW and other left-leaning industrial unions, especially those affiliated with the Congress of Industrial Organizations (CIO). In their studies of automobile

6 William H. Chafe, *The Unfinished Journey: America Since World War II* (6th ed.; New York, 2007), esp. 15–19; Richard Polenberg, *War and Society: The United States, 1941–1945* (Philadelphia, 1972), esp. 99–130; David Brody, "The New Deal and World War II," in John Braeman et al., eds., *The New Deal: The National Level* (2 vols.; Columbus, Ohio, 1975), I, 267–309. Also see Neil A. Wynn, *The Afro-American and the Second World War* (New York, 1976); and Barton J. Bernstein, "America in War and Peace: The Test of Liberalism," in Bernstein, ed., *Towards a New Past: Dissenting Essays in American History* (New York, 1968), 289–321.
7 Kersten, *Race, Jobs, and the War*, 4. Also see Reed, *Seedtime for the Modem Civil Rights Movement*, 9–10.

manufacturing, tobacco processing, rubber production, and meatpacking, these scholars contend that union support for equal employment was largely driven by an ideological commitment to racial equality that was itself premised on the need to organize the heavily interracial workforces of these industries.[8]

By contrast, the other side of this historiographical coin emphasizes the racial obstructionism practiced by many of the craft unions affiliated with the American Federation of Labor (AFL). One of the most oft-cited examples within this scholarly tradition is that of the West Coast boilermakers, whose decision to defy an FEPC order led to a California Supreme Court case in which the union's discriminatory membership practices were declared illegal.[9] Jacob Vander Meulen has extended a similar argument to the burgeoning southern aircraft industry by linking union opposition to the FEPC to the intense organizing struggles between rival AFL and CIO unions at the AVCO-Vultee plant in Nashville, Tennessee. In this case, the all-white IAM lodge (AFL) defended the company's discriminatory hiring practices and labeled the FEPC's investigations an attempt to help the racially integrated UAW (CIO) organize.[10] Other scholars have pointed out similar anti-FEPC activity among local unions affiliated with both the AFL and the CIO in the shipbuilding, refining, and oil tool industries as well.[11]

Both of these interpretations fail to offer a satisfactory explanation for the FEPC-friendly activities of unions in the Fort Worth aircraft plants. While the lily-white IAM District 776 certainly cannot be categorized as left-leaning, the segregated UAW Local 645 also never showed much of a penchant for

---

8 See, for example, Kersten, *Race, Jobs, and the War*, 5; Robert Korstad and Nelson Lichtenstein, "Opportunities Found and Lost: Labor, Radicals, and the Early Civil Rights Movement," *Journal of American History*, 75 (December 1988), 786–811; Robert Rodgers Korstad, *Civil Rights Unionism: Tobacco Workers and the Struggle for Democracy in the Mid-Twentieth-Century South* (Chapel Hill, 2003), 142–250; Michael K. Honey, *Southern Labor and Black Civil Rights: Organizing Memphis Workers* (Urbana, 1993), 177–213; and Rick Halpern, *Down on the Killing Floor: Black and White Workers in Chicago's Packinghouses, 1904–54* (Urbana, 1997), 167–218. On the sources and frequent ambiguity of the CIO's racially egalitarian ideology, see Michael Goldfield, "Race and the CIO: The Possibilities for Racial Egalitarianism during the 1930s and 1940s," *International Labor and Working-Class History*, no. 44 (Fall 1993), 1–32; and Bruce Nelson, "Class, Race, and Democracy in the CIO: The 'New' Labor History Meets the 'Wages of Whiteness,'" *International Review of Social History*, 41 (December 1996), 351–74.

9 On the boilermakers' challenge, see Reed, *Seedtime for the Modern Civil Rights Movement*, 267–317; William H. Harris, "Federal Intervention in Union Discrimination: FEPC and West Coast Shipyards during World War II," *Labor History*, 22 (Summer 1981), 325–47; and *James v. Marinship Corporation*, 25 Cal. 2d 721 (1944). For a comparative account of the boilermakers' experience on both the West and the East Coasts, see Andrew E. Kersten, *Labor's Home Front: The American Federation of Labor during World War II* (New York, 2006), 68–99.

10 Jacob Vander Meulen, "Warplanes, Labor, and the International Association of Machinists in Nashville, 1939–1945," in Robert H. Zieger, ed., *Southern Labor in Transition, 1940–1995* (Knoxville, 1997), 37–57.

11 "Reed, "FEPC, the Black Worker, and the Southern Shipyards"; Nelson, "Organized Labor and the Struggle for Black Equality in Mobile"; Ernest Obadele-Starks, *Black Unionism in the Industrial South* (College Station, Tex., 2000), 101–27; Emilio Zamora, *Claiming Rights and Righting Wrongs in Texas: Mexican Workers and Job Politics during World War II* (College Station, Tex., 2009), 125–203; Zamora, "Failed Promise of Wartime Opportunity"; Michael R. Botson Jr., *Labor, Civil Rights, and the Hughes Tool Company* (College Station, Tex., 2005), 13336. Also see Bruce Nelson, "'CIO Meant One Thing for the Whites and Another Thing for Us': Steelworkers and Civil Rights, 1936–1974," in Zieger, ed., *Southern Labor in Transition*, 113–45; Robert J. Norrell, "Caste in Steel: Jim Crow Careers in Birmingham, Alabama," *Journal of American History*, 73 (December 1986), 669–94; Nancy L. Quam-Wickham, "Who Controls the Hiring Hall? The Struggle for Job Control in the ILWU during World War II," in Sally M. Miller and Daniel A. Cornford, eds., *American Labor in the Era of World War II* (Westport, Conn., 1995), 120–44; Eileen Boris, "'You Wouldn't Want One of 'Em Dancing With Your Wife': Racialized Bodies on the Job in World War II," *American Quarterly*, 50 (March 1998), 77–108; and Katherine Archibald, *Wartime Shipyard: A Study in Social Disunity* (Berkeley, 1947). Broader accounts of the ambiguous relationship between the FEPC and the labor movement can be found in Herbert Hill, *Black Labor and the American Legal System. Vol. I: Race, Work, and the Law* (Washington, D.C., 1977), 173–381; Philip S. Foner, *Organized Labor and the Black Worker, 1619–1973* (New York, 1974), 238–74; and Paul D. Moreno, *Black Americans and Organized Labor: A New History* (Baton Rouge, 2006), 196–219.

progressive racial ideology during the war. Nor did either local ever have to contend with a large African American workforce, the presence of whom in other circumstances helped moderate the institutional racism of certain unions. Considered within this context, what inspired the racially moderate actions of these two locals? Why, in the absence of either ideological or organizational motives, did neither of these unions emulate the blatant racism of more exclusionary labor organizations?

This article argues that the actions of organized labor in behalf of African Americans at Convair and North American need to be viewed from a more practical standpoint. As Alex Lichtenstein has demonstrated in an essay on Florida's wartime shipyards, when considering working-class race relations and the efficacy of the FEPC it is best to focus on such contextual factors as the strength of local unions, the attitudes of union officials, and the level of hostility toward organized labor that existed among plant management.[12] This observation rings true when considering the unique situation that prevailed among the unions at Convair and North American. In both settings, newly formed locals of the IAM and the UAW worked alongside the FEPC not out of ideological affinity for racial equality but rather to advance their own organizational strength in the face of determined managerial resistance. So long as they refused to broach the taboo subject of social equality, the local leaders of these unions were able to conflate the economic grievances suffered by African Americans—who never presented a significant numerical challenge to the area's white aircraft workers anyway—with the managerial abuse visited on aircraft workers in general. These efforts to legitimate the unions' collective bargaining authority, self-serving though they may have been, nevertheless benefited both black workers and the FEPC. By demanding a workplace in which management's actions were constrained by a set of fairly negotiated contractual rules, local IAM and UAW leaders struck an important if unintended blow against the arbitrariness of wartime employment discrimination and situated themselves alongside the FEPC as agents of change in the segregated South.

The prelude to this unexpected alliance took place on June 25,1941, when President Franklin D. Roosevelt issued Executive Order 8802 "encouraging] participation in the national defense program by all citizens … regardless of race, creed, color, or national origin." Mandating that all defense training programs were to be administered free of discrimination and that all federal defense contracts were to contain a nondiscrimination clause, the order also established the FEPC to ensure that these orders were observed by employers in the bustling wartime economy. Black workers in Texas and across the country had every reason to celebrate this event: besides promising unprecedented federal support for struggles against economic inequality, the executive order also provided a psychological boost in that it was the brainchild of A. Philip Randolph, an African American and longtime labor activist. Almost immediately, letters from minority workers around the country poured into the FEPC's Washington office to ask for help battling the racism of employers, fellow workers, and unions. Unfortunately, the first year of the new antidiscrimination agency's life left these hopes largely unfulfilled. The organizational jurisdiction of the FEPC remained in flux until July 1942, when the committee was given a semipermanent home under the authority of the War Manpower Commission (WMC). As it turned

---

12 Alex Lichtenstein, "Exclusion, Fair Employment, or Interracial Unionism: Race Relations in Florida's Shipyards during World War II," in Glenn T. Eskew, ed., *Labor in the Modern South* (Athens, Ga., 2001), 135–57. This point is also made in Goldfield, "Race and the CIO"; and Robert Rodgers Korstad, "The Possibilities for Racial Egalitarianism: Context Matters," *International Labor and Working-Class History*, no. 44 (Fall 1993), 41–44. For a well-written work demonstrating that local conditions often colored race relations even within the most discriminatory unions, see Kersten, *Labor's Home Front*, 68–99.

out, WMC head Paul McNutt was little interested in Roosevelt's fair employment program and sought to marginalize the FEPC by cutting its already limited budget and denying it access to sorely needed staff resources. Although the committee did manage to hold several nationally publicized hearings on workplace discrimination, including one in Birmingham, Alabama, on southern industry, the obstacles placed in front of it by McNutt left it ill-suited to address the complaints of African Americans in Texas or any other area of the country throughout most of 1942.[13]

At the same time that the FEPC was attempting to establish itself as a viable antidiscrimination agency, the southern economy was undergoing a dramatic transformation. Through massive infusions of capital in the form of military contracts and construction subsidies, federal intervention thrust the region into the national economic mainstream and signaled to the world that Dixie was a crucial link in the production chain forged by the so-called Arsenal of Democracy.[14] Although it may be an exaggeration to argue, as some historians do, that this period was more important than the Civil War, there can be little doubt of World War II's economic impact on the South: by 1942 average wages had jumped by 40 percent over the 1939 figure, and manufacturing expanded by at least half during the conflict. Southern cities such as Fort Worth—the economy of which had depended heavily on the export of oil, cattle, and other raw materials before the war—suddenly became flush with new jobs and industry. Out of the $7.6 billion in defense contracts that Texas received, Dallas and Fort Worth took in approximately $2.3 billion, a massive sum that set the area apart as one of the South's greatest beneficiaries of wartime largesse.[15]

At the forefront of this federally financed industrial revolution were the massive Convair and North American aircraft plants. The story of north Texas's rise to prominence as an aircraft manufacturing center began in 1939 when Amon Carter Sr., Fort Worth's most prominent booster, began a propaganda campaign to recruit what was then known as the Consolidated Aircraft Corporation. Although the city had many things going for it (not the least of which was Carter's personal friendship with Consolidated president Reuben Fleet), the San Diego company initially set its sights on a tract of land west of Dallas near

---

13 Executive Order No. 8802, June 25, 1941, http://docs.fdrlibrary.marist.edu/od8802t.html (quotation); Reed, *Seedtime for the Modern Civil Rights Movement*, 10–15, 21–76; MacLaury, *To Advance Their Opportunities*, 94–99; Zamora, "Failed Promise of Wartime Opportunity," 329–30.

14 Chamberlain, *Victory at Home*, chap. 1. For an excellent historiographical essay on World War II and its impact on the South, see James C. Cobb, "World War II and the Mind of the Modern South," in Neil R. McMillen, ed., *Remaking Dixie: The Impact of World War II on the American South* (Jackson, Miss., 1997), 3–20. Also see Gregory Hooks, "Guns and Butter, North and South: The Federal Contribution to Manufacturing Growth, 1940–1990," in Philip Scranton, ed., *The Second Wave: Southern Industrialization from the 1940s to the 1970s* (Athens, Ga., 2001), 255–85; Bruce J. Schulman, *From Cotton Belt to Sunbelt: Federal Policy, Economic Development, and the Transformation of the South, 1938–1980* (New York, 1991), 88–111; Gavin Wright, *Old South, New South: Revolutions in the Southern Economy Since the Civil War* (New York, 1986), 239–74; George Brown Tindall, *The Emergence of the New South, 1913–1945* (Baton Rouge, 1967), 687–731; James C. Cobb, *The Selling of the South: The Southern Crusade for Industrial Development, 1936–1990* (2nd ed.; Urbana, 1993); and Gerald T. White, *Billions for Defense: Government Financing by the Defense Plant Corporation during World War II* (University, Ala., 1980). More recently, geographer Robert Lewis has questioned whether wartime manufacturing provided a basis for southern economic transformation. See Lewis, "World War II Manufacturing and the Postwar Southern Economy," *Journal of Southern History*, 73 (November 2007), 837–66.

15 "Morton Sosna, "More Important than the Civil War? The Impact of World War II on the South," in James C. Cobb and Charles R. Wilson, eds., *Perspectives on the American South: An Annual Review of Society, Politics, and Culture*, Vol. 4 (New York, 1987), 145–61; Schulman, *From Cotton Belt to Sunbelt*, 72; Kathryn Currie Pinkney, "From Stockyards to Defense Plants, the Transformation of a City: Fort Worth, Texas, and World War II" (Ph.D. dissertation, University of North Texas, 2003), 26–32, 51–52, 78–80; Richard F. Selcer, *Fort Worth: A Texas Original!* (Austin, 2004), 55–63, 67.

the farming community of Grand Prairie. Perhaps under pressure from Carter, however, Consolidated backed out of this deal, thus opening the way for the Defense Plant Corporation's decision to construct a more than $7 million plant on the site and lease it to North American in September 1940. Initially, this announcement appeared to offer a grim fate for Fort Worth's chances of securing its own aircraft factory; with a desire to spread both the nation's strategic resources and its wartime wealth, the Army Air Corps favored a more distant site in Oklahoma. But this situation only stiffened the resolve of the pugnacious Carter, who responded by pressing the city's case with influential bureaucrats, legislators, and even Roosevelt himself. Finally, after several tense months, on January 3, 1941, the War Department compromised by announcing that it would build aircraft factories in both Fort Worth and Tulsa. On April 18, 1941, less than two weeks after the North American facility in Grand Prairie was dedicated, a silver spade broke ground for the $10 million plant in Fort Worth. Leased by the government to Consolidated—which was subsequently purchased by the Vultee Aircraft Corporation and became popularly known as Convair—the Fort Worth plant became the largest fully automated aircraft factory in the world when it was completed in April 1942.[16]

With the opening of North American and Convair, north Texas joined what was already becoming one of the largest and most important segments of the nation's defense effort. Throughout the country, prime military aircraft manufacturers employed more than 750,000 workers, with subcontractors employing another 250,000. While much of this workforce was concentrated on the West Coast, the residents of Dallas, Fort Worth, and their environs also contributed mightily to building up the nation's airpower. By the end of the war, North American's Grand Prairie facility was employing nearly 39,000 workers, while Convair's payroll bulged with some 30,500 employees. As was the case throughout the nation, these two plants became increasingly dependent on women as military service sent men overseas. Within a year after North American hired its first female production workers in November 1941, at least 30 percent of the plant's employees were women. Female employment statistics at Convair were equally impressive, with nearly 11,600 women (approximately 38 percent of the workforce) engaged in assembly work by the end of the war.[17]

For these thousands of men and women, life in the North American and Convair plants was both exciting and daunting. Though parts of the manufacturing process shared a great deal in common with other mass-production industries such as automobile assembly, aircraft workers had to adopt new methods peculiar to the industry. To begin with, the size and complexity of finished aircraft made it impractical to operate a single, constantly moving assembly line. Instead, workers erected scaffolding and jigs around stationary planes and then swarmed over and around each other to complete their

16 "Huge Airplane Plant Dedicated by Knudsen," Dallas *Morning News*, April 8, 1941, pp. 1, 4; "Dirt Broken in Rain for Plane Plant," *ibid.*, April 19, 1941, pp. 1, 6; Roger Bilstein and Jay Miller, *Aviation in Texas* (Austin, 1985), 94–95; Pinkney, "From Stockyards to Defense Plants," 80–95. On the Defense Plant Corporation's financing of aircraft facilities, see White, *Billions for Defense*, chap. 6. The best biography of Carter is Jerry Flemmons, *Amon: The Life of Amon Carter, Sr. of Texas* (Austin, 1978).
17 Wayne Biddle, *Barons of the Sky: From Early Flight to Strategic Warfare: The Story of the American Aerospace Industry* (New York, 1991), 271; Roger E. Bilstein, *The American Aerospace Industry: From Workshop to Global Enterprise* (New York, 1996), 73–74; John B. Rae, *Climb to Greatness: The American Aircraft Industry, 1920–1960* (Cambridge, Mass., 1968), 151; V. Dennis Wrynn, *Forge of Freedom: American Aircraft Production in World War II* (Osceola, Wis., 1995), 12. For more detailed discussions of women aircraft workers, see Sherna Berger Gluck, *Rosie the Riveter Revisited: Women, the War, and Social Change* (Boston, 1987); Constance Reid, *Slacks and Calluses: Our Summer in a Bomber Factory* (Washington, D.C., 1999); and Chester W. Gregory, *Women in Defense Work during World War II: An Analysis of the Labor Problem and Women's Rights* (New York, 1974), 67–79.

various tasks before the plane was moved to the next assembly position. The variety of jobs these workers performed was astounding—in addition to a virtual army of riveters and buckers, aircraft plants also employed thousands of metal press operators, drillers, deburrers, subassembly installers, electricians, welders, carpenters, toolmakers, jig builders, and inspectors, to name but a few. For periods ranging from forty-eight to sixty hours and more per week, the members of this industrial juggernaut worked at their tasks under a flood of artificial light and amid ear-piercing mechanical sounds. The physicality and repetitiveness of life in the plants no doubt led many to agree with the statement of one young man that aircraft work "[is] like a jail sentence … and after the war, we'll be out."[18]

While likening aircraft manufacturing to incarceration may have been an exaggeration—most workers were simply glad to have a job after the travails of the Great Depression—such statements reflected the very real power that Convair's and North American's supervisors retained over their employees. Better known throughout the plants as "Damn Red Button[s]" due to the color of their identification badges, company officials guarded their managerial prerogatives and adamantly opposed anything that might impede their authority. This tendency was especially evident in the dim view that the aircraft manufacturers took of unions and labor relations in general. In California, where the industry was strongest, the antiunion sentiment of aircraft plant managers put them in the vanguard of the struggle to retain the state's reputation as "the white spot of the open shop."[19] In the summer of 1941, this antagonism toward employees was demonstrated in dramatic fashion at North American's main plant in Inglewood, California. Just as the first aircraft began rolling off the production line in Grand Prairie, managers at North American's West Coast facility had enlisted the support of Roosevelt and the army in putting down a Communist-inspired strike by employees who accused the company of refusing to bargain with their representatives. Besides serving notice on unions throughout the nation that production disruptions would not be tolerated during the war, the outcome of the Inglewood strike also provided a preview of the hard-nosed style that North American officials subsequently employed in their dealings with both black and white workers at the new plant in Texas.[20]

Convair's prewar history lacked the same dramatic confrontations with employees, but the attitude of its managers was no better than that of their North American counterparts. This antagonistic stance was perhaps best personified by Convair's chairman of the board, Tom M. Girdler. Well before the aircraft industry began its rise to prominence in Fort Worth, Girdler had earned a reputation as a fierce opponent of labor unions who was not above inciting violence to avoid working-class organization. The most famous example of these tactics occurred in 1937 when Girdler, who was then serving as head of Republic Steel, masterminded the defeat of the CIO's Little Steel strike, the climax of which was the brutal killing of ten workers by Chicago police in the infamous Memorial Day Massacre. Not surprisingly, Girdler's distaste for organized labor and shared governance on the shop floor did not diminish when he entered the aircraft industry. In a speech before the Foremen's Club of Fort Worth, the Convair chairman

18 "Adroit Use of Manpower Claimed by Airplane Plant's Officials," Dallas *Morning News*, October 2, 1943, sec. II, pp. 1, 11; Jacob Vander Meulen, *Building the B-29* (Washington, D.C., 1995), 47, 51, 55; Reid, *Slacks and Calluses*, 52 (quotation).
19 Reid, *Slacks and Calluses*, 117 (first quotation); Jacob A. Vander Meulen, *The Politics of Aircraft: Building an American Military Industry* (Lawrence, Kans., 1991), 216 (second quotation).
20 Nelson Lichtenstein, *Labor's War at Home: The CIO in World War II* (New York, 1982), 57–63; James R. Prickett, "Communist Conspiracy or Wage Dispute? The 1941 Strike at North American Aviation," *Pacific Historical Review*, 50 (May 1981), 215–33. On the response of management to the challenges of labor during the 1940s, see Howell John Harris, *The Right to Manage: Industrial Relations Policies of American Business in the 1940s* (Madison, Wis., 1982), 41–89.

reminded his managerial subordinates that they were to act as the undisputed bosses of their respective departmental fiefdoms. "You are not in your department to win any popularity contests," he charged. "Get your workers to like you if you can, but be sure to have their respect. Without respect, and without the discipline that results from respect, you can never build a well-knit, smooth working combination of workers." In their interactions with employees, the managers at Convair, several of whom had worked for Girdler at Republic, took these instructions to heart and brooked little opposition to their authority.[21]

The reluctance of North American and Convair to countenance any assault on the managerial prerogatives of the supervisory staff provided a good indication of the uphill battle that African Americans and the FEPC would fight throughout the war. If FEPC officials entertained any hopes that it would be easier to gain the cooperation of the transplanted Texas management of these companies, the reality they faced offered a rude awakening. Though most hailed from the ostensibly less hostile racial environment of California, early managers at Convair and North American were unwilling to challenge the prevailing social order of the segregated South. Many feared that doing so would needlessly antagonize white workers; others presumably shared their employees' prejudices. One excuse often used by management to justify discrimination was the claim that union contracts prevented them from dealing fairly with African Americans. While such pretexts were particularly disingenuous in light of the aircraft manufacturers' antagonism toward labor and the iron grip that they tried to maintain on the shop floor, the limiting effect on African American job opportunities was still the same.[22]

Such excuses led to the industry's first run-in with the FEPC. In December 1942 L. Virgil Williams of the Dallas Negro Chamber of Commerce wrote to the committee, complaining about the quality of training facilities available to African Americans who hoped to work in the aircraft factories. Williams's grievance was far from unique: at the end of January 1942, only 194 of 5,630 southern training programs accepted black workers. Dallas's African American population had gained both a large training facility and a $46,000 grant for equipment in September 1942, but Williams maintained that these funds were being raided by white training officials, who used them to purchase materials and machinery for their own students. Williams also criticized the director of the black training program for not passing on the names of qualified graduates to the local office of the United States Employment Service, which itself was under a great deal of scrutiny for channeling African Americans into discriminatory jobs. Earl Bowler of the U.S. Office of Education, which as administrator of these training programs had already had its own run-in with the FEPC, agreed with Williams that placement of black graduates had so far been difficult because no employers in the area would hire them. According to Williams, this situation had become so bad that the supervisor of the black training school was urging graduating students to accept positions as janitors at North American. When Bowler brought this matter up with North American management, industrial relations director Nate Molinarro offered little more than a vague promise that the company would begin hiring African Americans as paid trainees once conditions in

21 "Address of Tom Girdler ... Before Foremen's Club, Fort Worth, Texas, Division," October 17, 1943, Folder 24, Box 1, International Association of Machinists and Aerospace Workers, District Lodge 776 Papers, AR 48 (Special Collections, University of Texas at Arlington Library), hereinafter cited as District 776 Papers (quotations); "Anti-Union and Labor Baiting Is History of CVAC Management Personnel," *Fort Worth Labor News*, April 26, 1946. On the Little Steel strike, see Robert H. Zieger, *The CIO, 1935–1955* (Chapel Hill, 1995), 60–63; and Tom M. Girdler with Boyden Sparkes, *Boot Straps: The Autobiography of Tom M. Girdler* (New York, 1943), 223–373.
22 It should be noted that not all industrial employers were as antagonistic toward African Americans and the FEPC as Convair and North American initially were. For examples, see Kersten, *Race, Jobs, and the War*, 29–30, 51–52, 80.

the plant warranted such action. The company also indicated that it would set aside at least two departments for black workers but gave no indication of when this might occur.[23]

Not surprisingly, Molinarro's weak assurances failed to spur any significant action. Though North American management attempted to neutralize criticism by hiring an African American as assistant personnel officer, black workers continued to find it difficult to gain entry into the plant throughout the first half of 1943. Nearly six months after Williams reported the discriminatory conditions, a frustrated Bowler opined that it might be time to scrap the black training program altogether and instead focus on the actual needs of the companies in the area, a recommendation that would leave job discrimination essentially untouched. Even as tales of North American's discrimination began to be broadcast throughout the state by the African American press, the FEPC could do little to help. Still controlled by the largely unsympathetic War Manpower Commission and centered in Washington, D.C., the committee did not have the resources to initiate a full-scale investigation of the situation in Dallas.[24]

The turning point for the area's African American workers came on May 27, 1943, with Roosevelt's decision to issue Executive Order 9346. Drafted in response to a growing number of complaints from civil rights leaders about WMC leader Paul McNutt's apparent lack of concern for fair employment, this new order removed the FEPC from the War Manpower Commission and made it directly responsible to the president. The order also significantly expanded both the jurisdictional and geographic scope of the committee, allowing it to investigate all firms whose work was deemed essential to the war effort and setting up a system of regional offices throughout the country. This latter decision proved especially important for aircraft workers in Texas, who were henceforth able to file complaints with the FEPC's new Region X office in Dallas. Led by Don Ellinger, Leonard Brin, and the distinguished historian Carlos Castaneda, investigators took up the cause of fair employment in Texas, focusing the bulk of their attention on the oil refining and shipbuilding industries of the Gulf Coast and the aviation industry in and around Fort Worth.[25]

As indicated in Table 1, the reorganization of the FEPC set off a rash of new complaints in Region X and breathed new life into the struggle for training facilities in north Texas. In late June 1943, Williams and the Negro Chamber of Commerce once again filed a formal complaint regarding North American's refusal to hire skilled blacks. Shortly thereafter, FEPC executive secretary George Johnson contacted North American president J. H. Kindelberger directly to complain about the situation in Texas. Johnson

23 L. Virgil Williams to George Johnson, December 15, 1942, Folder "North American Aviation, 10-BR-173," Box 8, Closed Cases, RG 228; Earl Bowler to E. G. Ludtke, January 22, 1943, *ibid.*; George M. Johnson to Walter White, January 13,1943, Folder 1, Box A265, Records of the National Association for the Advancement of Colored People (Manuscript Division, Library of Congress, Washington, D.C.), hereinafter cited as NAACP Records. On the aptly named "jobs movement" among African Americans in the wartime South and the FEPC's larger struggles to secure equal training facilities for them, see Reed, *Seedtime for the Modern Civil Rights Movement*, 175–204, esp. 184; and Chamberlain, *Victory at Home*, 40–68, 86–96. An interesting case study of African American struggles to gain adequate war training is offered by Merl E. Reed, "Bell Aircraft Comes South: The Struggle by Atlanta Blacks for Jobs during World War II," in Eskew, ed., *Labor in the Modern South*, 102–34.
24 Earl Bowler to E. G. Ludtke, May 28,1943, Folder "North American Aviation, 10-BR-173," Box 8, Closed Cases, RG 228; "Exodus of Negroes from Dallas Grows as Local War Plant Denies Them Jobs," Dallas *Express*, May 8, 1943, pp. 1, 8.
25 Reed, *Seedtime for the Modern Civil Rights Movement*, 112; MacLaury, *To Advance Their Opportunities*, 99–101. For information on Castañeda, see Félix D. Almaráz Jr., *Knight without Armor: Carlos Eduardo Castañeda, 1896–1958* (College Station, Tex., 1999), esp. chap. 8. On the FEPC's work in the Gulf Coast refining and shipbuilding industries, see Zamora, *Claiming Rights*, 158–203; Zamora, "Failed Promise of Wartime Opportunity," 323–50; and Obadele-Starks, *Black Unionism in the Industrial South*, 101–27.

Table 1 Summary of Activity for FEPC Region X, July 1, 1943–June 30, 1944

Cases Pending, July 1, 1943	Total Cases, July 1, 1943– June 30, 1944	Total Cases Closed	Cases Satisfactorily Adjusted	Cases Dismissed	Cases Pending, July 1, 1944
14	336	213	86	124	123

Source: Fair Employment Practice Committee, *First Report: July 1943–December 1944* (Washington, D.C., 1945), Appendix E.

made special note that the Grand Prairie plant had recently assumed control of a training school for white teenagers while black graduates were still unable to secure employment. This decision to go above North American's local leadership apparently had the desired effect. Following negotiations with black leaders and the War Manpower Commission, Molinarro announced in early July that North American would begin employing African American trainees directly as part of a new production-training program in such skills as drilling, painting, and subassembly installation. Once these students completed their instruction, Molinarro promised, they would be transferred into areas of the plant where they were needed.[26]

Despite the lengthy delays and the necessity of appealing to higher authorities within the company, the FEPC could tally its first experience at North American in the win column. During the four months after Molinarro's announcement, over three hundred African Americans were trained and employed in aircraft work through the program that North American established.[27] By comparison, the committee's earliest efforts at Convair were not nearly as successful. In June 1942 FEPC officials approached the management at the Fort Worth plant and urged division manager Roland G. Mayer to offer training for African Americans. Initially it appeared that Mayer might be willing to cooperate: he promised to establish a training program for placing blacks in the center wing section of the plant. Upon further investigation, however, FEPC officials discovered that this program had never been set up and no African Americans had been moved into the jobs supposedly set aside for them. A full two years later, in June 1944, Ellinger still could not report any progress on this front; in fact, he admitted that the situation had grown worse as Convair had ceased offering training programs of any kind throughout the entire plant.[28]

Fortunately for African Americans, Ellinger was not deterred by the opposition he faced at Convair. As a former organizer with the International Ladies' Garment Workers' Union (ILGWU) in St. Louis and Dallas, Ellinger had had more than his share of confrontations with management by the time he became an FEPC investigator. Hoping to correct Convair's discriminatory training situation, Ellinger secured a conference with Mayer; the company's director of labor relations, John Hassler; and an official from the Army Air Corps in August 1944. Ellinger pointed out to this group that of the 800 black employees at

---

26 A. Maceo Smith to Walter White, December 11,1942, Folder 1, Box A265, NAACP Records; Earl Bowler to W. D. Gallier, May 28,1943, Folder "North American Aviation, 10-BR-173," Box 8, Closed Cases, RG 228; George Johnson to J. H. Kindelberger, June 15, 1943, *ibid.;* "Final Disposition Report," February 5, 1944, *ibid.;* "North American Aviation Starts Paying Negro Trainees," Dallas *Express,* July 10, 1943, p. 1.

27 "Final Disposition Report," February 5, 1944, Folder "North American Aviation, 10-BR-173," Box 8, Closed Cases, RG 228. Perhaps because of North American's internal training program, Dallas's black defense-job training center was closed in September 1943 due to low attendance. See Chamberlain, *Victory at Home,* 66.

28 Don Ellinger to Will Maslow, June 29, 1944, Folder "Consolidated-Vultee Aircraft Corp., 10-BR-235," Box 2, Closed Cases, RG 228.

Convair, only 114 held skilled or semiskilled classifications and that not a single one of these workers had been hired at any position above janitor or laborer. Despite this evidence, both Convair officials accused the FEPC of stirring up trouble where none existed, and Mayer stated categorically that he would not mix black and white workers. Only after Ellinger threatened to call a public hearing did Mayer relent and request suggestions on how Convair might comply. Though this concession seemingly represented a breakthrough, Ellinger continued to doubt the company's sincerity, declaring that "the attitude expressed by [Convair] made such a proposal fruitless since it was clear that they intended to do nothing about it."[29]

Notwithstanding his misgivings, Ellinger submitted the FEPC's proposal to company officials several days after the meeting. Hoping to capitalize on the earlier success in Grand Prairie, he pointed out that even though the percentage of African American employees at North American was more than twice what it was at Convair, there had been no real racial trouble to speak of. "Our observation has been that friction between races in a plant does not develop unless it is deliberately stirred up," Ellinger stated. "Workers of both races have worked together for years in this region and no failure to utilize available needed skills can be justified on a fear of friction." Ellinger also reminded Mayer that the FEPC was neutral on the subject of physical segregation so long as any arrangements made did not restrict employment opportunities. As requested, the letter concluded with a number of specific recommendations for Mayer to consider. These included making a public announcement of Convair's commitment to fair employment, surveying the qualifications of all African Americans and determining where these workers could best be used, and establishing relations with a representative committee of black workers who could act as a liaison to management.[30]

Ellinger's entreaties to Convair reveal a great deal about how the FEPC and its staff approached their investigations in the South. To begin with, Ellinger's assertion that blacks and whites had "worked together for years" was somewhat disingenuous: workplace interracialism had almost never occurred under conditions of equality within the region. While the implications of this statement would not have been lost on a southerner, Ellinger may have hoped that Mayer, a Seattle native, would be more amenable to such arguments.[31]

Ellinger's suggestion that the FEPC might accept some type of segregated arrangement also indicated that he understood the delicate nature of his mission. Though the segregation of black workers in war plants would not become a major issue until May 1943, when it was used to quell a race riot in the shipyards of Mobile, Alabama, the practice presented problems for the FEPC. Virtually all the committee's field representatives maintained that geography had to be considered when reaching settlements, yet they also understood that doing so risked setting precedents that might carry over into other regions where such conditions were not the norm. Equally worrisome was that prominent civil rights groups such as the NAACP opposed such compromises. These critics argued that any arrangement condoning segregation not only limited the opportunities of African Americans but also ensured that they would

29 Memo to File, n.d., *ibid.* Biographical information on Ellinger was taken from "Heart Attack Takes Don Ellinger," Washington (D.C.) *Machinist,* February 24, 1972, pp. 1, 7.

30 Don Ellinger to R. G. Mayer, September 11, 1944, Folder "Consolidated-Vultee Aircraft Corp., 10-BR-235," Box 2, Closed Cases, RG 228.

31 Biographical information on Mayer was derived from "Newman Quits Consolidated," Dallas *Morning News,* May 12, 1944, p. 3.

be quickly dismissed after the war through the wholesale liquidation of all-black departments. The FEPC was never able to find a satisfactory solution to this dilemma other than to insist that workplace segregation should never be allowed to interfere with black job prospects. With these vague instructions in hand, the committee's field representatives were left to use their judgment in determining when such arrangements were beneficial and when they constituted discrimination. In the case of Convair, Ellinger's decision to recommend segregated departments was likely informed by the fact that as early as 1942 the Dallas Negro Chamber of Commerce, one of the area's most prominent civil rights organizations, had suggested a similar arrangement at North American. Considered alongside the company's history of stonewalling, the group's stance seems to have been the key factor in convincing Ellinger that all avenues, even segregated ones, needed to be explored if black workers were to gain any concessions in the plant.[32]

Whatever hopes Ellinger had that Convair might be willing to accede to his recommendations were dashed with the evasive response that Mayer provided over three months later. Although Mayer admitted that retooling operations had prevented him from making an investigation, he stated bluntly that he could not agree with any of the allegations outlined and believed that the racial situation at North American was not nearly as rosy as Ellinger had painted it. No training programs were needed, he argued, because the Convair plant had increased its efficiency so much in recent months that it had terminated approximately a third of the workforce. Mayer also contended that Convair had a definite plan for upgrading its employees as well as a "highly-praised" grievance procedure and an industrial relations department where any individual could file a complaint if he or she were dissatisfied with his or her classification. In an operation as large as Convair, Mayer continued, it was impossible to police all supervisory employees to ensure that they were carrying out managerial policy "without allowing personalities to creep into the various transactions," a particularly disingenuous statement given the managerial philosophy of the company. Mayer concluded that in almost four years of operation, the Fort Worth plant had had virtually no labor difficulties, and he again restated his belief that the FEPC was in error. For his part, the normally resourceful Ellinger seems to have been taken aback by this intransigent response. Lacking the authority to issue hard sanctions, Ellinger could do little more than report to his superiors that Mayer was lying and that the company was actually behind schedule in fulfilling its contracts owing to a lack of manpower.[33]

As revealing as these prolonged confrontations between the FEPC and Convair were, training discrimination was but one of the many unfair practices that African Americans faced in the Fort Worth aircraft industry. Even after overcoming the daunting challenge of gaining entry into the plants, black workers continued to endure discrimination in the types of jobs they were offered, the pay they received, and the discipline that was meted out to them. One of the abuses inspiring the most complaints was the unwillingness of supervisors to properly classify African American workers. In one such case, a pair of black welders complained that although they were performing the same basic duties as whites in their department, North American refused to advance them any higher than the "C" classification. The labor relations department tried to cover itself by claiming that the men were accurately classified

32 Reed, *Seedtime for the Modern Civil Rights Movement*, 117–19; Chamberlain, *Victory at Home*, 59.
33 R. G. Mayer to Don Ellinger, November 18, 1944, Folder "Consolidated-Vultee Aircraft Corp., 10-BR-235," Box 2, Closed Cases, RG 228 (quotations); Don Ellinger to Will Maslow, December 12, 1944, *ibid.*; Don Ellinger to Clarence Mitchell, December 22, 1944, *ibid.*

according to the printed job descriptions, but this argument was discredited when the same company official admitted that "some things just can't be done" in Texas.[34]

In a similar case involving a group of black painters, one complainant who asked for an upgrade to an "A" classification recalled being told by his foreman that "here in the South, a nigger cannot be called a white man regardless of how good a worker he is." This case particularly worried the FEPC since a number of aggrieved African Americans had quit after realizing how limited their opportunities for advancement were. When Ellinger confronted North American management about the situation, director of labor relations F. J. Conlan again denied any discrimination and maintained that the company was within its managerial prerogatives to upgrade employees as it saw fit. Molinarro agreed, adding that many of the men had very poor attendance records and were therefore unfit for upgrades. Employing another frequently used tactic, Molinarro also questioned the character of one of the men by pointing out that he had allegedly abandoned his wife and children. Perhaps embarrassed by these revelations, Ellinger accepted the company's agreement to upgrade one of the complainants and put the others on notice that they would be considered for similar promotions if their attendance improved.[35]

The FEPC ran into this same stubbornness when it confronted management at Convair about its refusal to offer upgrades to African Americans. In particular, a number of black janitors and laborers testified that they had been denied the opportunity to upgrade into supervisory positions in their all-black department as well as into more skilled jobs elsewhere in the plant. An investigation by the Army Air Corps found that Convair's policy was to not upgrade blacks until there was a surplus in the pool of janitorial workers, a situation that apparently presented itself infrequently. The result was that inexperienced whites were hired off the streets for jobs that should have been open to these black workers based on their qualifications and seniority. Confronted by the FEPC, Convair management responded with "bristling hostility," contending that the black workers involved were both satisfied with their current positions and unqualified to take on supervisory duties. Faced with such uncompromising resistance, Ellinger again seemed at a loss. His only response was to suggest that blacks at Convair write letters to the company laying out their talents and ambition and to ask that all future decisions regarding upgrades be handled by the company's central personnel office rather than by individual foremen.[36]

All these problems were magnified exponentially when the applicant was an African American woman. Despite their confrontations with the FEPC over training and hiring practices, officials at both plants refused to hire black women in any but the most menial positions. This was the case for Elizabeth Myers, who wrote to the War Manpower Commission in June 1943 complaining that she had been unable to secure employment at North American despite having completed a war training course. "Is it true," she asked, "that colored women are allowed to sacrifice their time and energy in taking this training with no hope of gaining work in a plant? Not even a maid's job?" Each time she went to the local employment office to inquire, she was told to wait a few more days and then given minor domestic jobs to tide her over. After the matter was referred to the FEPC, it was discovered that North American was refusing to hire black women as production workers on the grounds that it did not have segregated

34 L. Virgil Williams to Carlos Castañeda, November 26, 1943, Folder "North American Aviation, 10-BR-160," Box 8, *ibid.*

35 "Final Disposition Report," September 26, 1944, Folder "North American Aviation, 10-BR-268," *ibid.;* F. J. Conlan to Don Ellinger, April 17, 1944, *ibid.;* Don Ellinger to F. J. Conlan, April 19, 1944, *ibid,* (quotation); Nate Molinarro to Leonard Brin, May 29, 1944, *ibid.;* Don Ellinger to F. J. Conlan, June 1, 1944, *ibid.*

36 Don Ellinger to Will Maslow, June 29, 1944, Folder "Consolidated-Vultee Aircraft Corp., 10-BR-235," Box 2, *ibid.*

facilities for them. It took over six months for the company to offer Myers a trainee job.[37] Many other potential female employees, such as Willie Mae Young and Carrie Tucker Buckner, were refused applications at the employment office while white women received jobs. Even when the FEPC investigated such complaints, the constantly fluctuating employment figures at the plants made it difficult to determine whether these and other aggrieved women had presented clear-cut cases of discrimination.[38]

The inflexibility of management was the root cause of most discrimination at the plants, but when attempting to settle complaints the FEPC also had to contend with the racial attitudes of white workers. Although officials at both North American and Convair often used threats of white backlash as a blanket excuse for refusing to make adjustments, such outbursts occurred frequently enough that Ellinger could not afford to ignore the matter. One such incident involved an African American named William Keele, who worked as an alignment operator in an all-black department on the night shift at North American. When this department was eliminated in the summer of 1943, Keele and two other employees were placed on the all-white day shift. Almost immediately, however, nearly two dozen white workers walked off the job rather than work alongside African Americans. In order to quell the disturbance, North American officials removed the trio from the alignment department and relocated them to a lower-skilled section of the plant without any reduction in pay. After his own protest to management yielded what he believed was an unsatisfactory offer of a different job, Keele filed a complaint with the FEPC alleging that his skills were being underutilized and he was being underpaid.[39]

Drawing on his experiences in the multiracial and multiethnic ILGWU, Ellinger realized that these issues had to be handled gingerly. On the one hand, in addition to minimizing the chance of another walkout, he wanted to avoid unduly antagonizing North American management—who, for once, appeared to be sincere in their efforts to adjust the situation—by demanding that they return Keele to the alignment department. On the other hand, Ellinger worried that pressing Keele to accept the company's offer would sanction the segregation of future black complainants into separate departments where their job opportunities would be circumscribed. Not knowing how to proceed, Ellinger wrote to the FEPC's director of field operations, Will Maslow, commenting that the outcome appeared bad no matter what course of action he took. In response, Maslow reminded Ellinger that the FEPC was not against segregation per se as long as it did not interfere with the rights of minority workers. Maslow recommended that unless there was to be some loss of seniority involved, Keele's acceptance of the company's transfer offer would be viewed as a satisfactory adjustment of his case. This advice came to naught when Keele once again refused to accept a transfer elsewhere in the plant. Given the situation, Ellinger's only hope was to prove to management that the white workers would not rebel again if an African American was placed among them. With the help of the alignment department foreman and a cooperative UAW shop steward, Ellinger devised a plan whereby Keele would be used to fill in for a temporarily absent white jig

---

37 Elizabeth Myers to Dr. Robert Weaver, June 19, 1943, Folder "North American Aviation, 10-BR-75," Box 7, *ibid,* (quotations); James Bond to Lawrence Appley, August 20, 1943, *ibid.;* "Final Disposition Report," February 11, 1944, *ibid.* On the experience of African American women in the workplace during World War II, see Maureen Honey, ed., *Bitter Fruit: African American Women in World War II* (Columbia, Mo., 1999), 35–125; and Karen Tucker Anderson, "Last Hired, First Fired: Black Women Workers during World War II," *Journal of American History,* 69 (June 1982), 82–97.
38 "Final Disposition Report," December 30, 1944, Folder "North American Aviation, 10-BR-449," Box 8, Closed Cases, RG 228.
39 "Statement of William Keele," April 12, 1944, Folder "North American Aviation, 10-BR-249," *ibid.;* Don Ellinger to Will Maslow, May 26, 1944, *ibid.;* "Final Disposition Report," August 9, 1944, *ibid.*

operator. Much to Ellinger's relief, the disturbances that the company had warned about never material-ized, and Keele was transferred back to the alignment department permanently, with a small pay raise.[40]

If William Keele's tribulations demonstrate what could be achieved with a little assistance from man-agement and a great deal of persistence by the FEPC, his experience also raises the important question of the role played by organized labor in the investigations at Convair and North American. Given the his-tory of unions in Fort Worth, one could certainly be forgiven for thinking that the UAW's cooperation with Ellinger was an aberration. Up to the beginning of World War II, conservative AFL craft unionists in the building trades and railroad brotherhoods dominated the local labor movement. With their main focus on improving wages and maintaining job security for skilled white workers, such unions had little use for African Americans or more progressive forms of civil rights unionism.[41]

Throughout the war, these exclusionary forces found a mouthpiece for their racial sentiment and voluntaristic pure-and-simple unionism in the octogenarian C. W. Woodman, publisher of Fort Worth's only labor journal, the *Union Banner*. Born during the Civil War, Woodman had been one of the original organizers of the Texas State Federation of Labor in 1900 and was a fifty-year member of the AFL-affiliated printing pressman's union, thus giving him plenty of time to imbibe the insular ideology of craft unionism. Besides boasting that Fort Worth had had no labor trouble in nearly two decades, Woodman also used the *Union Banner* as a sounding board for his views on race. The paper frequently carried editorials blasting the efforts of "carpetbaggers" from northern cities to stir up trouble among the South's black population. Like most white southerners, Woodman believed that whites and blacks in the region had "a perfect understanding," and he warned that overtures toward social equality from "crazy people" up north would surely result in the rebirth of the Ku Klux Klan and other extremist groups. These pieces became increasingly strident during the war as growing attention was focused on gaining jobs for African Americans.[42]

As important as Woodman's paper was for expressing craft union racism, the real bastion of an-tiblack sentiment in the Fort Worth labor movement was the Trades Assembly. Although this body nominally cooperated with the small number of African American union members in the area, its white leaders and delegates made very clear whom the junior partners in this relationship were. More than six months before the aircraft plants even opened, for example, an IAM member representing a small local foundry informed the body that black workers were seeking the same recognition as whites from

---

40 Don Ellinger to Will Maslow, May 26, 1944, *ibid.*; Will Maslow to Don Ellinger, June 8, 1944, *ibid.*; Memo to File, July 17, 1944, *ibid.*; "For the Files, Regarding 10-BR-249 and 10-BR-268," May 25, 1944, *ibid.*; "Final Disposition Report," August 9, 1944, *ibid.*

41 On the development of the pure-and-simple craft union ideology that dominated the AFL during the first half of the twentieth century, see William E. Forbath, *Law and the Shaping of the American Labor Movement* (Cambridge, Mass., 1991); Julie Greene, *Pure and Simple Politics: The American Federation of Labor and Political Activism, 1881–1917* (Cambridge, Eng., 1998); Joseph A. McCartin, *Labor's Great War: The Struggle for Industrial Democracy and the Origins of Modern American Labor Relations, 1912–1921* (Chapel Hill, 1997); and Howard Kimeldorf, *Battling for American Labor: Wobblies, Craft Workers, and the Making of the Union Movement* (Berkeley, 1999).

42 "Convention Program," Fort Worth *Union Banner,* June 19, 1942; "Breeding Race Trouble," *ibid.*, October 8, 1943 (first quotation); "The Negro We Know," *ibid.*, November 13, 1942 (second quotation); "Be Careful of Colored Problems," *ibid.*, August 11, 1944 (third quotation); "What Is Social Equality?" *ibid.* Biographical information on Woodman was taken from "*Union Banner* Completes 58th Year," *ibid.*, April 23, 1948.

Convair management. Appalled, the Trades Assembly went on record in agreement with one delegate's conclusion "that the negroes would not be on equality with the white at any time here in Texas."[43]

The elder statesmen of the Trades Assembly also did not look kindly on outside interference in their affairs, even when it came from within the labor movement. In February 1941 the assembly passed a motion instructing the AFL not to charter any so-called federal labor unions until local members had a chance to examine the application. For decades, the AFL had set up federal labor unions as a means of directly organizing less skilled workers who would otherwise have been overlooked by the labor movement because they did not qualify to join established craft unions. In practice, however, federal labor unions usually served as Jim Crow auxiliaries and offered the larger craft unions an opportunity to control African American workers without having to fully represent their interests or accept them as members. Although it is not clear why the Trades Assembly took this action, it may have been an attempt to prevent any top-down directive by the AFL—which during the war conceded the need for at least marginal equality—that would infringe on the privileges of white members. Less than a month later, in a vote that seemingly confirms this conclusion, the assembly carried another motion protesting the creation of a union for skilled black workers.[44]

The arrival of the aircraft industry in north Texas created a dilemma for Fort Worth's stagnant labor movement. Centered in small shops where labor relations remained something of a personal affair, the area's craft unions were ill-suited to the task of organizing the thousands of often unskilled workers newly employed in the massive facilities of North American and Convair. However, just as they gave rise to a new local economy, the construction of the aircraft plants also marked the beginning of an important shift for the Fort Worth labor movement. The task of organizing this new group of workers fell to international representatives of the UAW and LAM, which had emerged as the main rivals for collective bargaining rights in the aircraft industry.[45]

Born during the tumultuous CIO struggles of the 1930s, the UAW had gained a reputation as a progressive and militant industrial union that sought to organize all workers regardless of skill, race, or gender. Given the dynamism of this young organization, its interest in the newly emerging enterprise of aircraft manufacture came almost naturally. As auto companies began retooling UAW-organized factories for war production, union leaders recognized an opportunity to extend their organization's influence into aircraft plants across the country. This strategy took on added urgency after Roosevelt adopted UAW vice president Walter Reuther's slogan of "500 Planes a Day," serving notice that the mass-production techniques pioneered in automobile manufacturing would have to replace older batch methods of aircraft production.[46]

---

43 Minutes, October 9, 1941, Folder 8, Box 6, Fort Worth Trades Assembly Papers, AR 2 (University of Texas at Arlington Library).

44 Minutes, February 27, 1941, *ibid.*; Minutes, March 26, 1942, Folder 9, *ibid.* The record of this latter meeting gives no indication as to what industry the "Skilled Workers (colored)" were attempting to organize. On the early history of federal labor unions, see Robert H. Zieger and Gilbert J. Gall, *American Workers, American Unions: The Twentieth Century* (3rd ed.; Baltimore, 2002), 71–72, 78–79; and Foner, *Organized Labor and the Black Worker*, 92–93. On the AFL's wartime record on civil rights, see Kersten, *Labor's Home Front*, 68–99.

45 For information on the fierce wartime competition between the AFL and the CIO, see Kersten, *Labor's Home Front*, 139–65; and Zieger, *CIO*, 111–90.

46 Vander Meulen, *Politics of Aircraft*, 209; Lichtenstein, *The Most Dangerous Man in Detroit: Walter Reuther and the Fate of American Labor* (New York, 1995), 160–65 (quotation on 162).

By comparison, the IAM was an unlikely candidate for organizing aircraft workers. For decades after its founding in Atlanta in 1888, the IAM epitomized the old-line exclusionary craft unions of the AFL, with its base among highly skilled machinists in railroad repair shops. These labor aristocrats maintained strict control over the union and used it to protect their interests through conservative sweetheart contracts with employers. Having come out of the insular railroad shops themselves, the IAM's steadfast executive officers were initially opposed to organizing aircraft workers for fear that such efforts would weaken the tradition of craft unionism and dilute the bargaining power of more-skilled workers.[47]

This attitude began to change in 1936, however, when William Boeing, who was then seeking ways to limit competition in the cutthroat industry, offered the IAM a closed-shop contract covering all his Seattle workers. In exchange, Boeing demanded an ironclad no-strike pledge and assurances that the union would organize other aircraft companies as well. Not wanting to fall behind its increasingly aggressive UAW rival, the IAM gladly accepted Boeing's offer and launched its own organizing campaign among the nation's growing body of aircraft workers. Much to the chagrin of the union's old-timers, however, this new organizing effort slowly began to diminish the once clear lines that had existed between skilled and unskilled labor. As wartime mass-production techniques revolutionized the industry, the IAM simply could not afford to ignore the growing army of riveters, drop-press operators, and other semiskilled operatives who made up the bulk of the aircraft-manufacturing workforce. Though old railroad men continued to dominate the IAM's politics for some time to come, their conservative ideological influence began to wane.[48]

Despite the emerging parallels in their trade union philosophies, the two unions converged much more slowly on the treatment of African American workers. Even within the progressive CIO, the UAW was famous (or infamous, depending on one's location) for its leaders' public commitments to racial equality. In its hometown of Detroit, the union maintained close ties with the NAACP and used this alliance to great effect in organizing African American workers. This is not to say, of course, that all UAW locals and their members agreed with the international's racial program. Though the union's international officers tried to impress on the members the necessity of interracialism, the largely autonomous local leadership frequently rebelled against such strictures. At the North American plant in Grand Prairie, for example, one of the executive board members of UAW Local 645 forthrightly stated in the early months of the FEPC's investigations that "here in Texas there shall be no social equality," and that outsiders were not going to tell whites that they had to accept African Americans as equals.[49]

As revealing as such bigoted sentiments were, local UAW officers were nevertheless hard-pressed to ignore African Americans. In many instances, white leaders depended on black workers to carry out much of the work involved in organizing the union. Such was the case at North American, where Local 645 was organized on an integrated basis with a great deal of help from those at whom the board member's vitriol was directed. According to W. M. "Jack" Anderson, the local's first president, black

---

47 Mark Perlman, *Democracy in the International Association of Machinists* (New York, 1962), 11–24; Perlman, *The Machinists: A New Study in American Trade Unionism* (Cambridge, Mass., 1961), 105–12; Vander Meulen, *Politics of Aircraft*, 215–17.
48 Vander Meulen, *Politics of Aircraft*, 211–17; Perlman, *Machinists*, 107.
49 Zieger, *CIO*, 85, 153–56; Lichtenstein, *Most Dangerous Man in Detroit*, 207–11; Chamberlain, *Victory at Home*, 139 (quotation). On the UAW's often ambiguous relationship with African Americans, see David M. Lewis-Colman, *Race against Liberalism: Black Workers and the UAW in Detroit* (Urbana, 2008); August Meier and Elliott Rudwick, *Black Detroit and the Rise of the UAW* (New York, 1979); and Kevin Boyle, "'There Are No Union Sorrows That the Union Can't Heal': The Struggle for Racial Equality in the United Automobile Workers, 1940–1960," *Labor History,* 36 (Winter 1995), 5–23.

janitors were an indispensable part of the UAW's organizing drive at North American because their duties required them to wander throughout the plant. "These nigras [sic] was organizing everybody," Anderson recalled. "They not only organized the Black, they would talk to the people in these different departments." This effort accelerated even more rapidly after Anderson enlisted the support of the Dallas Negro Chamber of Commerce. Besides pleading with North American's black workers to extend the organizing drive, Anderson recalled, the leaders of that civic group also attempted to raise the moral indignation of all workers in the plant by advertising the deplorable conditions that many African Americans endured: "[The company] took a big wire ... mesh wire, oh it was twenty feet high. And people couldn't get in there to see these people, to talk to them. So there these Black people was in this screened-in department, like a bunch of animals. ... They kept them in there like a bunch of slaves. Just pitiful. Something very bad. So that was another selling point to get the people to sign the union card, to see how a human being was being treated." In short, Anderson concluded that had it not been for the African American workers, the local never would have gained enough signatures to call for an authorization election. Such interracial campaigns, even if they were undertaken for strategic reasons, put the UAW light-years ahead of most other unions in the South at the time.[50]

By contrast, the IAM has been frequently held up as a sterling example of the racist exclusionism prevalent among craft unionists. Foremost among the union's sins was its exclusion of African Americans as members. The mechanism for this discrimination was the IAM's not-so-secret induction ritual that pledged all new members never to recommend for membership anyone not of the white race. For years, this discriminatory language disqualified African Americans from even the most menial jobs in places where the IAM held closed-shop agreements. Such problems became especially acute during World War II with the rapid expansion of shipbuilding, aircraft manufacturing, and other industries in which the IAM was prominent. Boeing's closed-shop facility in Seattle provided perhaps the best example: out of a workforce of 41,000, there was not a single black employee in 1941. When confronted about such shameful episodes, the IAM's national leadership announced that while it was not opposed to the employment of African Americans, neither the FEPC nor any other government agency had the authority to compel it to accept black members. Similar records of discrimination could be found at IAM-organized aircraft plants in Missouri, Tennessee, California, and, of course, Texas.[51]

But change was coming to the IAM. Not even the discriminatory language of the union's ritual could escape the civil rights tide slowly spreading across the country during the war. Fueled by patriotism and a pragmatic desire to organize the growing number of unskilled aircraft workers, many of whom were African Americans, sentiment began to rise in the IAM's ranks for amending the discriminatory membership requirements. At the union's 1940 convention, delegates from New York, Pennsylvania, and California all advocated elimination of the ritual and the admission of African Americans; the matter was tabled, however, after the union's secretary-treasurer, a southerner, declared that local lodges would likely do as they wanted regardless of any official action. Perhaps drawing on the secretary-treasurer's

---

50 "Transcript of Tape on 'History of Local 645' Made by Jack Anderson in 1994," n.d., Box 1, UAW Local 848 Records, Accession 95–66 (University of Texas at Arlington Library).

51 Perlman, *Democracy in the International Association of Machinists*, 39; Perlman, *Machinists*, 108, 279; Hill, *Black Labor and the American Legal System*, 209–16; Reed, *Seedtime for the Modem Civil Rights Movement*, 35–36. At Boeing and a number of other companies with closed-shop IAM agreements, discrimination against African Americans was sometimes partly corrected by allowing the local lodge to issue work permits to African Americans if they would pay the equivalent of initiation fees and monthly dues.

words, a growing number of local lodges did indeed tackle the issue themselves. At the same time that the FEPC was investigating the massive Boeing lodge, for example, another lodge in Seattle tried to circumvent the union's membership prohibition by interpreting the whites-only clause as applying to an individual's character rather than his skin color. Sadly, these local officials were advised by the national leadership that their interpretation was in error, and the lodge ceased its efforts to recruit black members. A group of black workers who had been granted membership by an IAM lodge in St. Louis were afforded similar treatment once international officers discovered the local's transgression.[52]

These isolated rebellions gave way to a more widespread campaign against the union's membership policy in 1944 when the officers of District Lodge 727, which represented 35,000 workers at Lockheed Aircraft in Burbank, California, sent an open letter to lodges throughout the country. "Our membership believes," this communication read, "that the [all-white] clause in our ritual is unworthy of our great democratic association and opposed to the principles of democracy in the Constitution of the United States." Though District 727 was chastised for embarrassing the union with such public entreaties, its campaign garnered support for opening the IAM's ranks to African Americans: at the 1945 convention, a floor vote on whether to eliminate the ritual was defeated by the slim margin of 2,173 to 1,958. Not even Harvey Brown, who as president of the IAM was one of the staunchest defenders of its discriminatory policies, could deny the importance of these numbers.[53]

While there is no record of whether District 776 voted for elimination of the ritual during the 1945 convention, the Fort Worth union seems to have been among the growing number of IAM lodges that favored amending the union's discriminatory membership policies. Shortly after the leaders of Lodge 727 began circulating their antidiscrimination letter, District 776 president J. D. Smith informed the FEPC's Don Ellinger that many of the union's local leaders at Convair hoped the IAM executive council would follow the example of the International Brotherhood of Boilermakers and establish auxiliary locals for African Americans. Despite coming under scrutiny when the FEPC discovered that the boilermakers used this segregated arrangement to minimize black representation in union leadership, auxiliary locals fostered direct contact between local union leaders and African American members. By contrast, the AFL's federal labor unions usually depended on absentee AFL staff members to act as intermediaries, a situation that often resulted in underrepresentation of black workers and their interests.[54]

Of course, like their UAW counterparts at North American, District 776 leaders still showed definite limits to their racial moderation. While he favored the creation of segregated auxiliaries within the IAM, Smith made it clear that he would not take any action unless the Grand Lodge approved such arrangements throughout the nation. Even in the absence of official sanction, however, Smith did not

52 Perlman, *Machinists*, 278–79; Hill, *Black Labor and the American Legal System*, 214–15.

53 Dale O. Reed and W. M. Holladay to IAM recording secretaries, n.d., Folder 8, Box 4, District 776 Papers (quotations); Perlman, *Machinists*, 278–79. That a national campaign to repeal the IAM's ritual came out of Lockheed is not surprising given that in 1941 the company had been the first aircraft manufacturer to actively seek out black employees. See Reed, *Seedtime for the Modern Civil Rights Movement*, 39.

54 Don Ellinger to Clarence Mitchell, July 21, 1944, Folder "Consolidated-Vultee Aircraft Corp., 10-BR-336," Box 2, Closed Cases, RG 228; Harvey Brown to Dale Reed, February 16, 1944, International President's Office Records, International Association of Machinists and Aerospace Workers Records (Wisconsin Historical Society Archives, Madison), microfilm, reel 271; hereinafter cited as IAM Records, microfilm. On the use of Jim Crow auxiliaries by the boilermakers union and its conflicts with the FEPC, see Reed, *Seedtime for the Modern Civil Rights Movement*, 267–317; Kersten, *Labor's Home Front*, 68–99; and Hill, *Black Labor and the American Legal System*, 185–208.

ignore the organizational aspirations of Convair's black employees, who in 1943 chartered their own federal labor union with assistance from the local IAM aircraft industry organizing committee. Known as the Glover Colored Aircraft Workers Union, this AFL affiliate had the same drawbacks for African Americans as other federal labor unions, namely, its failure to provide its members with a voice in the affairs of their bargaining agent, District 776. Nevertheless, that Smith and his fellow IAM officers even considered such action was an important departure from the racism that had dominated the Fort Worth labor movement.[55]

International union policies aside, the true litmus test of the labor movement's wartime commitment to African Americans was found in how well union leaders performed their duty of representing workers at the local level. In the case of William Keele, it is tempting to dismiss the cooperation he received from his Local 645 steward as little more than a peculiarity. When this conclusion is considered alongside the full history of wartime representation by both Local 645 and District 776, however, the evidence suggests that Keele's positive experience was part of a broader pattern of accommodating relations between the FEPC and the local leadership of the aircraft unions. Throughout the war, Ellinger's correspondence with his colleagues in Washington was full of statements praising both UAW and IAM officials for their cooperation in adjusting African American complaints. This analysis is not to suggest, of course, that either union was an oasis of racially progressive thought: even as he praised their leaders, Ellinger voiced concerns about the willingness of these same men to condone segregation in their unions. Personal attitudes aside, union support was nevertheless instrumental to the FEPC's accomplishments in the Fort Worth aircraft plants. In the end, the single most important factor in explaining why both the UAW and IAM cooperated with Ellinger was the hostility they faced from management at North American and Convair. As the war dragged on, the leaders of Local 645 and District 776 recognized that the struggles of African Americans against arbitrary discrimination complemented their own battle for fair contracts and dignified treatment on the job.

The clearest evidence of the IAM and UAW's local approach to African Americans can be seen in the way they handled these workers' grievances. Because wartime unions lacked the power to sanction strikes or other protest actions that might disrupt production, the formalized grievance procedure was perhaps their most powerful tool for convincing workers of the unions' usefulness. Speaking to local union leaders in 1943, IAM Grand Lodge representative L. M. Fagan warned, "The most important thing is not a wage increase, but job protection and seniority rights. Your job is to sell Texas on your union, and your work will really begin when you win the election, for you must police your agreement with management." Though they might have found it disagreeable to assist African Americans, local leaders took Fagan's words to heart and recognized that even racial grievances had to be vigorously adjudicated if the aircraft unions hoped to maintain their legitimacy in a wartime environment where more militant actions were impossible.[56]

---

55 Don Ellinger to Clarence Mitchell, July 21, 1944, Folder "Consolidated-Vultee Aircraft Corp., 10-BR-336," Box 2, Closed Cases, RG 228; "Subject: Federal Labor Union No. 23394," December 11, 1953, International President's Office Records, IAM Records, microfilm, reel 108; "Glover Colored Aircraft Workers Union Charter," April 21, 1943, Folder 18, Box 6, District 776 Papers; Chamberlain, *Victory at Home,* 130.

56 "CIO Flayed by Dallas Union Man," Dallas *Morning News,* February 16, 1943, pp. 1, 9. For a case study outlining the importance of the grievance procedure in the institutional culture of industrial unions, see Korstad, *Civil Rights Unionism,* 211–23. On the centrality of the grievance procedure in the early history of Fort Worth's aircraft unions, see Kirk White, "The

One important grievance case involved R. C. Carroll, a black janitor at Convair, who served as president of the Glover Colored Aircraft Workers Union. Since being hired in 1942, Carroll had gained recognition as a hard worker and was often consulted for advice by foremen in the offices he cleaned. In June 1944 Carroll wrote labor relations director John Hassler to request consideration for either an upgrade to the position of leadman or a transfer to another department. Carroll's entreaties apparently did not please his white foreman, however, for Carroll began to receive disciplinary notices on trumped-up charges of insubordination and absenteeism. This treatment continued for several days until Carroll was discharged.[57] When Ellinger contacted Convair, he was told that Carroll had been let go due to a failure to maintain work standards and an alleged penchant for loafing. Ellinger remained suspicious, though, and continued to press the company for the real reason. His doubts were confirmed when a representative of Convair stated that Carroll was simply attempting to get a job in the maintenance department, where he would have the opportunity to work with whites. "All these niggers want," the official argued, "is a chance to work with white people."[58]

Faced with this rather forthright admission, Ellinger contacted District 776 president J. D. Smith to ask for his help in gaining Carroll's reinstatement. As fate would have it, Carroll's case came at an opportune time for the union. Since being recognized as the plant's sole collective bargaining agent in March 1943, District 776 had been engaged in a bitter battle with Convair's recalcitrant labor relations department to secure a contract. By the summer of 1944, members of the union had become so frustrated with the progress of negotiations that they filed a petition with the National Labor Relations Board (NLRB) for a strike vote under the War Labor Disputes Act.[59] This action placed District 776's leaders in an awkward position. On the one hand, the legitimacy of the local lodge depended on its officers' doing whatever it took to secure a contract, so for them to oppose the strike petition would risk rank-and-file abandonment of the union. On the other hand, these same leaders were also bound to honor the no-strike pledge signed by the AFL and the CIO in the opening days of the war. Relieving local leaders of their quandary, the national officers of the IAM took charge of the situation through a direct appeal to the membership in Fort Worth. After reminding the would-be strikers that given the recent invasion of Normandy their cooperation was more necessary than ever, Grand Lodge officials rescinded the petition.[60]

Development of IAM District Lodge 776 in Fort Worth, Texas, 1942–1946: A Case Study in the Growth of Organized Labor during World War II" (M.A. thesis, University of North Texas, 1999), 66–70, 77–82.

57 R. C. Carroll to John Hassler, June 6, 1944, Folder "Consolidated-Vultee Aircraft Corp., 10-BR-336," Box 2, Closed Cases, RG 228; R. C. Carroll to Don Ellinger, June 15, 1944, *ibid.*; Statement of J. L. Roberts, H. Avells, and A. Dudley, June 27, 1944, *ibid.*

58 Don Ellinger to Will Maslow, June 29, 1944, Folder "Consolidated-Vultee Aircraft Corp., 10-BR-235," *ibid.*

59 On the events leading up to District 776's strike petition, see White, "Development of IAM District Lodge 776," pp. 57–88. Under the War Labor Disputes Act, better known as the Smith-Connally Act, unions operating in essential war industries were required to give the government thirty days' notice of their intent to strike. It was hoped that this cooling-off period would allow enough time for disagreements to be more amicably resolved—in reality, tensions often increased significantly during the intervening period. If a strike were called without this official authorization, not only could the affected plant be seized by the government, but the union could also be held liable for any damages caused by its members. However, because even the threat of a strike was often enough reason for the government to seize a plant, union leaders began to use this tactic to leverage concessions from management. See James B. Atleson, *Labor and the Wartime State: Labor Relations and Law during World War II* (Urbana, 1998), 195–97.

60 H. W. Brown to J. D. Smith, June 8, 1944, International President's Office Records, IAM Records, microfilm, reel 345.

While the Grand Lodge's action ended the immediate threat of a strike, there still remained the issue of securing a contract and dealing with the even more frustrated District 776 membership. Carroll's termination took place within this tense atmosphere. Smith shrewdly recognized that Carroll's case could be used to keep the members' blood boiling by providing an example of the blatant discrimination that was possible when management went unchecked. Although the district president confided to Ellinger that Carroll had been out of line in requesting a job where he would have to work with whites, Smith nevertheless filed a grievance on the termination and took the case up with the plant grievance committee. At first, Convair refused to budge, but Smith turned the tables by threatening to initiate arbitration proceedings against the company. This warning took on even more significance when the union's paper, the *Cow-Town Plane Facts*, offered its public support for Carroll's reinstatement. Faced with the prospect of an expensive arbitration and an even more agitated workforce, Convair reinstated Carroll with full seniority rights and transferred him to the day shift. Though Ellinger admitted that the FEPC's influence with Convair may have helped, he concluded that "[the] adjustment affected was handled by the machinists and they deserve full credit for it."[61]

Carroll's case was not the only African American grievance that the all-white IAM became involved in. When janitor Ennis Dunkin was fired for substandard production in January 1945, he brought his complaint to Smith, who agreed to initiate a grievance even though the forty-eight-hour time limit for doing so had passed. Like Carroll, Dunkin had apparently been quite active in the union's organizing efforts and served as a trustee for the Glover auxiliary. Through Smith's assistance, Dunkin was eventually offered reinstatement in April, but he refused it on the grounds that he had secured a position as foreman with another company. Lest this decision be misunderstood as a condemnation of District 776, Dunkin declared that the union had done well by him and that Smith had personally called about returning to work at Convair.[62]

Even more impressive was the IAM's willingness to fight in behalf of African American women for higher wages. Following a lengthy struggle by the international office of the IAM, in July 1944 the War Labor Board ordered management at Convair to completely redo the company's wage rates. Under the so-called Southern California Airframe Industry (SCAI) plan, all workers in Convair's Fort Worth facility were to be reclassified and paid retroactively according to job descriptions established by a National Airframe Panel based on its observations of defense plant operations on the West Coast. As it had done in virtually all matters involving labor relations, however, Convair attempted to skirt the order when possible by working employees outside designated classifications for wages below those specified. Although there is no evidence that the company targeted African Americans, such tactics did fall hard on these workers since they were already concentrated in the lowest-paying jobs.[63]

---

61 Don Ellinger to J. D. Smith, June 16, 1944, Folder "Consolidated-Vultee Aircraft Corp., 10-BR-336," Box 2, Closed Cases, RG 228; Don Ellinger to Will Maslow, June 29, 1944, *ibid.*; Don Ellinger to Will Maslow, July 21, 1944, *ibid*, (quotation); "Convair Union Withdraws Strike Vote," June 16, 1944, International President's Office Records, IAM Records, microfilm, reel 345; "Robert Carroll Termination Case Headed for Arbitration," *Cow-Town Plane Facts*, July 14, 1944. This episode is also briefly mentioned in an essay by Merl Reed, but his conclusion that Carroll's reinstatement was brought about in part by a group known as the Fort Worth Negro Welfare Council is contradicted by Ellinger's account. See Reed, "Bell Aircraft Comes South," 127.
62 "Statement of Ennis Dunkin," January 13,1945, Folder "Consolidated-Vultee Aircraft Corp., 10-BR-462," Box 2, Closed Cases, RG 228; Ennis Dunkin to Don Ellinger, April 19, 1945, *ibid.*
63 C. Z. Lindsey to Benjamin Aaron, July 1, 1945, International President's Office Records, IAM Records, microfilm, reel 345; "Fort Worth Air Plant Wage Plan Decreed," Dallas *Morning News,* August 24, 1944, p. 6.

In July 1945 IAM Grand Lodge representative C. Z. Lindsey informed Smith that Convair had refused to upgrade its African American maids to the classification of janitor, even though they were already performing the duties of a janitor under the SCAI plan. Even worse, the company was paying these women up to twenty cents per hour less than the designated rate for janitors and had refused to give them the retroactive lump sum that other workers had received. When Lindsey asked Convair's Hassler why the women were not given the full pay owed them, the company official glibly responded that he was concerned about the consequences of an "economic disparagement within the Fort Worth colored colony" if highly paid maids were introduced there. In a statement rendered all the more impressive by its writer's apparent lack of racial prejudice, Lindsey advised Smith that District 776 "should lend every effort to secure justice for those whose rights have been so delibertly [sic] ignored by insisting they be classed as janitors."[64]

Smith took Lindsey's instructions to heart and approached Convair several times with requests that these African American women be properly classified. Each time he was met with a request that the union instead negotiate a stipulated agreement outside the regular SCAI plan allowing for maids to be paid less than janitors. In bringing the matter up with the National Airframe Panel, Lindsey said there was no way the union could agree to such a stipulation since "it would amount to a separate low rate of pay for females performing essentially the same duties as males at a higher rate." Faced with these untenable demands, Smith petitioned the NLRB for authorization to conduct a strike vote in July 1945, a shrewd tactic that took advantage of the War Labor Disputes Act's provision requiring unions to obtain the approval of their members before taking any kind of strike action. Although the disparity in maids' wages was not the sole issue about which Smith complained, it is quite telling that he included it among the five most important areas of disagreement between the union and Convair.[65]

Had Smith or any other union leader in Fort Worth threatened a strike in behalf of African American maids before the war, they likely would have been labeled as radicals and unceremoniously dismissed from their duties by angry white members. By the end of the war, however, such demands apparently no longer raised eyebrows among the thousands of IAM members who had struggled for a contract over the past three years. For these workers, the plight of a few black maids was another example of Convair's constant attempts to deal unfairly and unilaterally with its workforce. Smith's strike threat worked: in August 1945 the union withdrew its petition after Convair agreed to negotiate a permanent contract and clarify older areas of dispute.[66]

Although UAW Local 645 never had to resort to filing charges or petitioning the government for a strike vote in its battles with North American, it too became involved in a number of grievance cases in

---

64 C. Z. Lindsey to J. D. Smith, May 23, 1945, International President's Office Records, IAM Records, microfilm, reel 345 (quotations); C. Z. Lindsey to Benjamin Aaron, July 1, 1945, *ibid.*

65 J. D. Smith to Paul Herzog, July 10, 1945, *ibid.* The other areas of disagreement that Smith cited to the NLRB were the company's refusal to follow seniority in layoffs, the application of the six-month merit review, the replacement of production workers with downgraded supervisors, and the proper handling of grievances concerning hours and rates of pay. *Ibid.*

66 C. Z. Lindsey to Benjamin Aaron, July 1, 1945, *ibid.;* "IAM Lodge Withdrew Strike Petition After Reaching Agreement with Convair," *Cow-Town Plane Facts,* August 10, 1945. Although he does not mention African American women specifically, Andrew Kersten maintains that the IAM was one of the labor movement's most adamant supporters of equal pay for equal work during the war and consistently refused the attempts of management to create separate job classifications for men and women. See Kersten, *Labor's Home Front,* 124. For an account of black women's relationship with organized labor during the war and how it compared with the experience of white women, see Philip S. Foner, *Women and the American Labor Movement* (2 vols.; New York, 1979–1980), II, 360–93.

behalf of African American members, demonstrating in the process its commitment to the principles of strong, contract-focused unionism. One particularly incendiary incident took place in late 1943 and involved a black laborer named Willie Shields. At the end of his shift in North American's metal segregating department one evening, Shields was threatened by a group of white men when he tried to squeeze past them on his way to the time clocks. Having reported the encounter to his leadman, Shields believed the problem would be taken care of and thus attempted to take the same route the following night. This time, however, the white men were waiting, and when one of them struck him on the leg with a pipe, Shields picked up a brick and threatened to defend himself. The melee ended without any further violence, but Shields's troubles were just beginning. Reporting the confrontation to his leadman once again, a worried Shields asked whether he and other African American employees would be forced to carry guns to the plant in order to protect themselves from such thugs. Almost immediately after making this statement, the beleaguered black laborer was detained by plant security and terminated on charges that he had threatened a supervisor. When Shields protested his firing to North American's labor relations office, he was told to consider the dismissal a favor since he probably would be killed if management sided with him against a group of whites.[67]

Clearly, Shields's case was tailor-made for intervention, and both the UAW and the FEPC soon became involved. Grievance committee chairman Homer Davidson was the first person from the union to come to Shields's aid, filing a complaint that quickly worked its way through the established grievance procedure. In keeping with its past dealings with employees, management refused to budge on its decision, and the grievance was dropped from the committee's agenda. Suspicious that Davidson had not pressed the case hard enough, FEPC examiner Leonard Brin began looking into the operations of Local 645 as part of his investigation. Meeting with the local's executive council, Brin reported that half the leadership was sympathetic to the problems of blacks, while the other half was "either antagonistic or unable to see the core of the problems involved." Davidson himself admitted dropping Shields's grievance but said he had been forced to do so because he could not secure any African American witnesses to testify. The other officers present defended Davidson's actions and maintained that they handled cases on behalf of African Americans the same as other members. This apparently did not impress Brin, especially after he discovered that black members of the local were meeting separately from whites at the Negro YMCA in Dallas. When Davidson and the council urged him to convince these workers to return to the union hall, Brin refused, saying that it was not up to him to do the union's organizing for it. Although he officially concluded that the meeting had impressed the local leadership with the importance of the FEPC's program, Brin—who did not have a background in the labor movement and was thus much less concerned than Ellinger about embarrassing recalcitrant unions—stated confidentially that it might be necessary to call in the UAW's international officers to supervise the local.[68]

Hoping to avoid this drastic course of action and solidify relations between the FEPC and Local 645, Brin called on Ellinger to meet with the union's officers one more time. Following a conference with these leaders, Ellinger reported back that they had agreed Shields's firing was racially discriminatory

---

67 "Leonard Brin to Will Maslow, March 3, 1944, Folder "North American Aviation, 10-BR-156," Box 8, Closed Cases, RG 228; "Statement of Willie Shields," February 1, 1944, *ibid.*
68 "For the File: North American Aviation, Inc., of Texas," March 7, 1944, *ibid.*; "Memo to Maslow," n.d., *ibid,* (quotation). Biographical information on Brin can be found in Denton L. Watson, ed., *The Papers of Clarence Mitchell Jr.* Vol. II: *1944–1946* (Athens, Ohio, 2005), 767.

and would take any action necessary to sell this conclusion to the members and the public. The real trouble, they insisted, was getting North American to go along. The officers and Ellinger agreed that the crux of the problem for Shields and all other workers in the plant was the grievance procedure, which was weak and under management's control. Without the most airtight evidence, a grievance had almost no chance of coming successfully through arbitration, which explained the initial dismissal of Shields's case. Ellinger maintained that Shields was not the only member to suffer from the weakness of the contract: out of nearly two dozen cases recently filed, the union had won only two.[69]

In spite of his earlier lukewarm assessment, these updates convinced Brin that Local 645 was indeed fulfilling its obligations to African American members. The real issue was to show that this case (which had become less pressing because Shields had been drafted) was part of a larger pattern of discrimination that could only be adjusted by holding hearings on the situation at North American. Brin was therefore dismayed to learn that his superiors in Washington had contacted UAW president R. J. Thomas and criticized the local for supposedly refusing to reinstate Shields. Thomas responded by sending an international representative to Grand Prairie, a move that did little to put Brin in Local 645's good graces. In letters to Thomas and FEPC chairman George Johnson, Brin assured both men that the union's officers had been consistently helpful. Furthermore, based on his own frustrating communications with North American, he doubted that any offer of reinstatement had ever been made to Shields. Even more important, Brin concluded that the consequences of a solitary adjustment in Shields's case, which was now a moot point, would only "serve to bury for all time the vicious situation in this plant where supervisory employees kick minority groups around, apparently with the consent of higher authority." What was needed was a hearing to publicly expose North American's discrimination and compel its compliance. Despite this impassioned plea for broader action by the FEPC, Brin's superiors in Washington were confident that the episode had taught North American a much-needed lesson, and they refused to call the requested hearing.[70]

Like its IAM counterpart at Convair, UAW Local 645 was also concerned about North American management's arbitrary use of classifications and wage scales. Regardless of its members' personal feelings about African Americans, the union had to confront any and all violations of the contract lest such actions embolden the company to commit further abuses. In the midst of Shields's case, another complaint came into the FEPC from Joseph Brown, a truckman's helper, alleging that African Americans in North American's transportation department were not being offered upgrades. In addition to Brown's complaint that he was being worked as a truck driver for ten cents an hour below the proper rate, a number of his fellow workers were unhappy at having to train new white workers who would then advance ahead of the black employees. There was also a great deal of dissatisfaction with the foremen in the transportation department, especially a former prison guard named Sells who allegedly bragged about shooting black prisoners. Hoping to adjust the matter through the union rather than the FEPC, Ellinger convinced Brown to gather other black workers for a meeting with grievance committee chairman Davidson and Local 645 president O. H. Britt. Both union officers assured the men that they were welcome in the union hall and urged them to make use of the grievance procedure when such discrimination took place. Ellinger concurred, telling the gathered workers that the union's regular shop

---

69 Don Ellinger to Leonard Brin, March 23, 1944, Folder "North American Aviation, 10-BR-156," Box 8, Closed Cases, RG 228.
70 Leonard Brin to George Johnson, April 19, 1944, *ibid,* (quotation); Leonard Brin to R. J. Thomas, April 19, 1944, *ibid.*; "Final Disposition Report," August 9, 1944, *ibid.*

procedure was the best place for them to seek redress since it had broader coverage than the FEPC. Davidson also agreed to appoint more African Americans to positions as union stewards and selected a man on the spot. For their part, Brown and his coworkers decided to hold a monthly meeting in order to convey their problems directly to Davidson and the grievance committee. When news of this gathering and the union's support for it reached the general foreman of the transportation department, he quickly agreed—over the objections of North American's labor relations director F. J. Conlan—to remove foreman Sells, appoint three black leadmen, and further investigate Brown's pay discrimination claims.[71]

Impressive as the UAW's and the IAM's local representation of African Americans was, skeptics will no doubt point out that official actions by union leaders reveal relatively little about the attitudes of rank-and-file members. And indeed, certain events do suggest that the racial attitudes of white aircraft workers did not soften significantly during the war—both the violence meted out to Willie Shields for pushing past a group of white workers at North American and the refusal of white employees to work alongside William Keele at Convair bear witness to this. Shameful as these episodes were, however, they must be considered alongside contrary examples. Though they had to be persuaded by District 776 leaders that it was in their interest, Keele's white antagonists did eventually accept him into their department without further protest. If the violence at North American was disturbing, it must also be remembered that according to Local 645 president W. M. Anderson, black janitors enjoyed great success in organizing white workers during the union's early efforts at the plant. Even more telling is that the IAM's much-publicized campaigns to reinstate R. C. Carroll and secure equal wages for black female janitors apparently did not elicit any reaction from the thousands of white rank and filers who read about the initiatives in the *Cow-Town Plane Facts*. While it would be going too far to argue that this quietude indicates the absence of racism, it does suggest that white workers were developing a basic sense of economic fairness with regard to their African American counterparts. At a time when the union was struggling to secure an organizational foothold at Convair, District 776's leadership would certainly not have advertised these racial grievances if they did not feel that such action enjoyed at least some support from the all-white membership.

One other important incident at Convair reveals the slow but steady breakdown of exclusionary racial sentiment among the plant's white rank-and-file union members. In February 1944 a white worker named J. D. McNeely was laid off by Convair, and his job was taken over by a group of less senior African Americans. Supported by the statements of at least six of his coworkers, McNeely filed a grievance with District 776 complaining about this situation. While it is tempting to view this complaint as being racially motivated, McNeely seems to have considered the incident from a less-biased perspective and laid bare the issues at stake with admirable clarity: "When [assistant foreman] Smith told me he didn't have enough work for me I said to him that I thought the ones who had been there for some time should have preference over the newer ones. He told me seniority didn't count with him, that he would keep the ones he wanted to. Apparently that is what he did because he kept men who had been employed less than six months." For McNeely, the race of the individuals who replaced him was secondary to the clear violation of the seniority principle that he and other District 776 members were demanding in the union's contract negotiations.[72]

---

71 "Don Ellinger to Leonard Brin, April 25, 1944, Folder "North American Aviation, 10-BR-288," *ibid.;* "Special Meeting of Dept. 59: Colored People," April 13, 1944, *ibid.*
72 "Statement of J. D. McNeely," n.d., Folder 15, Box 3, District 776 Papers.

This same sense of economic injustice was shared by the coworkers who testified in McNeely's behalf. Though they all made the point that "a Negro" had taken McNeely's job, these witnesses seemed more concerned that the black replacement was doing the same work for the minimum rate of sixty cents per hour. Notably, unlike their counterparts in the Keele case, these white witnesses stayed on the job after McNeely's black replacement entered the department. In short, the same goal that compelled union leadership to take up the grievances of African Americans and cooperate with the FEPC also drove the various participants in McNeely's case: a pragmatic desire to counter the arbitrary authority of the aircraft manufacturers. In this bitter industrial struggle, white aircraft workers had little choice but to recognize that their welfare and the strength of their union depended on maintaining such color-blind economic principles as seniority and equal pay for equal work.[73]

As much as racial attitudes and union practices had evolved, neither the rank and file nor their leaders were in a position to address the looming problem of unemployment facing all defense workers at the end of the war. Proponents of fair employment were equally fearful that even the minor gains won by African Americans would vanish once industries shut down and veterans returned from overseas. FEPC officials began preparing for the inevitable downturn as early as the summer of 1944 but found themselves cut off from high-level discussions about reconversion to a peacetime economy. The impact of this falling economic tide on the FEPC's already limited bargaining power was particularly pronounced at Convair. As the final year of the war began, Ellinger had at last managed to gain some movement from management on training and upgrading African Americans. The turning point came in February 1945 when the army ordered Convair to comply with the FEPC's program. While still denying that his company had ever practiced discrimination, Convair's director of labor relations, John Hassler, agreed to set aside the foundry, drop hammer, and plaster departments for African Americans and to reassign the whites holding these jobs. Hassler also assured the FEPC that seniority and employee evaluations would govern who would receive transfers. Though Ellinger cautioned that his superiors were likely to reject the plan if they thought that segregated departments would serve to limit black opportunities, given the frustrating history of negotiations at Convair he was willing to recommend Hassler's idea on a trial basis in order to prove that African Americans could work in higher classifications. Just as expected, the FEPC's national office expressed concern about the arrangement, but ultimately officials there too agreed that it should be temporarily accepted "as a prelude to complete compliance."[74]

Initially, the upgrading program seemed to work quite well. According to Jackson Valtair, a consultant sent by Ellinger to meet with Hassler in late March 1945, management at Convair was "fairly satisfied" with the progress being made and had already conducted two training classes consisting of close to one hundred black employees under the supervision of skilled white sheet metal workers. Although Hassler contemptuously asserted that efficiency among the transferred black workers had fallen off after several weeks, Valtair confirmed that this slowdown was due to a change in the materials used. The black workers and their representatives in the Glover colored lodge also expressed their satisfaction

---

73 "Statement of Five Workers," March 4, 1944, *ibid.*; "Statement of H. C. Huff," March 6, 1944, *ibid.* It is not clear exactly what action, if any, IAM officials took or whether McNeely was reinstated.

74 Reed, *Seedtime for the Modern Civil Rights Movement*, 321–26; Don Ellinger to Clarence Mitchell, February 8, 1945, Folder "Consolidated-Vultee Aircraft Corp., 10-BR-235," Box 2, Closed Cases, RG 228; Don Ellinger to Clarence Mitchell, February 9, 1945, *ibid.;* "Outline of Plan Relative to Increasing Employment of Negro Men and Women," n.d., *ibid.*; Clarence Mitchell to Don Ellinger, February 28, 1945, *ibid.*; Don Ellinger to John Hassler, March 6, 1945, *ibid.* (quotation).

with the program even as they urged continued vigilance on the part of the FEPC. By early May, African American employees of various skill levels represented over half of the workforce in the drop hammer department. Even more important, ninety of these workers had proved themselves in skilled classifications, leading Convair's fabrication superintendent, C. J. Petrick, to conclude that the program should be extended when the need for additional workers arose.[75]

By the time Petrick made this recommendation, however, the employment situation at Convair had already begun to deteriorate. Since initiating the upgrade plan in February 1945, close to 2,400 employees had been terminated due to decreasing workloads, and serious talks were being held on the prospect of cutting the workweek back to forty hours in order to avoid more layoffs. In light of these changes, Hassler reported that "the company does not feel that it would be justified in terminating qualified, experienced, white employees in order to make jobs for Negroes." More disturbing was the announcement in late May that the army was cutting back its purchases of aircraft by some 17,000 planes. As a result, by the end of September the workforce at Convair, which stood at roughly 23,000 at the beginning of the year, was scheduled to be slashed by another 10,000 employees. Having already produced a large surplus of parts, Convair's fabrication operations were particularly hard hit. In an ominous signal of the hard times to come, the company announced that the drop hammer department into which many African Americans had recently transferred was scheduled for elimination. Whether there was any sinister intent behind this decision is difficult to say, but Ellinger immediately realized that it devastated the FEPC's program. Given that more than 4,000 of the fabrication workers being laid off were white, Ellinger concluded that "[it] seems … we have no acceptable complaint because of the one hundred Negroes who were included in the reduction."[76]

The situation was even bleaker at Grand Prairie, where in mid-August 1944 the army decided to curtail North American's existing prime contract for bombers. Although the plant retained some sub-contracting work, the announcement meant that more than half of the roughly 30,000 total employees still on the company's payroll were to be laid off by the end of the year in line with their seniority. With hundreds of workers leaving every week, it was not long before African Americans got caught up in the fray. In December, Volney Phillips, one of the three black men promoted to the position of leadman in the transportation department case earlier that year, received word that he was being demoted to truck driver and replaced by a less-senior white employee. When Phillips asked why, his foreman forthrightly told him that due to cutbacks and departmental rearrangements there was no longer an all-black crew for Phillips to lead. Ellinger sent off a letter protesting this decision and requesting access to the company's employee evaluations so that he could determine for himself whether Phillips was entitled to remain in the position. Rather than dispute the FEPC's charges, however, North American's labor relations director, F. J. Conlan, simply replied that the company had utilized as many African Americans as it could and would continue to do so "when practical." Ellinger could do little in response—in July 1945, southern legislators had managed to cut the FEPC's budget in half, virtually crippling its field operations.

---

75 "Jackson Valtair to Don Ellinger, March 26, 1945, Folder "Consolidated-Vultee Aircraft Corp., 10-BR-235," Box 2, Closed Cases, RG 228 (quotation); Jackson Valtair to Don Ellinger, May 11, 1945, *ibid.*; John Hassler to Capt. M. H. Baugh, May 12, 1945, *ibid.*; "Present Status of Plan for Employment of Negro Workers at Consolidated-Vultee Aircraft Corp.," n.d., *ibid.*

76 "Present Status of Plan for Employment of Negro Workers at Consolidated-Vultee Aircraft Corp.," n.d., *ibid,* (first quotation); Don Ellinger to Will Maslow, May 31, 1945, *ibid.*; "Reverting to 40-Hours Week Is Now Being Considered," *Cow-Town Plane Facts,* May 11, 1945 (second quotation); "Cutback Starts in Fort Worth," *ibid.,* June 1, 1945; Chamberlain, *Victory at Home,* 157.

Given these circumstances and the acceleration of layoffs in the plant, Ellinger conceded that the case was no longer adjustable. Two weeks later, in the wake of the Japanese surrender, North American announced that the Grand Prairie plant was to be shut down completely and all of its remaining 15,000 employees let go.[77]

Given that the eviscerated FEPC was unable to mount even a feeble campaign against the wholesale liquidation of black workers during the final months of the war, how are its investigations at North American and Convair to be evaluated? Any answer to this question must take into consideration the hard-fought gains Ellinger and his counterparts had achieved for African Americans over the previous years. When the Region X office was first opened, North American had refused to hire black workers for any other than janitorial and labor positions. But by mid-1944, over 2,300 African Americans worked in fifty-seven different classifications, including over four dozen black leadmen and assistant foremen. Though hundreds of these employees were still concentrated in unskilled work, for many others who gained work as riveters, assemblers, and inspectors, both the FEPC's and UAW Local 645's help were crucial. Unfortunately, the record of achievement at Convair, where a harder-nosed managerial style prevailed much longer than at North American, was more mixed. As late as October 1944, the Fort Worth plant employed only about 600 African Americans out of a total workforce of some 20,000, and all these workers were concentrated in a mere seven classifications. By the time the FEPC and its local allies in the IAM gained the backing of the military to force Convair to create an upgrading plan, wartime cutbacks had made this step a moot point. As the war in the Pacific entered its final weeks, Ellinger stated that regrettably Convair had given the committee "the shadow of a satisfactory adjustment without its substance." When one considers the wholesale terminations that took place throughout the country in all the defense industries the FEPC investigated, Ellinger's conclusion provides important insight into a national issue.[78]

The bleakness of the war's final days for black aircraft workers continued during the immediate postwar years. With the downsizing of Convair and the closing of North American, only a severely limited pool of jobs remained open to African Americans in the Fort Worth plants—brooms and shovels quickly replaced rivet guns and metal presses as the main tools for those lucky enough to remain in aircraft production. Furthermore, the FEPC's loss of its congressional battle for permanence in 1946 deprived African Americans of a symbolically important ally in their struggle for equality on the job.[79] Not until 1953, with the creation of Dwight D. Eisenhower's President's Committee on Government Contracts, did fair employment again become a priority for the federal government.[80]

---

77 "Memo to File," January 23, 1945, Folder "North American Aviation, Inc., 10-BR-454," Box 8, Closed Cases, RG 228; Don Ellinger to F. J. Conlan, February 6, 1945, *ibid.;* "Memo to File," July 30, 1945, *ibid.;* F. J. Conlan to Don Ellinger, February 19, 1945, Folder "North American Aviation, 10-BR-76," Box 7, *ibid,* (quotation); "17,000 More Workers at NAA Face Layoff by Mid-November," Dallas *Morning News,* August 17, 1944, pp. 1, 11; "North American Receives Shutdown Order," *ibid.,* August 16, 1945, pp. 1–2; Reed, *Seedtime for the Modem Civil Rights Movement,* 328.

78 "Final Disposition Report," October 19, 1944, Folder "Consolidated-Vultee Aircraft Corp., 10-BR-127," Box 2, Closed Cases, RG 228; Don Ellinger to Clarence Mitchell, July 16, 1945, Folder "Consolidated-Vultee Aircraft Corp., 10-BR-235," *ibid,* (quotation).

79 "On the final days of the FEPC, see Reed, *Seedtime for the Modern Civil Rights Movement,* 321–43.

80 For information on the President's Committee on Government Contracts and equal employment during the 1950s, see Robert Frederick Burk, *The Eisenhower Administration and Black Civil Rights* (Knoxville, 1984), 89–108; Paul D. Moreno, *From Direct Action to Affirmative Action: Fair Employment Law and Policy in America, 1933–1972* (Baton Rouge, 1997), 180–88; Ronald Alan Schlundt, "Civil Rights Policies in the Eisenhower Years" (Ph.D. dissertation, Rice University, 1973), 59–91; and

Perhaps most tragic, in the absence of the FEPC, IAM District 776, Fort Worth's only remaining aircraft union, rapidly lost interest in the special problems facing black workers. As national IAM leaders struggled to revise the union's discriminatory initiation ritual and define its place in the emerging postwar civil rights coalition, local IAM leaders focused on the day-to-day shop-floor struggles essential to forging a vigorous union and a strong contract. Though they did not completely turn their backs on African Americans, these more organizationally secure union leaders made little effort to link the racial grievances of an underrepresented minority group to the broader economic interests of the entire membership. In short, as the nation entered this uncertain readjustment period, those who believed in the moral and economic imperatives of fair employment faced a long and daunting battle to make their voices heard.

Joseph Abel, "Sunbelt Civil Rights: Race, Labor, and Politics in the Aircraft Manufacturing Industry of Texas, 1940–1980" (Ph.D. dissertation, Rice University, 2011), chap. 3.

"Race" and Sport

Critical Race Theory

By Kevin Hylton

Our capabilities in sport are often described in physical or psychological terms, 'natural' differences. These 'gifts' are often identified as the difference between those who are likely to succeed in a given sport and those who are not. This discourse of superiority and inferiority in sport is not dissimilar to other debates in wider society which revolve around genetics and intelligence, and ultimately underpin imperialist ideologies (Goldberg 1993, Essed and Goldberg 2002, Omi and Winant 2002). There is a popular perception in sport that our genes and to a degree our cultural background dictate the prowess of an individual sportsman or woman. This discourse of advantage and of course disadvantage in sport is invariably reduced to 'harmless' racial differences, a deduction that suggests, however, a more sinister undercurrent: 'race' logic (Coakley 2001), racial discourse (Goldberg 1993), racial formations (Omi and Winant 1994), raciology (Gilroy 2000) and racialisation (Murji and Solomos 2005).

In this reading I consider some key concepts for the analysis of 'race' and sport and later outline five key tenets of Critical Race Theory (CRT) as an important framework to critically consider issues related to 'race', racism and sport. CRT is presented as a starting point for developing a critical 'race' consciousness and defended as a useful political standpoint for racial transformations in sport. For Armstrong and Ng (2005: 35) 'race is the social construction, but the act and effect of this construction (racialisation) have produced actual divisions between people'. In hard populist terms what 'race' often boils down to is physical differences, and in particular physiognomy. Whereas many believe that they can tell the difference between people born in continents and countries across the world, the ability to distinguish social groups according to this notion of 'race' is beyond the most advanced minds and computers, the truth being we are as much collapsed into one 'race' as pieces in a jigsaw: we all may look different but we all fit together to make the one picture. Malik's (1996) argument that humanity is not a Dulux colour chart with everyone falling into discrete categories is reiterated here.

RACIALIZED ASSUMPTIONS

Assumptions that have endured are those that argue humans could be divided into a few biologically and phenotypically detached 'races'; the similarities within these groups could be reduced to ability, behaviour and morality; these differences would be naturally passed from one generation to the next; and racial hierarchies exist with white people at the top and darker 'races' at the opposite end (Fenton 2003). The 'Jack Nicklaus syndrome' typifies the example of this unconscious, benign acceptance of differences in sport premised upon biology or psychology. In 1994, before Tiger Woods had established himself as the best golfer in a generation, Nicklaus was reported to have argued that African American golfers could not succeed at the highest level of golf because of their muscle structure (Hatfield 1996). The 'Nicklaus syndrome' has been evident at all levels of sport, and its related impacts replicated internationally. St Louis (2004) accepts that this racist orthodoxy exists while positing that the perception of racial Others as being particularly strong in motor rather than psychological terms, and that evidence of conspicuous success in high-profile sport is evidence of this, provides for many a prima facie case for the existence of racialised propensities. These racial differences that emerge from a flawed social Darwinism begin and end in a biological reductionist morass.

They give support to Younge's contention that these views (2000: 24) suggest that if (black) people are naturally talented at sport then they are naturally less equipped intellectually. The ability to generate stereotypes of this kind in itself points towards the insidious prejudices, 'race' thinking and social positioning of dominant hegemonic actors within sport and academe.

Turning to popular culture, in 1993 Jon Turtletaub's film *Cool Runnings*, the story of the Jamaican bobsleigh team competing in the Olympic Games, was written as a comedy that was underpinned by the conception and stereotype that black people cannot do winter sports, they do not like the cold and are quite superficial characters. Also, in Jon Shelton's *White Men Can't Jump* (1992) where the narrative is even more obvious, the film carries still a benign subtext that not only has the white man who couldn't jump, jumping, but shows him managing it only when he needs to and only after a lot of hard work! Here racial stereotypes prevail again with many racialised ideologies, concepts and stereotypes remaining intact and unchallenged. What was not considered in any respect was the corollary of these arguments which Coakley (2001) alludes to in his examination of race logic in sport as he points to the unlikelihood of commentators explaining the achievements of Swiss skiing from a biological viewpoint. This racial thinking in sport is perpetuated by four weak theoretical propositions (St Louis 2004: 32):

1. Sports are based on theoretical principles of equality.
2. The results of sporting competition are unequal.
3. This inequality of results has a racial bias.
4. Therefore, given the equality of access and opportunity, the explanation of the unequal results lies in racial physicality.

RACISM

Fredman (2001, cited Bhavnani et al. 2005: 15) conceptualizes racism as a process that can be recognised by its penchant for stereotyping which may lead to violence if not prejudice. In Italy's top football leagues Carroll (2001) observed incessant racist chanting, crowd violence and racism on the pitch resulting in an institutional ambivalence that effectively condones this behaviour through a lack of action. (The decision not to act is not unusual in relation to racism in sport organisations. This then leads to cycles of inequality and disadvantage that finally negate the culture of the groups concerned. For Anthias and Yuval-Davis (1993: 2) racisms need to be recognised as 'modes of exclusion, inferiorization, subordination and exploitation that present specific and different characters in different social and historical contexts'. Racism is often articulated in a plural sense (racisms) as in policy terms it is acknowledged as negatively impacting specific social groups at different levels, but also because we experience racism in often quite different ways.

Racism is often described as operating in the dialectic between individual, institutional and structural forms (Miles 1989, Mason 2000). Although any of these racially motivated discriminations can be direct or indirect, against individuals or groups in society, it is institutions like sport that legitimate these actions and embed them in what seemingly become benign practices. When institutions like sport become complicit in institutionalised racist acts it no longer takes the efforts of rogue actors or right-wing organisations when racism is intentionally or unwittingly perpetuated. Institutional racism is often marked by its more subtle covert incarnation as opposed to the more overt expressions of behavior by individual actors (Wieviorka 1995). Structural or societal-level racism reinforces the pervasive embedded nature of racism in the major arenas of our social lives. The interconnectedness of these domains—education, employment, housing, health, policing, legal system, politics—leads us to a chronic disempowering of some social groups that marks their existence in a way that requires more of a contest with the system for them to succeed, often despite the system. These processes lead critical race theorists to support the view that racism is effortlessly reproduced and perpetuated in sport and society.

ETHNICITY, NATION AND NEW RACISM

Solomos and Back (2001) suggest that more recent conceptualisations of racism have shifted debates in a more positive direction. They argue that earlier work zealously overlooked the status of 'race' as a social construct and often reinforced the notion of 'race' and its implicit meanings for themselves and racialised others in their enthusiasm to tackle racism (cf. Cashmore and Troyna 1982). The emergence of whiteness critiques and other metonymic analyses in the new racism debates, media investigations and other influential racial formations have helped to move narrower static conceptualisations of racism into more fluid and critical descriptions and analyses of social relations in diverse and late modern times. Importantly, an analysis of racialisation processes would not be complete without a consideration of ethnicity and identities and their contribution to the way racism is constructed and experienced and the way racial ideologies are (re)created. Ethnicity is a term often used in the social analysis of sport, and has been presented as a more palatable alternative when considering human diversity (Mason 2000). What 'race' and ethnicity share are boundary making properties that are socially constructed, can be self-imposed or externally imposed or both, and can be rooted in explanations that can be reduced to territory, culture, biology or physiognomy.

'Ethnicity' is often used uncritically in vernacular and political parlance and as such they imply clear objective boundaries between groups. On one hand they reinforce the differences between people that can on the one hand lead to the xenophobic, nationalistic, and racist behaviour evidenced in sport and wider society over recent years (MacClancy 1996), and on the other hand assume static incarnations of ethnic groups that remain as defined and identifiable from generation to generation (Mason 2000, Jenkins 1997). There is much evidence in sport today that ethnic identities are fluid, strategic, and under constant revision. Jenkins (1994: 198) usefully summarises this problematic: Ethnicity is not an immutable bundle of cultural traits which it is sufficient to enumerate in order to identify a person as an 'X' or a 'Y' or locate the boundary between ethnic collectivities. Rather, ethnicity is situationally defined, produced in the course of social transactions that occur at or across (and in the process help to constitute) the ethnic boundary in question. In sport any examination of ethnicity like those of Burdsey (2004a), King (2004), and Ismond (2003) is welcome, but the message is 'proceed with caution'.

The subtleties of ethnicity and racism have led to the coining of a new term: 'cultural racism', in some cases 'new racism'. This term is often used by those decrying particular racialized populations where little recourse is made to explicit biological differences. Solomos and Back (2001) argue that this type of racism is often categorized by 'metonymic elaborations' as a consequence of racisms being affected through coded signifiers. In this case references to cultural differences reify distinctions between powerful and less powerful groups that present an argument for exclusion, prejudice or hatred. Excluded groups are therefore not the victims of more traditional and overt racism but more subtle incarnations of even more insidious practices. In sport these discourses have been used as a majoritarian device to set newer communities apart from others by questioning national allegiances through cultural and civic preferences. A constant aspect of this new racism is its ability not to be recognised as the explicit or overt racism of the past as it transforms itself into debates about citizenship, immigration, nationhood. A 'safe' distance emerges for these discourses from the more identifiable biological or phenotype explanations of racial hierarchies and inferiority or superiority, and results in amorphous types of racism that are difficult to detect and much easier to deny. The imagined communities as exemplified by Anderson (1991) become a property that is then defended, resisting any perceived differences that would come only from those who have been described in the past as ultimately different in essentializing biological terms. In some cases, who people cheer for when their country of residence plays their country of family origin is an acid test for many public figures. In the UK this has been labelled the 'Tebbit test' after Lord Tebbit, who challenged Asian communities to stand with English national teams against the country of their heritage as a test of their social integration, citizenship and loyalty to the nation. In this one 'test' debates on immigration and xenophobia become metaphors for a debate on 'Britishness' and nationhood.

The absence of some social groups in the writing of sport literature is not only raced but also gendered, as sports writers have failed to include black women in their analyses. Writers such as Scraton 2001, Watson and Scraton (2001), Birrell (1989) and Hargreaves (1994) have been critical of social science's recidivism in this area. In particular, sports feminists have been reticent in engaging with the leisure lifestyles and sporting experiences of black women and as a result we know far less about black women than we do about black men in sport. Black women are invisible in sports writing in academic and everyday contexts. Where women are given attention in either academic or even sports feminist writing, then the focus is mainly reflective of a white perspective about (white) women in general (Mirza 1997). Writing on 'race' and ethnicity has made the black male as conspicuous in sport as the white woman in mainstream gender theorizing, therefore making our understanding of the black woman's leisure and sporting lifestyles a mystery (Scraton 2001, Birrell 1989). These hierarchies in our epistemologies are reflective of wider raced, classed and gendered power processes that seek to structure our knowledge and intellectual development (Goldberg 1993). Goldberg (1993) recognises the bias of discourses and their ability to normalise vocabularies, thus privileging some whilst marginalizing others. The view that sports feminists have regularly dealt in stereotypes of women in sport as white, middle-class and heterosexual is further emphasised in Mirza's (1997) work on black feminism which alerts us to this marginalizing process in sport theorising.

Given the significance of 'race' and racism and the contested arena of these debates in sport, another paradox emerges to challenge the critical sociologist, the antiracist, student and practitioner. The paradox is, can we really ignore 'race', as much as we may want to? Can we somehow reject it out of hand to somehow begin the process of debunking it as a form of social categorisation? If we do this, then how can we effectively transform racialised relations of power structured by racial projects underpinned by reductionist 'racial' thinking? Given the imperative to resist racism, how can we do this without recourse to the lexicon of 'race' even with the warnings of those advocating racialisation as a possible way forward? For even with a racialisation framework we still must revert with caution to 'race', racial signification and representation in sport to challenge racism. 'It is impossible to organize, maintain, or transform social structures without simultaneously engaging in racial signification' (Omi and Winant 2002: 128).

CRITICAL RACE THEORY

CRT has been described as exciting, revolutionary and an intellectual movement (Roithmayr 1999). It can be summarised as a framework from which to explore and examine the racism in society that privileges whiteness as it disadvantages others because of their 'blackness'. CRT also confronts 'race-neutrality' in policy and practice and acknowledges the value of 'the black voice' that is often marginalised in mainstream theory, policy and practice. CRT challenges past and present institutional arrangements in sport that racially discriminate, subjugate and oppress (Nebeker 1998, Delgado and Stefancic 2001). CRT has also been described as a hybrid discipline as it draws from a number of necessarily relevant disciplines to incorporate a transdisciplinary approach to the development of theory and praxis in relation to racism in society (Stovall 2005).

Like the law, sport is an institution deemed to lessen or eradicate racist dysfunction when it rears its head within this hallowed cultural construct. Research agendas dominated by what could be viewed as an elitist Eurocentric social science are a target for part of this transformation as critical writers such as Goldberg (1993) reiterate how the success of any standpoint on 'race' and racism must depend on its ability to offer resistance to racism(s). CRT has the potential to interrupt and transform social structures and racial power to further an agenda of 'racial emancipation' (Roithmayr 1999: 1). CRT can also be seen as a configuration of alternative accounts in sport that challenge orthodoxies, canons and dogma. The utility of CRT in our analyses of sport can be drawn analogously to Mirza's (1999) critique of liberal 'race' reform in the US. Here Mirza's frustration with the discourses of assimilation, integration and 'colour-blindness' can be equally levelled at sport where few sports or sport theorists have taken a proactive, radical stance to the construct of 'race' and racism in their arenas of expertise. In agreement with Mirza (1999: 112), racial inequality in sport, as in the law, is often seen as 'exceptional and irregular rather than routinely ubiquitous and deeply ingrained'.

Five precepts of CRT are outlined as a framework to consider as an emergent development in sport and leisure theorising. It has been generally agreed that critical race theory is a theoretical framework that has emerged from the writing predominantly of black scholars in North America (Crenshaw et al. 1995, Delgado 1995, 2000, Nebeker 1998, Parker 1998). Not only does CRT have the potential to shape the discourses of minds closed to racism-centred perspectives, it also wishes to influence the lethargy in liberal critiques of those debates. Sport can be observed as a key tool in the subjugation of black people and the magnification of the place of 'race' as a major mediating factor within society; in sport many have made these connections (Lapchick 2001, Carrington and McDonald 2001, Marqusee 2003). Sport, like the law, is supposed to be a 'level playing field'; however there is a body of knowledge to suggest otherwise. Sport is another racially contested arena which is used as a 'ring to wrestle' for academics, participants and policy makers. As much as our cultural background is mediated by the intersection of gender and class, critical sport sociology is beginning to focus on these and other more conventional fronts concerning racial formations and related processes around gender, identity, nation, racism(s) and policy (Marqusee 1994, 2003, MacClancy 1996, Watson and Scraton 2001, Carrington and McDonald 2001); racism(s) (Shropshire 1996, Polley 1998, Long 2000, Lapchick 2001); and policy (Horne 1995, Swinney and Horne 2005, Gardiner and Welch 2001, Hylton 2003).

'Race' and Sport: Critical Race Theory (Hylton, 2008) supports Singer's (2005a) view that a dialogue should be encouraged with academics, students, practitioners and policy makers to think beyond their everyday opinions and ideologies. In relation to 'Race' and Sport: Critical Race Theory, CRT offers an alternative way of knowing and an alternative vocabulary and discourse from which to understand research. Authors such as Stanfield II (1994), Twine and Warren (2000), Coates (2002), Gunaratnam (2003) and Bulmer and Solomos (2004) argue that researchers and writers need to urgently centralise 'race' and racism(s) as core factors in the study of wider social relations. Such actions improve and enhance the bodies of knowledge pertinent to 'race', racialisation and racial formations, as they 'challenge and transform' epistemologies and ways of thinking about the world (Gunaratnam 2003). This has the effect of questioning the everyday assumptions about socially constructed groups that often become the foundation for myth and folklore. Stanfield II's (1994) challenge is that we all should establish new lines of inquiry whilst criticising traditional epistemologies, rather than acquiescing to their hegemony. As Leonardo (2005, xi) contends, CRT writers explore social issues with 'race' (and racism) as 'the point of departure for critique … not the end of it'.

'Race' is neither an essence nor an illusion, but rather an ongoing, contradictory, self reinforcing, plastic process, subject to the macro forces of social and political struggle and the micro effects of daily decisions … terms like 'black' and 'white' are social groups, not genetically distinct branches of humankind. (Haney-Lopez, 2000: 65)

FIVE PRECEPTS OF CRITICAL RACE THEORY

A CRT perspective as outlined below acts as an umbrella for a range of views. The points discussed here are presented as a foundation for approaching the issues related to 'race' and sport. It is useful at this juncture to point out that CRT perspectives should be as fluid and dynamic as the problems they attempt to tackle. To present an overview of CRT five significant aspects are drawn out of the main ideas of CRT writers such as Crenshaw et al. (1995), Parker et al.(1999), Solorzano and Yosso (2001, 2005), Delgado and Stefancic (1995, 2000, 2001) and Ladson-Billings (1998, 2003).

1) Centralizing 'Race' and Racism

The first tenet involves centralising 'race' and racism in sport at the same time as recognizing their connection with other forms of subordination and oppression (Ladson-Billings 1998, Parker 1998).

For example, class cannot be theorised in isolation from 'race', as Marxists might wish, as 'race' must be central to the theorising of class relations from a CRT viewpoint (Nebeker 1998). It has further been argued that, although there is some recognition amongst writers and researchers that 'race' and racism are a significant area of study, they have done little more than acknowledge this as they wander on to more familiar theoretical terrain (Anthias 1998). Stanfield II (1993) also asks researchers to consider less the question of methodology but more the notion of an epistemology that gives a more accurate picture of the black experience in society. Back et al. (2001) are keen to follow this advice as their investigations into racism in football demonstrate the need for innovation and diversity to show how racism is a 'multiply inflected and changing discourse … this involves understanding how forms of inclusion and exclusion operate through the interplay of overt racist practice and implicit racialised codings' (Back et al. 2001: 6).

The careful centering of 'race' and racism in our analyses of sport should engage a thoughtful consideration of racial processes that explore and examine further, past and present processes and practices in sport that are neither inevitable nor accidental. Rather, they can be seen as part of a cycle of activity that can at the very least be broken or disrupted. CRT can develop a political lexis that can heed the advice of Tate IV (1999) and others that is conscious of the clumsy use of systemic racism as a beginning and end in a world that cannot be reduced into homogeneous experiences and polemic binaries. For example, when the talented young golf prodigy Kiran Matharu stated that she had been the victim of racism at golf clubs where she was refused membership, she clearly had grounds to base such an assumption as other less successful juniors were being admitted (Guardian 2007). However we will see further when we explore the fifth tenet of CRT how it encourages us to explore such issues even further as an intersectional analysis of racialisation and racist acts. In Matharu's case as a young Asian woman from a working-class background, her exclusions from these clubs could be due to a mix of racial discrimination and/or golf's gender relations which have been the subject of many controversies owing to its patriarchy. In addition golf has been accused of its membership policies relying on social networks and cultural capital as criteria for entry.

Peters (2005) has witnessed CRT become an inclusive and pluralistic framework that resists racism in complex, multidimensional ways. The intersections of 'race' and culture, gender, class, space, whiteness, politics, history, community, identity and nation, for example, have ensured a more sensitive theorising of social issues. McDonald and Birrell (1999) see many benefits to moving from single-issue theory and debates to a critical theoretical approach that converges issues and relations of 'race', class, gender and sexuality. Similarly a reading of the experiences of Serena and Venus Williams on the tennis circuit would be bereft of its various complexities without a consideration of racialisation, racism, gender, sexuality, class and whiteness (Spencer 2004).

2) Challenging Convention and Colour-Blindness

Secondly, CRT challenges traditional dominant ideologies around objectivity, meritocracy, colour-blindness, race-neutrality and equal opportunity (Nebeker 1998, Solorzano and Yosso 2001, Gardiner and Welch 2001). Two founder proponents of CRT, Richard Delgado and Jean Stefancic (2001), identified patterns of criticism of CRT in relation to meritocracy and the challenge to objectivity. The challenge to dominant ideals and philosophies is not a pointless one. In effect sport as a racial formation becomes the subject of many challenges across its many racial projects. The academy, practitioners, policy makers, the media and the law join sport in the contested racialised arena of society, each maintaining dominant viewpoints, racial hierarchies, racial inequalities and 'truths' open to reinterpretation. An alternative reading of sport and its history for example is likely to challenge the existing orthodoxies surrounding it of cultural pluralism, fairness, integration, racial harmony, colour-blindness and other social benefits. Just as the law, policing, education, health, housing, social welfare and politics cannot afford to be colour-blind, neither can those in sport as managers, policy makers, the media or academics.

Color-blind racism revolves around issues of liberalism or ambivalence to matters of racism; the mechanism of cultural rather than biological arguments to support prejudicial views or racial projects that maintain recruitment and employment patterns, sports participation, sports policy exclusions; the utopian ideal that owing to effective opposition over the years racism is now a marginal or insignificant issue (Bonilla-Silva 2002). This colour-blindness takes a more sophisticated strategy to expose and tackle for 'race' critics as the nature of these issues is so divisive because they can seem so innocuous. There are numerous examples in sport where some racialised groups have a higher level of acceptance than others and in some instances are held as exemplars of successful integration. Color-blindness, like the new racism noted earlier, is a device that maintains dominant hegemonies and social hierarchies by regularly ignoring discriminatory criteria for inclusion.

Similarly, a CRT examination of employment practices in sport management, media, education, sport participation and spectatorship reveals parallel findings to those in CRT and education where the notions of meritocracy and color-blindness are much more closely aligned to a defense of the status quo and racist practices that many would want to distance themselves from.

3) Social Justice

The Third tenet posits that CRT has a clear commitment to social justice that incorporates elements of liberation and transformation (Solórzano and Yosso 2001, 2005). With Bernal (Solórzano and Bernal 2001), Solórzano posits that the core variant of transformational resistance is social justice. For a politics of social change to have any value, the praxis of CRT must culminate in a process of social transformation which in sport might result in radical employment practices that value black people in sport management whether it involves professional clubs or local authority providers; practice in each of these arenas has been woefully inadequate in the UK and North America. Similarly, racism occurs at every level of sport ranging from innocuous exclusions at local clubs to discrimination in sports policy and practice and racist behaviour in the stands and in our living rooms when watching, listening to or reading media sources. CRT's emphasis on social justice in terms of policy would align itself with radical, proactive forms of policy discourses that would cite racism, amongst other concerns, as the cause of the need for the manipulation and redistribution of resources (Parker 1998). The short-term impact of these policies on some over others may seem inequitable but are necessary if ahistorical conceptions of provision and the concept of a level playing field are to be rejected and the material differences between those disadvantaged in society are thought through in terms of how they are balanced out, leading to a 'de-cloaking' of color-blind ideologies and institutional arrangements.

A critical ontology ensures that where writers or researchers are conscious of the crucial social processes that structure their worlds they take those ideas forward as their starting point. That is, where racism and the distribution of power and resources disproportionately marginalize the racialized Other and their position in society, sport, local government and any other major social structures, then they will ensure that those issues stay at the centre of their investigations, or lens, rather than at the comfortable rim.

4) Centralizing Marginal Voices

The Fourth tenet reflects this centralizing of the marginalized voice that is often tabled as a significant contributory aspect of CRT but is also seen as a potential weakness by some according to Delgado and Stefancic (2000). CRT encourages us to explore what sport means to those whose experiences and identities are inadequately represented in the various conceptions of sport policy and practice. The 'lived experiences' (Hylton 1995, 2003, Solórzano and Bernal 2001) of those voices rarely heard in sport, such as black academics, black spectators, black referees, Asian darts players, African Caribbean swimmers, Latina managers and white people talking about whiteness in sport, are highly valued. A criticism of this approach is that the recognition of the black voice has an essentializing effect on the black experience. It suggests that views from racialised individuals somehow represent the experiences of all black people and is open to conventional criticisms around validity, reliability and representativeness. CRT encourages counter-storytelling methodologies such as the centering of a black or racialised 'voice' seen as 'race'-centered research tools that can effectively voice the marginalised experiences of the Other in a bid to present different or competing versions of reality that is often the prerogative of white social scientists (Delgado 1995).

CRT is an empowering framework that encourages Others traditionally excluded from the dominant perspectives to put forward views that have not been heard before. Lorde's (1979) assertion that the master's tools will never dismantle the master's house is thought provoking in the extreme as she encourages us to challenge tradition with different viewpoints and methodologies, and not be afraid to present experience as valid resources and knowledge to supplement and challenge established epistemologies. The 'voice' aspect of CRT should be viewed as 'an asset, a form of community memory, a source of empowerment and strength, and not as a deficit' (Villalpando 2004: 46). Henderson (1998) supports this as a major thrust of enlightened meaningful social analysis. A CRT viewpoint allows us to get a clearer understanding of the major structures involved in the organization of sport, which is crucial when racism is the ultimate target. An emergent counter-narrative helps us to focus on established power processes, white hegemony, racism and equality that have been consistently ignored by mainstream theorists.

5) Transdisciplinarity

The Fifth element posited by CRT writers involves the transdisciplinary nature of CRT. In the spirit of challenging dogma and orthodoxies it is incumbent on CRT advocates to adopt a resistance to ahistorical, unidisciplinary models of analysis. As much as CRT, sport and leisure studies are necessarily multidisciplinary, it is argued that they, like CRT writers, should be wary of utilizing a familiar and/ or narrow multidisciplinary straitjacket that might constrain them in explaining modern (or historical) phenomena (Coalter 1998, Delgado and Stefancic 2001). A criticism angled at CRT, according to

Delgado and Stefancic (2001) and reinforced by critical Marxists Darder and Torres (2003, 2004), is whether CRT has taken enough account of globalization, and economic democracy. Darder and Torres rely on a critical Marxist analysis that effectively subsumes all oppressions under those of class that traditional Marxists attempted many years ago. The view that racism is integral to the accumulation of capital and that racialized populations that benefit the least from globalization is one that they would argue generate, little attention from social scientists. This lack of attention to global racialised processes confirms their argument that some racism theorizing can be parochial in nature and reductionist in perpetuating a dominant black/white binary in the centralizing of 'race' as an analytical category. Darder and Torres (2003) go on to accuse 'race' critical writers of considering class too superficially and almost in passing. Their reference to CRT writers who emphasize the need to consider the intersections of oppressions does not bring class into sharp enough relief for them and they see this as a failure of CRT. The notion of intersectionality is also seen by them as a smokescreen for avoiding class as a central issue of racism theorizing. A weakness of presenting 'race' as a central political construct, and therefore ignoring 'the class struggle', is to separate the two spheres—'A move that firmly anchors and sustains prevailing class relations of power' (Darder and Torres 2003: 248). Darder and Torres's (2003, 2004) fear is that ahistorical, apolitical, classless analyses of homogeneous rather than culturally pluralistic societies prevail, thus presenting narrow and static views of racism and racialized politics.

Delgado and Stefancic (2001) suggest that these criticisms are justified to a degree. However I have yet to see a theoretical framework that has satisfactorily tackled all of the crucial issues of its time. CRT is clearly metamorphosing in North America in terms of critical subjects ranging from critical race feminism and whiteness to Latino/a critiques (Lat/Crit) which emphasize crucial issues for our time, or for specific racialised populations. In some places like Europe, CRT is only just emerging as a valid framework and so it is not extraordinary that some important questions are yet to be fully explored (Gillborn 2005, Hylton 2005). Delgado and Stefancic (2001) add that this situation reflects the resources and emphasis to date but things change as CRT's ability to offer important contributions is only strengthened by external and internal reflections.

The need to draw ideas from multiple disciplines will assist this process of growth for CRT, and so in their cultural analysis of sport McDonald and Birrell (1999) go as far as to describe transdisciplinarity as 'anti-disciplinary'. For want of a better term they attempt to emphasize the need for writers to engage constantly in an intellectual project to broaden their theoretical and methodological frames. CRT draws on necessary critical epistemologies to ensure that their social justice agenda intersects to highlight related oppressive processes or the 'multidimensionality' of oppression that affect gender, social class, age or disability (Harris 1999). In this respect, CRT challenges orthodoxies and dominant ideologies congruent with critical approaches to complex social issues. Where this, albeit limited, transdisciplinary stance has been employed in sport and leisure, the strengths of critical 'race' analyses have been evident. The crossing of epistemological boundaries forces us to shift from and ultimately 'unlearn' the domain assumptions and orthodoxies that many have in their 'home' disciplines and opens the door to other innovative ideas and worldviews.

The principles of a CRT approach make up an essential framework from which to invite sport and leisure academics to reconsider their own positions on 'race' and racism. Research and writing that adopt CRT principles have been considered to be at the cutting edge of emergent critical black and cultural studies research (Stanfield II 1993, West 1995, Parekh 2000, Gillborn 2005). The target for CRT activists is not just the conservative right but also the liberal left who put their trust in a system with the vain hope that it will somehow ensure fairness. According to West (1995), CRT challenges both liberals and conservatives whose assumptions are such that they reconstruct white privilege. Also, those seen as radicals who have marginalized or stayed silent on 'race' and racism in society are prime targets. This has serious implications for local authority sport providers who refuse to accept a collectivist perspective on race equality (Horne 1995, Clarke and Speeden 2000, Hylton 2003).

CONCLUSION

Critical race theory has the potential to challenge sport and leisure theorizing through its fundamental belief in its transformative capacity. CRT can be used effectively to generate a useful theoretical vocabulary for the practice of progressive racial politics in sport and leisure theorizing, in addition to understanding the essential formations of racial power and ideologies. CRT rejects orthodoxies as a challenge to mainstream paradigms. In the study of 'race' and racism in sport it can be used to reject the notion of neutral objective detachment from issues for more personal political perspectives. Crenshaw et al. (1995) and sports writers such as MacClancy (1996) consider writing about 'race' and racial processes as a site where racial power can be reconstructed, therefore redefining it as an arena from which paradigms can be challenged. CRT facilitates analyses of sport and leisure phenomena from a starting point that is 'race'-conscious. From an example of policies that have had integrationist, assimilation, multicultural or color-blind viewpoints, CRT shifts those paradigms to a 'race'-centered one. 'Race' and Sport: Critical Race Theory progresses from the standpoint that we live in a fundamentally racist and unequal society where processes systematically disenfranchise and limit the potential of black (and white) people. We therefore have a racist society that impinges on all aspects of our lives (Macpherson 1999, Parekh 2000). The academy is one such network that is affected by naturalized systems of order, often where research practice is flawed owing to epistemological (in)consistencies that make claims to the nature and order of things. Delgado and Stefancic (1995: 206) refer to this as a DNA-like process as knowledge bases have a tendency to replicate themselves endlessly, easily and painlessly—knowledge being one of those processes that is regularly modified and recreated through the hegemony of mainstream agendas. This is replicated in other key social institutions.

CRT applied to sport and leisure focuses on core social relations and processes of power. 'Race' and racism are central to any CRT focus, and its transdisciplinary nature ensures that disciplinary borders and conventions do not preclude appropriate methodologies or epistemologies from being applied. CRT's political agenda of challenge, change and transformation contributes to the ability of sport and leisure communities to re-examine critically how 'race', and racialised processes and formations are incorporated into their theory and practice. The CRT framework is presented here for serious consideration.

References

Anderson, B. (1991) *Imagined Communities,* London: Verso.

Anthias, F. (1998) 'Rethinking social divisions: some notes towards a theoretical framework'. *The Sociological Review,*505–535. Anthias, F. and Yuval-Davis, N. (1993) *Racialized Boundaries,* London: Routledge.

Armstrong, J. and Ng, R. (2005) 'Deconstructing race, deconstructing racism'. In J. Lee and J. Lutz, eds, Situating *'Race' and Racisms in Space and Time and Theory: Critical Essays for Activists and Scholars,* London: McGill-Queens University Press.

Back, L., Crabbe, T. and Solomos, J. (2001) *The Changing Face of Football,* Oxford: Berg.

Bhavnani, R., Mirza, H. and Meetoo, V. (2005) *Tackling the Roots of Racism,* Bristol: The Policy Press.

Birrell, S. (1989) 'Racial relations theories and sport: suggestions for a more critical analysis'. *Sociology of Sport, 6,* 212–227.

Bonilla-Silva, E. (2002) 'The linguistics of color blind racism: how to talk nasty about blacks without sounding "racist"'. *Critical Sociology,* 28 (1–2).

Bulmer, M. and Solomos, J., eds (2004) *Researching Race and Racism,* London: Routledge.

Burdsey, D. (2004) 'Obstacle race? "race", racism and the recruitment of British Asian professional footballers'. *Patterns of Prejudice, 38 (3),* 279–299.

Carrington, B. and McDonald, I. (2001) *'Race', Sport and British Society,* London: Routledge.

Carroll, R. (2001) 'Racist, violent, corrupt: welcome to SerieA', *OSM,* May, 38–45.

Cashmore, E. (1982) *Black Sportsmen,* London: Routledge and Kegan Paul.

Cashmore, E. and Troyna, B., eds (1982) *Black Youth in Crisis,* London: Routledge and Kegan Paul.

Clarke, J. and Speeden, S. (2000) *Measuring Up: Report of a Study of the Adoption and Implementation of Racial Equality Means Quality, the CRE's Standard for Local Government.* Liverpool: Centre for Local Policy Studies, Edge Hill College.

Coalter, F. (1998) 'Leisure studies, leisure policy and social citizenship: the failure of welfare or the limits of welfare?' *Leisure Studies,* 17, 21–36.

Crenshaw, K., Gotanda, N., Peller, G. and Kendall, T., (eds) (1995) *Critical Race Theory: The Key Writings that Formed the Movement,* New York: New Press.

Darder, A. and Torres, R. (2004) *After Race,* London: NYU Press.

Darder, A., Baltodano, M. and Torres, R., eds (2003) *The Critical Pedagogy Reader,* London: Routledge Falmer.

Delgado, R. (ed) (1995) *Critical Race Theory: The Cutting Edge,* Philadelphia: Temple University Press.

Delgado, R. and Stefancic, J. (1995) 'Why do we tell the same stories? Law reform, critical librarianship, and the triple helix dilemma'. In R. Delgado and J. Stefancic, eds, *Critical Race Theory: The Cutting Edge,* pp. 206–216. Philadelphia: Temple University Press.

Delgado, R. (2000) 'Storytelling for oppositionists and others: a plea for narrative'. In Delgado, R. and Stefancic, J., eds, *Critical Race Theory: The Cutting Edge,second ed.,* Philadelphia: Temple University Press.

Delgado, R. and Stefancic, J. (2001) *Critical Race Theory: An Introduction,* New York: NYU Press.

Essed, P. and Goldberg, D., eds (2002) *Race Critical Theories,* Oxford: Blackwell.

Fenton, S. (2003) Ethnicity,Cambridge: Polity Press.

Fredman, S. (2001) 'Combating racism with human rights: the right to equality'. In S. Fredman, ed., Discrimination and Human Rights: The Case of Racism, Oxford: Oxford University Press.

Gardiner, S. and Welch, R (2001) 'Sport, racism and the limits of "color-blind" law'. In B. Carrington and I. McDonald, eds, *'Race', Sport and British Society*, pp. 133–149. London: Routledge.

Gillborn, D. (2005) 'Education policy as an act of white supremacy: whiteness, critical race theory and education reform'. *Journal of Education Policy*, 20(4), July, 485–505.

Gilroy, P. (2000) *Against Race: Imagining Political Culture beyond the Color Line*, Cambridge, MA: Harvard University Press.

Goldberg, D. (1993) *Racist Culture*, Oxford: Blackwell.

Guardian, (2007) 'I'm Asian and different—it's good', 27 January,
http://www.guardian.co.uk/g2/story/0,,1991894,00.html#article_continue.

Gunaratnam, Y. (2003) Researching *'Race' and Ethnicity: Methods, Knowledge and Power*, London: Sage.

Haney-Lopez, I. (2000), "The social construction of 'race'". In R. Delgado and J. Stefancic, eds, *Critical Race Theory: The Cutting Edge*, pp. 163–175. Philadelphia: Temple University Press.

Hargreaves, J. (1994) *Sporting Females: Critical Issues in the History and Sociology of Women's Sports*, London: Routledge.

Harris, A. (2003) 'Race and essentialism in feminist legal theory'. In A.K. Wing, ed., *Critical Race Feminism*, pp. 34–41. London: NYU.

Hatfield, D. (1996) 'The Jack Nicklaus syndrome', *Humanist*, July-August, 1.

Henderson, K. (1998) 'Researching diverse populations'. *Journal of Leisure Research*, 30 (1), 157–174.

Horne, J. (1995), 'Local authority black and ethnic minority provision in Scotland'. In M. Talbot, S. Fleming and A. Tomlinson, eds, *Policy and Politics in Sport, Physical Education and Leisure*, LSA Pub. 95, pp. 159–176. Edinburgh: Moray House Institute/Heriot-Watt University.

Howe, D. (2004) 'It was not a lapse: Atkinson was up to his neck in football's endemic.'

Hylton, K. (1995) 'A "Lived Experience"'. In J. Long, ed., *Nightmares and Successes: Doing Small Scale Research in Leisure*, Leeds: LMU.

Hylton, K. (2003) *Local Government 'Race' and Sports Policy Implementation*, unpublished PhD Thesis, Leeds Metropolitan University.

Hylton, K. (2005) '"Race", sport and leisure: lessons from critical race theory'. Leisure Studies,24(1), January, 81–98.

Hylton, K. (2008) *'Race' and Sport: Critical Race Theory*, London: Routledge.

Ismond, P. (2003) *Black and Asian Athletes in British Sport and Society: A Sporting Chance?* Basingstoke: Palgrave Macmillan.

Jenkins, R (1997) *Rethinking Ethnicity: Arguments and Explorations*, London: Sage.

King, C. (2004) 'Race and cultural identity: playing the race game inside football'. *Leisure Studies*, 23 (1), 19–30. 30

Ladson-Billings, G. (1998) 'Just what is critical race theory and what's it doing in a nice field like education?' *Qualitative Studies in Education*, 11(1), 7–24.

Ladson-Billings, G., ed. (2003) Critical *Race Theory: Perspectives on Social Studies*.

Lapchick, R. (2001) *Smashing Barriers: Race and Sport in the New Millennium*, London: Madison Books.

Leonardo, Z., ed. (2005) 'Foreword'. In *Critical Pedagogy and Race*, Oxford: Blackwell.

Long, J. (2000) 'No racism here? A preliminary examination of sporting innocence'. *Managing Leisure*, 5(3), 121–133.

Lorde, A. (1979) 'The master's tools will never dismantle the master's house'. In C. Lemert, ed., (1999) *Social Theory: The Multicultural and Classic Readings,* Boulder: Westview Press.

MacClancy, J., ed. (1996) *Sport, Identity and Ethnicity,* Oxford: Berg.

McDonald, M. and Birrell, S. (1999) 'Reading sport critically: a methodology for interrogating power'. *Sociology of Sport Journal,* 16, 283–300.

Macpherson, Sir William, of Cluny (1999) *Report of the Stephen Lawrence Inquiry* (Cm4262-I), London: The Stationery Office.

Malik, K. (1996) *The Meaning of Race,* London: Macmillan Press.

Marqusee, M. (1994) *Anyone But England: Cricket and the National Malaise,* London: Verso.

Marqusee, M. (2003) 'Racism—one step forward'. *The Guardian,* 18 December, 32.

Marqusee, M. (2005) *Anyone But England: An Outsider Looks at English Cricket,* London: Aurum Press.

Mason, D. (2000) *Race and Ethnicity in Modern Britain,* Oxford: Oxford University Press.

Miles, R. (1989) *Racism,* London: Routledge.

Mirza, H. (1997) *Black British Feminism: A Reader,* London: Routledge.

Mirza, Q. (1999) 'Patricia Williams: inflecting critical race theory'. *Feminist Legal Studies,* 7, 111–132.

Murji, K. and Solomos, J., eds (2005) *Racialization: Studies in Theory and Practice,* New York: Oxford University Press.

Nebeker, K. (1998) 'Critical race theory: a white graduate student's struggle with this growing area of scholarship'. *Qualitative Studies in Education,* 11(1), 25–41.

Omi, M. and Winant, H. (1994) *Racial Formation in the United States: From the 1960s to the 1990s,* London and Boston: Routledge.

Omi, M. and Winant, H. (2002) 'Racial formation'. In P. Essed and D. Goldberg, eds, *Race Critical Theories,* Oxford: Blackwell.

Parekh, B. (2000) *The Future of Multi-ethnic Britain,* London: Runneymede Trust.

Parker, L. (1998) '"Race is race ain't": an exploration of the utility of critical race theory in qualitative research in education'. *Qualitative Studies in Education,* 11(1), 43–55.

Parker, L., Deyhle, D. and Villenas, S., eds (1999) *Race Is … Race Isn't: Critical Race Theory and Qualitative Studies in Education,* Boulder: Westview Press.

Peters, M. (2005) 'Editorial—critical race matters'. In Z. Leonardo, ed., *Critical Pedagogy and Race,* Oxford: Blackwell.

Polley, M. (1998) *Moving the Goalposts: A History of Sport and Society Since 1945,* London: Routledge.

Roithmayr, D. (1999) 'Introduction to critical race theory in educational research and praxis'. In L. Parker, D. Deyhle and S. Villenas, eds, *Race Is … Race Isn't: Critical Race Theory and Qualitative Studies in Education,* Boulder: Westview Press.

St Louis, B. (2004) 'Sport and common sense racial science'. *Leisure Studies,* 23(1), January, 31–46.

Scraton, S. (2001) 'Reconceptualising race, gender and sport: the contribution of black feminism'. In B. Carrington and I. McDonald, eds, *'Race', Sport and British Society,* pp. 170–187, London: Routledge.

Shropshire, K. (1996) *In Black and White: Race and Sports in America,* London: New York University Press.

Singer, J. N. (2005a) 'Addressing epistemological racism in sport management research'. *Journal of Sport Management,* 19(4), 464–479.

Solomos, J. and Back, L. (2001) 'Conceptualizing racisms: social theory, politics and research'. In E. Cashmore and J. Jennings, eds, *Racism: Essential Readings,* London: Sage.

Solórzano, D. and Bernal, D. (2001) 'Examining transformational resistance through a critical race and LatCrit theory framework: Chicana and Chicano students in an urban context'. *Urban Education,* 36(3), May, 308–342.

Solórzano, D. and Yosso, T. (2001), 'Critical race and Latcrit theory and method: counter-storytelling'. *Qualitative Studies in Education,* 14(4), 471–495.

Solórzano, D. and Yosso, T. (2005) 'Maintaining social justice hopes within academic realities: a Freirean approach to critical race/LatCrit pedagogy'. In Z. Leonardo, ed., *Critical Pedagogy and Race,* Oxford: Blackwell.

Spencer, N. (2004) "Sister act VI: Venus and Serena Williams at Indian Wells: 'sincere fictions' and white racism". *Journal of Sport and Social Issues,* 28(2), May, 115–135.

Stanfield II, J. (1993) *Race and Ethnicity in Research Methods,* London: Sage.

Stanfield II, J. (1994). "Ethnic Modeling in qualitative research" in N.K. Denzin and Y.S. Lincoln (eds), *Handbook of Qualitative Research* (pp. 175–188). Thousand Oaks, CA. Sage Publications.

Stovall, D. (2005) 'A challenge to traditional theory: critical race theory, African-American organizers, and education'. *Discourse Studies in the Cultural Politics of Education,* 26(1), March, 95–108.

Sugden, J. and Tomlinson, A. (2002) *Power Games: A Critical Sociology of Sport,* London: Routledge.

Swinney, A. and Horne, J. (2005) 'Race equality and leisure policy: discourses in Scottish local authorities', *Leisure Studies,* 24(3), July, 271–289.

Tate IV, W. (1999) 'Conclusion'. In L. Parker, D. Deyhle and S. Villenas, eds, *Race Is … Race Isn't: Critical Race Theory and Qualitative Studies in Education,* Boulder: Westview Press.

Twine, F.W. and Warren, J., eds (2000) Racing Research Researching Race: Methodological Dilemmas in Critical Race Studies, *London: New York University Press.*

Villalpando, O. (2004) 'Practical considerations of critical race theory and Latino critical theory for Latino college students'. *New Directions for Student Services,* 105, Spring, 41–50.

Watson, B. and Scraton, S. (2001) 'Confronting whiteness? Researching the leisure lives of South Asian mothers'. *Journal of Gender Studies,* 10(3), 265–277.

West, C. (1995) 'Foreword'. In K. Crenshaw, N. Gotanda, G. Peller and T. Kendall, eds, *Critical Race Theory: The Key Writings that Formed the Movement,* New York: New Press.

Wieviorka, M. (1995) *The Arena of Racism,* London: Sage.

An Unmistakably Working-Class Vision

Birmingham's Foot Soldiers and Their Civil Rights Movement

By Max Krochmal

That evening I got off work at three o'clock. I got on the bus, and it was a seat vacant beside this white fellow. It was so crowded that people were standing on the bus. All the rest of the black folk was sitting in the back or standing up. ... And at this particular stop this white lady got off the bus. Where she had been sitting beside this white gentleman, I sat down beside him. ... He grabbed me and said no nigger was going to sit by him. ... He tried to push me out of the seat, and I held on. ... [The driver] stopped the bus, got off, and made a phone call, right there on Twenty-sixth Street and about Twentieth Avenue in North Birmingham. He stopped at a telephone booth and called the police. ... So the police came. ... [and] arrested me, taking me in, and locked me up. I could see the faces of some of them [black passengers], how happy they were. ... Nobody else had the nerve to sit beside a white person on the bus.

Jimmie Louis Warren

T his remarkable story sounds a lot like the familiar tale of Rosa Parks, the tired woman who ignited the civil rights movement when she refused to give her bus seat to a white passenger. But this was Birmingham, not Montgomery, and the year was around 1960, not 1955. Jimmie Louis Warren, an African American man who worked in paper and pipe manufacturing, seamlessly melded his civil rights activism in the community with campaigns for justice on the job.[1] Like Rosa Parks, Warren represented only the tip of a much larger iceberg. Outside the view of Birmingham's white authorities—and

---

1 Jimmie Louis Warren interview, in Horace Huntley and David Montgomery, eds., *Black Workers' Struggle for Equality in Birmingham* (Urbana, 2004), 199–200. Also see Transcript of Jimmie Louis Warren, interview by Horace Huntley, May 17, 1996, pp. 14–15, Birmingham Civil Rights Institute Oral History Project (hereinafter BCRIOHP) (Birmingham Civil Rights Institute Archives, Birmingham, Ala.; hereinafter BCRI). Throughout this article I cite oral history interviews in which subjects use unconventional forms of English grammar. I have left these "errors" intact, making corrections only to ensure clarity. To make the text more readable, I have refrained from marking "[*sic*]" on each occasion. The author thanks Horace Huntley and Laura Caldwell Anderson for their guidance with the BCRIOHP transcripts and archives; William H. Chafe and Sarah Deutsch for their aid throughout the writing and revision process; and Blair L. M. Kelley, the four anonymous *Journal of Southern History* reviewers, and many others who provided written commentary or oral feedback on previous incarnations of this article—all of which improved it immeasurably. Thanks also to Paul Ortiz and Dana Frank for getting me into the history business, and to Courtney for helping me sustain it.

beyond the gaze of most historical accounts—countless working-class black activists quietly engaged in a decades-long battle for access to good jobs, desegregation of social spaces, and the right to vote.

In fact, African American trade unionists and other workers developed and sustained an expansive vision of social change that placed economic justice issues at the center of Birmingham's larger black freedom struggle. Informal networks of black workers rooted in daily fights for equality on the job formed critical hubs around which the more familiar civil rights organizations often pivoted. Similarly, the most visible black leaders such as Fred L. Shuttlesworth, Arthur D. Shores, and Emory O. Jackson all based their own advocacy in the militant organizing tradition of African American labor activists. Black workers swelled the ranks of the Alabama Christian Movement for Human Rights (ACMHR), playing key roles both behind the scenes and in public demonstrations. The flowering movement throughout the city in turn reinvigorated the struggle of black workers on the job and within their white-dominated unions. From the 1930s through the 1960s, community- and workplace-based civil rights activism consistently dovetailed. Often orchestrated by the same individuals, struggles in one arena gained strength from and simultaneously emboldened the other.

At the core of all of it was the belief that human rights included not only the desegregation of public space but also the right to improve one's economic condition. Surprisingly, this principle survived the onslaught of the early cold war and persisted during even the darkest days of Jim Crow Alabama. The idea remained muted in the official pronouncements of civil rights leaders, and it proved anathema to most white officers of Birmingham's biracial unions. But it dominated the worldview of most black workers, and for that reason it became the linchpin of the entire black freedom struggle.

Jimmie Louis Warren's one-man bus sit-in was not a singular occurrence, nor did it come out of thin air. Rather, it represented just another manifestation of a well-documented African American protest tradition. If its ancestral roots are to be found in resistance to slavery, this tradition's modern lineage in the Birmingham area began with the formation of interracial unions in the mining industry. Both Brian Kelly and Daniel Letwin have shown that black workers before 1921 seized the opportunity to join the United Mine Workers (UMW), but their white counterparts often proved unsteady allies, causing the incipient union movement to founder.[2] In Alabama, as around the country, organized labor achieved renewed strength during the Great Depression. Under the leadership of William Mitch, the UMW finally united thousands of black and white coal miners and brought them under union contracts. The newly formed Congress of Industrial Organizations (CIO) extended into industries related to its UMW origins, which in Alabama included ore mining, steel mills, and other heavy metal manufacturing. World War II and expanding industrial operations accelerated the unionization process, and black workers shared, albeit unevenly, in the spoils of the growing movement. The American Federation of Labor (AFL) and the railroad brotherhoods also expanded so that by the end of the war, high union density in Birmingham's heavy industries made the Magic City more closely resemble Pittsburgh than Atlanta, its nearest New South rival.[3]

2 Brian Kelly, *Race, Class, and Power in the Alabama Coalfields, 1908–21* (Urbana, 2001): Daniel Letwin, *The Challenge of Interracial Unionism: Alabama Coal Miners, 1878–1921* (Chapel Hill, 1998).

3 Robert H. Woodrum, *"Everybody Was Black Down There": Race and Industrial Change in the Alabama Coalfields* (Athens, Ga., 2007): Glenn Feldman, "Alabama Coal Miners in War and Peace, 1942–1975." in Edwin L. Brown and Colin J. Davis, eds., *It Is Union and Liberty: Alabama Coal Miners and the UMW* (Tuscaloosa, 1999), 84–110. See also Judith Stein, "Southern Workers in National Unions: Birmingham Steelworkers, 1936–1951." in Robert H. Zieger, ed., *Organized Labor in the Twentieth-Century South* (Knoxville, 1991), 183–222; Stein, *Running Steel, Running America: Race, Economic Policy, and the Decline of Liberalism*

The Great Depression and World War II also provided new opportunities for civil rights organizing in Alabama and across the country. Robin D. G. Kelley has shown that some African American sharecroppers, farmers, and industrial workers joined the Communist Party and many more participated in party activities throughout the 1920s and 1930s. The Communist Party's advocacy in behalf of the Scottsboro defendants positioned the party as a radical alternative to the National Association for the Advancement of Colored People (NAACP) and, Kelley suggests in his epilogue, helped lay the foundation for black working-class civil rights activism in the postwar period.[4] For its part the NAACP experienced little growth until the beginning of the war, when the message of its "Double V" campaign—for democracy's dual victories over fascism both abroad and at home—contributed to a nationwide explosion of the group's membership rolls. Many black workers joined the association while serving in the military, and they returned home ready to expand the fight for full citizenship in their own communities.[5]

For a decade following the late 1930s, many of these disparate elements briefly coalesced into a loose coalition that scholars have termed "civil rights unionism."[6] African American workers formed the core of this broad movement, but they were joined by Communists of all colors as well as the left wing of the CIO. For these activists, writes Jacquelyn Dowd Hall, "neither race nor class trumped the other, and both were expansively understood." But the "decisive first phase" of the "long civil rights movement" reached its peak in the late 1940s, when organizers failed to respond effectively to the rise of the cold war paired with a powerful employer and stale-led offensive against both unions and civil rights.[7] In Alabama, civil rights unionism found its fullest expression in the International Union of Mine, Mill, and Smelter Workers (often known as Mine-Mill). Horace Huntley has shown that Mine-Mill's leadership actively fostered black activism within the union, and rank-and-file black workers consequently rose to positions of prominence in both the local and the international union leadership. Some of these leaders also came to be identified with the now ostracized Communist Party, and the union's controversial support of Henry A. Wallace's left-wing presidential race against Harry S. Truman in 1948 drew the ire of national CIO leaders. The United Steelworkers of America (USWA) began a series of raids against Mine-Mill, decimating the latter union and ultimately capturing nearly all of its remaining membership.[8]

(Chapel Hill, 1998); Robert J. Norrell, "Caste in Steel: Jim Crow Careers in Birmingham, Alabama." *Journal of American History,* 73 (December 1986), 669–94; Bruce Nelson, *Divided We Stand: American Workers and the Struggle for Black Equality* (Princeton, 2001); Nelson, "Class, Race and Democracy in the CIO: The 'New' Labor History Meets the 'Wages of Whiteness,'" *International Review of Social History,* 41 (December 1996), 351–74; and Nelson, "'CIO Meant One Thing for the Whites and Another Thing for Us': Steelworkers and Civil Rights, 1936–1974," in Robert H. Zieger, ed., *Southern Labor in Transition, 1940–1995* (Knoxville, 1997), 113–45.

4 Robin D. G. Kelley, *Hammer and Hoe: Alabama Communists During the Great Depression* (Chapel Hill, 1990), esp. 228–31.

5 Beth T. Bales, "'Double V for Victory' Mobilizes Black Detroit, 1941–1946," in Jeanne Theoharis and Komozi Woodward, eds., *Freedom North: Black Freedom Struggles Outside the South, 1940–1980* (New York, 2003), 17–39. Many of the BCRIOHP interviews with veterans include narratives of black servicemen joining the NAACP during the war. See, for example, Transcript of George Price, interview by Horace Huntley, March 24, 1995, pp. 6–7, BCRIOHP. There is a voluminous literature on the NAACP; for a recent survey see Gilbert Jonas, *Freedom's Sword: The NAACP and the Simple Against Racism in America, 1909–1969* (New York, 2005), esp. chap. 6 on World War II.

6 Robert Rodgers Korstad, *Civil Rights Unionism: Tobacco Workers and the Struggle for Democracy in the Mid-Twentieth-Century South* (Chapel Hill, 2003).

7 Jacquelyn Dowd Hall, "The Long Civil Rights Movement and the Political Uses of the Past," *Journal of American History,* 91 (March 2005), 1233–63 (quotations on 1245–46).

8 Horace Huntley, "Iron Ore Miners and Mine Mill in Alabama: 1933–1952" (Ph.D. dissertation, University of Pittsburgh, 1977).

Other histories document the rise and fall of civil rights unionism in cities across the South and nation, and all tell remarkably similar stories.[9]

By the 1950s black workers played a diminished role in the labor movement, and in most scholarly accounts they seemingly disappear from the scene altogether. Robert Korstad and Nelson Lichtenstein aptly summarize the change in a now-classic article published in 1988: the unions that survived the early cold war grew increasingly bureaucratic and narrowly focused their efforts on winning improvements to wages and working conditions through collective bargaining. Organized labor turned its back on black workers, and African American civil rights activists charted an alternative course. The movement that emerged in the late 1950s and 1960s, Korstad and Lichtenstein write, possessed a "different social character and an alternative political agenda" that depended not on trade unions "but the black church and independent protest organizations."[10]

Yet while the institutional home of the civil rights movement may have shifted during the mid-1950s, the degree to which both the "social character" and the "political agenda" of the freedom struggle changed remains less clear. John Dittmer and Charles M. Payne argue that in Mississippi "local people" stood at the forefront of the movement, both dominating its rank-and-file constituency and determining, to a great extent, its overall vision and particular campaigns. In the Delta, sharecroppers like Fannie Lou Hamer drew on an indigenous "organizing tradition" to help the Student Nonviolent Coordinating Committee (SNCC) develop a statewide voter registration initiative.[11] Emilye Crosby has shown that to the south, in Claiborne County, conflicts over land and labor dating to Reconstruction produced a continuous struggle that began with "a little taste of freedom" during the New Deal and climaxed in the form of mass boycotts against white merchants in the late 1960s.[12] Similarly, Greta de Jong's study of African American laborers in rural Louisiana over a seventy-year period demonstrates that ordinary blacks there preserved the teachings of the Communist Party and carried them directly into the postwar civil rights battles organized by the Congress of Racial Equality.[13] Most recently, William P. Jones is uncovering the vibrant movement of black unionists in New York City that, under the banner of the Negro American Labor Congress, put forth a radical noncommunist vision that paralleled the earlier civil rights unionism at the most classic of classical phase moments: the 1963 March on Washington for Jobs and Freedom in the nation's capital.[14] In all these cases, black workers—defined here broadly to encompass all nonprofessional African American laborers in industrial, public sector, domestic, informal, and even agrarian contexts—advanced a political agenda that was often different from the one articulated in the official pronouncements of church-based national and local civil rights leaders.

---

9 See, for example, Michael K. Honey, *Southern Labor and Black Civil Rights: Organizing Memphis Workers* (Urbana, 1993); Martha Biondi, *In Stand and Fight: The Struggle for Civil Rights in Postwar New York City* (Cambridge, Mass., 2003); and Robert O. Self, *American Babylon: Race and the Struggle for Postwar Oakland* (Princeton, 2003).

10 Robert Korstad and Nelson Lichtenstein, "Opportunities Found and Lost: Labor, Radicals, and the Early Civil Rights Movement," *Journal of American History*, 75 (December 1988), 786–811 (quotations on 811).

11 John Dittmer, *Local People: The Struggle for Civil Rights in Mississippi* (Urbana, 1994); Charles M. Payne, *I've Got the Light of Freedom: The Organizing Tradition and the Mississippi Freedom Struggle* (Berkeley, 1995).

12 Emilye Crosbv, *A Little Taste of Freedom: The Black Freedom Struggle in Clairborne County, Mississippi* (Chapel Hill, 2005).

13 Greta de Jong, *A Different Day: African American Struggles for Justice in Rural Louisiana, 1900–1970* (Chapel Hill, 2002).

14 Author's notes on William P. Jones, "Gender, Jobs, and Freedom: Black Trade Unionists and the 1963 March on Washington," presented at the conference "The Long Civil Rights Movement: Histories, Politics, Memories," University of North Carolina at Chapel Hill, April 3, 2009. Video of this presentation can be found on the Publishing the Long Civil Rights Movement blog. https://lcrm.lib.line.edu/blog/index.php/2009/07/28/video-of-the-week-will iam-p-jones/.

In the case of Birmingham, scholars recognize that the Alabama Christian Movement's "social character" necessarily reflected the city's demographics: according to Glenn T. Eskew, the churches and parishioners who formed the basis of the ACMHR were predominantly working class. But despite all the detailed evidence that historians have uncovered about Eugene "Bull" Connor's police dogs and fire hoses, Shuttlesworth's oratory, and the tensions between the local and national movements, historians still know relatively little about the "local people" who gave the Birmingham struggle its own unique flavor.[15] We know still less about these people's "political agenda"—about the expansive vision that underlay their commitment to racial equality.

And at a more basic level, we know virtually nothing about what happened to their once vibrant civil rights unionism or about their ongoing efforts to win economic inclusion.

The struggle in the Magic City looks different from the perspective of the black workers at the center of the civil rights storm. From their vantage point, some opportunities may have been lost in the late 1940s, but they nonetheless carried the fight for both social and economic justice from the New Deal and war years into the postwar period, infusing both the ACMHR and the larger struggle with a distinctly black working-class politics.

The experiences of African Americans at the work site shed some light on the nature of the organizing tradition in Birmingham. Soon after the bombing of Pearl Harbor brought the United States into World War II, black workers across the country intensified their fight for equal access to good jobs. In the South, they also challenged the segregation of company space and accommodations. The wartime Fair Employment Practice Committee (FEPC) offered southern black workers a formal process to file complaints against their employers, but most companies ignored the committee's directives, leaving skilled and supervisory positions all-white well into the 1960s."[16]

After World War II, most black workers in Birmingham remained confined in the city's worst, dirtiest, and lowest-paying jobs. Except for the few professionals who served black patrons and achieved status if not great wealth in the black community, most African Americans remained workers, broadly defined. Most of them lacked regular employment and frequently moved from one unskilled, often menial occupation to another. The Magic City's steel mills, railroad yards, and coal and iron ore mines offered the best blue-collar employment available to black men, while teaching, nursing, and clerical work offered the best opportunities for black women who hoped to transcend kitchens and laundries. Racial segregation further shaped each of these already gendered areas of occupational advancement. In heavy industry, black men performed undesirable, often dirty, and at times physically dangerous tasks, ranging from shoveling coal and digging ditches to janitorial service and, at best, the position of "helper" to a white craftsman. Skilled positions continued to be the exclusive purview of white workers, despite the frequent presence of interracial labor unions. For their part, black women laboring as

15 Glenn T. Eskew, *But for Birmingham: The Local and National Movements in the Civil Rights Struggle* (Chapel Hill, 1997), 6–11, 14–17, 124–28; Andrew M. Manis, *A Fire You Can't Put Out: The Civil Rights Life of Birmingham's Reverend Fred Shuttlesworth* (Tuscaloosa, 1999); Aldon D. Morris, *The Origins of the Civil Rights Movement: Black Communities Organizing for Change* (New York, 1984); David J. Garrow, ed., *Birmingham, Alabama, 1956–1963: The Black Struggle for Civil Rights* (Brooklyn, N.Y., 1989); Marjorie L. White and Andrew M. Manis, eds., *Birmingham Revolutionaries: The Reverend Fred Shuttlesworth and the Alabama Christian Movement for Human Rights* (Macon, Ga., 2000); Diane McWhorter, *Carry Me Home: Birmingham, Alabama: The Climactic Battle of the Civil Rights Revolution* (New York, 2001).
16 Woodrum, *"Everybody Was Black Down There,"* 99–100; Robert H. Zieger, *For Jobs and Freedom: Race and Labor in America since 1865* (Lexington, Ky., 2007).

teachers taught in all-black schools; black nurses attended black patients; and most black clerks worked for black-owned businesses. With the exception of education and casual manual labor, public sector employment for both men and women at the municipal, county, state, and federal levels was restricted to white civil servants.[17]

Despite these disparities, as Robert Korstad has shown, collective bargaining agreements at times entitled black workers to some degree of fair treatment and racial egalitarianism on the job—even as they were denied equality with whites in other areas of life. For example, the democratic processes of some interracial unions allowed African Americans, who were largely unable to participate in formal electoral politics outside the union, to vote in internal elections and to partake in creating organizational policy. In addition, unions in the South, as elsewhere in the nation, challenged the autocratic independence of white foremen who for decades had arbitrarily hired, fired, directed, and disciplined workers of all races without reference to any standards of fairness or guidance from a central human resources administration. Union contracts instead required foremen to follow specific procedures for promotions and transfers and only permitted disciplinary action in cases of "just cause." Contracts further established grievance procedures that allowed black workers to demand a hearing with upper management. In the Jim Crow South, such provisions represented a deep symbolic challenge to white supremacy since they undermined the racial hierarchy that sanctioned white reprisals against black mobility both inside and outside the workplace. Most important, unions offered black workers unusual job security. Labor's record on the racial front was checkered, to say the least, but participation in unions still afforded some African American workers an unprecedented degree of "shop floor democracy" that replaced the "racial etiquette, paternalism, [and] personalism" customary in the segregated South with "a new language of rights and obligations" understood by workers and managers alike.[18]

More generally, civil rights unionism remained a powerful ideal among black workers even as their unions suffered the stinging defeats that quickly followed World War II.[19] Black workers continued to mobilize around both racial and economic justice from the late 1940s through the 1960s. They fought for access to lucrative "skilled" jobs, organized for dignity and respect at work, filed lawsuits to open new opportunities, demanded higher pay, and walked off the job in protest. These struggles at work primed Birmingham's black workers for action by the time the classical phase of the movement picked up steam in the late 1950s.

At the Louisville & Nashville Railroad (L&N) yard in Birmingham, for example, black union leaders Colonel Stone Johnson and Reuben Davis contested the age-old segregation of jobs on the shop floor. Railroad workers had a long tradition of unionization, but black workers had been almost entirely

---

17 For a history of black employment in Birmingham, see Bobby M. Wilson, *America's Johannesburg: Industrialization and Racial Transformation in Birmingham* (Lanham, Md., 2000). Black workers faced similar challenges across the country. See Zieger, *For Jobs and Freedom*, 140–47.

18 Korstad, *Civil Rights Unionism*, chap. 8 (first quotation on p. 217; second quotation on p. 211; third and fourth quotations on p. 214).

19 The passage of the antiunion Taft-Hartley Act in 1947 represented the most devastating of labor's many well-known defeats after World War II. Labor also failed to limit inflation by extending wartime price controls, lost a wave of national strikes in most major industries, and gradually abandoned the demand for power over corporate management and on the shop floor, culminating in 1950 in the so-called Treaty of Detroit, an agreement between General Motors and the United Auto Workers. For a ease study of the postwar situation, see *ibid.*, chap. 12. For an overview, see Nelson Lichtenstein, *Labor's War at Home: The CIO in World War II* (Cambridge, Eng., 1982), 178–245.

excluded from the all-white railroad craft "brotherhoods." African American laborers nonetheless saw the benefits of unionization, and they joined segregated auxiliaries that remained subordinate to the all-white unions in each trade. Johnson helped organize an all-black local of the Brotherhood of Railway Clerks at the L&N, while Davis helped lead the company's black auxiliary of the Brotherhood of Firemen and Oilers.[20]

Though their unions proved separate and unequal, black railroad laborers nonetheless worked through their auxiliaries for dignity on the job. Interviewed nearly fifty years after a series of incidents in the late 1940s, Johnson blurred together the details of several similar grievances that defined his experience as chairman of the union's Protective Committee. White workers at the L&N "had a bad habit," Johnson remembered; "I've seen them kick [black] fellows just like they kick a dog. They called [it] playing." When a white foreman kicked a recently hired black laborer, "something in me just reared. ... I couldn't take it."[21] The company typically ignored blacks' grievances against whites; the letters wound up in "file 13," the trash can in the superintendent's office. But Johnson's persistence and reputation as a staunch unionist gained him a hearing with upper management on many occasions. In one instance, Johnson's supervisor pleaded with him to withdraw a grievance against a white worker who stood to lose his job for kicking a black worker. In a complete reversal of Jim Crow etiquette, Johnson demanded that the white worker apologize and promise to never kick another African American laborer. Moreover, the union leader refused to seek out the guilty party, demanding instead that the white worker come to him to make amends. Johnson recalled the following (probably reworded) exchange with his boss: "'He ever done anything to you?' And I said, 'No, but I'm my brothers' keeper. I'm head of the union. How can I represent a man and turn my head when [the white worker] is kicking a man ... ?'" The supervisor agreed to the deal, the white worker apologized, and Johnson went to the personnel office and removed the grievance from the offender's file. 'And I took it and threw it in the wastebasket,' Johnson added, and "I never heard about another Black fellow being kicked. ..."[22]

The all-black auxiliary unions also helped Johnson and Reuben Davis, a leader of another all-black union auxiliary at the L&N, demand access to better-paying, safer, and cleaner jobs. Davis's father was an oiler at the L&N, and Reuben went to work at the yards as a laborer right out of high school. Looking back, he remembered that he wanted to be a locomotive engineer—despite the fact that no African Americans held that post. He left his job to serve in the U.S. Navy during World War II, but there too he encountered employment discrimination. Relegated to performing domestic service for white officers, Davis grew angry, but he also found the courage to protest. "I had decided that I was a person," he recalled. When he returned to Birmingham to work at the L&N, he asked for training as an apprentice machinist. His request was ignored, so he filed a federal suit demanding access to an apprenticeship program. In court his foreman admitted that Davis had the ability, merit, and seniority to begin training, but the foreman also told the judge that Davis was "hot headed." The case was dismissed.[23] Still, Davis continued to apply pressure, this time pushing management to promote several black laborers to more

---

20 Colonel Stone Johnson interview, in Huntley and Montgomery, eds., *Black Workers' Struggle for Equality in Birmingham*, 36–37. On African Americans and railroad unionism, see Eric Arnesen, *Brotherhoods of Color: Black Railroad Workers and the Struggle for Equality* (Cambridge, Mass., 2001).
21 Transcript of Colonel Stone Johnson, interview by Horace Huntley, January 6, 1995, p. 9, BCRIOHP.
22 *Ibid.*, 12–13.
23 Transcript of Reuben Davis, interview by Horace Huntley, March 20, 1996, pp. 7–13 (first quotation on 12; second quotation on 13), BCRIOHP.

lucrative posts working on the steel gang.[24] "So Reuben was called a troublemaker," Johnson explained, "but all the men in Reuben's union were upgraded to helpers, and then from helpers to car repairmen or journeymen."[25] Davis never became an apprentice and was fired in 1950 because of his activism, but the L&N's African American workers continued to labor in their new posts and move up the occupational ladder.[26] For his part, Davis fought the capricious dismissal and was reinstated three years later with back pay.[27]

Both Johnson and Davis owed a great debt to another black toiler on the L&N lines, a man who a decade earlier had served as the lead plaintiff in a pathbreaking court case that forced the all-white brotherhoods to provide fair representation to black workers in their respective crafts.[28] Eric Arnesen has thoroughly narrated the story of Bester William Steele's suit against the L&N and the Brotherhood of Locomotive Firemen and Engineers (BLFE), but a few details of the action bear repeating. *Steele v. Louisville & N. R. Co.* (1944), like *Brown u Board of Education* (1954) and other well-known civil rights cases, represented a single piece of a larger civil rights litigation strategy. Unlike *Brown*, however, *Steele* sprang not from the NAACP but from a small, independent industrial union of black railroad workers. The all-black International Association of Railway Employees (IARE) counted fewer African American members than did the white-dominated brotherhoods, but it played a critical role in the struggle for jobs. B. W. Steele, a Birminghamian who began working on the L&N lines in 1904, served on the executive board of the IARE in 1941, when the company and the BLFE reached an agreement that gave white workers the traditionally dirty and dangerous (and all-black) "fireman" job on new, cleaner, safer diesel engines. The IARE attempted in vain to resolve the dispute through negotiations with the railroad and union; Steele sat in these meetings along with the association's president and its general counsel, Arthur Shores. A lifelong resident of the Magic City, Shores was at that time the only black attorney on the Alabama bar, and his clients included the city's Mine, Mill, and Smelter Workers Union locals, NAACP chapters, and various black community organizations. Charles H. Houston, who achieved national prominence litigating *Brown* ten years later, took over as lead counsel for *Steele* when the case reached the U.S. Supreme Court in 1944, but Shores remained intimately involved.[29]

Thanks to Steele and Shores, the IARE found and won its test case and forced the BLFE and L&N back to the bargaining table. In 1951 they reached an agreement through which black firemen regained their posts on many of the longest diesel runs, though they continued to lose ground overall.[30] The expansion of union auxiliaries such as those led by Johnson and Davis can be seen as yet another legacy

---

24 Reuben Davis interview, in Huntley and Montgomery, eds., *Black Workers' Struggle for Equality in Birmingham,* 119–20.

25 Colonel Stone Johnson interview, *ibid.,* 39.

26 Reuben Davis interview, *ibid.,* 120–22.

27 Transcript of Reuben Davis interview, pp. 13–15, 20–21, BCRIOHP.

28 *Steele v. Louisville & N. R. Co.,* 323 U.S. 192 (1944).

29 "Meeting of the Committee from the Personnell [*sic*] Board of the L&N Railroad Company ..." July 31, 1941, pp. 1–2, Folder 2, Box 7, Arthur D. Shores Papers, 97–062 (BCRI). For more background, see Boxes 5–7 of the Shores Papers; Arnesen, *Brotherhoods of Color,* 205–9; and David Montgomery, "Introduction," in Huntley and Montgomery, eds., *Black Workers' Struggle for Equality in Birmingham,* 13–14. Steele was chairman of IARE's General Committee for the L&N. See B. W. Steele to Emory O. Jackson, December 28, 1947, AR1102.1.1.2, *Birmingham World* Office Files, Correspondence Series (Department of Archives and Manuscripts, Birmingham Public Library; hereinafter BPL). At the BPL, the final two segments of the identifier represent the box and folder number, respectively. On IARE, see Arnesen, *Brotherhoods of Color,* and Ernest Obadele-Starks, *Black Unionism in the Industrial South* (College Station, Tex., 2000), 63–67.

30 "Agreement of Settlement," November 26, 1951, pp. 1–3, Folder 2, Box 7, Shores Papers.

of the *Steele* case. Propelled by this and other early victories, Shores became the preeminent civil rights attorney in Birmingham. B. W. Steele continued to advocate for black railroad workers until his death in 1955.[31] But perhaps most significant, *Steele* again highlights the broad appeal of civil rights unionism to black workers in Birmingham over several decades. The case further illuminates the close connections between the shopfloor battles of trade unionists and the mass movement that emerged in the streets of the Magic City in the late 1950s and early 1960s.

The struggle for access to the best jobs remained a central component of black activism in Birmingham even as the classical phase of the civil rights movement began to gain momentum. In 1956 Emory O. Jackson, former executive secretary of the Birmingham NAACP and editor of the city's most important black newspaper, helped black members of the United Auto Workers at Hayes Aircraft Corporation file a complaint before the President's Committee on Government Contracts that resulted in the upgrading of a small number of black workers into classifications formerly reserved for whites.[32] Burford York, a worker at Hayes, again filed a complaint before the committee in 1962.[33] In the early 1960s Jimmie Louis Warren—who got arrested in the bus incident recounted in the epigraph—and other black laborers at the U.S. Pipe Company began to bid on vacancies in previously all-white positions.

In many cases they were unsuccessful, but on other occasions, when no white workers bid for the open positions, management awarded the posts to black workers.[34] Even without the FEPC, black workers continued to fight to desegregate the clean, skilled, previously all-white departments of Birmingham's major industries.

Struggles for upgrading to better jobs at times dovetailed with efforts to organize nonunion firms. When workers at the American Cast Iron Pipe Company (ACIPCO) attempted to join the UMW and unionize in 1958 and again in 1960, they faced employer reprisals, paternalism, and union busting. ACIPCO kept wages a few cents above those of its unionized competitors like U.S. Pipe, and the company offered sizable bonuses and sponsored recreational activities like baseball teams.[35] Such policies convinced Charles Gratton, an African American worker, that ACIPCO offered blacks the best employment opportunity since they were never "really bothered with layoffs or strikes" and did not have to pay union dues.[36] Other employees like Lloyd Harper saw the union as a potential vehicle for winning access to skilled positions. "Someone told us that if you got a union, a union will stop all of this [job discrimination]," Harper recalled. The organizing campaigns floundered. Harper added, because management

---

31 Arnesen, *Brotherhoods of Color*, 205.

32 J. Francis Pohlaus to Herbert Hill, April 3, 1957, Box A-177, Part III, National Association for the Advancement of Colored People Records (Manuscript Division, Library of Congress, Washington, D.C.), hereinafter NAACP Papers; Herbert Hill, "Report to NAACP Annual Meeting by the Labor Secretary," January 5, 1959, Box A-309, *ibid.* Note the year (1956) of this complaint and presidential committee. Established by Dwight D. Eisenhower's administration and overseen by Vice President Richard M. Nixon, this committee was the predecessor to John F. Kennedy's President's Committee on Equal Employment Opportunity, created by Executive Order 10925 in 1961. Huntley and Montgomery, eds., *Black Workers' Struggle for Equality in Birmingham*, 112n3.

33 Burford York to R. B. Troutman Jr., February 16, 1962, Box A-182, Part III, NAACP Papers.

34 Jimmie Louis Warren interview, in Huntley and Montgomery, eds., *Black Workers' Struggle for Equality in Birmingham*, 202.

35 Lloyd Harper interview, *ibid.*, 56–58.

36 Charles Gratton, interview by Tywanna Whorley, Birmingham, Alabama, June 22, 1994, pp. 26–27, Box TR 3. Behind the Veil: Documenting African-American Life in the Jim Crow South Records (Rare Book, Manuscript, and Special Collections Library, Duke University, Durham, N.C.), hereinafter Behind the Veil. The page numbers for citations to the Behind the Veil Oral History Project interviews refer to the pagination of the unedited, restricted-use transcriptions in the collection's Transcript Series. To confirm the exact quotations, listen to the tapes in the Use Tapes Series.

held separate meetings with white workers where the company convinced them that the union would force the bosses to replace the whites with African Americans.[37] One worker recounted a story in which management, faced with a union drive, pandered to black workers as well, offering them handfuls of silver dollars during an emotional meeting steeped in religiosity and overseen by a large portrait of black Jesus that had been mounted on the wall specially for the occasion.[38] Both the 1958 and 1960 campaigns failed, as did a third effort in 1975.[39]

The presence of labor unions and the nature of heavy industry may have contributed to black workers' activism, but the battle for justice on the job was not confined to blue-collar men in Birmingham's mines and mills. Black teachers also contested the terms of their employment by demanding parity with their white counterparts. Education played a critical role in African American society in the age of Jim Crow, and teaching represented a highly respectable occupation for the black women who dominated the profession. Still, black schools remained underfunded and marginalized by state and local authorities. African American community leaders struggled throughout the period of segregation to win more resources and supplies for their schools.[40]

For many black teachers, the issues of funding and community development became closely intertwined with a more bread-and-butter complaint: their own low pay in comparison with that of white teachers doing the same job in white schools. In April 1945 the United Public Workers of America (UPW), an affiliate of the CIO, won a decision in an Alabama federal court declaring that black and white teachers should receive "equal pay for equal work, regardless of race or color." Seizing this ruling, local units of the union began negotiating with school boards across the state. The Birmingham local grew impatient with the school board's inaction and sued for contempt of court in 1947. Two black women teachers who testified in this case were promptly removed from duty. The Birmingham school district fired Ruby Jackson Gainer, president of the UPW and the Jefferson County Negro Teachers Association, while the independent suburban Fairfield district forced Maenetta Steele, also a UPW local president, to resign.[41]

The women's responses to their dismissals drew on family ties and the vibrant black labor movement surrounding them. Gainer's brother was Emory Jackson, who in addition to his roles as an NAACP activist and local editor served as an officer of the National Negro Publishers Association. For her part, Steele came from "a family of members of the Steel Workers Union" (though it appears she was not related to B. W. Steele of the L&N suit). CIO locals and NAACP chapters across the country rallied behind the two educators, and the black press spread their story to Atlanta, New York, Chicago, and beyond.

Jackson spearheaded a drive to raise money for the two women, who hired attorney Arthur Shores to tile a new suit demanding their reinstatement. Gainer spoke at innumerable public engagements to promote her own cause, while her brother and union leaders directed a national publicity campaign.

---

37 Lloyd Harper interview, in Huntley and Montgomery, eds., *Mack Workers' Struggle for Equality in Birmingham*, 57–58 (quotation on 57).

38 Harvey Lee Henley Jr. interview, *ibid.*, 111–12.

39 Lloyd Harper interview, *ibid.*, 57; Harvey Lee Henley Jr. interview, *ibid.*, 111. Also see Montgomery, "Introduction," 5.

40 On the struggle to build African American educational institutions in the South, see James D. Anderson, *The Education of Blacks in the South, 1860–1915* (Chapel Hill, 1988). On educators, see Adam Fairclough, *A Class of Their Own: Black Teachers in the Segregated South* (Cambridge, Mass., 2007).

41 Malcolm Cotton Dobbs to All CIO International Unions, October 20, 1947, AR1102.1.3.2. *Birmingham World* Office Files, Correspondence Series.

Gainer's and Steele's cases bounced around the court system until the Alabama Supreme Court finally forced the districts to reinstate both women in early 1949—eighteen months after their termination. Gainer had by then moved to Pensacola. Florida, to take another teaching job, so she resigned her post in Birmingham immediately after being reinstated. But the court gave Steele her job back in Fairfield retroactive to the fall of 1947, including a right to back pay.[42]

African American workers at the very bottom of the Jim Crow occupational hierarchy likewise contested the terms of their employment, demanding both higher wages and a degree of dignity on the job. In 1951 approximately 350 black garbage collectors, street cleaners, tree trimmers, and "sewer maintenance men" staged a brief sit-down strike to demand a pay increase. These dirtiest of municipal government jobs represented the only foothold other than education for African Americans in the public sector, but city leaders took great care to make sure that even such limited government work did not translate into black economic gains. The city classified the men as "day laborers" despite the fact that most had worked the same routes for years. Likewise, their status as casual employees denied the garbage men and other black workers in the Streets Department access to the civil service system and its accompanying guarantees of job security and retirement pensions. Most critically, city law prohibited the municipality from engaging in collective bargaining with any of its workers.[43]

The black sanitation workers, almost all of them garbage collectors, probably had all of this on their minds when they sat down instead of starting up their trucks. Still, they appointed a committee of leaders and demanded to be heard. Public Works Commissioner James Morgan surely also knew that collective bargaining was illegal when he went to the yards to meet with the workers and negotiate a tentative cease-fire. The laborers returned to their posts and resumed work while their committee, led by Manuel Hines, laid out their demands to the city commissioner. When a week passed without a raise, the sanitation workers staged a full-scale strike. Garbage trucks stood idle in Birmingham and surrounding suburbs. The few African American men who sought to replace the strikers faced verbal insults and physical assaults; both daily newspapers highlighted the violence directed toward strikebreakers, including one incident in which a striker threw a watermelon rind at a scab. Several days passed before the city achieved even reduced levels of service. As the stoppage wore on, the strikers joined a CIO public

---

42 *Ibid.*, (quotation); Ruby Jackson Gainer to Birmingham Branch of the N.A.A.C.P., June 27, 1948, AR1102.1.1.3. *Birmingham World* Office Files, Correspondence Series; Emory Jackson to Hartford Knight, May 5 and 12, 1947. AR1102.1.1.16. *ibid.* Also see other letters of support and memos in this collection in these two folders. Jackson's network of black publishers resulted in extraordinary national newspaper coverage for this kind of dispute. See the Baltimore *Afro-American,* January 31, 1948, April 23 and May 5, 1949; Atlanta *Daily World,* May 13 (p. 6) and 29 (p. 2), June 10 (p. 1) and 17 (p. 6), July 3 (p. 5), August 14 (pp. 5–6), and October 25 (p. 4), 194, and February 3 (p. 2), March 2 (p. 1) and 19 (p. 1), April 20 (p. 2), and September 29 (p. 3) and 30 (p. 2), 1948, and January 4, 1949, p. 6; Chicago *Defender,* February 8 (p. 7), May 31 (p. 4), June 28 (p. 2), September 20 (p. 9), and October 4 (p. 10), 1947, and February 21 (p. 15) and October 2 (p. 3), 1948; New York *Amsterdam News,* June 21, 1947, p. 7, and January 24, 1948, p. 11; Philadelphia *Tribune,* January 18, 1949; and Pittsburgh *Courier,* April 19 (p. 1) and 26 (p. 5), May 10 (p. 1), 17 (p. 13), 24 (p. 5), and 31 (p. 1), June 21 (p. 1), July 5 (p. 1) and 12 (p. 5), and August 16 (p. 1) and 23 (p. 1), 1947, January 24 (p. 1) and April 3 (p. 1), 1948, and January 8 (p. 5) and February 26 (p. 5), 1949. In January 1949 the Jefferson County Board of Education reinstated Gainer in an out-of-court settlement in anticipation of the Alabama Supreme Court's final ruling. The Fairfield board did not settle with Steele, and the court ruled in her favor on February 17, 1949. See Atlanta *Daily World,* January 4, 1949, p. 6; and Pittsburgh *Courier,* January 8 (p. 5) and February 26 (p. 5), 1949.

43 "Garbage, Trash Men Ask Pay Hike after Brief Stoppage," Birmingham *News,* August 20, 1951 (quotations); "Garbage Collectors oil Strike over Pay," *ibid.,* August 27, 1951; both collected in AR1922.8.35. James L. Baggett Research Files on Eugene "Bull" Connor (BPL). The author thanks Mr. Baggett for drawing the author's attention to the sanitation worker strikes and for sharing these and subsequently cited files.

workers' union en masse. Morgan agreed to meet with CIO leaders even while he refused to recognize the union. A week later the commission quietly settled with the strike committee, and the garbage collectors resumed working with a greater than 10 percent pay increase and an unprecedented recognition of their permanent service: five and a half days of sick leave per year of work.[44]

More than a decade before Bull Connor and Martin Luther King Jr. brought Birmingham into the national spotlight, three hundred black workers performing the least desirable of tasks had demanded and won a little respect from the Jim Crow town. A year later, in 1952, the workers again struck successfully, this time winning the reinstatement of workers fired for joining the CIO.[45] But the city also passed a new ordinance requiring the immediate termination of any worker engaged in a work stoppage. By 1960 the city's black sanitation workers had formed Local 1184 of the American Federation of State, County, and Municipal Employees (AFSCME), an institution that must have given them some confidence when they again walked off the job to protest cuts to their weekly work hours. As student civil rights sit-ins raged across the South, the all-white city commission made good on its threat and fired all four hundred black so-called day laborers. The majority-white Birmingham Labor Council rallied behind the black workers, and representatives of the USWA and UMW sought to mediate the conflict. Yet the city held firm and successfully replaced the strikers, agreeing to rehire individuals only gradually and only at the reduced number of hours.[46]

The rise and fall of the sanitation workers' unions may at first appear to represent little more than a run-of-the-mill labor conflict, but it in fact was far from routine. African American workers at the bottom of Jim Crow hierarchies of race and class served as the cornerstone of the white supremacist South. Expected by whites to remain invisible as well as docile, they nonetheless performed essential tasks without which the white side of the segregated order could not function. The garbage collectors' strike forced white elites to bargain with the most despised of laborers, while ordinary whites had to cope with interrupted or reduced municipal services. The reports in daily mainstream newspapers underscored these tensions. The workers were always identified as "Negroes," while the inconvenienced white "citizens" and "housewives" remained racially unmarked. Meanwhile the account of the watermelon incident served to reinforce white stereotypes of blacks' innate recourse to violence and their inherent minstrel-like buffoonery. When strikers threw a Molotov cocktail into the home of a black scab in 1960, the Birmingham *News* ran a full-spread feature on the injured replacement worker and his family. Such a sympathetic response stood in stark contrast to the general indifference of the daily paper toward the house bombings of Fred Shuttlesworth, Arthur Shores, and other civil rights activists. The garbage collectors' strikes brought central contradictions of Jim Crow society to the fore, even though they did not expand into a city wide movement on the scale of Memphis in 1968.[47]

---

44 Birmingham *News,* August 20, 26–31, and September 1–3, 5, 8–9, 1951; Birmingham *Post-Herald,* August 21, 27–31, and September 1, 4, and 5, 1951; all collected in AR1922.8.35. Baggett Research Files.

45 "B'ham Negroes Back on Jobs after Strike," Atlanta *Daily World,* August 27, 1952, p. 1.

46 "Striking Garbage Handlers Fired," Birmingham *News,* April 20, 1960. See additional articles in the Birmingham *News,* March 28–30, April 2–3, 5, 20, 24, and 26–27, July 25 ad 27, and August 5, 1960; and Birmingham *Post-Herald,* March 15–16, 22, and 29–30, April 4, 6, 20–23, and 27, and July 26, 1960; all collected in AR1922.10.34. Baggett Research Files.

47 On the house bombing, see the articles in the Birmingham *News* on April 26 and 27, 1960, especially the spread of photographs and the short article "Fire Bomb Tossed in Negro's Home," *ibid.,* April 26, 1960. Also see the sources in the preceding three notes. On Memphis in 1968, see Michael K. Honey, *Going Down Jericho Road: The Memphis Strike, Martin Luther King's Last Campaign* (New York, 2007).

African American economic justice organizing clearly attracted people from throughout the black working class, from unionized miners and railroad workers to teachers, garbage collectors, and street sweepers. Even domestic service workers fought for dignity on the job, though they could not look to unions for support and their experiences largely failed to enter the written record. Mattie C. Haywood was just one of the countless black women who worked in white households for wages that lagged well behind even those of the garbagemen. "You [were] always that Colored girl [who] got to go to the back," she remembered in an oral history interview in 1996. "And I don't care how much they grin in your face, you still a Colored person. ... [But] That's all Black women could do. Even if they got to the 12th grade they still couldn't get nothing but a maid in a hospital or domestic work." Looking back at her experiences in the 1950s and 1960s, Haywood remained defiant but not bitter. "Well, now they treat you pretty good as long as folks just stay in your place," she recalled; "But, when they made me mad, I would walk off the job."[48] Haywood protested with her feet many times. One employer refused to give her a day off on a single Sunday each month so she could go to church. Haywood said nothing but quietly quit. On another occasion, the man of the house scolded her for bringing food to the table but not serving it. "'You know how to serve the food, you supposed to serve on this side,' [he said]. And I just set the plate down on the table and walked out," Haywood added. The employer then talked to Haywood's husband to plead for her return; the latter took his wife's place for the rest of the day, but she "never did go back."[49]

Haywood had no union to protect her, no ability to draw on the strength of the solidarity of three hundred or more fellow workers. But she nonetheless struggled to assert her dignity on the job, and her experiences at work in the white homes of Birmingham soon led her—like so many other black workers—directly into the civil rights movement.

"It was from my activism with the union that I really understood the way racism worked," recalled Colonel Stone Johnson, one of the leaders of the black brotherhoods at the L&N rail yards. "Then, in the 1950s, when the movement started, I was basically primed for it, because I had already been doing this kind of work."[50] Johnson's story typifies the experiences of many black workers. African Americans organized on the job, slowly gaining access to skilled positions and fighting for improvements in wages and working conditions. Yet many of these same activists also helped organize the civil rights movement in their community. Black workers contributed to the larger freedom struggle by joining and taking leadership positions in its most important local organization, the Alabama Christian Movement for Human Rights. They also engaged in direct action demonstrations to desegregate public accommodations and led the effort to register voters. This activism ultimately fueled another critical component of the struggle: forming shop floor and citywide caucuses to bring the fight back to work.

Seen from the perspective of the black workers at the movement's core, many of its iconic participants, including both students and religious leaders, begin to look a little different. George Holloway, a black worker and union leader from Memphis, explained, "The CIO really contributed to the civil rights movement. ... The CIO brought better wages, so parents got interested in schooling, and began to send kids to college."[51] Historian David Montgomery adds, "Many of the high school and college

---

48 Transcript of Mattie C. Haywood, interview by Binnie Miles, March 1, 1996, p. 7, BCRIOHP.
49 *Ibid.*, 7–9 (quotations on 8).
50 Colonel Stone Johnson interview, in Huntley and Montgomery, eds., *Black Workers' Struggle for Equality in Birmingham*, 40–41.
51 George Holloway, interview by Michael Honey, Baltimore, Maryland, March 23, 1990, p. 50, Box TR 3, Behind the Veil.

students arrested for demonstrating against segregation in Birmingham's streets … were daughters and sons of these union members."[52] From this perspective, the labor movement contributed significantly, but indirectly, to the civil rights movement by creating a stable, upwardly mobile class of workers who could afford for the first time to educate large numbers of their children.

Of course, many of those young people were themselves workers. Local NAACP leader W. C. Patton recalled that Autherine Lucy, the black woman who famously confronted Governor George C. Wallace by enrolling in the University of Alabama, worked at a restaurant chain franchise until the radio picked up on her story, causing her white bosses to fire her the next day.[53] Similarly, Lola Hendricks, who became a well-known local leader of the Birmingham movement, was the daughter of a "laborer at the coal yard" and a domestic servant. Although she experienced poverty in her youth, she nonetheless became the first person in her family to attend college, and she worked as an insurance clerk during the movement before becoming one of the first African Americans employed by the federal government in Birmingham.[54] Among those arrested at the landmark children's march of 1963 were the children of UMW leader Leon Alexander, L&N union activist Nims Gay, and domestic worker Mattie Haywood.[55]

Fred Shuttlesworth, the Birmingham movement's most famous local religious leader, also came from the working class. In fact, when Colonel Stone Johnson helped organize the Brotherhood of Railway Clerks auxiliary at the L&N, he and other workers elected Shuttlesworth's uncle, August U. Morris, to the local union's presidency. According to Johnson, Morris and his wife raised their niece, Shuttlesworth's wife, Ruby, as their own. The reverend and Johnson became so close that when the Shuttlesworths' house was first bombed. Johnson recalled, "it was as if they had bombed my house."[56] Shuttlesworth's working-class roots extended beyond his marriage and into his congregation. Reuben Davis, who led the light for promotions at the L&N, also played a role in bringing the reverend to Birmingham. As a member of Bethel Baptist Church, Davis "could recommend various ministers to the chairman of the pulpit committee," he recalled. Having heard at work that Morris's nephew wanted to move from his current job in Selma. "I recommended that they invite Reverend Shuttlesworth" to come to Birmingham, Davis added.[57]

Historian Glenn Eskew argues that Shuttlesworth's ACMHR remained a distinctly working-class organization. Shuttlesworth organized the ACMHR in response to the state of Alabama's decision to ban the NAACP by injunction on May 20, 1956. About two weeks later, on June 5, over one thousand largely working-class African Americans attended the ACMHR's founding mass meeting at Sardis Baptist Church.[58] Birmingham's traditional black middle-class leadership, headed by the Reverend J. L.

52 Montgomery, "Introduction," 21. Montgomery also cites the Holloway interview as it appears in Michael Keith Honey, *Black Workers Remember: An Oral History of Segregation, Unionism, and the Freedom Struggle* (Berkeley, 1999), 170.
53 William C. Patton, interview by Tywanna Whorley, Birmingham, Alabama, June 14, 1994, p. 46, Box TR 3, Behind the Veil.
54 Lola Hendricks, interview by Tywanna Whorley, Birmingham, Alabama, June 22, 1994, p. 3, Box TR 3, Behind the Veil. See also *ibid.,* 10–11, 23–31.
55 Leon Alexander, interview by Paul Ortiz, Tuskegee, Alabama, June 21 and 27, 1994, p. 60, Box TR 3, Behind the Veil: Transcript of Mattie C. Haywood interview, p. 9, BCRIOHP; Transcript of Nims Gay, interview by Horace Huntley, April 6, 1995, p. 14. BCRIOHP.
56 Colonel Stone Johnson interview, in Huntley and Montgomery, eds., *Black Workers' Snuggle for Equality in Birmingham,* 37–11 (quotation on 41).
57 Reuben Davis interview, *ibid.,* 129.
58 Glenn T. Eskew, "'The Classes and the Masses': Fred Shuttlesworth's Movement and Birmingham's Black Middle Class," in White and Manis, eds., *Birmingham Revolutionaries, 34–38."*

Ware, opposed both the meeting and the organization born from it. According to Eskew, such dissent resulted from both personal jealousy (Ware feared the emergence of a new leader) and class politics. Instead of targeting the "'professional people" who composed the Birmingham NAACP, the ACMHR sought to organize "respectable working class black people." Eskew adds that 15 percent of the ACMHR's employed members worked in highly skilled positions, while only a third filled completely unskilled positions "such as maids and janitors." The remainder, who made up the majority, engaged in semiskilled industrial work constrained only by the "glass ceiling black people hit under segregation." It was no coincidence that Reuben Davis, Colonel Stone Johnson, Lloyd Harper, Nims Gay, Mattie Haywood, and countless other black workers became active in the ACMHR. Rather, the Alabama Christian Movement itself—like its leader—was the product of working-class organizing.[59]

Black workers in Birmingham also contributed to the civil rights movement directly, as its "foot soldier[s]," an aphorism USWA lawyer Buddy Cooper attributed to Johnson.[60] Indeed, such on-the-ground activism on the part of black workers occurred often before the founding of the ACMHR in 1956. Mine worker Earl B. Brown brought the message of the NAACP to the shop floor, spreading information about the organization to the black members of the UMW.[61] At the risk of being llred from his nonunion job, ACIPCO worker Lloyd Harper raised money outside the plant first for the Montgomery Bus Boycott and later for the ACMHR, while Harvey Lee Henley Jr., another ACIPCO employee, clandestinely passed the hat to seek contributions on the shop floor. Though neither of them were fired. Henley remembered being the recipient of constant harassment from the plant superintendent: "If you attended the mass meetings, you would be reported to the company. I was reported, and the superintendent said, 'Harvey, you involved in that mess going on down in Birmingham?' I said, 'I'm not directly involved, I'm an observer.' He said, 'Well, Harvey, we don't need that kind of stuff. You too good a man to be tied up in that old communist stuff.'"[62] While both the boss and the worker played their prescribed roles in this exchange, the threat lingered nonetheless. Harper likewise remembered that ACIPCO promised to automatically fire any worker jailed in civil rights demonstrations.[63]

Such intimidation may help explain why few readily identifiable workers assumed formal leadership positions in the ACMHR. Like Henley and Harper, many industrial workers, domestic servants, and educators feared termination From their jobs or harassment at work as the possible price for visible participation in the movement. They nonetheless attended mass meetings and joined large demonstrations,

59 Ibid., 36–38 (first quotation on 36: second and third quotations on 37; fourth quotation on 38). Eskew notes that Bethel Baptist's tour hundred members, including Reuben Davis, were also all part of the working class. The NAACP was not entirely middle class: several other working-class ministers who had, like Shuttlesworth, served on the NAACP board joined him in establishing the ACMHR. They saw themselves as a new leadership group answering the call of ordinary black Birminghamians who had grown frustrated with J. L. Ware's cadre. Eskew also notes that, despite opposition from Ware, Shuttlesworth steadfastly advocated the hiring of black policemen both before and alter the creation of the ACMHR. Ibid., 34, 39.
60 Jerome "Buddy" Cooper interview, in Huntley and Montgomery, eds., Black Workers' Struggle for Equality in Birmingham, 144; Colonel Stone Johnson interview, ibid., 44–15.
61 Earl B. Brown, interview by Paul Ortiz, Mulga, Alabama, June 28, 1994, pp. 11–12, Box TR 3, Behind the Veil.
62 Loyd Harper interview, in Huntley and Montgomery, eds., Black Workers' Struggle for Equality in Birmingham, 58; Harvey Lee Henley Jr. interview, ibid., 109.
63 Lloyd Harper interview, ibid., 60; Harvey Lee Henley Jr. interview, ibid., 110.

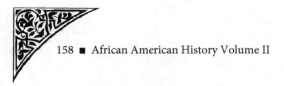

but they often made known from the outset that they could not afford to be arrested and detained away from work for a protracted period.[64]

Movement organizers recognized the obstacles faced by their workingclass members, so they found other community members to take the most public of stands, including possible beatings or apprehension by police. In 1963 the movement called on workers' children to face down Bull Connor's police dogs and fire hoses. On other occasions, workers at businesses serving the black community, or sometimes the owners of these establishments, served as the struggle's shock troops. For example, Lincoln Hendricks had no need to fear economic reprisal since he worked at his family's delicatessen, which served black customers in one of Birmingham's industrial suburbs.[65] Scholars have long observed that black reverends took on leadership roles in the civil rights movement, but less commonly noted is the fact that when they did so, they drew strength from the support of the working-class congregations who paid their salaries. In contrast, as Charles Payne has shown, black preachers at churches without independence from surrounding economic elites tended to shy away from the struggle.[66]

Defying this general trend of workers' avoiding formal leadership posts, George Price took on extraordinary and revealing roles. After growing up in Birmingham, Price attended college for a year before entering the service during World War II. A black officer told Price's battery that the enlisted men were earning too much money, so the officer urged them to join the NAACP and contribute their surplus wages to the association. Price returned to Alabama and graduated from the Tuskegee Institute, and he got a job as an iron inspector at Connors Steel. It was there that he first joined a union and served as a shop steward. At his next job he became a committeeman for the Mine, Mill, and Smelter Workers Union. "I've always, wherever I worked, if there was a labor union available, I always joined," he recalled. Price's participation in the labor movement dovetailed with his ongoing membership in a Birmingham-area NAACP chapter. "Blacks would always be underpaid, but the union made it so where blacks received what whites received [for] doing the same type of work," Price remembered. "The union made all the difference in the world. Without the union, they would run off anybody they want to and do what they wanted to do." Mine-Mill's radical civil rights unionism included a requirement that African Americans fill some of its top leadership posts, and Price soon rose to the post of vice president of Local 836. He managed to survive the USWA's takeover of Mine-Mill relatively unscathed, continuing as vice president of USWA Local 6612. Such a transition required strong support among rank-and-file black workers, but he also must have steered clear of the Communist Party. He thus served as a bridge between the radical organizing traditions of Mine-Mill and the liberal, anticommunist USWA. When the state of Alabama banned the NAACP in 1956. Price was uniquely positioned to serve as the de facto labor representative of the ACMHR. He became a board member of the Alabama Christian Movement,

64 For another striking example of workers' reluctance to he publicly named as part of the ACMHR, see Transcript of Colonel Stone Johnson interview, p. 20, BCRIOHP.

65 Transcript of Lincoln Hendricks, interview by Horace Huntley, June 9, 1995, p. 7, BCRIOHP. His older brother Elias Hendricks Sr. worked at Armour Packing and served as an officer of his local and district units of the United Packinghouse Workers of America. Elias avoided the civil rights demonstrations, not out of fear, but because of his temper and aversion to nonviolence. Elias Hendricks Sr. interview, in Huntley and Montgomery, eds., *Black Workers' Struggle for Equality in Birmingham*, 63–67.

66 Payne, *I've Got the Light of Freedom*, 191–201.

charged with directing its voter registration initiatives—a task that blended seamlessly with his role in the USWA.[67]

Yet most of the movement's working-class members stayed out of visible roles and served as foot soldiers, sometimes in the literal sense. In addition to attending mass meetings and direct action demonstrations, many worked as guards to protect movement leaders from violent attacks. Colonel Stone Johnson, chair of the grievance committee at the L&N railroad yard, remembered,

> [Shuttlesworth's uncle August] Morris said, "Johnson, you know Shuttlesworth can't get anybody to watch his house and the church? … You've got a lot of influence with the men out here in the union, and during the meeting nights ask some of the fellows to volunteer" … I had a good friend that was president of a mine local; his name was Will Hall. They called him John L. Lewis because he represented the miners union, and he was real tough. … The Lord fixed it for us to get together. We organized a watchmen group, and in those days you wouldn't have survived calling yourself a "watchmen group" or a "security group," so we were labeled "ushers" for the Alabama Christian Movement for Human Rights.[68]

Johnson helped create a rotating schedule where different men took responsibility for weekly shifts guarding Bethel Baptist Church, the attached parsonage where Shuttlesworth lived, and other potential targets. Another movement participant, Robert Revis, lived across the street from Bethel Baptist and donated the use of his enclosed porch as an ad hoc guard station. One evening in June 1958 someone slipped by the "ushers" on foot and planted a bomb next to the church. Johnson remembered,

> That was the bomb. It was in a fresh paint can, and the fuse was lit, which made the paint smoke. … We rushed out when we saw the smoke. Will Hall and myself. We got up close to it and I said, "John L., that's some dynamite." … He was experienced with fuses that are in mines. He says, "Yeah, it's some dynamite." "Let's get it," he said, and both of us reached for it about the same time, and we caught the [handle] of the five-gallon paint can and walked it about eight to ten feet and set it in the gutter. … We backed off another eight to ten feet, and it went off. … BOOM! … The bomb blew all the glass out of the church, and for five to six blocks around, dishes broke … and windows broke … but the church still stood.[69]

As this story suggests, working as an "usher" for the ACMHR could be dangerous business, but such labor represented the movement's core defense against white supremacist violence.

Civil rights historians often note that crude dynamite attacks like this one became so frequent that the city earned the nickname "Bombingham." But the black workers who sat armed with shotguns on

---

67 George Price interview, in Huntley and Montgomery, eds., *Black Workers' Struggle for Equality in Birmingham,* 161–70 (quotations on 162). Also see Transcript of George Price interview, pp. 2, 4, BCRIOHP.

68 Colonel Stone Johnson interview, in Huntley and Montgomery, eds., *Black Workers' Struggle for Equality in Birmingham,* 42. Originally a leader of the UMW, Lewis was the first president of the CIO and one of the country's most famous union leaders at the time. Will Hall's nickname invoked Lewis's fierce brand of militant unionism.

69 *Ibid.,* 43–44. For a slightly different telling of this incident, see La Verne Revis Martin interview, in Horace Huntley and John W. McKerley, eds., *Foot Soldiers for Democracy: The Men, Women, and Children of the Birmingham Civil Rights Movement* (Urbana, 2009), 89–90.

porches like Robert Revis's all over town have all but disappeared from popular memories and histories of the Birmingham movement. The near miss that evening at Bethel Baptist nonetheless won recognition among contemporaries in the ACMHR. Fearing further harassment, Johnson asked that his name be left out of the official account, so the miner alone received credit for removing the dynamite.[70] Beneath a photograph labeled "Mr. John L. Lewis (Mr. Will Hall)," the commemorative program for the ACMHR's second anniversary notes that his "daring courage saved the church from destruction."[71]

Like Johnson and Hall, most of the "ushers" were industrial workers recruited through the networks established over decades by black union activists. Reuben Davis took his turn doing guard duty for the movement, as did ACIPCO activist Lloyd Harper.[72] The informal network connecting these men represented a critical foundation on which the ACMHR was built. Religious leaders and students played important roles in the Birmingham civil rights movement, but black workers like Johnson and Hall did much of the nitty-gritty work that sustained it. L&N unionist Nims Gay even served as the first director of the ACMHR choir![73]

In turn, Shuttlesworth and the ACMHR leadership acknowledged the importance of jobs and other working-class concerns through their actions. Battles for spatial desegregation often went hand in hand with the economic issues at the heart of black Birminghamians' decades-long fight against discrimination.

The fight over segregated buses offers one example. As Robin Kelley has pointed out, buses had long been a frequent site of black resistance and white violence.[74] General unrest became mass defiance after the ACMHR demanded that the Birmingham Transit Company follow the example of Montgomery and integrate its coaches. In July 1956 Shuttlesworth wrote to the city commission asking for the body's views on "the two basic issues involved (the hiring by the Bus Company of Negro Operators, and the Federal Court Injunction against Bus Segregation). ..." Of course, the two demands were intertwined; black bus drivers would presumably be less likely than whites to violently confront black passengers, as had been the case far too often since at least World War II. But the movement's demand went deeper

---

70 Transcript of Colonel Stone Johnson interview, p. 20, BCRIOHP.

71 "Two Years of Progress of the Alabama Christian Movement for Human Rights" (second anniversary commemorative program), 1958, p. 11, AR1102.2.4. *Birmingham World* Office files (BPL). Note that the "Office files" collection, AR1102, is distinct from what I call the "Office Files, Correspondence Series," which is cataloged as AR1102.1; both are followed by box and folder numbers per the archive's citation and retrieval guidelines.

72 Not all of the "ushers" were union men, but most if not all were workers. Charles Grafton—who opposed unionization at ACIPCO—worked as a guard on a weekly basis. The "ushers" protected other potential targets, including the home of Arthur Shores. Charles Grafton interview, pp. 34–35, Behind the Veil: Reuben Davis interview, in Huntley and Montgomery, eds., *Black Workers' Struggle for Equality in Birmingham*, 129–30; Transcript of Llovd Harper, interview by Horace Huntley, June 12, 1996, p. 15, BCRIOHP. Nims Gay was also part of this network, though he did not mention in his interview whether he served as a guard. Transcript of Nims Gay interview, p. 20, BCRIOHP.

73 Transcript of Nims Gay interview, p. 11, BCRIOHP. Gay, who watched his son get assaulted by Bull Connor's fire hoses during the 1963 march, grew up in the milieu of Birmingham's Communist Party. He recalled the Scottsboro case and his uncle's close relationship to the party. Gus Hall, who later ran for president on the Communist Party of the United States of America ticket, stayed at Gay's uncle's home whenever Hall visited the Magic City. See *ibid.*, 8–9, 14. Gay thus served as an inter-generational link between the Old Left and the civil rights movement in its classical phase.

74 Robin D. G. Kelley, "Congested Terrain: Resistance on Public Transportation," in Kelley, *Race Rebels: Culture, Politics, and the Black Working Class* (New York, 1994), 55–76.

than that: "Know, Sirs, that we are deeply concerned about receiving a more just and equitable share of this city's economy, both in better jobs and better opportunities," Shuttlesworth continued.[75]

These issues pointed to another, related question: "We would appreciate also if you would take some position on the much needed matter of [hiring] Negro Policemen."[76] Immediately after its founding in 1956, the ACMHR approached the city to request this change. As one pamphlet published in 1959 put it, "The new organization's first effort was directed toward getting the city of Birmingham to hire Negroes on its police force. When petitions and delegations to officials failed, a suit was tiled in October, 1956, against the Personnel Board demanding the right of Negroes to take examinations for all civil service jobs—police, clerical, etc. The Personnel Board later removed the 'white only' designation from all jobs, and Negroes were allowed to take examinations. None, however, have ever been hired, and new court action is now being prepared."[77] In his annual ACMHR report in June 1959, Shuttlesworth called on movement members to continue the fight by testing the new system: "Negroes must now take all examinations—and should do so in large numbers. This is necessary to the second step of proving discrimination in hiring."[78]

Both the demand to hire bus drivers and the campaign for black police officers proved to be protracted fights. The Alabama Christian Movement had not yet engaged in direct action when terrorists first bombed Bethel Baptist on Christmas night in 1956. The very next day Shuttlesworth led a mass action in which twenty-two black protesters were jailed tor defying segregation on the bus. The civil rights organization filed suit soon after but lost the case when the city and the private transit company changed the laws to comply with federal statutes but nonetheless gave the drivers the power to seat passengers and maintain the practice of segregation. At an October 1958 mass meeting, ACMHR members approved a series of resolutions opposing this legal end around, demanding "courtesy" from white drivers, and renewing the call for "company employment of some Negroes as Drivers by December 15, 1958 to demonstrate appreciation for patronage and continued cooperation." Thirteen movement members again defied the new law and company rules, leading to their arrest.[79]

Despite a justifiable fear of reprisal, black workers joined the bus fight as it raged on into the early 1960s. The ACMHR produced a series of pamphlets giving riders instructions on how to conduct themselves as they challenged the segregated buses, and the foot soldiers took these lessons to heart.[80] As recounted above, paper and iron worker Jimmie Louis Warren got arrested when he sat in the white

75 Copy of letter from F. L. Shuttlesworth and N. H. Smith Jr. to Birmingham City Commission, July 26, 1956, pp. 1–2, AR1102.1.1.1. *Birmingham World* Office Files, Correspondence Series.
76 *Ibid.*, 2.
77 They Challenge Segregation at Its Core," brochure published by Alabama Christian Movement for Human Rights, in cooperation with the Southern Conference Educational Fund, n.d. [1959], AR1102.2.4. *Birmingham World* Office Files.
78 Copy of "President's Annual Report." June 5, 1959, p. 2. AR1102.2.3. *Birmingham World* Office Files; emphasis in original. See also "Two Years of Progress of the Alabama Christian Movement for Human Rights" (second anniversary commemorative program). 6, 28.
79 "Resolutions Adopted at Mass Meeting." October 16, 1958. pp. 1–2 (quotations on 1). AR1102.2.4. *Birmingham World* Office files: Emory O. Jackson to Rev. F. I., Shuttlesworth, October 15, 1958, AR1102.1.1.1. *Birmingham World* Office Files. Correspondence Series: "Two Years of Progress of the Alabama Christian Movement for Human Rights" (second anniversary commemorative program), 6; Copy of "President's Annual Report," 1; "They Challenge Segregation at Its Core," 2–3.
80 "What You Should Know About Riding the Buses." n.d. [ca. 1960]; untitled ACMHR bulletin. n.d.; both in Alabama Christian Movement for Human Rights Collection, 97–005 (BCRI). Oral history interview subjects frequently mention that they had received instructions from the ACMHR prior to taking action. See, for example, Transcript of Jimmie Louis Warren interview, p. 13. BCRIOHP.

section of a Birmingham bus in 1960. That same year Lloyd Harper, who twice tried to unionize ACIPCO, participated in an ACMHR-sponsored test of Birmingham's segregated bus system. With his two children in tow, he boarded a bus and sat in the white section. The bus driver overlooked the infraction. Harper remembered, but a white passenger demanded that the driver kick the black family off the bus. Harper requested and received a refund of his fare despite the fact that drivers typically claimed that they were unable to make change. Harper and his children stepped off the bus and caught the next one, again sitting in the white section. This time the whites merely grumbled, but a black friend asked him to "come back here where you belong."[81] On another occasion local union vice president and ACMHR board member George Price boarded a bus downtown and sat near the front. The driver skipped Price's stop and then "was kind of nasty" when Price wrote down the identification numbers of both the bus and its operator.[82] The demand for black drivers remained tied to the push to desegregate seating as late as the famed confrontation beginning in April 1963. Days before the children's march, three African Americans applied for jobs as drivers, and movement leaders planned yet another meeting with company officials.[83] Price remembered that it took constant tests, a delegation of white students willing to challenge the color line, and endless negotiations with the bus company before Birmingham finally desegregated its public transit system.[84]

Black workers served on the front lines as the ACMHR gradually extended the direct action campaign from the buses to other public spaces. Soon after his arrest on the bus, Jimmie Louis Warren and his friend Wilson Brown attended a University of Alabama football game at Legion Field in Birmingham. The two black men were the only African Americans in the stadium except for "those that had on white coats [concessions workers]." Throughout the game white spectators jeered at Warren and Brown, and when it ended, a mob of white fans chased them from the stadium, throwing punches at Warren as he lied—straight into a police car. The police took him downtown for questioning but never charged him, but neither did they investigate his white assailants. The incident was reported on the radio and in local papers, and Warren's employer, the Birmingham Paper Company, later fired him as a result.[85]

When the Alabama Christian Movement turned to the desegregation of lunch counters during the climactic civil rights campaign code-named "Project C" in April and May 1963, economic justice issues remained paramount. Historians frequently include the movement's appeal for jobs at downtown department stores on a long laundry list of ACMHR demands, but few scholars add further comment.[86] Yet viewed within the context of a decades-long struggle for the best jobs in town, the appeal for

---

81 Lloyd Harper interview, in Huntley and Montgomery, eds., *Black Workers' Struggle for Equality in Birmingham*, 59–60 (quotation on 60). The year 1960 for both actions is an educated guess based on Harper's and Warren's interviews. Both could have taken place as early as 1959 or as late as 1961. Regardless of the exact date, their protests took place during this discrete phase of the bus campaign, between the October 1958 mass meeting and the 1963 demonstrations.
82 George Price interview, *ibid.*, 167.
83 "Three Seek Bus Driver Jobs in Birmingham, Ala.," Atlanta *Daily World.* April 30, 1963. p. 1.
84 George Price interview, in Huntley and Montgomery, eds., *Black Workers' Struggle for Equality in Birmingham.* 167.
85 Jimmie Louis Warren interview, *ibid.*, 197–99 (quotation on 199). According to one report, these events took place on September 22, 1962, at a game against the University of Georgia. Warren remembered it taking place at a game against Georgia Tech in 1961, which according to Alabama football records was played on November 18 of that year. See "Ala. fan Beaten after Grid Game." Chicago *Daily Defender* (Daily Edition), September 25, 1962, p. 2. The date of the 1961 game can be found by downloading the 1961 season recaps from the archives page of the University of Alabama Official Athletic Site, http://www.rolltide.coni/spoils/m-foothl/arehive/alah-nvlootbl-archive.html.
86 See, for example, Morris, *Origins of the Civil Rights Movement,* 250–62 (quotation on 257).

employment probably played a central role in helping the ACMHR win the support of the black community. On April 9, just six days into the unprecedented wave of demonstrations. Wyatt Tee Walker sent out a press release boasting that the city's Baptist Ministers Union had endorsed the ACMHR's actions. "Chief among the Negro requests are the immediate desegregation of lunch counter facilities and the establishment of fair hiring practice and job upgrading on a nondiscriminatory basis," the statement read.[87] The push for equal employment opportunity clearly helped the Alabama Christian Movement gain legitimacy with a politically diverse group of black ministers, and it aided the mobilization of black workers and their families. The demonstrations and boycott did not cease until early May, when downtown merchants agreed to desegregate and hire at least one black clerk within ninety days.[88] The following year the ACMHR again took to the streets with a selective buying campaign aimed at forcing the hand of retailers who had ignored the 1963 agreement, and for the next several years movement leaders repeatedly extended their call to move away from token hiring of black workers toward fully nondiscriminatory employment practices.[89]

Meanwhile, black workers also continued to engage in direct action in the years after Project C. Jimmie Louis Warren joined with several black coworkers from his new job at U.S. Pipe to test the newly integrated Dobbs House restaurant at the Birmingham airport. Shuttlesworth had first requested service there in 1960, and a court ruling in 1962 ordered that the restaurant serve all customers since it was involved in interstate commerce. The Civil Rights Act of 1964 extended racial integration to all private establishments. Although the exact date of their action remains unclear. Warren and his coworkers certainly had the law on their side when they went to the airport one Sunday afternoon. They were also armed with instructions from the ACMHR and joined by Jim Hendricks. Lola's brother-in-law, whom Warren had met at the Hendricks family deli, a popular gathering place for movement participants. When the four men arrived at Dobbs House, Warren recalled, the wait staff initially refused to serve them, claiming that the restaurant had closed. The activists pointed out that the white customers were getting service, so management reluctantly agreed to feed the black men as well. "We all got a ham sandwich and a Coke, and they charged us ten dollars apiece for a ham sandwich," Warren remembered. "So we sat there and ate and paid for it. Jim [Hendricks] said he wasn't going to eat his—he was going to take it home, keep it, and put it in the freezer, and he did." But as the other black men ate, the restaurant turned away new incoming customers and then closed for the day.[90]

87 "Negro Ministers Give Full Backing to Movement," ACMIIR press release, April 9, 1963, AR1102.2.3, *Birmingham World* Office Files.

88 Quarterly report of Alabama Council on Human Relations to Southern Regional Council. July 16, 1963, p. 5, AR41.1.35, Southern Regional Council/Alabama Council for Human Relations Records (BPI.). Aldon Morris writes that the settlement stipulated that "Negroes would be hired and upgraded on a nondiscriminatory basis throughout the industrial community of Birmingham." See Morris. *Origins of the Civil Rights Movement,* 271.

89 "Special Notice!" ACMHR Selective Buying Campaign flyer, 1964. AR1102.2.3, *Birmingham World* Office Files. Also see Rev. F. L. Shuttlesworth to Friend of Freedom, March 6, 1964, AR1102.1.1.1, *Birmingham World* Office Files. Correspondence Series. On later years, see, for example. "Tenth Annual Address to the ACMHR, B'ham, Ala.," delivered by F. I. Shuttlesworth, June 6, 1966, AR1102.2.3, *Birmingham World* Office Files.

90 Jimmie Louis Warren interview, in Huntley and Montgomery, eds., *Black Workers' Struggle for Equality in Birmingham,* 201–2. Surprisingly, Warren was unaware of the prior history at the Dobbs House; he believed that his was the first sit-in at the airport. On Shuttlesworth's earlier attempt, see copy of "Brief in Support of Defendant's Motion to Dismiss," *Shuttlesworth el al., v. Dobbs Houses, Inc.,* Civil Action No. 9765. United Stales District Court, Northern District of Alabama, Southern Division, in Alabama Christian Movement for Human Rights Collection; and "Dobbs House Must Serve Everybody," Baltimore *Afro-American,* July 28, 1962, p. 18.

Black workers also took the lead in the decades-long voter registration campaign, a key component of Birmingham's "long civil rights movement." As early as the 1930s Earl Brown and other UMW leaders began helping union miners, both black and white, register to vote. Leon Alexander remembered that Walter Jones, the black UMW organizer who rebuilt the union during the Great Depression, had a saying that "when the company's kicking ass they don't look to see whether the ass is black or white they just started kicking ass and if it happen to be a white ass he get kicked just like the black one."[91] Motivated by this ethos of interracial solidarity, Alexander and Brown encouraged white miners to pay their poll taxes while simultaneously encouraging black workers to register to vote. Up until the NAACP was banned in 1956, Brown helped the organization by canvassing the mine and asking black miners whether they were registered. He invited those who were not to attend educational meetings at church after work.[92] Likewise, Alexander worked with NAACP chief W. C. Patton to organize similar seminars at his church and in people's homes, and steelworker Roosevelt Williams taught some of the classes.[93] Union leader George Price became the ACMHR's director of voter registration after the injunction against the NAACP. Between 1956 and 1964, when the NAACP returned to Alabama, Price's campaign was credited with registering over seventeen thousand voters.[94]

While the NAACP and the ACMHR both contributed to the registration of black voters in the Birmingham area, the most durable institution was the Bessemer Voters' League (BVL), another working-class organization, located in an industrial suburb. Black leaders of the left-leaning Mine, Mill, and Smelter Workers Union helped found the BVL and served as officers of the Bessemer branch of the NAACP. Asbury Howard Sr. led both groups in addition to fulfilling his duties as the international vice president and southeastern regional director of Mine-Mill. Organized in the late 1940s, the BVL offered voter education classes and helped African Americans go to the county courthouse to register to vote. Asbury Howard and Mine-Mill came under attack for having Communist sympathies, but the BVL survived the half decade of devastating USWA raids on the union. As the BVL continued its work of registering black voters, the charges of Communist infiltration gradually subsided. In 1953 NAACP labor secretary Herbert Hill, a staunch anticommunist, recommended that the national office remove Howard and the rest of the Bessemer leadership.[95] But NAACP regional secretary Ruby Hurley expressed a different view that emphasized the nuts and bolts of the struggle. She contended that the Mine-Mill workers had led the association's activities in the area and had done nothing to violate NAACP policy. The USWA-CIO people, in contrast, were "doing the griping without going to the Branch to work. ..."[96] Helped by Hurley's intervention, the Bessemer branch continued to function under the same BVL leadership into the 1960s. Their voter registration work formed an integral part of the larger civil rights movement, and their contributions did not go unrecognized. The Birmingham *World* took note

91 Leon Alexander interview, p. 15, Behind the Veil.
92 Earl Brown interview, pp. 12–15, Behind the Veil.
93 Leon Alexander interview, pp. 24–26. Behind the Veil: Roosevelt Williams, interview by Paul Ortiz. Birmingham, Alabama. June 24, 1994, pp. 21–23. Box TR 3. Behind the Veil.
94 George Price interview, in Huntley and Montgomery, eds., *Black Workers' Struggle for Equality in Birmingham,* 165. He also remembered that some forty thousand people were turned down by voter registrars in a three-year span.
95 "Confidential Memorandum to Walter White, from Herbert Hill," May 8–17, 1953, Box A-343, Part II, NAACP Papers; Montgomery, "Introduction," 15.
96 "Memorandum to Mr. Cluster B. Current from Mrs. Ruby Hurley, Regional Secretary." July 17, 1953, Box A-9, Part II, NAACP Papers.

of a ceremony in which the Bessemer Baptist Ministers Conference and the West Jefferson County Coordinating Council honored the BVL's leader by declaring February 12, 1960. "Asbury Howard Day."[97] Howard's work earned another kind of recognition from white supremacist terrorists, who in 1957 fire-bombed his house and in 1959 severely beat him as he left a Bessemer courtroom.[98]

Howard, Johnson, Warren, and untold others served as the foot soldiers of the civil rights movement, making an invaluable contribution to the struggle. Black workers led the battle for access to skilled jobs, joined the ACMHR, formed the unit of "ushers" who protected the movement against violent attack, conducted direct action demonstrations in cafeterias and on buses, and registered voters. They also gave the larger movement its esprit de corps, its gestalt, or, for lack of better words, its vision, mission, and even its meaning. And as the great civil rights organizations began to fizzle and search for new directions in the mid-1960s, black workers continued to carry their organizing tradition back to the shop floor.

By 1964 the Alabama Christian Movement listed "some upgrading by stores and numerous industrial concerns" among its long list of accomplishments. Yet for many black workers, "some" was not good enough. As the ACMHR called for "More in '64," black workers in Birmingham continued the fight for access to the best jobs available.[99] Nancy MacLean has ably demonstrated that African Americans seized the opportunity presented by Title VII of the Civil Rights Act of 1964 to demand inclusion at the workplace. The new bill gave black workers unprecedented legal power to achieve this goal, and it created a federal agency with the capacity to enforce the new order.[100] But the legislation did not create the demand, nor did it entirely meet the lofty expectations of African American laborers who had struggled toward the same end for decades. Still, the passage of Title VII and the flowering of the movement that won it did embolden black workers to engage in yet another round of protests for justice on the job.

Colonel Stone Johnson credited his union activism with preparing him for the civil rights movement, but other black workers reversed his formula, believing that their activism on the job stemmed from their training in the movement. For example, Jimmie Louis Warren recalled. "And so the Christian Movement [ACMHR] kind of gave me an insight on how to handle myself out there on the job." When he got fired from Birmingham Paper Company. Warren and his friend Wilson Brown left town to attend a series of SNCC training seminars. "I had this little training from Talladega and Atlanta from SNCC about how to move up when things come open," Warren remembered, so when he got the job at U.S. Pipe, he was ready to begin the fight for access to the good jobs reserved for whites. In addition to bidding for those posts. Warren and other black U.S. Pipe workers staged a sit-in during a union meeting, refusing to sit in the "so-called black side" of the hall and instead intermingling with the white members. Warren and his peers later filed a series of Equal Employment Opportunity Commission (EEOC) complaints against both the company and the union, the Molders and Allied Workers, and the black workers eventually won and forced the removal of Jim Crow signs from the union hall. But the union remained in the same space at the time of Warren's oral history interview in 1996, leaving dual

---

97 "Asbury Howard Sr. Honored," Birmingham *World,* March 9, 1960, pp. 1, 8.

98 "Alabama Drops Case," Baltimore *Afro-American,* February 7, 1959, p. 2; Patrick Murphy Malin, American Civil Liberties Union, to E. O. Jackson, August 1959, AR1102.1.1.11, *Birmingham World* Office Files, Correspondence Series. Howard was not at his home when it was bombed in 1957; he was in Washington. D.C., preparing for the national Prayer Pilgrimage for Freedom, held on May 17.

99 "Eight Years of Progress of the Alabama Christian Movement for Human Rights" (eighth anniversary commemorative program), p. 5. AR1102.2.4, *Birmingham World* Office Files.

100 Nancy MacLean, *Freedom Is Not Enough: The Opening of the American Workplace* (New York, 2006).

water fountains and dual restrooms as durable signs of past discrimination (all workers used both sets of facilities by 1996).[101]

In the early and mid-1960s, black workers at ACIPCO brought the civil rights movement back to the job despite the fact that their plant remained nonunion. Harvey Lee Henley Jr. remembered that both Andrew Young of the Southern Christian Leadership Conference and Stokely Carmichael of SNCC often tried to recruit black industrial workers to participate in their organizations. "They would meet with us and talk about labor's untold story," Henley recalled.[102] Early in the decade Henley led a pair of efforts aimed at winning access to jobs and desegregating plant facilities. Since ACIPCO received government contracts, Henley and other black workers filed complaints with the President's Committee on Equal Employment Opportunity in 1961. Henley remembered that the agency initially gave them "the runaround," so they continued to write letters until government investigators came to the plant in 1963. Still, the committee's attempt "to get good faith agreements" stalled, and the case remained in limbo. The passage of the Civil Rights Act in 1964 allowed Henley and his coworkers to sue ACIPCO in court, where they ultimately won their case. On the shop floor Henley and his coworkers formed a caucus called the Committee for Equal Job Opportunity, which then staged a sit-in at the plant cafeteria. "When the sit-ins were going on downtown, we were sitting in at the ACIPCO restaurant. Those were bold moves because we didn't have no union," Henley recalled. Management tore down the wall that had divided the cafeteria, and the change in the plant's race relations was palpable, Henley remembered. "We would come out of the shop, all sweaty and dirty, and go to the restaurant and sit next to white people who were dressed in suits." On one occasion a white carpenter threatened the black workers with a hammer, but they walked past him without incident, and the cafeteria remained integrated.[103]

Black workers did not carry out their struggles in isolation from one another. Rather, their personal and political relationships overlapped to create a loose network of like-minded activists. Colonel Stone Johnson, for example, organized the watchmen group by drawing on his union and industrial community contacts. By the mid-1960s these informal networks had produced at least one formal organization of activist black workers. Initially, Jimmie Louis Warren and coworker Willie Hicks formed a committee of black workers at U.S. Pipe that met on Sundays at a nearby YMCA. Warren remembered, "We had a secretary and treasurer, president, and things like that. And so we would get blacks to come and educate them about what they can do." Later workers from other plants joined the U.S. Pipe committee for the Sunday meetings. Black workers from ACIPCO, U.S. Steel, Stockham Valve, and others joined together to coordinate their campaign for access to skilled jobs.

---

101 Jimmie Louis Warren interview, in Huntley and Montgomery, eds., *HI tick Workers' Struggle for Equality in Birmingham,* 200–205 (first and second quotations on 202: third quotation on 203). The Equal Employment Opportunity Commission was created by Title VII of the Civil Rights Act of 1964.

102 Harvey Lee Henley Jr. interview, *ibid.,* 110–12 (quotation on 111). Henley narrated the stories of these actions and dated them around 1963. He also listed 1963 as the peak of the movement. But he paradoxically concluded that "if you don't have the national government supporting you, it don't mean anything." *Ibid.,* 112. His story suggests that the Civil Rights Act allowed him and his colleagues to solidify and extend the gains won through earlier fights.

103 *Ibid.,* 110–11. See note *32* regarding the President's Committee on Equal Employment Opportunity.

"We had people from each plant," Warren recalled. Members of this city wide caucus began filing complaints even before the creation of the EEOC. Warren claimed that they tiled so many charges that the EEOC was forced to establish a branch in Birmingham in order to process their cases.[104]

Despite this ongoing activism, the struggle for justice on the job remained far from over. Conflicts over the integration of company bathhouses raged at mines, mills, and yards in the Birmingham area into the late 1960s. According to several black workers, most white workers refused to bathe or share locker rooms with blacks for years after passage of the Civil Rights Act. Some whites initially responded by leaving work without showering. Black workers fondly remember that this strategy failed because the white workers' wives protested their husbands' smell in the car on the way home from their shifts. At one mine, white workers then rented their own trailer in order to bathe and change clothes there rather than rub shoulders with their black counterparts.[105]

In 1966 the labor and industry committee of the NAACP Birmingham branch conducted a study of ongoing violations of the Civil Rights Act in and around the Magic City. Focusing its efforts on government contractors in heavy industry, the committee received over five hundred complaints tiled by black workers against their employers and unions. Of these, over three hundred originated at the Tennessee Coal, Iron & Railroad Company (TCI) or other U.S. Steel facilities. In one egregious case, a union representative at TCI told a black worker with a grievance to "get the hell out."[106] "Nearly all major corporations in Birmingham" maintained segregated locker rooms, pay lines, and cafeteria sections by assigning numbers to employees based on race, the committee reported. At the U.S. Pipe Company, management created a numbering system to prevent the integration of the bathhouses. Workers numbered 1–900 were black and used one set of facilities, while white workers were labeled 1,000 and up and used another.[107] Hayes Aircraft hired black workers frequently but for only weeks at a time in order to doctor its aggregate numbers to mislead government regulators into thinking the firm hired equally across racial lines. ACIPCO—like all the unionized plants—maintained separate facilities, used racially biased or often rigged examinations to determine promotions, and counted seniority based only on time of service in a given occupation rather than overall time employed in the plant. This last practice, common both before and after the Civil Rights Act, guaranteed that layoffs disproportionately affected black workers who had either just arrived in skilled jobs or continued to toil in the rapidly disappearing unskilled positions. The NAACP committee called for immediate "positive and affirmative action in rectifying these discriminatory abuses."[108] The association's call went unheeded. As Judith Stein, Nancy

---

104 Jimmie Louis Warren interview, in Huntley and Montgomery, eds., *Black Workers' Struggle for Equality in Birmingham*, 203–4.

105 These stories recur frequently in the oral history interviews and can be thought of as the black workers' oral tradition. The best account is Leon Alexander interview, pp. 3–8, 55–58, Behind the Veil. Also see Transcript of Jimmie Louis Warren interview, p. 24, BCRIOHP; Earl Brown interview, pp. 5–6, Behind the Veil; and notes on author's unrecorded conversation with Colonel Stone Johnson, Birmingham, Alabama, October 10, 2008, in author's possession.

106 John W. Nixon et al., "Report of the Labor and Industry Committee of the Birmingham Branch of the National Association for the Advancement of Colored People," 1966, pp. 1, 8 (quotation), 9, AR1102.1.1.6, *Birmingham World* Office Files, Correspondence Series.

107 Ibid., 6.

108 *Ibid.,* 4–5 (quotation on 4).

MacLean, and others have shown, it took numerous EEOC complaints and copious court battles before the steel industry settled these grievances in a "consent decree" in 1974.[109]

Yet the string of complaints, lawsuits, and negotiations do not entirely explain the eventual shift toward racial equality at work sites across Birmingham. Rather, the change also required that Johnson, Davis, Warren, Henley, and myriad other black workers engage in a wide range of struggles on the shop floor and in the union hall. They did so before the formation and during the heyday of the Alabama Christian Movement as well as before and after the Civil Rights Act, in all cases drawing strength from networks and caucuses with their fellow black workers. Their daily activities helped shape the black freedom struggle in all of Birmingham while providing on-the-ground enforcement of court rulings and federal laws. If Project C helped create the Civil Rights Act, as is commonly assumed, black workers helped first to write the landmark law and then to define its meaning.

African Americans' struggle for jobs and justice persisted throughout Birmingham's "long civil rights movement." Economic issues, often recognized as paramount during the Great Depression and World War II, did not simply disappear in the late 1940s. Nor did they suddenly reappear after 1964. Rather, despite the rising anticommunism of the cold war, occupational mobility continued to serve as a rallying cry for black activists in Birmingham—and perhaps elsewhere. It is true, in the words of Robert Korstad and Nelson Lichtenstein, that some opportunities were in fact lost. As Jacquelyn Hall has recently reasserted, during the "classical phase," black activists "could not ground their battle in growing, vibrant, social democratic unions" and instead relied on "independent protest organizations."[110]

But the innumerable examples of black working-class activism recounted above suggest that this moment of rupture and this dichotomy at an organizational level might not have been as sharp and severe as many historians have assumed. Indeed, these stories highlight a marked continuity of vision, tactics, and personnel at the level of on-the-ground activists. Black trade unionists in Birmingham both led and populated the ACMHR, a so-called independent protest organization. Black participation in the labor movement remained sufficiently robust in 1958 that the Alabama Christian Movement celebrated a hero nicknamed John L. Lewis without the need to further explain what the honorific epithet meant.

More generally, from teachers to industrial workers to maids to garbage men, African American workers fought for and often won access to better jobs and a degree of dignity at work throughout the long postwar period, including before the Civil Rights Act. Drawing on one, two, or more decades of experience, many black working-class activists were well primed to extend their struggle into new arenas by the time the so-called classical phase of the movement began in the mid-1950s. In Birmingham, the outlawing of the NAACP opened up space for new leadership in the black community, and African American workers helped propel Fred Shuttlesworth to fill the vacuum. This working-class preacher, with the support of his laboring congregation, laid out an agenda that foregrounded the ongoing organizing tradition in Birmingham's industrial areas. The ACMHR he led fought nearly all of its battles with one eye toward expanding economic opportunities, a goal that no doubt sprang from the expansive political agenda of many rank-and-file movement participants.

Black workers became the foot soldiers of the struggle, physically protecting its leaders and taking its campaigns to desegregate public spaces to the streets, often at great personal cost. African American

109 Stein, *Running Steel, Running America*; MacLean, *Freedom Is Not Enough*, 127–33 (quotation on 131).
110 Hall, "Long Civil Rights Movement," 1253.

laborers brought the struggle for racial equality to work and the fight for economic justice to the larger community. Each arena of struggle reinforced and strengthened the other, and both profited from the exchange of people and ideas from work site to community and back again. The *short* civil rights movement in Birmingham was a product of protracted working-class organizing even as it spurred new demands and protests on the job. Black workers did not merely contribute to a movement led by preachers and students; the workers built it. And in so doing, they endowed it with an unmistakably working-class vision.

THE MISSISSIPPI CIVIL RIGHTS MOVEMENT AND ITS LEGACY

By Kenneth T. Andrews

Do social movements matter? When people come together to challenge inequalities and face powerful authorities and opponents, what hope can they have of bringing about significant changes? This question has puzzled movement participants and observers throughout history. There are numerous examples to inspire confidence in the power of social movements, and there are equally plentiful cases to support a pessimistic assessment that movements are more likely to fail, invite repression, become co-opted, or produce polarization and violence than to achieve success.

The civil rights movement has raised the same questions for its participants and subsequent observers. John Lewis, one of the early SNCC leaders from Nashville, argues that "so many things are undeniably better. … But there is a mistaken assumption among many that these signs of progress mean that the battle is over, that the struggle for civil rights is finished, that the problems of segregation were solved in the '60s and now all we have to deal with are economic issues" (1998, 490). Mary King is critical of a flippant view, writing:

> Those who sardonically claim "not much has changed for American blacks" must not know how bad it was. Such a comment reveals … that the speaker was not on the front lines in the southern civil rights movement and never experienced the brutality that was directed against blacks and their supporters at that time. (1987, 544)

Others have painted a less optimistic assessment, pointing to the limited gains, continuing inequality and injustices, and the costs that were suffered through the fierce struggles of the movement. Annie Devine, a legendary activist from Canton, Mississippi, wonders whether "all we may have done through the civil rights movement is open Pandora's box" (quoted in Dent 1997, 347).

L. C. Dorsey, a civil rights leader from Bolivar County, observes that "to the optimist, things are beautiful and even the small changes take on grand dimensions. For the pessimist, the changes may seem miniscule when viewed from eyes that expect the rubble from the fallen walls of racism already to be cleared away" (1977, 41). From the perspective of the activist, change can be measured relative to the goals that were sought or against the conditions that prevailed before the movement began. In this study, I use the tools of historical and social scientific analysis to shed new light on the legacy of the civil rights movement.

Many scholars of social movements assume that movements are, at least under certain conditions, effective agents of social change, especially for poor and powerless groups. This belief in the efficacy of protest and collective action underlies much of the scholarship by historians and social scientists on social movements. This is especially true for scholars of the civil rights movement. In fact, many studies of the origins and development of the movement have been justified by pointing to its success in challenging and transforming the southern system of racial domination. For example, Aldon Morris, in *The Origins of the Civil Rights Movement,* argues that the movement had "a profound impact on American society" (1984, 266). Similarly, Dennis Chong points to the movement as "the quintessential example of public-spirited collective action in our time" that "spark[ed] radical changes in American society" (1991, 1). Although these and many other scholars make strong assertions about the success of the civil rights movement, they do not examine this basic question. Surprisingly, we know more about the origins and early development of the civil rights movement than about the role the movement played in transforming the institutions and social relations of the South.

Adding to the confusion are disagreements about how movements influence social change. Some scholars locate the power of movements in disruptions and threats that force concessions from powerful opponents and authorities. In contrast, other scholars see movements as engaged in a form of persuasive communication designed to bring about change by appealing to the "hearts and minds" of bystanders. In this view, effective protest can win influential allies and secure much-needed resources. Finally, another line of argument claims that movements are efficacious when they adopt the organizational forms, institutionalized tactics, and rhetorical frameworks of interest groups and abandon the "politics of protest." Professionalization and moderation are the necessary steps to winning new advantages as groups make the transition from outsiders to insiders. These alternatives were well represented within the civil rights movement as leaders debated the strengths and weaknesses of strategies built around the basic mechanisms of disruption, persuasion, and negotiation as tools of social change.

In this study, I address these long-standing questions about the impacts of social movements through a multilayered study of the Mississippi civil rights movement. Mississippi stood most firm in its resistance to the civil rights movement and federal efforts to enforce racial equality. Tom Dent, a native of New Orleans who worked in the Mississippi movement for many years, tells us that "if racial change and justice meant anything anywhere, change in Mississippi, to the degree it existed, would be … the surest barometer of progress in the American South" (1997, 338). By examining this historically important case, I clarify our broader understanding of the ways in which movements transform social and political institutions as well as the constraints and obstacles that movements face when they try to do so. Through this analysis, I shed light on the movement building that took place in Mississippi and the resilience of the movement in the face of massive repression. I trace the movement's development beginning in the early 1960s, and I analyze its impact and setbacks during the 1970s and 1980s. This time period includes the expansion of voting rights and gains in black political power, the desegregation of public schools and the emergence of "white flight" academies, and the rise and fall of federally funded antipoverty programs. I chart the movement's engagement in each of these arenas as well as the tactical interaction between local civil rights movements and white power holders.

Research on the civil rights movement has focused primarily on the period up to the passage of the Voting Rights Act in 1965, often regarded as the final chapter of the southern phase of the black movement. However, many important struggles took place after 1965 as local movements tried to shape electoral politics, increase access to and improve the quality of public schools, and secure public resources like Head Start and community action programs.

Furthermore, historians of the civil rights movement have focused most heavily on the national leaders, the major civil rights organizations, and a handful of key protest campaigns. These are, of course, appropriate topics for research. However, this disproportionate focus on the national level of the movement obscures the depth and breadth of the civil rights struggle. Moreover, this focus locates the potential impacts of the movement in major court decisions and legislative reforms without asking whether or to what extent these legal changes were realized in the institutions throughout the South. The major legal reforms of the civil rights era only beg the question of whether the implementation of new laws and policies made the functioning of politics, schools, and social policies more equitable in the post-civil rights South.

Movements rarely, if ever, achieve all of their goals, but they can and do generate enduring consequences. Sidney Tarrow notes that "protest cycles do not simply end and leave nothing but lassitude or repression in their wake; they have indirect and long-term effects that emerge when the initial excitement is over and disillusionment passes" (1994, 172). Tarrow's observation is widely regarded as accurate by scholars of social movements and contentious politics. This study broadens and refines our understanding of movement impacts. Underlying this study is an argument that explains how movements have long-term and short-term impacts. I claim that focusing at the local level provides the best opportunity and the most important barometer for examining the consequences of social movements. In addition, I show that there is continuity between the heyday of movement activity and the period of movement decline.

Clayborne Carson, one of the leading historians of the civil rights movement, wrote an incisive essay about the historical scholarship on the movement, making three major criticisms that have influenced my argument. Carson observes that "because the emergent goals of American social movements have usually not been fulfilled, scholars have found it difficult to determine their political significance" (1986, 19). From this complexity and causal ambiguity, some scholars assume that movements are important and others assume that they are inconsequential. Some scholars assume that professional interest groups and routine political processes are the key actors because they are more likely to persist once mass mobilization wanes.[1] Second, there is the assumption "that the black struggle can best be understood as a protest movement, orchestrated by national leaders in order to achieve national civil rights legislation" (Carson 1986, 23). This assumption leads to an inaccurate view of the tactics, organizations, leaders, goals, and impacts of the movement. Throughout the civil rights movement, campaigns and tactics targeted change at the local level. In a small handful of campaigns such as in Birmingham and Selma, there was a complex effort to use local mobilization to leverage federal action. These highly visible cases represent a small fraction of the broader civil rights struggle. The assumption of a national movement effecting national legislation leads to a third error—"the prevailing scholarly conception … that [the movement] ended in 1965" with the passage of the Voting Rights Act (Carson 1986, 27). Rather, Carson argues that there is substantial continuity alongside transformation in the broader struggle by blacks after the Voting Rights Act.

Clayborne Carson's insights are a key starting point for this study of the continuity and transformation of the Mississippi civil rights movement from the early 1960s through the early 1980s. This focus allows us to better understand the consequences of social movements. In short, to understand the

history of the black freedom struggle, we must examine in detail the ongoing conflicts after the major legislative victories of the civil rights movement. The question here is a rather direct and obvious one, and it grows out of a straightforward concern on the part of social movement participants and observers to understand the consequences of social movements. While the question is generally acknowledged to be important, research and theory remain sparse.[2] Many barriers stand in the way of insightful research on the impacts of movements—both methodological and conceptual. In the next section, I describe the research that has allowed me to address these challenges and develop my analysis of the impact of the civil rights movement.

Overview of the Study

The argument developed through this study demonstrates the importance of movement dynamics for explanations of political change. In addition to the actions of elites, courts, legislatures, and counter-movements, social movements can and sometimes do play a key role in the process of social change. I show how the Mississippi movement built indigenous organizations and facilitated the growth of new leadership. I call this combination of leaders, indigenous resources, and local organizations the "movement infrastructure," and I demonstrate that long-term patterns of institutional change are shaped by variations in the emergence and continuity of a community's movement infrastructure. The cultivation of local leadership and the building of effective organizations are crucial steps in developing the capacity for ongoing social change efforts.

In this study, I employ two major research strategies to examine the trajectory and impact of local civil rights movements in Mississippi. First, I have assembled a quantitative county-level data set to examine the movement's impacts on electoral politics, primary and secondary schools, and social policies. Second, I completed intensive examination of three communities using archival data and informant interviews to examine *how* movements matter and the interaction of movements, opponents, and authorities. These strategies are complementary, and both are essential if we are to understand the complex dynamics of the civil rights movement and its legacy. The quantitative analysis allows for precise estimates of movement impacts and other forces shaping change, such as the social and economic characteristics of the community, the role of violence by whites, and the intervention of federal agencies and courts. The comparisons of all counties by level of movement activism present the broad patterns. The quantitative data described above carries the burden of making systematic comparisons across communities by summarizing major relationships, including patterns over time and among variables. The qualitative case studies explore the process of movement building, the tactical interaction between movements and countermovements, and many other dynamics that cannot be measured quantitatively across all counties. The case studies examine variations among counties, all of which had high levels of activism in the early 1960s, and demonstrate what these changes looked like and how they came about in specific contexts. The key strength of the case studies is to illustrate major characteristics of communities and organizations, to provide insight into the motivations and social relationships within those communities, and to demonstrate processes of change or mechanisms through which change occurs. (See appendix A for a more detailed description of the research design.) The following map (fig. 1.1) shows the patterning of movement activity in Mississippi and identifies the three case studies. Mississippi counties are grouped into three major categories of sustained, episodic, and non-movement

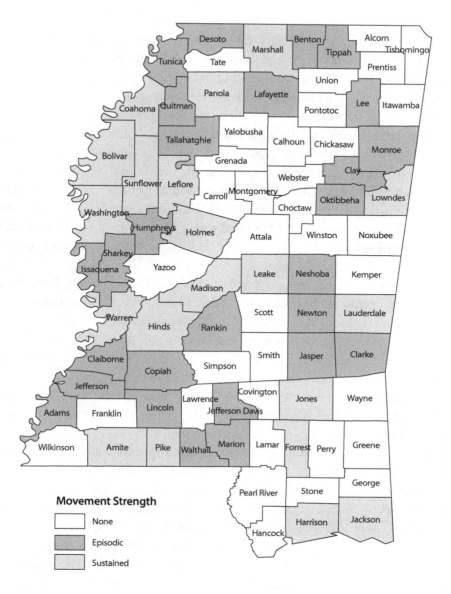

Movement Strength

(white)	None
(dark gray)	Episodic
(light gray)	Sustained

Figure 1.1. Map of Movement Counties

counties based on indicators of movement activity and organization in the early 1960s. (The indicators used for these comparisons are described in detail in chapter 4.)

Dimensions of Movement Infrastructure

I propose a movement infrastructure model for examining whether and, if so, how movements have enduring impacts. Three components of a movement's infrastructure must be examined to explain a movement's influence on social change: leadership, organizational structure, and resources. Strategies and tactics are shaped by the configuration of a movement's leadership, organization, and resource capacities. Leaders and organizations often carry particular repertoires of action and ideologies that influence the ability of movements to have lasting impacts. Infrastructures that allow the movement to employ multiple mechanisms of influence including disruption, persuasion, and bargaining will have the greatest impact across outcomes because movements must engage a complex and changing environment. This ability is crucial because, as Daniel Cress and David Snow argue, most of the impacts that movements have operate through "multiple pathways rather than through one surefire pathway or set of conditions" (2000, 1096). At a general level, I claim that the autonomy and continuity of the infrastructure are key factors explaining the long-term viability and impact of the movement, sustaining a movement through shifts in the broader political environment (Andrews 1997; Rupp and Taylor 1987). A strong movement infrastructure can spur political elites to initiate policy concessions in response to the perceived threat of the movement. Often that threat rests on the belief that a movement has the capacity to institute more substantial change through parallel, autonomous institutions (Clemens 1998; Schwartz 1976).

This argument dovetails with the work of scholars who have focused on the organizational survival of social movements (Edwards and Marullo 1995). I focus on the process by which organizational consolidation is achieved in one locale and organizational collapse occurs in another. This is based on the assumption that organizational survival is a key intervening link that allows activism to be sustained during periods of limited opportunity (Clemens 1998; Minkoff 1993; Tarrow 1994; Taylor 1989). As Debra Minkoff notes, "The very existence of associations in which people can participate should have some discernible, if not easily measurable, impact on society and, ultimately, social change" (1993, 905). The key limitation of the research on organizational persistence is the assumption that survival is associated with later influence—a claim that is rarely demonstrated.

In my argument, leadership is important for movement impact in ways that differ from most conventional accounts of organizational leadership. Rather than the individual properties of leaders, I give greater attention to the social relations of leaders to one another, to movement participants, and to the institutions targeted by the movement (for a general discussion of leadership in movements, see Aminzade, Goldstone, and Perry 2001). I draw on the arguments advanced by Aldon Morris and Belinda Robnett about civil rights leadership that emphasize the linkage between leaders and community institutions. For Morris (1984), successful movement leadership is rooted in "indigenous" organizations. This link makes leaders more responsive and less easily co-opted when they negotiate with authorities and opponents. Hence, the structural location of black ministers within community institutions made them an effective leadership base during many civil rights campaigns.

Leaders and organizations must be embedded in indigenous, informal networks. In her study of gender and leadership in the civil rights movement, Robnett (1996) distinguishes between formal leaders (e.g., ministers) and an intermediate layer of "bridge leaders" who stand at nodal points within the informal networks of a community. Movements with a simple structure of formal leaders and mass base are unlikely to be successful because bridge leaders are needed to expand participation throughout the community. Bridge leaders make co-optation of formal leaders less likely because bridge leaders can effectively connect to the demands and expectations of a movement's broader constituency. This type of leadership structure can generate ongoing tension within the movement. However, it also can provide advantages, such as innovation (Stepan-Norris and Zeitlin 1995). A differentiated leadership structure allows for communication to various audiences, including participants, potential recruits, opponents, and state actors (Klandermans 1997). A leadership structure with a diversity of skills and experiences will be better able to use mass-based tactics as well as routine negotiation with other groups, including authorities (Ganz 2000; Gerlach and Hine 1970).

The critical role of preexisting organizations and resources has been established in the emergence of social movements. To persist over time, movements must forge new organizational forms and establish independent resource flows (McAdam 1982; Schwartz 1976). In the mobilization process, the informal structure of relationships among activists and organizations must be expansive across communities and subgroups. In the policy-making process, formal organizations become a necessary vehicle for advancing a group's claims. Organizational structures can alter the routine operation of the political process when they are perceived as legitimate and/or threatening by established political actors (Clemens 1997; Gamson 1990).

Movements that rely primarily on the mobilization of people rather than on externally generated financial resources are more likely to continue using protest tactics (Schwartz and Paul 1992). As a result, their strategic and tactical options are often broader (Ganz 2000). Ultimately, movements require substantial contributions of participants to maintain organizations and launch protest campaigns. This is seen most clearly at the local level, where movement organizations are less likely to maintain a paid professional staff.

The importance of indigenous resources does not preclude the possibility that external resources can facilitate the movement or its efficacy. However, dependence on external resources makes movements vulnerable to shifts in the discretion of external actors (Jenkins and Eckert 1986; McAdam 1982). In addition, external resources often entail obligations that can constrain the movement's strategy and tactics and increase the chance of co-optation.

In the movement infrastructure model, strategy and tactics depend to a large degree on a movement's leadership, organization, and resources. This contrasts with alternative explanations that view effective protest and formal organization in conflict with one another or ignore the role of organization. Strategy and tactics are conceptualized broadly in the infrastructure model and range from protest to the building of counter-institutions. Consistent with this line of argument, Marshall Ganz (2000) has shown how the United Farm Workers were able to organize California farmworkers where more resource-rich organizations failed. According to Ganz, the UFW's leadership and organizational structure generated greater strategic capacity "if a leadership team includes insiders and outsiders, strong and weak network ties, and access to diverse, yet salient, repertoires of collective action and also if an organization conducts regular, open authoritative deliberation, draws resources from multiple constituencies, and roots accountability in those constituencies" (2000, 1005; see also Delaney, Jarley, and Fiorito 1996). Ganz's argument refers to the characteristics of a single organization, but these characteristics can also be properties of a broader field of organizations. For most social movements, the impact of the movement will be more closely tied to the collective properties of multiple organizations rather than a single challenger.[3] As a property of a single organization or set of groups, strategic capacity facilitates the ability of movements to develop creative solutions to collective problems.

In sum, strong movement infrastructures have diverse leaders and a complex leadership structure, multiple organizations, informal ties that cross geographic and social boundaries, and a resource base that draws substantially on contributions from their members for both labor and funds. These characteristics provide movements with greater flexibility that allows them to influence the policy process

through multiple mechanisms including disruption, persuasion, and negotiation. This argument differs from the main alternatives among sociologists and political scientists. I will briefly outline three major alternatives by highlighting areas of convergence and divergence with the movement infrastructure argument.

Disruption: Securing Concessions from Threat

One of the most common ways of conceptualizing movement efficacy focuses on the short-term potential of protest to win victories. The first two models of movement efficacy focus on protest, but they specify alternative mechanisms through which protest influences change—disruption and persuasion. In both arguments, mobilization has the momentary potential through an "action-reaction" process to leverage change by mobilizing political elites, electoral coalitions, or public opinion.

In the first argument, movements are dramatic, disruptive, and threatening to elites, which prompts a rapid response—typically either concessions and/or repression. Frances Fox Piven and Richard Cloward have been the primary proponents of this view, arguing that "the most useful way to think about the effectiveness of protest is to examine the disruptive effects on institutions of different forms of mass defiance, and then to examine the political reverberations of those disruptions" (1977, 24). The independent influence of protest is constrained by its role in a sequence of events. In *Poor People's Movements* (1977), Piven and Cloward raise questions about the independent impact of protest because it "wells up in response to momentous changes in the institutional order. It is not created by organizers and leaders" (36). Protest is one link in a sequence, and once the sequence is initiated, protesters have little control over the policy response. The authors conclude that "whatever influence lower-class groups occasionally exert in American politics does not result from organization, but from mass protest and the disruptive consequences of protest" (36).[4]

Organizations, particularly mass-based membership organizations, are doomed to failure because powerless groups can never mobilize as effectively as dominant groups in a society. As a result, organizations can only lessen the disruptive capacity and efficacy of protest (Piven and Cloward 1984, 1992; also see Gamson and Schmeidler 1984; A. Morris 1984). Elite reaction is ultimately focused in a self-interested way on ending protest. Analyzing urban policy changes in the 1960s, Ira Katznelson argues that "the targets of these public policies were not objects of compassion, but of fear born of uncertainty" (1981, 3). Policy makers caught off guard by protest attempt to quickly assemble a strategy of repression, concessions, or a combination of the two that will end the protest wave (Tarrow 1993). Disruption models focus on the limitations of protest on policy making beyond the agenda-setting stage.

Persuasion: Generating Support Through Symbolic Protest

In the second model, movements are dramatic and generate support from sympathetic individuals and groups that take up the cause of the movement. The intervening role of "third parties," "bystander publics," or "conscience constituents" is critical. In a classic essay, Michael Lipsky argues that "the 'problem of the powerless' in protest activity is to activate 'third parties' to enter the implicit or explicit bargaining arena in ways favorable to protesters" (1968, 1145). Lipsky claims that "if protest tactics are not considered significant by the media ... protest organizations will not succeed. Like the tree falling unheard in the forest, there is no protest unless protest is perceived and projected" (1151; also see Benford and Hunt 1992).[5]

David Garrow (1978) argues that civil rights campaigns, especially in Selma, Alabama, generated momentum for the 1965 Voting Rights Act. For some theorists, repression is an intervening link. For example, Garrow contends that attacks by southern officials on civil rights activists further solidified the support of bystanders. Paul Burstein (1985) shows that the movement did not reverse the direction of public opinion on race and civil rights. He argues instead that movements are probably unable to have such a substantial impact on opinion. Rather, protest increased the salience of the civil rights issue through protest, demonstrating the injustice of southern racism and violence. As civil rights became more important in the eyes of the American public, political representatives acted on louder and clearer signals from their constituents (Burstein 1999). In this view, protest is a form of communication, and persuasion is the major way that movements influence policy (Lohmann 1993; Mansbridge 1994).

The first two arguments focus on similar aspects of movements, but they differ on key points. The disruption model emphasizes disruptive and often violent action forcing a response from political elites, and the persuasion model proposes that protest can mobilize sympathetic third parties that advance the movement's agenda by exerting influence on political elites (see also McAdam and Su 2002 on disruptive and persuasive movement activity). Both of these action-reaction arguments share the assumption that (1) large-scale dramatic events shape the process of change by (2) mobilizing more powerful actors to advance the movement's cause, and (3) that (implicitly) movements have little or no direct influence beyond this initial point. In both models, the primary focus is on the communicative aspects of public protest events rather than on organizational form or capacity within a movement.

Negotiation: The Routinization of Protest

The negotiation model, a third major approach, argues that the determinant of movement efficacy is the acquisition of routine access to the polity through institutionalized tactics. This approach typically describes a drift toward less disruptive tactics, such as electoral politics, coalitions, lobbying, and litigation. Organization and leadership figure prominently in this model. Organizational changes parallel the tactical shift, including increasing centralization and bureaucratization of movement organizations. In order to achieve influence, social movements generate organizations that evolve into interest groups. In the negotiation model, the organizational and tactical shifts are accompanied by an increase in influence over relevant policy arenas. In contrast, the action-reaction model would predict that movement influence declines as tactics become routinized and organizations become incorporated. Most important, the access-influence model argues that disruptive tactics have little independent impact on institutional change. Rufus P. Browning, Dale Rogers Marshall, and David H. Tabb, in their study of the impacts of black and Hispanic political mobilization on a variety of policy outcomes, argue that protest and electoral strategies were used together effectively, but "demand-protest strategies by themselves produced limited results in most cities" (1984, 246).

Negotiation models also assert that securing insider status is more consequential than pursuing a single, specific policy objective. Thomas Rochon and Daniel Mazmanian (1993) argue that the antinuclear movement, by advocating a single piece of legislation, was unsuccessful. In contrast, the environmental movement, especially antitoxic groups, attempted to become a legitimate participant in the regulatory process. By gaining access, the movement has been able to have a substantial long-term impact on policy (also see Costain 1981; Sabatier 1975). In this vein, Mario Diani argues that "social movement outcomes may be assessed in terms of the movement's capacity to achieve more central positions in networks of social and political influence" (1997, 133; see also Laumann and Knoke 1987). In contrast to this negotiation model, movement organizations may achieve positions that are merely symbolic, and movements can generate leverage without directly bargaining with state actors or other authorities (Burstein, Einwohner, and Hollander 1995; Schwartz 1976).

The negotiation model has fewer proponents than the disruption and persuasion models among the sociologists who study social movements. However, the notion that "routine" tactics are most efficacious is consistent with pluralist theories of democracy that view the political system as relatively open to citizen influence. This argument would find greater support among the political scientists who study interest groups, political parties, and the policy process. From this perspective, organization building (especially professionalization, bureaucratization, and centralization) provides movements with the necessary tools to operate in the interest group system, where bargaining is the key mechanism of influence.

Comparing the Models

The movement infrastructure model that I have proposed builds on the insights of the prior three models. First, it assumes, like the disruption and persuasion models, that there are key moments when movements can be especially efficacious. Further, it assumes that disruptive tactics are important for movements to have an impact, especially when they are creatively injected into routine political processes. The movement infrastructure model differs from the others because it emphasizes the building and sustaining of movement infrastructures as an important determinant of the long-term impacts of social movements (in contrast to short-term impacts, like agenda setting). Furthermore, unlike the access-influence model, movements have the greatest impact when they maintain their ability to use both "outsider" and "insider" tactics. Litigation, lobbying, and electoral politics can be effectively employed by social movements. However, movements lose key opportunities for leverage in the political process when they quickly adopt the strategies and tactics of "interest groups" and abandon "insurgent" forms.

Although much of the debate turns on the question of the types of organizational forms that are most efficacious, organization as a concept gets used loosely in arguments and criticisms. For example, Piven and Cloward's (1977) argument is cast as a broad critique of organizations, but their real target is national membership organizations. If we distinguish forms of organizations, we can see that there is variation, with some playing a more direct role in facilitating disruption. In his analysis of the 1963 Birmingham campaign, Morris (1993) illustrates the importance of organizing for large dramatic campaigns. Forman (1972) argues persuasively that SCLC's campaign at Selma (and Albany) depended on the organizing of SNCC field-workers in Selma and nearby Lowndes County. In many cases, especially the most repressive settings, building organizations is disruptive and can be a necessary step before other forms of collective action are possible. SNCC's own measure of success was "the extent to which the people they helped bring into political activity became leaders themselves" (Payne 1995, 318). As a result, building organizational structures was itself a strategic vehicle of the movement.[6] In this study, I pursue these questions about the efficacy of different organizational forms.

Table 5.1. Voter Participation and the Level of Movement Activity

	Movement Counties		Non-Movement Counties	State
	Sustained	Episodic		
Voter Registration				
Registered black voters, 1967	4,183	1,844	992	2,025
Registered black voters, 1967 (%)	53.1	53.6	47.1	50.7
Registered white voters, 1967	10,166	5.753	5,070	6,493
Registered white voters, 1967 (%)	70.6	71.2	64.6	68.2
Black Candidates for County-level office				
Black candidates, 1967	3.0	1.5	0.5	1,4
Black candidates, 1971	6.5	3.6	1.5	3.4
Voter Turnout				
Clifton Whitley, 1966	1,661	637	240	705
Clifton Whitleym, 1966 (%)	17.8	16.7	9.7	13.9
Whhite voter turnout, 1966 (%)	42.4	48.3	44.2	45.2
Differential (white voter turnout minus black voter turnout) (%)	24.6	31.6	34.6	31.2
Charles Evers,	3,705	1,740	1,057	1,906
Charles Evens, (%)	40.2	41.4	42.5	41.6
White voter turnout, 1971 (%)	65.9	73.8/	76.4	73.1
Differential (white voter turnout minus black voter turnout) (%)	25.7	32.4	33.9	31.5
Number of counties	19	27	35	81

Note: This table reports mean values for counties.

I argue that movements are most influential when they can create leverage through multiple mechanisms. The prior three models focus on a single mechanism as the primary means by which movements create change—disruption, persuasion, or negotiation. The movement infrastructure model accounts for the ability of movements to impact political change through multiple mechanisms, and this change can occur when a movement's leadership and organization allow for strategic flexibility and innovation.

The pattern of outcomes for a movement may depend on processes described by each of these models. For example, the negotiation and persuasion models focus on agenda setting as the primary outcome that movements can influence. In contrast, access-influence and movement infrastructure models examine later stages in the policy-making process. Ultimately, researchers should use these models to compare across different types of social movements and political contexts. However, the main patterns

identified in this study demonstrate the utility of the movement infrastructure model as applied to the Mississippi civil rights movement and for understanding movement impact more broadly.

Local Movements and Electoral Participation in Mississippi

Did counties where the movement was most active have higher levels of electoral participation in the late 1960s and early 1970s than those that did not? We can begin to answer this question by looking at the summary statistics in table 5.1. Here, there are data on three forms of political participation—voter registration, the number of black candidates running for office, and voter turnout—covering the period from 1966 to 1971. In 1967 the number of black registered voters is greater in sustained movement counties than in episodic or non-movement counties. However, the actual number is influenced by the size of the black voting-age population. The percentage measure shows that counties with sustained and episodic movements have very similar levels of voter registration.

The second set of indicators presents the number of black candidates running for county-level office in 1967 and 1971. In the South, counties are the most important local political body, and it is possible to compare the efforts to win elected office. Here, the relationship of black candidates and the level of movement activity is very strong, with movement counties having much higher levels of political mobilization. Although these candidates rarely won elections during this period, their campaigns represented an important development in the longer struggle toward greater black political power.

Finally, I estimate the voter turnout for blacks and whites in two elections by candidates for statewide office—Clifton Whitley in 1966 and Charles Evers in 1971. Both candidates had been involved in civil rights organizing. Whitley, for example, held state-level leadership positions in the Mississippi Freedom Democratic Party and was an MFDP delegate to the 1964 Democratic National Convention. Evers's relationship to the movement was more controversial. His brother, Medgar Evers, had been the NAACP's field secretary in Mississippi and was shot down outside his home by Byron de la Beckwith in 1963. Charles Evers returned to Mississippi shortly thereafter, and he began building a political base in the southwest part of the state. While he was never fully embraced by many civil rights activists, he was a prominent state-level leader by the late 1960s. In the Whitley election, we see a pattern similar to voter registration where movement counties (sustained and episodic) had higher levels of black electoral participation than non-movement counties. In the Evers election, there is very little difference between the counties based on the level of movement activity (a pattern I examine more carefully below). Finally, note the indicators of turnout differential—the gap between white voter turnout and black voter turn out. The pattern here shows that increases in voter turnout in movement counties are not offset by increases in white voter turnout. Surprisingly, this differential is narrowed in movement counties, suggesting that there are relative gains for black turnout in these counties. This evidence contradicts the expectation that local civil rights activity escalated white countermobilization.[7] In the following sections, I examine these patterns of political participation in a more systematic manner to determine whether these relationships hold under more rigorous analyses.

Voter Registration

In much of the South, black voter registration had been increasing since World War II. However, in Mississippi voter registration campaigns produced very minimal increases in the early 1960s. The Justice Department had already filed suits against the registrars in several Mississippi counties, and the Southern Regional Council's Voter Education Project spent $12.13 for each new voter added between 1962 and 1964 (Lawson 1976, 284). Voter registration in Mississippi increased dramatically following the passage of the Voting Rights Act. The period from 1965 to 1971 saw substantial increases in black political participation but minimal increases in black office holding.

In 1968 the U.S. Commission on Civil Rights consolidated data on voter registration in a comprehensive report, *Political Participation*. The report documents the number of newly registered black voters in Mississippi counties, and it also indicates whether a county was assigned federal examiners between 1965 and 1967. Federal examiners were usually sent to counties that were known for their discrimination against black registrants. Deep South counties were the target of the vast majority of federal examiners, with Mississippi receiving examiners in thirty-one counties by 1967 (USCCR 1968, 244–47).[8] These data provide an initial indication of the emerging patterns of black political participation in Mississippi.

We have already seen that movement counties had slightly higher levels of black voter registration, but it is important to use techniques that account for additional factors that may influence registration levels. In table 5.2, I use an OLS (ordinary least squares) regression model to examine the factors that influence black voter registration. In addition to measures of social movement activity, I measure the impact of federal examiners and white violence on black voter registration. The size of the black voting age population in 1960 is used as a control variable in analyses for the total number of registered blacks in 1967.

The Voter Education Project argued that federal examiners had a more substantial impact on black registration rates than movement organization (Black and Black 1987, 135). The analysis I present in table 5.2 shows a greater effect for local organizing than for examiners.[9] Most significantly, I find that both organizing during Freedom Summer and NAACP membership are better predictors of a county's level of black voter registration than the presence of federal examiners, with Freedom Summer being by far the most powerful predictor.[10] These findings suggest that the resources (Freedom Summer staff and volunteers) and results (NAACP organization) of the early period of organizing were primary factors in shaping higher levels of voter registration after the Voting Rights Act.

In the next sections, I examine other forms of black political participation that have received less attention—specifically, voter turnout and the campaigns by black candidates for office. Registration is an intermediate outcome because it does not reflect particular gains for the black community but is preliminary mobilization aimed at achieving other goals.[11]

Electoral Mobilization: Voter Turnout and Black Candidates

Movement activists ran for office in several statewide elections. Often this was a strategy for unifying the local campaigns where black candidates had a much more realistic opportunity to win office. The statewide campaigns provide a way to gauge the turnout of black voters. For electoral mobilization, I have used votes cast for two black candidates, Clifton Whitley in 1966 and Charles Evers in 1971, in their campaigns for statewide office.[12]

Table 5.2. Coefficients from OLS Regression Predicting Electoral Mobilization: Voters Registered in 1967 and Votes for Two Black Candidates for Statewide Office

	Voter Registration, 1967	Whitley, 1996	Evers, 1971
Freedom Summer volunteers and staff, 1964	.358***	.229*	−.003
	(51.339)	(14.864)	(−.344)
NAACP membership, 1966	.135*	.138*	.191***
	(98.800)	(45.595)	(110.632)
Violent Resistance Index, 1960–69*	.100	.115	.022
	(15.914)	(8.235)	(2.825)
Feder5al examinersm, 1965–67	.119*	.246***	.054
	(437.704)	(408.363)	(158.858)
Black voting-age population, 1970	.400***	.423***	.796***
	(.190)	(.091)	(.301)
Percentage urban, 1970	−.066	−.050	.019
	(−5.278)	(−1.785)	(1.228)
Constant	—	—	—
	(500.937)*	(−61.768)	(149.620)
R-squared	.683	.649	.867
Adj. R-squared	.657	.621	.856

$* = p < .05; ** = p < .01; *** = p < .001$ (one-tailed tests)
Note: The standardized coefficient is presented followed by the unstandardized coefficient in parentheses.
a Although the index covers the period 1960–69, only 2 incidents out of 657 occurred after 1966.

Treating the votes cast for black candidates as an indicator of black voter turnout raises some potential questions. For example, could whites have voted for these candidates, or could blacks have voted for white candidates? Extensive research has documented the persistence of "racial bloc voting" or "racially polarized voting" throughout the South and in major cities during this period (see, for example, Loewen 1990; McCrary 1990; and Murray and Velditz 1978).[13] With votes cast for Whitley and Evers, I am assuming that only blacks voted for these candidates. Undoubtedly, some blacks voted for white candidates, as documented by the cases in which white poll watchers or employers have manipulated the black vote for white candidates (Berry 1973; Loewen 1981; Salamon 1972a), but no systematic data on such manipulation of the black vote is available by county. Moreover, votes cast for black candidates for statewide office is a useful indicator of black electoral strength because it suggests the degree to which the votes of black citizens can be coherently and effectively marshaled in support of state-level black candidates.

Like the changes in voter registration, voter turnout is examined in terms of the impact of the movement, federal registrars, and other variables noted above. The results of the analysis are presented in table 5.2. The results for the Clifton Whitley campaign are quite similar to those found for voter registration in 1967. The movement (Freedom Summer and NAACP) and federal examiners have significant positive effects on the number of votes cast for Clifton Whitley. In fact, examiners have a slightly greater effect than Freedom Summer. In 1971 the Evers campaign shows an important difference—the effects of Freedom Summer volunteers and federal examiners are no longer statistically significant. The short-term impact of federal examiners is consistent with James Alt's study of voter registration across the South that found "the absence of a significant effect [for examiners] after 1967 … [which] suggests that the relative impact of federal examiners' presence on black registration rates wore off over time" (1994, 371).

The Evers campaign for governor in 1971 appears to be a departure from the Whitley campaign in that the movement base of the early 1960s does not play a significant role; however, the NAACP variable, measuring mid-to-late 1960s movement strength, does have a significant positive effect. The pattern of black political mobilization in Mississippi did not follow a linear path through the late 1960s and 1970s, underscoring the need for multiple outcome measures. As mayor of Fayette in Jefferson County, Charles Evers's political strength was concentrated in several majority-black counties in southwest Mississippi (e.g., Claiborne, Wilkinson, Jefferson) that had had little civil rights activity from 1961 to 1965 (Berry 1973).[14] While the electoral successes of these counties have continued at the local level, they represent a different pattern of mobilization than that found in pre-1965 movement counties.

The 1967 county and state elections in Mississippi were widely viewed as the first opportunity for black Mississippians to make significant gains in office holding by building on the massive gains in registered voters. Over a hundred candidates ran for office in twenty-six counties with twenty-two candidates winning office in the November general election. While the victories were important, they were also disappointing, leading Frank Parker to conclude that "the 1967 election results were a substantial victory for Mississippi's massive resistance to black political participation" (1990, 73). As we saw in Holmes County, despite the importance of Robert Clark's election, many local leaders were surprised and disappointed by the results of the 1967 election.

In which counties were blacks most likely to launch campaigns for elected office? Table 5.3 presents the results of an OLS regression analysis predicting the number of black candidates running for office in 1967 and 1971. The same set of independent variables is used from the earlier analyses with two exceptions. The control variable, black voting-age population, is now included as a percentage of the total voting-age population.[15] A measure of voter turnout for Clifton Whitley is used as an indicator of mass participation in electoral politics in the immediate aftermath of the Voting Rights Act.

The most interesting results of the analysis are that federal examiners had no significant impact, Freedom Summer and NAACP had significant positive effects, and that violent resistance had a significant negative effect. The positive effects of Freedom Summer and the NAACP are clear indicators that the movement infrastructure had expanded to support electoral campaigns and leaders.

The statistical nonsignificance of federal examiners is interesting because the presence of examiners should indicate a greater "openness" of the polity. However another dimension of the political opportunity structure is the use of repression by elites and other actors. Here we see that the use of violence by local whites decreases the number of black candidates for office. This probably operated through a variety of avenues. Black candidates would have been more likely to experience harassment and violence in highly repressive counties, and some potential candidates may have withdrawn from elections or avoided electoral politics completely. In addition, a broader infrastructure of organizations and leaders was less likely to develop in highly repressive communities. In sum, repression minimizes the development of the movement infrastructure used to launch local campaigns.

Table 5.3. Coefficients from OLS Regression Predicting Number of Black Candidates Running for Office in 1967 and 1971

	Black Candidates, 1967	Black Candidates, 1971
Freedom Summer4 volunteers and staff, 1964	.369***	.342***
	(.081)	(.161)
NAACP membership, 1966	.159*	.193**
	(.177)	(.461)
Violent Resistance Index, 1960–69	–.192*	–.211**
	(–.047)	(–.110)
Federal examiners, 1965–67	–.091*	–.017
	(–.510)	(–.209)
Percentage vote for Whitley, 1966	.372***	.013
	(9.294)	(.676)
Proportion of the black voting-age population as total, 1970	.371***	.577***
	(6.119)	(20.351)
Percentage urban, 1970	—.061	.012
	(.007)	(.003)
Constant	—	—
	(–2.081)***	(–4.643)***
R-squared	.596	.606
Adj. R-squared	.558	.568

* = p < .05; ** = p < .01; *** = p < .001 (one-tailed tests)
Note: The standardized coefficient is presented followed by the unstandardized coefficient in parentheses.

Racial Disparities in Voter Turnout

I have already noted the impact of white violence on the number of black candidates running for office. More routine tactics were available to white Mississippians to counter black political power, including voting for segregationist candidates for local, state, and federal office. The analyses of voter registration and turnout reported above indicate absolute levels of black participation. However, electoral power is a matter of relative power, so a key indicator of change is the level of black political participation relative to white participation.

Voting patterns can be used to assess the tactical interaction between black and white mobilization. Given the persistence of racial bloc voting, we can assume that increases in white registration undermined the potential power of black voters. The trend is striking for the 1960s where "three new whites were enrolled in the Deep South for every two blacks." Earl Black and Merle Black note that "it is difficult to say how much of this huge increase … can be attributed to racism" (1987, 139). In a multivariate analysis for the entire South, James Alt finds that white registration increases were greatest in counties with high black proportions, "suggesting a continuing fear among whites of the possibility of black electoral dominance" (1994, 354). Data on white voter registration is limited for Mississippi. Instead of using the limited voter registration data, I have analyzed white voter turnout in statewide elections—the same elections reported above: Clifton Whitley's campaign for the Senate in 1966 against the incumbent James Eastland and Charles Evers's campaign for governor in 1971. I estimate white voter turnout as the votes cast for white candidates as a proportion of the white voting-age population.

Table 5.4. Coefficients from OLS Regression Predicting White Turnout Advantage in 1966 and 1971

	1966	1971
Freedom Summer4 volunteers and staff, 1964	.332**	−.049
	(−.004)	(−.0004)
NAACP membership, 1966	.134	−.231*
	(.008)	(−.011)
Violent Resistance Index, 1960–69	.022	.019
	(.0002)	(.0002)
Federal examiners, 1965–67	−.222*	−.111
	(−.064)	(−.027
Proportion black of the voting-age population, 1970	.564***	.421***
	(.478)	(.298)
Percentage urban, 1970	−.163	−.350**
	(−.001)	(−.002)
Constant	—	—
	(.208)***	(−.296)***
R-squared	.392	.359
Adj. R-squared	.343	.308

* = p < .05; ** = p < .01; *** = p < .001 (one-tailed tests)
Note: The standardized coefficient is presented followed by the unstandardized coefficient in parentheses. The racial disparity measures are determined by the proportion white turnout minus the proportion black turnout. Negative coefficients indicate smaller differences in turnout rate.

The relationship between white and black turnout is estimated by taking the difference in these two proportions. In all counties, white turnout exceeds black turnout, so this measure provides an estimate of the overall disparity in black and white electoral mobilization. This measure allows for a refinement in the earlier analysis by assessing black and white mobilization in relation to one another. For example, movement mobilization may increase black turnout and simultaneously increase white turnout at even greater levels. The same is true for federal examiners or any other of the variables analyzed above. Table 5.4 presents the results of the OLS regression models for the 1966 and 1971 elections. The primary independent variables from earlier equations are included in the analysis: early (Freedom Summer) and late (NAACP) movement organization, white violence, presence of federal examiners, and percentage urban. In addition, the proportion black of the voting-age population measures whether turnout disparities were different as the relative size of the black population increased. For the equations, negative coefficients indicate smaller differences in the level of voter turnout; in other words, the gap between black and white turnout is narrowed.

In both elections, the turnout disparity was positively related to the proportion black, which could indicate depressed rates of black turnout in these counties or increased white turnout. The latter is the case in Mississippi. In fact, black turnout is positively correlated with the proportion black in a county for both elections. For example, during the Whitley campaign, the correlation coefficient is 0.37. White turnout is related to the proportion black at an even greater magnitude; the correlation coefficient between white turnout and proportion black during this same election was 0.70. These results suggest

that the electoral threat posed by a larger black electorate generated huge turnouts by whites in 1966 and 1971.

In the Whitley campaign of 1966, the presence of federal examiners and the civil rights movement resulted in smaller disparities between white and black voter turnout. The earlier analysis showed that these two variables predicted higher levels of black voting. Importantly, examiners and movement organization also narrow the gap between black and white voting levels. Here again, the movement has a larger impact than federal examiners on the disparity. For the 1971 elections, NAACP organization and percentage urban predict smaller disparities in turnout. In short, the results reported in table 5.4 confirm that local movement organization resulted in relative gains (by narrowing the gap between black and white turnout) as well as absolute gains (more black voters). Nevertheless, white turnout rose dramatically as the proportion black in a county increased.

Study Design

In this appendix, I describe the research strategy that I have used to study the various impacts of the Mississippi civil rights movement. Building on the conceptualization of movement outcomes presented in chapter 2, I present a more detailed consideration of the empirical dilemmas for research on outcomes. This initial methodological discussion applies generally to studies of movement outcomes. In addition, I consider the Mississippi movement as a case study in terms of its strengths and limitations. The majority of the chapter focuses on the two components of the research design: the qualitative case studies and the quantitative data set of Mississippi counties. The analysis that flows from these two distinct research strategies is complementary. In fact, I argue that both are essential because each answers different types of questions about the potential impacts of movements on outcomes.

Broad Themes

Levels of Mobilization and Levels of Analysis

Like many social movements, the civil rights struggle included a combination of local, regional, and national organizations and campaigns. In this study, I give primary consideration to the local dimensions of mobilization, countermobilization, and impact. This focus is important for two reasons. First, the movement itself was based in local movement centers, despite the historiographical bias toward treating the movement as if it were a nationally coordinated movement "from above" (Morris 1984).[16] Second, by examining these smaller units, we can study the variation across the state. Here, James Button's assertion that there was local variation in mobilization and impact becomes a methodological point of leverage (1989). In an assessment of strategies for improving the explanatory power of case studies, Edwin Amenta (1991) suggests that analysis of "subunits" of the case has important advantages. His example is the distribution of New Deal programs across states. Lee Ann Banaszak (1996) follows the same strategy in her comparative study of the women's suffrage movements in the United States and Switzerland by examining state-level variation in the United States and canton-level variation in Switzerland. Obviously, for this design strategy to work, there must be variation and the subunits must be "meaningful." For example, the processes that take place within that unit must be consequential for explaining variation. With the civil rights movement, this is the case, and it turns out to be a useful strategy for examining movement outcomes in many other cases.

While keeping the primary focus on the local level, there are processes that must be examined at the state and national level to understand local movements and their consequences. These include the broader dynamics of movements, such as shifts in ideology, funding, or tactics, and changes in the opportunity structures that operate at these broader levels. For example, the collapse of COFO in the mid-1960s and the MFDP in the late 1960s originated at the state level, but these changes in movement organization impacted local movements. White resistance to black electoral power through vote-dilution tactics occurred in state legislatures as well as the municipal and county political bodies. Another example is the aggregate decline of the War on Poverty funding, which has important consequences at the local level. The rule of thumb used in this study is that I have examined these types of state and national processes when they impact on the local level in important ways. A more comprehensive explanation of the rise and decline of the War on Poverty or any other of these large-scale shifts is beyond the scope of this study.

Mobilization and Context

The questions examined in this study call for a research design that can capture the underlying dynamics of conflict and the variation from case to case. This includes the multiple actors who enter into the struggles with and against social movements. In short, the extensive collection of historical data is necessary before a balanced analysis can be made about the role of local organizing and other factors in producing social and political change. I have used two complementary research strategies for studying the movement in Mississippi, each of which corresponds to different sets of data and modes of analysis. They are as follows:

1. A quantitative county-by-county data set to examine three major groups of outcomes: (a) electoral politics, including participation and black office holding; (b) federal antipoverty programs; and (c) schools and desegregation.
2. A set of three case studies examining the variation in the patterns of movement development after 1965 at the county level. The case studies combine further archival research and informant interviews with local activists, politicians, and citizens.

The two research strategies allow for the combination of distinctive strengths found in each approach. The quantitative assessment of all Mississippi counties allows for a multivariate analysis with refined estimates of movement impact. The qualitative case studies allow us to situate these patterns in specific locales and explore the internal dynamics of the community in greater detail, especially the interplay between the movement organizations and the social infrastructure that sustains or undermines it.

The Outcome Arenas Studied

One of the major difficulties in studying the outcomes of social movements is determining exactly what outcomes to examine. This study centers on three major "outcome arenas"—electoral politics, federal poverty programs, and educational institutions. Each of these outcome arenas falls within the overall purview of local civil rights movements; however, the relative importance of each "goal" varied within the Mississippi movement as a whole and across local movements. From its origins in the early 1960s, electoral politics was the central focus of the Mississippi movement; as such, it represents a major and enduring goal, more than the other arenas. Underlying electoral politics and many of the other strategies pursued by the movement were a concern with the economic problems facing black Mississippians. The War on Poverty, then, was another arena in which local movements directed considerable energy. However, this is a more ambiguous case because movements were reluctant, fearing possible cooptation. Finally, with educational institutions, there was far less effort placed in attacking institutional inequalities in this arena.

Within each outcome arena, I have measured different types of outcomes at different points in time (following the theoretical argument I make in chapter 2). By looking at many dependent variables, I can examine differences between outcomes (voter registration vs. black elected officials) and over time. Further, increasing the number of dependent variables in this way increases the overall reliability of the study, providing greater confidence in the theoretical conclusions (Campbell 1975).

Mississippi as a Case Study

Mississippi is well suited for a study of the consequences of the civil rights movement in the South. First, the historical significance of Mississippi alone makes it worthy of close examination. During the modern civil rights movement, Mississippi was a trailblazer in developing strategies of resisting the emergence of the movement. In the period after the Voting Rights Act, Mississippi once again developed new strategies for minimizing the political power of black Mississippians. Hence, Mississippi can be treated as a test case for the South as a whole.

Second, there is sufficient variation among counties on all of the key variables to allow for careful generalization to the civil rights movement in other parts of the South (including the extent of mobilization and countermobilization, the size of the black population, class structure, and urbanization). V. O. Key, in his classic study of southern politics (1949), argued that there were "many Souths." I argue similarly that Mississippi is not monolithic. Examining one state poses certain limitations, but it also has the methodological advantage of "holding constant" variation at the state level. This is especially useful given my primary interest in local patterns of conflict and change.

However, Mississippi's "exceptionalism" should be noted. First, the coordination of a statewide movement in the early 1960s and the wide array of strategies pursued by the movement make the Mississippi case unique. In most other states, the movement worked on a city-by-city basis[17] rather than coordinating and confronting racial inequality statewide as in Mississippi. In terms of the data available, this is a clear advantage because it means that comparable evidence can be used to examine varying levels of mobilization across the state. Second, the strategies used to resist the movement were more intense and more varied than in other areas.

Unit of Analysis

For the quantitative analysis and case studies, I use counties as the unit of analysis. There are three major reasons for using counties rather than municipalities. First, the movement mobilized at the county level in Mississippi. There was often variation in the county in terms of which areas had greater levels of participation in the movement. Fortunately, the case studies allow me to examine this variation. Nevertheless, counties were a primary organizational unit because they were the most important political unit in Mississippi containing, for example, the County Board of Supervisors, the most significant political body in local southern politics (see Black and Black 1987; and Krane and Shaffer 1992). This leads to a second reason for using counties as the unit of analysis—substantially important outcomes can be measured at the county level. Finally, a large body of political research uses counties as the unit of analysis dating back (at least) to Donald Matthews and James Protho's classic study *Negroes and the New Southern Politics* (1966). Following in this tradition, the results of this study can be compared to this broader body of research (see, for example, Alt 1994, 1995; Black and Black 1987; Colby 1986; Davis 1987; James 1988; Roscigno and Tomaskovic-Devey 1994; Salamon and Van Evera 1973; Stewart and Sheffield 1987; Timpone 1995 on electoral politics; Conlon and Kimenyi 1991 on schools; and Colby 1985 on poverty programs).

Counties are useful units. However, there are some measurement difficulties to be addressed especially with educational and poverty program variables. For schools, districts are the unit by which students and resources are distributed. In Mississippi many districts are contiguous with county boundaries. However, in some cases, there are multiple districts within the same county; (there is one multicounty district for Sharkey and Issaquena counties because of the low populations in these counties). For these multidistrict counties, data can be aggregated to the county level.[18] For the multicounty district, estimates can be determined using census reports for the school-age population for blacks and whites in each county. Multiple districts were not used primarily for the purposes of segregation; rather, racially separate schools were contained within each district. Typically, in a multidistrict county, there would be a district for the county seat and a rural school district. I have tested for possible bias by comparing the single and multidistrict counties.

With poverty programs, counties were again an important unit for distributing programs and resources. However, there were some statewide and multicounty programs. Where it is possible to make county-level estimates of the distribution of poverty program funds, I have done so. For a small number of cases, statewide programs cannot be disaggregated into county-level appropriations from the information included in the Office of Economic Opportunity reports.

There is one final methodological issue concerning the county data set. Hinds County includes the state capital, Jackson, and it is a statistical outlier on many variables. For this substantive and statistical rationale, I have excluded it from the quantitative date reported throughout the book.

Statewide Quantitative Data

In this section, I describe the quantitative data set with attention directed toward the analytic issues that have been addressed with the data. The specific variables and their sources are reported in appendix D. The richness of the data set described below allows me to examine hypotheses concerning movements, conflict, and change.

First, I describe the groups of outcome measures in detail. The first set of outcomes focuses exclusively on electoral politics with four groups of indicators: (1) voter registration; (2) votes cast for black candidates in statewide elections; (3) the number of black candidates in early elections; and (4) the

number of county-level black elected officials for the years between 1974 and 1984 (before this point the numbers were too low to be meaningful at an aggregate level).

The second group of outcomes examines the expansion and distribution of public services in relation to the black community. Indicators of public services include community action programs (CAPS) and Head Start programs. Frances Fox Piven and Richard Cloward argue that political elites use public expenditures to diminish protest (1977; see also Colby 1985). Following a similar line of argument, John Dittmer argues that federal funding was initially directed toward the movement (in part because white politicians rejected the funding) but was shifted to "safer" hands as those resources became a base of power for community organizing (1993 and 1994; see also Quadagno 1994). This struggle played out over the funding for Head Start programs, and this case raises central issues concerning the constraints faced by local activists in dealing with federally funded programs. Collections of the Office of Economic Opportunity at the National Archives and Records Administration were consulted for documentation of CAP and Head Start programs in the state.

The third group of outcomes examines schools as an arena of conflict and includes measures of the extent of desegregation and the formation of private academies. The key indicator of desegregation is the dissimilarity index for selected years, and private academies are measured as the proportion of white school-age children attending these white-flight school[s]. This data provides the basis for analyzing how schools, as institutions, are shaped by the ongoing and historical residues of political conflict (see Andrews 2002).

There are two types of measures for the local movement: (1) indicators of local organizational strength and (2) indicators of the movement's capacity to mobilize the local community. Measures include the number of Freedom Summer volunteers, number of votes cast in the 1964 Freedom Vote (a mock election), number of Mississippi Freedom Democratic Party (MFDP—an independent movement-based political party) organizers in the county (1965), the number of COFO field-workers in the county prior to and following Freedom Summer, the number of NAACP members, and the amount of NAACP dues collected for the years between 1961 and 1970.

The intervention of the federal government, in this case the Justice Department, is measured by the presence of federal examiners and the number of people registered by federal examiners. This allows me to test to what extent factors external to the county impact on black electoral participation.

Measures of white resistance to the movement falls into four major categories: (1) organizations explicitly directed toward resisting the movement (e.g., Citizens' Council and Ku Klux Klan organizations); (2) violent actions taken by whites toward the movement to intimidate or stop local mobilizing; (3) the establishment of counterinstitutions to subvert the goals of the movement; and (4) "legal" resistance such as the changing of electoral procedures or boundaries.

For organizational measures, I use indicators of Citizens' Council and Ku Klux Klan organizations in the county For the summer and fall of 1964, several indicators are used that measure white harassment and violence against civil rights workers, including threats, physical assault, and shots fired at civil rights workers; here, the relative impact of different resistance strategies can be assessed. For 1960 to 1969, I have used the number of attacks of civil rights workers compiled by David Colby (1987) from organizational records and newspapers.

Finally, I have compiled many variables measuring the local social structure. In order to account for variation in demographic and economic variables among the counties, data is available from census reports and city and county data books. I have compiled data on the income and occupational structure of blacks and whites in the county, urbanization, and absolute and relative size of the black and white population (and the voting-age population).

Community Studies

In this section, I discuss the logic of case selection, describe the three communities, review the types of data used, and outline the major questions that can be answered by the community studies. Many dimensions of the development and transformation of local movements are difficult, if not impossible, to measure quantitatively for all counties. The following issues are given primary consideration through the case studies: (I) early movement strength and early participant-leaders; (2) continuity or change in the movement base leading to late movement strength or internal factionalism; (3) a changing set of participants—in terms of class position, organizational affiliations, et cetera.; (4) external movement connections—links to national organizations and resources; (5) changing demographic basis and class structure; (6) role of federal funding of poverty programs; (7) federal intervention in electoral politics—federal examiners, Justice Department suits, et cetera; (8) violent repression by whites; and (9) non-violent resistance/opposition by whites.

I utilized the same mix of data sources for each case study. Informant interviews with key participants have helped to make up for a sparse literature on the period after 1965. The interview list was constructed to tap different target groups. Major groups include movement activists from different points in time and with different organizational affiliations. In addition, elected officials and community leaders were interviewed. I employed a uniform interview protocol that focused on the level and forms of political conflict. Interview data was supplemented with a review of local weekly newspapers. Last, archival sources (described in appendix B) were examined to formulate profiles of the "movement infrastructure" that developed in the early and mid-1960s. These profiles have been assembled based on published historical work and archival research with the SNCC, CORE, and NAACP papers and the manuscript and oral history collections at Tougaloo College.

The community studies significantly strengthen the research design by focusing on the same set of outcomes (electoral politics, education, and social policies) while extending the range of data. On the question of movement strategy and infrastructure, the community studies include data about tactics that cannot be captured for all Mississippi counties, such as the formation of community centers (in Holmes and Madison), rural health clinics (Bolivar), and farming and manufacturing cooperatives (Bolivar and Holmes). It is noteworthy that the movement strategies listed here are both characteristics of mobilization and outcomes. Further, the community studies provide additional insight into the strategies used by whites toward the movement, such as the redrawing of electoral boundaries (Parker, Colby, and Morrison 1994). Last, the community studies shed light on the ways in which local social structure shaped political mobilization and consequently changes in local institutions.

Data Sources

The research for this study was derived from four major sources: (1) archival collections of participants, civil rights organizations, and government agencies; (2) informant interviews; (3) newspapers; and (4)

reports and documentation of various organizations and agencies such as the United States Commission on Civil Rights. Let me describe each in turn, highlighting the limitations and strengths of each.

Archival Collections

By far, the most valuable source of data for this study was the archival collections that document mobilization at the local level. The major collections consulted for this study are listed in appendix B. Nevertheless, one limitation of the archival collections is the almost exclusive documentation of major civil rights organizations (e.g., CORE and SNCC) and the early 1960s; this limitation is reflected in the historical scholarship. However, for the period from 1965 to 1970, extensive documentation is available in smaller collections. For an understanding of the Mississippi movement during this period, one of the most valuable collections is the Civil Rights Litigation Records at Tougaloo College. In addition to the original documents, there is a set of 170 microfilm reels, including the case and office files for the major civil rights legal organizations working in Mississippi. The activities of many local movements find their way into the Litigation Records. To paraphrase one of the activists interviewed for this study, there were civil rights lawyers behind every bush back then. The collections of various organizations were examined, including SNCC, CORE, NAACP, CDGM, and the MFDP. The Freedom Information Service Archives was another particularly valuable collection for the post-Voting Rights Act period. In addition, the collections of many individuals are available and were examined, including Fannie Lou Hamer, Ed King, Rims Barber, Charles Horowitz, and James Loewen. In addition to these movement sources, I have examined the documents of various government agencies, including the Office of Economic Opportunity, the Department of Justice, and the United States Commission on Civil Rights.

Interviews

Informant interviews provided another source of documentation that was especially important for the community studies. In each community, I conducted open-ended interviews with key participants. Individuals were selected who could comment on specific areas of the local movement and community history. In other words, I attempted to interview individuals representing different periods and organizations. A uniform interview protocol was used to provide comparable information about the internal dynamics and trajectory of local movements. Topics covered in the open-ended interview were key organizations, leadership, internal conflicts, major tactics, repression, early electoral campaigns, and participation in the War on Poverty. However, I tailored the interview to the respondent's experience and expertise, such as Head Start, the history of litigation in the community, or a specific movement organization. Using interviews to establish a community history is a difficult task, and researchers face a number of potential problems. The most important problem is the limitations of memory over an expanded time frame. This was especially acute for my study, where I was interested in establishing sequencing and detailed accounts of major events such as boycotts.

The interviews also provided data on the relations between different organizations, a (retrospective) account of the high and low points of mobilization, and the forms of repression and their effects. I conducted the interview research in tandem with the other research for this study. Like all forms of data, the interviews are strengthened when they are scrutinized in relation to other forms of data.

For example, prior to conducting the interviews, a preliminary profile and history was established for each community based on archival research and prior studies. If a respondent discussed an event or organization that I did not already have documentation on, I returned to the archival collections and local newspapers to search for independent confirmation and further documentation on a particular time period or organization.

In addition to the interviews I collected, I have drawn on interviews that have been conducted by prior researchers. These include the Tom Dent Oral History Collection conducted in the late 1970s and early 1980s, the Civil Rights Documentation Project at Howard University, and Stanford University's Project South Oral History Collection of taped meetings, discussions and interviews from 1965. Because many of these interviews were conducted in the 1960s and 1970s, they help address the memory problem in my interviews. In addition, some of the recordings are with individuals who have since died or of meetings that obviously cannot be re-created.

Newspapers

Like interviews, newspapers come with particular strengths and limitations. Newspapers were used for a number of different reasons. When reporters interviewed key informants, they can be used much as the interviews noted above to assess the ideas and tactics of key actors in the midst of conflict. In the case of Mississippi, local newspapers have to be treated with special care because they can vary widely between towns depending on the local editor. For example, in Holmes County the *Lexington Advertiser* reported extensively on movement activity, going as far as announcing meetings of the MFDP and NAACP. In Madison and Bolivar counties, local newspapers were openly hostile to the movement. In both cases, the newspapers reported infrequently on the movement. The newspapers also participated in openly repressing the movement. The *Bolivar Commercial* listed the names of parents sending their children to formerly all-white schools, inviting economic pressure and violence on these families. The *Madison County Herald* listed the names of individuals who had registered to vote in the past week as an act of intimidation. Neither paper reported movement activity beyond vague rumors. For example, in the mid-1960s, the *Bolivar Commercial* reported a rumor that civil rights activists were working in Shaw. More common were diatribes in response to events covered in the national press. The *Bolivar Commercial* pursued the "outside agitator" theory by blaming organizations like the Delta Ministry (a group sponsored by the National Council of Churches) or "Yankee" lawyers for any local activity In short, the Madison and Bolivar papers were not helpful sources for news on major campaigns (which were generally not reported) during the 1960s. For Bolivar County, the *Delta Democrat Times* from Greenville in nearby Washington County reported on movement activity. For example, the Shelby school boycott of 1968 generated numerous articles in the *Delta Democrat Times,* in contrast to the *Bolivar Commercial,* which only commented on the boycott after it ended.

For this study, I have collected extensive newspaper coverage for each of the three cases. Part of that coverage was collected from newspaper clippings in the subject files at the Mississippi Department of Archives and History (MDAH) under a broad range of topics. These subject files proved particularly helpful for the period from 1970 to 1985. By this period the major newspapers in the state, the *Clarion-Ledger* and the *Jackson Daily News,* began to report on black politics and protest more systematically. The subject files also include articles from regional and local newspapers and articles from the *Jackson*

Advocate (a black-owned newspaper), the *New Orleans Times-Picayune,* the *Memphis Commercial Appeal,* and the *Washington Post.* These files, though limited, were helpful in establishing a baseline of major protest events, political battles, and litigation within each of the communities. I followed up on key events reported in state or regional newspapers (e.g., a boycott sponsored by the United League of Holmes County in 1978) by examining local newspapers and by interviewing central actors.

In addition to the subject files, I made intensive investigation of local newspapers for selected points in time. I conducted a review of newspapers in each community during the following periods: Freedom Summer, the implementation of freedom of choice school desegregation, poverty program implementation, the formation of CAP boards, and full-scale school desegregation (for this period a search was also conducted of the *New York Times,* which reported widely on the *Alexander v. Holmes* decision and the implementation of school desegregation). In addition, searches were conducted for other periods of local mobilization and local elections.

A final methodological point on the use of newspapers: generally speaking, newspapers report on events, but not on organizations, or only incidentally on organizations as sponsors of events. For example, the *Delta Democrat Times* covered in minute detail the school boycott in Shelby during the spring and summer of 1968. The coverage was especially detailed concerning legal developments such as the curfew. The Shelby Educational Committee was noted as a sponsor of the boycott, but little investigation was made concerning the origin or development of this organization. An organization like the North Bolivar County Farm Cooperative never received substantial coverage in the local or regional press. The important point is that these limitations in the data, unless duly noted and addressed, can lead to analytic errors. The most serious error is to reproduce the notion that the civil rights movement was a series of "events" without addressing the underlying organizational developments in particular locales.

Reports and Government Documents

The last source of documentation of the Mississippi movement is reports and data generated by government agencies and other organizations. These include reports by the United States Commission on Civil Rights, the Joint Center for Political Studies, and congressional hearings. More familiar sources such as census documents are used frequently, especially for the quantitative data set; and reports published by the state of Mississippi were used for education, election returns, and other county-level data. Many of these state documents are located at the Information Services Library of Jackson State University.

NOTES

1. Numerous studies have attempted to determine the impact of key court decisions and legislative changes, including Davidson and Grofman (1994) on the Voting Rights Act, Grofman (2000) on the 1964 Civil Rights Act, and Rosenberg (1991) on major Supreme Court decisions.

2. Over the past four decades, leading scholars have reviewed the relevant literature on social movements and have noted the limited amount of systematic research on outcomes (Diani 1997; Eckstein 1965; Giugni 1998; Marx and Wood 1975; McAdam, McCarthy, and Zald 1988; Tarrow 1998). Burstein, Einwohner, and Hollander observe that "the field of social movements grew tremendously in the 1970s and 1980s, but the study of movement outcomes did not. ... [The result

is] that we still know very little about the impact of social movements on social change" (1995, 276). In the past five to ten years, this has been a growth area, and in chapter 2, I discuss recent trends in studies of movement impact in detail.

3. This may be one of the ways that unionization campaigns differ from other forms of contentious politics.

4. The literature responding to Piven and Cloward's thesis is quite extensive; see the 1993 edition of their *Regulating the Poor* for a bibliography. Two important critiques from movement scholars are Gamson and Schmeidler's "Organizing the Poor" (1984) and Morris's *The Origins of the Civil Rights Movement* (1984). See also Piven and Cloward's responses in (1984) and (1992).

5. These models of movement influence are connected to methodological strategies. For example, Rucht and Neidhardt argue that media-reported protest is a meaningful barometer of all protest: "Insofar as we are interested in those protests which are an input for the political system, media-reported protests have a higher validity than the whole range of actual protests" (1998, 77).

6. For more detailed discussion of movement organization, see Conell and Voss (1990), Minkoff (1995), Schwartz (1976), Schwartz and Paul (1992), and Staggenborg (1988).

7. This is true at least for the counties where the movement operated. Arguably, the movement could have had an impact on communities without a local movement, although it would be very difficult to determine whether or not this type of impact occurred.

8. See U.S. Commission on Civil Rights, *The Voting Rights Act: The First Months* (1965), for a detailed description of the role of federal examiners.

9. I measured the presence or absence of federal examiners in the county. Examiners provided a parallel registration process that was intended to eliminate discrimination. The Voter Education Project report (and other researchers) used the total number of blacks listed by federal examiners as an indicator of the effect of examiners. This conflates the outcome (number of registered blacks) with the facilitative role played by examiners and overestimates the effect of examiners.

10. Although direct effects of examiners were limited, there may have been indirect effects. For example, the presence of examiners may have moderated the resistance of examiners in other counties. If this were true, then the cross-sectional estimates would underestimate the overall impact of examiners.

11. A second reason for moving to other outcome measures is that the data on voter registration is the least reliable measure of political participation. Voter registration records are not kept by race, so the data used are estimates of various kinds either by local registrars or self-reported in census data. Even aggregate data on voter registration tends to be inaccurate because registrars fail to purge records on a regular basis for deaths, migration, and felony conviction (Lichtman and Issacharoff 1991).

12. Clifton Whitley ran for the U.S. Senate in the Democratic primary in August and in the general election as an independent candidate. Voter turnout in these two elections is highly correlated (r = 0.797), so I have used an average of the two as an indicator of mid-1960s black electoral mobilization.

13. "Racial bloc voting" refers to the tendency in biracial elections for whites to vote for white candidates and blacks for black candidates. In legal cases concerning discriminatory redistricting, racial bloc voting research has been important for establishing the discriminatory effect of at-large election systems.

14. These counties had no Freedom Summer projects. By 1966 Claiborne County had 1,316 adult members of the NAACP; Jefferson and Wilkinson had 924 and 889, respectively.

15. The two variables (the size and proportion of the black voting-age population) cannot be entered into the same equation without generating multi-colinearity. In table 5.2, the dependent variables require a control for the absolute size of the black electorate. In tables 5.3 and 5.4, the dependent variables require a control for the relative size of the black electorate.

16. See Payne's essay at the end of *I've Got the Light of Freedom* (1995) and Carson's essay "Civil Rights Reform and the Black Freedom Struggle" (1986) for more thorough developments of this idea. For historical analyses that focus on local patterns of mobilization, see Ceselski (1994), Chafe (1980), Dittmer (1994), Eskew (1997), and Norrell (1985).

17. The SCLC's strategy reflected this pattern by focusing on particular cities, for example, Birmingham, Selma, and Chicago. Even SNCC's work outside Mississippi was focused on one town rather than statewide.

18. Studies examining school desegregation and politics in urban areas have followed a similar strategy of aggregating across school districts to compare cities to each other.

"This is Harlem Heights"

Black Student Power and the 1968 Columbia University Rebellion

By Stefan Bradley

Introduction

This is an account of the forces of race and power and how students and community members used their race to gain power from a white American institution. More specifically, this is a story about black students on the campus of Columbia University in the City of New York allying themselves with local black politicians as well as black working class and poor residents from Harlem, the black enclave just adjacent to the school. Taking place on the Morningside Heights campus of Columbia, this tale's primary theme deals with the achievement of Black Power, which, in the late 1960s, was the goal of many young African Americans across the nation.

In essence, the second generation of the black bourgeoisie that sociologist E. Franklin Frazier described in his classic piece, *Black Bourgeoisie,* met with what may be called the "black proletariat."[2] Attempting to move away from the trappings of Frazier's first generation of black bourgeoisie members, black students (or members of the intelligentsia), who attended an Ivy League school, employed what this historian refers to as "Black Student Power."[3] The practice of Black Student Power included (but was not exclusive to) the use of the philosophies and strategies of Black Power to force predominantly white universities to capitulate to a variety of demands.

According to Stokely Carmichael (Kwame Ture) and Charles V. Hamilton, authors of *Black Power,* the achievement of Black Power for black people meant going through the processes of "self definition" and "political modernization."[4] In order to attain self-definition, black people would have to take pride in their blackness and take ownership of the issues that confronted the race. In an effort to define themselves, some black organizations in the late 1960s purged their ranks of white members and leaders, leaving black people to decide on black matters.

The process of political modernization involved three steps: "(1) questioning old values and institutions of society; (2) searching for new and different forms of political structure to solve political and economic problems; and (3) broadening the base of political participation to include more people in the decision-making process."[5] Indeed, in 1968, black students questioned white institutions and made an attempt to keep institutions of higher education from inhibiting the economic and political rights of black people. Furthermore, at places like Columbia, black students sought to give more representation and power to those whom white American institutions had previously used and neglected.

On American college campuses, some of the more popular demands of those protesters who applied the principles of Black Student Power typically involved increases in the number of black students and faculty members on campus, black studies courses and programs, black culture centers, and in the case of Columbia's protesting black students, respect and power for the neighboring black community.[6] The ultimate goal of Black Student Power was the cessation of the institutional racism that schools, colleges, and universities perpetuated as white institutions in America. In the late 1960s, black protesters like those on Columbia's campus used their status as students as a means to advance the Black Freedom struggle.

The study of black student protesters and Black Power is in no way new. Clayborne Carson, in his coverage of the Student Non-Violent Coordinating Committee (SNCC), did quite well to denote the changing philosophies of black college activists in the 1960s.[7] Similarly, William Van Deburg made a good contribution to the field in his work on the cultural victories of Black Power. In *New Day in Babylon*, Van Deburg offered useful empirical data regarding black militancy on college campuses.[8] In the 1970 work, *Black Students,* sociologist Harry Edwards also chronicled the infusion of Black Power strategies into campus life.[9] He also wrote a valuable piece concerning the rise of black militancy in the realm of collegiate and professional athletics.[10] These works, and many others, provide background literature to the campus unrest that occurred across the country in the late 1960s.

Concerning predominantly white universities in the North, several authors have ably described the black student movement. In an effort to detail the action of black students at the University of Illinois, Joy Ann Williamson has most recently published her work, *Black Power on Campus*. In it, she explains that because white institutions of higher education fostered a sense of racial hostility, black students proactively unified into black activist organizations to forge an identity for themselves in order to effect changes in "curricula, policies, and structure[s]."[11] With his 1985 piece, *Paradoxes of Protest,* William Exum focused on the issues that affected black students in a mostly white academic environment as well.[12] In a similar fashion, Richard McCormick's book, *The Black Student Movement at Rutgers,* dealt with student demonstrations on Rutger's Newark campus.[13]

Regarding activity on Ivy League campuses, several authors have come to the forefront. Wayne Glasker, in *Black Students in the Ivory Tower,* described the incidents that occurred as young black protesters demonstrated on the campus of the University of Pennsylvania.[14] Werner Sollors, Caldwell Ticomb, and Thomas Underwood constructed a documentary of *Blacks at Harvard* that covered black student activity in Cambridge, Massachusetts.[15] With his extremely thorough monograph, *Cornell '69,* Donald Downs depicted the 1969 scene that involved gun-toting demonstrators from Cornell University.[16]

In dealing with Columbia University, no one work has been devoted to the efforts of black students on the Morningside Heights campus. Authors like Jerry Avorn, who was a student at the time of the 1968 protest, have discussed in detail the role of the Columbia chapter of radical New Left organization, Students for a Democratic Society (SDS), but these authors have not gone into great detail about the work of the black student group, Students' Afro-American Society (SAS).[17] The same is true for Roger Kahn, author of *The Battle for Morningside Heights*.[18] Although Kahn points to Columbia's historically tenuous relationship with its Harlem neighbors, he does not present an in-depth analysis of SAS. Another scholar, Robert Liebert, who acted as an instructor of psychiatry at the time of the protests, did devote a good section of his volume, *Radical and Militant Youth,* to SAS's role; however, much of the discourse on the black group involved its relationship with the white students and not SAS's distinctive role in the demonstrations.[19]

Part of the reason for this neglect is the fact that these authors completed their work shortly after the 1968 protest. At the time, many protesters refused to participate in interviews (although they would later).[20] Some of the black protesters refused on the grounds that they were unsure of what repercussions university officials planned to level at the young demonstrators for their disturbance. Another reason for the relative lack of information on the activity and role of SAS rests in the over-inflated role that these authors envisioned the members of SDS playing. Granted, SDS gained national attention for the protest by drawing violence, destroying school property, and by pushing for an end to the Vietnam War and an increase in student power; however, the most tangible victory of the 1968 protest concerned SAS's tactics in blocking construction of Columbia University's proposed gymnasium in Morningside Park (the only land mass that separated the university from the neighborhoods of Harlem).[21]

This article has several purposes. First, it will highlight the efforts of black student activists on Columbia University's campus. The fact that young black people, who had the opportunity to attend an elite Ivy League university, chose to risk their chances of economic, political and social success in America for the sake of advancing the Black Freedom movement is truly remarkable and should be noted. Second, the article will show how even an Ivy League school like Columbia could not escape or shut out the invasiveness of the social movements of the 1960s; particularly, the tenets and philosophies of Black Power to confront the power and authority of university officials. Finally, this article will illustrate a tangible victory for Black Power.

As William Van Deburg pointed out in *A New Day in Babylon,* many of Black Power's victories were cultural in nature, e.g., cultural identification, redefinition, and cultural pride. Admittedly, the tangible achievements of Black Power have not always been so apparent. With that in mind, SAS's and the Harlem community's ability to keep the university from building the gym in Morningside Park marked one of those tangible victories. By forcing the university not to build a gym in the park, the black protesters won not only space for the Harlem community, but also the respect of Columbia University decision makers who could never approach the Harlem community in the same way again.

COLUMBIA AS A NEIGHBOR

To understand this controversy, it is necessary to note the relationship of Columbia to the city of New York and black residents. Originally, Columbia University had not been located on Morningside Heights, which stretches from 110th to 125th street on its west side and from Morningside Park to the Hudson River on its east side. As early as 1775, the institution, then known as King's College, actually sat on the land of the Trinity Episcopal Church at Broadway and Wall streets. Later in 1897, it moved to what was known as Morningside Heights because, according to George Nash, author of *The University and the City,* Columbia University was attempting to "escape" the encroachment of the city onto the campus.[22]

Until World War II, the neighborhoods of Morningside Heights remained starkly white in population. As black southerners migrated to the North during the first and second Great Migration, some found their way to Morningside Heights while most moved to nearby Harlem.[23] The fact that blacks chose to live in an area that had traditionally been reserved for Columbia's faculty members and students motivated the university to intensify its efforts to "escape" certain elements of the city. In 1967, Jacques Barzun, a provost at Columbia University, believed that the neighborhoods that surrounded the school were becoming "uninviting, abnormal, sinister, and dangerous."[24] Along the same lines, the Faculty Civil Rights Group of Columbia University, which did a study on the university's policy in regards to the

Morningside Heights neighborhood, quoted one of the university planners as stating: "We are looking for a community where the faculty can talk to people like themselves. We don't want a dirty group."[25]

As Columbia did not employ one full-time black faculty member until 1969, it is clear what the planner meant by "people like themselves." It is also clear, given the rising population of black and Puerto Rican residents of Harlem and Morningside Heights, that the planner was referring to the non-white dwellers of the surrounding community as elements of the "dirty group." Whiteness and white privilege for staff members like Barzun and the university planner had made it possible for them to see whiteness as somehow culturally clean or natural and blackness as otherness.[26] In essence, the statement implied that the arrival of so many blacks and Puerto Ricans "dirtied up" the once clean (white) group of Morningside Heights residents. Consequently, it became one of the objectives of the university to clean up the "sinister" and "dirty" area surrounding the school.

To sanitize the nearby neighborhoods, Columbia embarked upon a project—purchasing a great deal of land and buildings in Morningside Heights and Harlem neighborhoods. Ostensibly, the purpose for these purchases was to create more space for the students and to construct more campus buildings. Incidentally, more than a few of the edifices that the university bought had provided homes for poor and minority residents. The fact that Columbia owned Single Room Occupancy (SROs) buildings would later fuel the controversy between the university and Harlem residents, who believed that the school was using its power to take homes and space away from black people.

SROs were originally apartment buildings, but because of the weakness of the market, in the late 1940s and early 1950s, they were separated and rented out as rooms.[27] Initially, students used these SROs as dwellings; however, later, poorer and more elderly people took over the residences because of the inexpensive rent. Some of the tenants were those who had had troubles with the law, such as prostitutes and various roguish types. As Gilbert Osofsky noted in *Harlem: The Making of a Ghetto,* Harlem was once the home of a renaissance, but with the decline of municipal services, the influx of drugs, and the removal of job opportunities for its residents, the black enclave withered rapidly. Within this declining economy, land values became even cheaper. This cheapness of land provided an impetus for Columbia University to expand its domains.

The relationship between Columbia and city residents was further weakened by the university's alleged landlord policies. Roger Kahn, who wrote about the 1968 controversy, claimed that Columbia was one of "the largest and most aggressive landlords on earth," and that more than half of its assets ($280 million) were in land, buildings, and mortgages.[28] Maintaining that the trustees of the university were the invaders, *The Worker,* a socialist paper, alleged that "Columbia made war on its Harlem neighbors" without regard to their need for shelter and homes.[29] While the word "war" might have been an extreme description of Columbia's acquisition policies, it was quite clear that the university intended to expand its holdings in spite of the complaints and concerns of residents and neighbors.

Bolstering the arguments of *The Worker* article, several residents of Columbia-owned SROs decried the removal tactics that Columbia used on those who dwelled in the university's buildings. One resident, Yvelle Walker, explained that after the university told her to move from her apartment, she subsequently found a wax-like substance in her lock, preventing her from re-entering her home.[30] Another tenant observed that the university would ask residents to leave and if they did not leave fast enough, then the residents would find themselves without the use of heat, which was the case in one of the university's buildings during the winter of 1967–1968.[31]

The results of Columbia's efforts to remove tenants in the Morningside Heights and Harlem areas are notable. Robert Liebert, who also documented the 1968 rebellion, found that in the decade of the 1960s, the university purchased ISO housing units used mostly by blacks and Puerto Ricans. During that period, the university facilitated the displacement of 7,500 people, approximately 85 percent of whom were black or Puerto Rican.[32] When the university appointed a committee to find out the causes of the 1968 protest, the commission found that one of the primary causes regarded Columbia's insensitivity in tenant removal. It pointed to one university publication that stated "Morningside Heights has been cleaned up. … All but two of the worst SRO houses have been eliminated, and nobody really regrets their passing."[33] Surely somebody regretted "their passing."

Concerning space, Columbia University further antagonized the residents of Harlem and Morningside Heights with its use (rather misuse) of Morningside Park. During the 1950s, the university leased five acres of land from the city to construct softball fields in the park.[34] The school would use the fields for the recreation of its undergraduate men. The city authorized the lease of the land, but only under the stipulation that Columbia make the fields open to the public free of charge. Early on, Columbia upheld its end of the bargain by sponsoring community little league play.[35] In fact, at that point, the university had invested nearly $25,000 into the community athletic program.

Toward the end of the 1960s, however, the situation changed when the fields were all too frequently locked and unavailable to the community.[36] Needless to say, seeing the locks on the gates of the fields embittered the black residents of Harlem and Morningside Heights who also needed recreational space. By making the field available to only university affiliates, Columbia was using its economic prowess to place its need for space above that of black city residents. Many feared that the construction of a gymnasium in the park would end with the same results.

This scene, along with national turmoil, precipitated the events that came to a head in 1968. The Black Power movement did not occur in a vacuum; it was the result of building racial tension in America. During the 1960s, Harlem, and many other black communities throughout America experienced civil unrest. In 1960, in Greensboro, North Carolina, black students from North Carolina A&T attempted to integrate the city through lunch-counter sit-ins.[37] Three years later, Lee Harvey Oswald assassinated President John F. Kennedy, whose constituency included many African Americans. At the same time, the black Muslim movement thrived, and civil rights leader Martin Luther King, Jr. articulated his dream of racial harmony. Although Congress had passed the Civil Rights Act of 1964, the long hot summer of that year saw yet another riot in Harlem after an off-duty police officer killed a black youth.[38] The next year, as King marched in the South, several black Muslim men assassinated Malcolm X in Harlem, and, that summer, the Watts section of Los Angeles exploded with racial violence.[39]

A CHANGE IS COMING

Between 1965 and 1968, racial tension in the United States spiked. In the mid and late 1960s, the government increasingly called upon many young black men to fight the Vietnam War, and those not drafted struggled to find employment.[40] This and many other factors spurred the birth of Black Power, which advocated separation along racial lines. By 1968, Black Power had reached its pinnacle, and unrest among many black people appeared especially intense. Moreover, the April 4, 1968, murder of

King further unsettled many black communities. In the neighborhoods of Harlem, which sit adjacent to Columbia University, people poured into the streets, rioting and grieving the murder of their leader.[41] Many black citizens blamed the prejudice and discrimination of white America for these incidents. The black people, who lived next to the Ivy League school in Manhattan, saw the institution as a representative of white oppression, and the university subsequently became a target of their frustration.

Using this frustration as fuel, the black community members would eventually lash out at the multimillion-dollar gymnasium that Columbia planned to build in Morningside Park. The fact that Columbia, in order to compete with other Ivy League universities, needed to build a new gymnasium brought the school into direct confrontation with residents of Harlem, who also wanted to enjoy the recreational space that the park provided.[42] To deal with this, Columbia, under pressure from city officials, offered to allow non-university affiliates use of two of the ten floors of the structure the school would build.[43] When the plan was submitted in 1958, there was little controversy involved because of the relatively mild political climate and because the school had not brought the idea to the community.[44]

By 1967, the political and social atmosphere of Harlem and the rest of the nation had changed a great deal, and because of this, the idea of a predominantly white private institution building a structure in a public, predominately black, community park, did not go over so well. Part of this rising controversy had to do with the fact that Columbia, although making provision to allow city residents use of the facility, had misrepresented the amount of space that would be allotted for community use. Instead of the 20% of the structure that many residents expected to have available (Columbia had previously set aside two of ten floors), the facility really only offered 12.5 percent of the space for the community.[45] Making matters worse was the fact that the community part of the structure had an entirely different entrance than university affiliates would use. Reminiscent of the days of legalized public segregation, this prompted some city officials, residents of Harlem and Morningside Heights, and students to refer to the university's proposed recreational facility as "Gym Crow."[46]

At this point opposition to the gymnasium grew steadily.[47] A part of the opposing contingent was Black Power activist H. Rap Brown, who, at one point, headed up SNCC, the organization that took the lead in the Black Power movement. In 1967, Rap Brown, at a Harlem community rally against the gym, offered some advice to residents concerning university builders and the gym. He said: "If they build the first story, blow it up. If they sneak back at night and build three stories, burn it down. And if they get nine stories built, it's yours. Take it over, and maybe we'll let them in on the weekends."[48] Although Rap Brown used references to explosions and burning as rhetoric, it would not have been difficult for Columbia officials to recall riots that took place in Harlem in which several white-owned businesses were burned and destroyed[49] In this way, the potential for the destruction of the gymnasium, if built against the will of the community, became very real for the university.

The Road to Black Student Power

Starting in the late 1960s, emissaries from SAS had been attending local meetings to find out the issues that affected the neighboring black community.[50] While at these local gatherings, the members of SAS learned of the gym controversy and decided to take on the community's protest as their own. SAS saw the proposed gym in the park as a symbol of racism and as a struggle for control over land in the adjacent neighborhoods.[51] Because of the school's proximity to a black community, the nearly one hundred black students at Columbia who made up SAS could readily become activists for the Black Freedom struggle.

One observer of SAS believed that the black group had ulterior motives in taking up the protest against the gym. The observer claimed that the role of SAS in the 1968 controversy "was to dramatize the unresponsiveness of the University primarily to them," and not necessarily that toward the community of Harlem.[52] To be sure, like many black student groups across the nation, when Columbia's SAS started in 1964, it did strive to create an identity for itself.[53] To do so, it protested for an increased number of black students and faculty, as well as changes to the university's curriculum. The idea, however, that the group took on the gym to bring attention to itself was unfounded. Furthermore, in the view of the black students, they struggled for more than their own advancement. Their larger concern was for the interests of their race, because of the commonality of their race, the students and community members shared a bond in their battle.[54]

By 1968, another campus group, SDS, had taken on the gymnasium as a protest issue.[55] As a chapter of the nationwide organization, Columbia's SDS, led by Mark Rudd, a junior from New Jersey, had previously demonstrated against the presence of an ROTC program on campus, the arrival of CIA recruiters, as well as Columbia's ties to the Institute for Defense Analysis (IDA).[56] IDA was a consortium of higher level universities that received funding from the government to research war weaponry and strategy. These issues, SDS believed, brought the university into a direct relationship with the controversial war in Vietnam. While the radical group might have been correct in its assessment of the university's relationship with the war effort, until 1968, none of the organization's protest efforts had stirred the mostly apathetic student body on Columbia's campus to social action. Because of this, SDS needed an issue that directly affected the students on campus.[57] That issue became the gymnasium in the park.

SDS's timing in inserting the gym as an issue on its protest platform was impeccable. The April 4, 1968, death of King and the riots that occurred afterward weighed heavily on the hearts of a great many Americans and more than a few college students. Taking advantage of this situation, at a memorial for King, SDS leader Rudd pointed to the university as a racist institution for attempting to honor the fallen civil rights activist and at the same time continuing with its plans to build the gym in the park.[58] This was a view that SDS and SAS shared.

Although the two groups had never worked together before, SDS and SAS would come together during a campus protest on April 23, 1968. SAS members such as Raymond Brown and Cicero Wilson, both undergraduates, and William Sales, a graduate student, watched and listened at the sundial in the middle of campus as members of SDS denounced the university and its implicit relationship to the war as well as the university's poor treatment of its black neighbors.[59] From the start, the black group made clear what its role in the protest would be. After gaining the attention of the growing crowd of mostly white students, SAS leader Cicero Wilson explained that "this is Harlem Heights, not Morningside Heights," implying that Columbia University was part of a mostly black residential area and that the residents in that area had just as many rights as the university to make decisions that would affect their homes and community.[60] He continued by asking the mostly white crowd what it would do if somebody tried to commandeer its property.[61]

While at the sundial, Rudd suggested that the crowd stage an indoor protest in Seth Low Library, the university administration building. When that effort was blocked, Rudd urged the crowd to take the protest to the construction site of the gymnasium. After an altercation between the protesters and the police took place there, Rudd, at the encouragement of another SDS leader, led the crowd back to campus.[62] It was apparent that SDS's leadership did not have a clear plan as to how the protesters would implement their demonstration. Consequently, the members of SAS had grown frustrated with the back and forth decision making that SDS used.[63] In a reactionary moment, SAS's leadership further clarified its role. Venting its frustration, Wilson intimated that his group intended to take over the demonstration: "SDS can stand on the side and support us … but the black students and the Harlem community will be the ones in the vanguard."[64]

Rudd, who had just been upstaged, asked Wilson what his proposals were.[65] Wilson responded that SAS had not "proposed" to do anything but to keep the university from building the gymnasium.[66] Furthermore, he stated, the idea that proposals were necessary for the protest inferred that white leaders wanted to decide which path black people should take to end construction on the gym, and that would be unacceptable.

In 1966, that very same sentiment amongst the white leadership of SNCC struck a militant cord amongst many black participants, who, until that point, had been willing to share the leadership of the organization.[67] The result of that controversy culminated in the group's purging itself of white membership and calling for Black Power. Wilson's statements about taking the vanguard and allowing the community to decide for itself what was best were very much in line with the tenets of Black Power, which advocated that blacks take the leadership in matters that would primarily affect them and their communities. At that point, it became clear to all the protesters that SAS's main concern was with the gymnasium and the university's mistreatment of the adjacent neighborhoods.

Wilson's statements took Rudd and many of the white protesters by surprise because they believed that blacks and whites would attack Columbia together as an integrated front.[68] In turn, SAS members began to wonder if SDS was using them to enhance its ideological "revolution."[69] Taken aback by Wilson's inferences, Rudd maintained that SDS was indeed serious about helping to end racism, but that its style of leadership was just different. He exclaimed that it was not indecisiveness that led the protesters back and forth; instead, it was the radical group's adherence to participatory democracy, a leadership style that allowed the members of a group to have as much decision making power as the leader(s).[70]

This particular style was markedly different from the styles and strategies that Black Power groups employed. By the late 1960s, members of Black Power organizations like SNCC, Congress of Racial Equality (CORE), the Black Panthers, as well as predominantly black groups in general, tended to elect their leadership. After the leaders took their offices, the leaders would develop plans with the people who elected them in mind. These group leaders even asked for contributions from the various memberships; however, once the leadership solidified its plans, then the groups typically adhered to the plan.[71] Furthermore, discipline was extremely essential to the operation of Black Power and black organizations, and this trait was not wasted on the members of SAS, who urged the white leadership of SDS to practice more of it.

One of the comments that university officials frequently made about the black student protesters concerned SAS's strict discipline and determination to carry out goals. Part of this was undoubtedly due to the fact that many of the members of SAS participated in civil rights organizations as well as black Greek-letter organizations even before the protest.[72] Concerning the white radical group, some school officials claimed they had absolutely no respect for the SDS led protesters, who often destroyed school property, participated in violence, or refused to discuss the demands that the radical group had set.[73]

As far as the current protest was concerned, SAS leadership, seeing the potential effectiveness of a black-white coalition decided to go along with SDS a little while longer.[74] Although the philosophy of Black Power advised black groups against making coalitions with radical white groups, the philosophy clarified that it was not advisable to do so if the black group is less powerful than the white.[75] In this case, it was very probable that at the time the members and leadership of SAS believed that, with the backing of the Harlem community and various other city officials, SAS had at least as much power as the SDS led white protesters.

After reassessing the situation, Rudd and SDS led the expanding group of 400 protesters into Hamilton Hall, a classroom building. There, the army of demonstrators surrounded a dean's office, in essence forcing the dean to remain there.[76] What happened afterward, really pointed up the influence that Black Power had on the leadership of SAS. While the racially mixed group had entered the building as one, that situation soon changed. SAS and SDS disagreed over which tactics to take in securing the building. SDS's leadership wanted to hold a sit-in, allowing people to come in and out of the building. Conversely, SAS leadership wanted to barricade the doors and not allow anybody in or out of the building.[77] At the time, SAS's strategy of barricading the building and disallowing traffic was fairly new to campus protest; furthermore, it was a significantly more militant stance than was the sit-in.

The matter was settled late into the night when Black Power leader H. Rap Brown arrived with a Harlem contingent. To the group of onlooking white demonstrators he stated: "I'd like to tell you that the Harlem community is now here and we want to thank you for taking the first steps in this struggle." Moreover, he asserted, "the black community is taking over."[78] After some befuddlement, and some encouragement from the black leadership, SDS left Hamilton and eventually entered four more campus buildings.[79] SAS and Rap Brown had made the point; in this situation Black Power would prevail and the black protesters would not confuse the community issues with those of the radical white group.

While SDS leadership had placed the gymnasium at the top of its list of protest demands, there were several more items on the list that could have clouded the issue. Some of those items included amnesty for the current protesters and protesters involved in previous demonstrations; the creation of a tripartite disciplinary board that allowed students, faculty members, and administrators to make decisions involving students; and finally, SDS demanded that the school cut ties to the Institute for Defense Analysis.

Granted, these demands were extremely valid and important, but as SAS leadership realized, those were not demands directly related to the neighboring black community and the way that Columbia was using its power to take advantage of black people. To focus the attention on the issues of the community, the members of SAS believed that only they and their invited guests should occupy Hamilton Hall. With that in mind, SAS released the dean from his office and bid SDS farewell.[80]

For the next week, SAS maintained it own separate protest in Hamilton as the ousted white demonstrators took over four other buildings. While in Hamilton, the members of SAS enjoyed the support and assistance from Harlem well-wishers. At the onset of the protest, SAS sent emissaries to Harlem to inform the community of the protest and to ask for food and monetary donations. From patrons in local clubs and restaurants, the black group, within hours, received more than $100 in donations.[81] Throughout the week, families from the community dropped off food donations at Hamilton Hall. While standing outside of Hamilton Hall on the rainy second night of the students' occupation, one mother from Harlem explained that "rain or no rain, I don't care. We must support these young people. They went out on a limb for us. ... I for one am coming back and bringing them hot, nourishing food."[82]

Furthering the cause, black politicians, activists, and high school students came to join SAS's efforts. Politicians such as Basil Paterson and Percy Sutton appealed to then Mayor John Lindsay and school officials to end construction on the gymnasium.[83] Members of black militant organizations from Harlem such as the Mau Maus and the United Black Front also arrived on campus to protest the gym with the black students.[84] Activists like H. Rap Brown and Stokely Carmichael used their fame to help the black student demonstrators. Although SAS leadership would not allow the two activists to make decisions on behalf of the student group, Rap Brown and Carmichael assisted by relaying the demands and messages of the group to the media when the press imposed a "black out" on the students in Hamilton Hall. When speaking to the press, the activists declared their support for the group inside. "If the university doesn't deal with our brothers in there, they're going to have to deal with the brothers out on the streets," explained Carmichael.[85] At one point during the week, black high school students with bats, clubs, and sticks marched onto campus to help SAS in its protest. Although the members of SAS had to tell the high school students to "cool it," the student group appreciated the generosity of the community. Other community members offered moral support.

The Harlem community enveloped the black student protesters with support. As one Harlem resident, the Reverend Sam, thought about the actions of the black students, he commented that when SAS commandeered Hamilton Hall, it was like "the invasion of the ivory tower."[86] Similarly, letters and articles in the black newspaper, the *New Amsterdam News*, expressed pride in the maturity and determination of the black student protesters.[87] Highlighting the support of the community, one *New Amsterdam News* headline read: "Harlem Backs Columbia Sit-in."[88]

This particular protest over the gymnasium was able to do what few protests in the history of black America could effectively do. It brought together black people from different socioeconomic backgrounds and black people who fell on opposite sides of the political spectrum to accomplish one goal. As the politically moderate black senator, Basil Paterson, admitted, he "would stand with anyone [including the likes of H. Rap Brown] against the racist gym."[89] This was remarkable, and it displayed the quintessence of Black Power.

For centuries, white people had practiced and maintained "white power" by crossing lines of class and coming together along racial lines. After Nathaniel Bacon's Rebellion in 1676, white people were able to ally themselves along racial lines to assert their place in society.[90] The same occurred when the Ku Klux Klan mustered members from the ranks of both politicians and sharecroppers to deal with blacks during Reconstruction and even into the twentieth century.[91] This carried on during the Jim Crow era, and even into modern politics, when presidential candidates like Richard Nixon used his "southern strategy" to stabilize a white southern constituency at the expense of black progress.[92]

With the gym protest that SAS maintained, black people coalesced in much the same way, and the effects were crippling for the university. On April 25, the pressure of the black protesters forced school officials to suspend construction on the gymnasium indefinitely. When school officials, in an effort to end the ever-growing demonstration of student power, brought 1,000 police officers onto campus, the protest turned sour. At this point, black students saw the university acquiescing to SAS's demand for the end of gym construction, so the black group decided to leave the building non-violently and without incident. In fact, several black lawyers were present to ensure that the mostly white police force did not mistreat the students as the students were being arrested.[93]

Meanwhile, the mostly white student protesters, who had left Hamilton and taken over four other campus buildings, met with danger. For the SDS led demonstrators in those buildings, the situation was not the same as it was for the black students in Hamilton. In the newly occupied buildings, violence erupted between students and police officers, who in an effort to clear the buildings, used their batons to beat male and female students. By the morning of April 30, some 700 students had been arrested and countless more had been traumatized by the violence. The result of the incident was a six-week student strike that shut the university down.[94]

CONCLUSION

Columbia University witnessed a tremendous show of power during the spring protest of 1968. It saw determined students who believed in their demands regarding student power and an end to school ties to the Vietnam War. It also observed concerned black students who would not allow a white institution to take advantage of black people. These children of the black bourgeoisie sacrificed their class stability to advance the cause of their race. In this rare case, members of SAS, by taking on the gym in Morningside Park as an issue, brought together community residents, local black politicians, and militant black activists for a single purpose. Together, the group of anti-gym activists exercised the essence of Black Power.

The members of SAS, using what they had learned from the growing Black Freedom movement, advanced the movement by employing Black Student Power. For this protest, that meant separating from white protesters to allow black people to define the goals and strategies of black people, as well as taking over buildings to disturb university operations and to draw attention to a particular issue. Subsequently, these would be tactics that protesting black students would use at other Ivy League schools in the North.[95] In the end, the group achieved its goal of halting the gym's construction, and SAS won respect for the neighboring black community. Because of these black students' efforts, Columbia, although still powerful and rich in land holdings, could never approach Harlem in the way it did before the protest in 1968.

In a larger sense, the protest marked a tangible victory for the national Black Freedom movement. The Columbia Rebellion taught American universities and institutions that black people would use their collective power to protect what black people perceived as "their" space. The battle to end "Gym Crow" showed that, in spite of their class differences, black people would actively confront institutional racism and they would look to their race as a form of empowerment. In the end, Columbia never built the gym in Morningside Park, but there are those who still remember when Black Power "invaded the ivory tower."[96]

NOTES

1. Stefan Bradley is an Assistant Professor in the Department of Historical Studies at Southern Illinois University, Edwardsville.

2. E. Franklin Frazier, *Black Bourgeoisie* (New York: The MacMillan Company, 1970), 193–194.

3. For an interesting discussion regarding the second generation of the black bourgeoisie, see Paula Giddings, *When and Where I Enter: The Impact of Black Women on Race and Sex in America* (New York: William Morrow and Company, Inc., 1984), 272–273.

4. Kwame Ture and Charles V. Hamilton. *Black Power: The Politics of Liberation* (New York: Vintage Books, 1967,1992), 34–39.

5. Ibid.

6. For discussion on the topic of black student activism in America, please see *The Journal of African American History*, vol. 88, no. 2, spring 2003.

7. Clayborne Carson, *In Struggle: SNCC and the Black Awakening of the 1960s* (Cambridge: Harvard University Press, 1981).

8. William Van Deburg, *A New Day in Babylon: The Black Power Movement and American Culture, 1965–1975* (Chicago: University of Chicago Press, 1993), 64–81.

9. Harry Edwards, *Black Students* (New York: Free Press, 1970).

10. Harry Edwards, *Revolt of the Black Athlete* (New York: Free Press, 1970).

11. Joy Ann Williamson, *Black Power on Campus: The University of Illinois, 1965–1975* (Champaign: University of Illinois Press, 2003), 1.

12. William Exum, *Paradoxes of Protest: Black Student Activism in a White University* (Philadelphia: Temple University Press, 1985).

13. Richard P. McCormick, *The Black Student Protest Movement at Rutgers* (New Brunswick: Rutgers University Press, 1990).

14. Wayne Glasker, *Black Students in the Ivory Tower: African American Student Activism at the University of Pennsylvania, 1967–1990* (Amherst: University of Massachusetts Press, 2002).

15. Werner Sollors, Caldwell Titcomb, and Thomas Underwood, eds., *Blacks at Harvard: A Documentary History of African-American Experience at Harvard and Radcliffe* (New York: New York University Press, 1993).

16. Donald Downs, *Cornell '69: Liberalism and the Crisis of the American University* (Ithaca: Cornell University Press, 1999).

17. Jerry Avorn, *Up Against the Ivy Wall: A History of the Columbia Crisis*, (New York: Atheneum, 1968).

18. Roger Kahn, *The Battle for Morningside Heights: Why Students Rebel* (New York: William Morrow and Company, Inc. 1970).

19. Robert S. Liebert, *Radical and Militant Youth: A Psychoanalytic Inquiry* (New York: Praeger Press, 1971).

20. Joanne Grant, *Confrontation on Campus: The Columbia Pattern for the New Protest* (New York: Signet Books, 1969), 111.

21. Frederic Law Olmsted, Jr. and Theodore Kimball, *Frederick Law Olmsted, Landscape Architect, 1822–1903* (New York: GP Putnams, 1922); SB Sutton, *Civilizing American Cities, A Selection of Frederick Law Olmsted's Writing on City Landscapes* (Cambridge: MIT Press, 1971).

22. George Nash, *The University and the City: Eight Cases of Involvement*, (New York: McGraw-Hill Book Company, 1973), 95.

23. For a discussion of the rise and results of the Great Migration and Harlem, see Gilbert Osofsky, *Harlem: The Making of a Ghetto* (New York: Harper and Row Publishers, 1963), 15–34.

24. Nash, *The University and the City*, 97.

25. Ibid.

26. David Roediger, *The Wages of Whiteness and The Making of the American Working Class* (New York: Routledge, Chapman, and Hall, 1991), 14 and 19; Roediger, *Colored White: Transcending the Racial Past* (Berkeley: University of California Press, 2002).

27. Daniel Bell and Irvin Kristol, eds., *Confrontation: The Student Rebellion and the Universities* (New York: Basic Books, 1968), 110.

28. Kahn, *The Battle for Morningside Heights*, 82–83.

29. *The Worker* (New York), 17 May 1968.

30. Kahn, *The Battle for Morningside Heights*, 86.

31. Douglas Davidove, Assadour Tavitian, Teymour Darkhosh, and Michael Stama te Latos, "What do the Tenants of the Occupied Buildings Say?" 17 May 1968, Columbiana Collection, Columbia University, New York.

32. Liebert, *Radical and Militant Youth*, 36.

33. *Crisis At Columbia: Report of the Fact-Finding Commission Appointed to Investigate the Disturbances at Columbia University in April and May 1968* (New York: Random House 1968), 39. Hereafter *Cox Commission Report, Crisis at Columbia.*

34. Roger Starr, "The Case of the Columbia Gym," *The Public Interest,* 107; Peter Millones, "Gym Controversy Began in Late 50's," *New York Times,* 25 April 1968, 50.

35. *Partners in the Park* (New York), March 1968, Columbiana Collection, Columbia University, New York.

36. Dwight C. Smith, "Letter to the Editor," *New York Times,* 20 May 1966, 46.

37. John Salmond, *"My Mind Set on Freedom": A History of the Civil Rights Movement, 1954–1968* (Chicago: Ivan R. Dee, 1997), 81–84.

38. *Kerner Report: Report of the National Advisory Commission on Civil Disorders* (New York, 1968), 206.

39. For a complete discussion on Watts riots, see Jerry Cohen and William Murphy, *Burn, Baby, Burn: The Watts Riot* (New York: Avon Books, 1966).

40. Wallace Terry, *Bloods: An Oral History of the Vietnam War by Black Veterans* (New York: Ballantine Books, 1984), xiii.

41. Terry Anderson, *The Movement and the Sixties: Protest in America from Greensboro to Wounded Knee* (Oxford: Oxford University Press, 1995), 192.

42. Columbia Gymnasium Committee, "The New Columbia Gymnasium," Columbiana Collection of Columbia University, New York.

43. Bell and Kristol, eds., *Confrontation,* 118.

44. Kahn, *The Battle for Morningside Heights*, 92.

45. Starr, *The Public Interest,* 114–116.

46. Ibid., 118.

47. Opposition to the gym included then Democratic Mayor John Lindsay, Parks Commissioner Thomas Hoving, Senator Basil Paterson, Manhattan Borough President Percy Sutton, and numerous community environmental and civic groups. "Politicians Would Prevent Construction in Morningside Park," *New York Times,* 17 May 1966, 49; Kahn, *The Battle for Morningside Heights,* 94; "M. M. Graff to the Editor of the *New York Times*" 25 April 1968, Collins Collection of the Archives, Schomburg Center for Research in Black Culture, New York Public Library, New York; Sara Slack, "Columbia Students In Siege," *Amsterdam News,* 27 April 1968, 37.

48. Avom, *Up Against the Ivy Wall,* 20.

49. *Kerner Report, 35; 206.*

50. William Sales, interview by author, 25 March 1999, telephone interview, Columbia, Missouri.

51. Stephen Donadio, "Columbia: Seven Interviews," *Partisan Review,* vol. 25, no. 3 (1968) p. 376.

52. *Cox Commission Report, Crisis at Columbia,* 17.

53. "Black and Latin at Columbia," Barnard College Archives, Barnard College, New York.

54. Sales interview

55. Kahn, *The Battle for Morningside Heights,* 108.

56. *Cox Commission Report, Crisis at Columbia,* 63–69.

57. Alan Adelson, *SDS: A Profile* (New York: Scribner's Sons, 1972), 7.

58. Kahn, *The Battle for Morningside Heights,* 108.

59. Ronald Fraser, *1968: A Student Generation in Revolt* (New York: Patheon Books, 1988), 171–172.

60. Avorn, *Up Against the Ivy Wall,* 40–41.

61. Ibid.

62. Grant, *Confrontation on Campus,* 45. [6]

63. Sales Interview.

64. Avorn, *Up Against the Ivy Wall*, 41.

65. Kahn, *The Battle for Morningside Heights*, 126.

66. Avorn, *Up Against the Ivy Wall*, 47.

67. James Forman, *The Making of Black Revolutionaries* (New York: The MacMillan Company, 1972), 497–504; Carson, *In Struggle*, 191–214. William Van Deburg, ed., *Modern Black Nationalism: From Marcus Garvey to Louis Farrakhan* (New York: New York University Press, 1997), 123–124.

68. Avorn, *Up Against the Ivy Wall*, 47.

69. Twenty years after the 1968 rebellion, Rudd recalled that he had actually "bought into the fantasy of a revolution." Keith Moore, "Only Make-Believe Says Student Rebel," *New York Daily News,* 22 April 1988, 1. SAS leader Ray Brown claimed that from the start of the protest, the members of SAS had no pretenses about a revolution, instead they were fighting to stop the construction of a gymnasium. Raymond Brown, interview by author, 24 November 1999, telephone interview, Columbia, Missouri.

70. Adelson, *SDS,* 207.

71. For a thorough discussion of SNCC's leadership, see Forman, *The Making of Black Revolutionaries,* 411–444.

72. Raymond Brown Interview.

73. David Truman, interview by John Wooter, 4 October 1968, Oral History Collection, Columbia University, New York, NY.

74. Sales interview.

75. Ture and Hamilton, *Black Power,* 59–84.

76. Grant, *Confrontation on Campus,* 46.

77. Raymond Brown interview.

78. Grant, *Confrontation on Campus,* 58.

79. Avorn, *Up Against the Ivy Wall,* 187–189.

80. Raymond Brown interview.

81. *Columbia Revolt,* produced and directed by the students of Columbia University, 60 min., Third World Newsreel, 1968, video cassette.

82. Allon Schoener, ed., *Harlem on My Mind: Cultural Capital of Black America, 1900–1968* (New York: Random House, 1968), 238.

83. Avorn, *Up Against the Ivy Wall*, 182–183.

84. David Bird, "300 Protesting Columbia Students Barricade Office of College Dean," *New York Times* (New York) 24 April 1968, 1; 30.

85. Columbia *Daily Spectator* (New York) 27 April 1968, 1.

86. Reverend Samuel N. Brown, interview by author, 22 November 1997, New York, hand-written notes, the "Pan Pan" restaurant, Harlem, New York.

87. *Amsterdam News,* 11 May 1968, 18.

88. Ibid., 4 May 1968, 1.

89. Kahn, *The Battle for Morningside Heights,* 96.

90. Edmund Morgan, *American Slavery, American Freedom: The Ordeal of Colonial Virginia* (New York, 1975), 266–267.

91. Nancy MacLean, *Behind the Mask of Chivalry: The Making of the Second Ku Klux Klan* (Oxford: Oxford University Press, 1994), 52–53.

92. Kenneth O'Reilly, *Nixon's Piano: Presidents and Racial Politics from Washington to Clinton* (New York: The Free Press, 1995), 6–8, 279–329.

93. Grant, *Confrontation on Campus,* 93.

94. "Six Weeks that Shook Morningside: A Special Report," *Columbia College Today,* spring 1968, 65–66.

95. See Sollors, Titcomb, and Underwood, eds., *Blacks at Harvard*; Lawrence Eichel, *The Harvard Strike* (Boston: Houghton, Mifflin, 1970); Downs, *Cornell '69* ; Glasker, *Black Students in the Ivory Tower.*

96. Reverend Sam Interview.

BLACK FEMINIST THOUGHT

BLACK FEMINISM, KNOWLEDGE, AND POWER

By Patricia Hill Collins

BLACK FEMINIST THOUGHT AS CRITICAL SOCIAL THEORY

Even if they appear to be otherwise, situations such as the suppression of Black women's ideas within traditional scholarship and the struggles within the critiques of that established knowledge are inherently unstable. Conditions in the wider political economy simultaneously shape Black women's subordination and foster activism. On some level, people who are oppressed usually know it. For African-American women, the knowledge gained at intersecting oppressions of race, class, and gender provides the stimulus for crafting and passing on the subjugated knowledge[1] of Black women's critical social theory (Collins 1998, 3–10).

As an historically oppressed group, U.S. Black women have produced social thought designed to oppose oppression. Not only does the form assumed by this thought diverge from standard academic theory—it can take the form of poetry, music, essays, and the like—but the *purpose* of Black women's collective thought is distinctly different. Social theories emerging from and/or on behalf of U.S. Black women and other historically oppressed groups aim to find ways to escape from, survive in, and/or oppose prevailing social and economic injustice. For African-American women, critical social theory encompasses bodies of knowledge and sets of institutional practices that actively grapple with the central questions facing U.S. Black women as a collectivity.

The need for such thought arises because African-American women as a *group* remain oppressed within a U.S. context characterized by injustice. This neither means that all African-American women within that group are oppressed in the same way, nor that some U.S. Black women do not suppress others. Black feminist thought's identity as a "critical" social theory lies in its commitment to justice, both for U.S. Black women as a collectivity and for that of other similarly oppressed groups.

Historically, two factors stimulated U.S. Black women's critical social theory. For one, prior to World War II, racial segregation in urban housing became so entrenched that the majority of African-American women lived in self-contained Black neighborhoods where their children attended overwhelmingly Black schools, and where they themselves belonged to all-Black churches and similar community organizations. Despite the fact that ghettoization was designed to foster the political control and economic exploitation of Black Americans (Squires 1994), these all-Black neighborhoods simultaneously provided a separate space where African-American women and men could use African-derived ideas to craft distinctive oppositional knowledges designed to resist racial oppression.

As mothers, othermothers, teachers, and churchwomen in essentially all-Black rural communities and urban neighborhoods, U.S. Black women participated in constructing and reconstructing these oppositional knowledges. Through the lived experiences gained within their extended families and communities, individual African-American women fashioned their own ideas about the meaning of Black womanhood. When these ideas found collective expression, Black women's self-definitions enabled them to refashion African-influenced conceptions of self and community. These self-definitions of Black womanhood were designed to resist the negative controlling images of Black womanhood advanced by Whites as well as the discriminatory social practices that these controlling images supported. In all, Black women's participation in crafting a constantly changing African-American culture fostered distinctively Black and women-centered worldviews.

Another factor that stimulated U.S. Black women's critical social theory lay in the common experiences they gained from their jobs. Prior to World War II, U.S. Black women worked primarily in two occupations—agriculture and domestic work. Their ghettoization in domestic work sparked an important contradiction. Domestic work fostered U.S. Black women's economic exploitation, yet it simultaneously created the conditions for distinctively Black and female forms of resistance. Domestic work allowed African-American women to see White elites, both actual and aspiring, from perspectives largely obscured from Black men and from these groups themselves. In their White "families," Black women not only performed domestic duties but frequently formed strong ties with the children they nurtured, and with the employers themselves. On one level this insider relationship was satisfying to all concerned. Accounts of Black domestic workers stress the sense of self-affirmation the women experienced at seeing racist ideology demystified. But on another level these Black women knew that they could never belong to their White "families." They were economically exploited workers and thus would remain outsiders. The result was being placed in a curious *outsider-within* social location (Collins 1986), a peculiar marginality that stimulated a distinctive Black women's perspective on a variety of themes (see, e.g., Childress 1986).

Taken together, Black women's participation in constructing African-American culture in all-Black settings and the distinctive perspectives gained from their outsider-within placement in domestic work provide the material backdrop for a unique Black women's standpoint. When armed with cultural beliefs honed in Black civil society, many Black women who found themselves doing domestic work often developed distinct views of the contradictions between the dominant group's actions and ideologies. Moreover, they often shared their ideas with other African-American women. Nancy White, a Black inner-city resident, explores the connection between experience and beliefs:

> Now, I understand all these things from living. But you can't lay up on these flowery beds of ease and think that you are running your life, too. Some women, white women, can run their husband's lives for a while, but most of them have to … see what he tells them there is to see. If he tells them that they ain't seeing what they know they *are* seeing, then they have to just go on like it wasn't there! (in Gwaltney 1980, 148)

Not only does this passage speak to the power of the dominant group to suppress the knowledge produced by subordinate groups, but it illustrates how being in outsider-within locations can foster new angles of vision on oppression. Ms. White's Blackness makes her a perpetual outsider. She could never be a White middle-class woman lying on a "flowery bed of ease." But her work of caring for White women allowed her an insider's view of some of the contradictions between White women thinking that they are running their lives and the patriarchal power and authority in their households.

Practices such as these, whether experienced oneself or learned by listening to African-American women who have had them, have encouraged many U.S. Black women to question the contradictions between dominant ideologies of American womanhood and U.S. Black women's devalued status. If women are allegedly passive and fragile, then why are Black women treated as "mules" and assigned heavy cleaning chores? If good mothers are supposed to stay at home with their children, then why are U.S. Black women on public assistance forced to find jobs and leave their children in day care? If women's highest calling is to become mothers, then why are Black teen mothers pressured to use Norplant and Depo Provera? In the absence of a viable Black feminism that investigates how intersecting oppressions of race, gender, and class foster these contradictions, the angle of vision created by being deemed devalued workers and failed mothers could easily be turned inward, leading to internalized oppression.

But the legacy of struggle among U.S. Black women suggests that a collectively shared, Black women's oppositional knowledge has long existed. This collective wisdom in turn has spurred U.S. Black women to generate a more specialized knowledge, namely, Black feminist thought as critical social theory. Just as fighting injustice lay at the heart of U.S. Black women's experiences, so did analyzing and creating imaginative responses to injustice characterize the core of Black feminist thought.

Historically, while they often disagreed on its expression—some U.S. Black women were profoundly reformist while more radical thinkers bordered on the revolutionary—African-American women intellectuals who were nurtured in social conditions of racial segregation strove to develop Black feminist thought as critical social theory. Regardless of social class and other differences among U.S. Black women, all were in some way affected by intersecting oppressions of race, gender, and class. The economic, political, and ideological dimensions of U.S. Black women's oppression suppressed the intellectual production of individual Black feminist thinkers. At the same time, these same social conditions simultaneously stimulated distinctive patterns of U.S. Black women's activism that also influenced and was influenced by individual Black women thinkers. Thus, the dialectic of oppression and activism characterizing U.S. Black women's experiences with intersecting oppressions also influenced the ideas and actions of Black women intellectuals.

The exclusion of Black women's ideas from mainstream academic discourse and the curious placement of African-American women intellectuals in feminist thinking, Black social and political theories, and in other important thought such as U.S. labor studies has meant that U.S. Black women intellectuals have found themselves in outsider-within positions in many academic endeavors (Hull et al. 1982; Christian 1989). The assumptions on which full group membership are based—Whiteness for feminist thought, maleness for Black social and political thought, and the combination for mainstream scholarship—all negate Black women's realities. Prevented from becoming full insiders in any of these areas of inquiry, Black women remained in outsider-within locations, individuals whose marginality provided a distinctive angle of vision on these intellectual and political entities.

Mammies, Matriarchs, and Other Controlling Images

Intersecting oppressions of race, class, gender, and sexuality could not continue without powerful ideological justifications for their existence. As Cheryl Gilkes contends, "Black women's assertiveness and their use of every expression of racism to launch multiple assaults against the entire fabric of inequality have been a consistent, multifaceted threat to the status quo. As punishment, Black women have been assaulted with a variety of negative images" (1983, 294). Portraying African-American women as stereotypical mammies, matriarchs, welfare recipients, and hot mommas helps justify

U.S. Black women's oppression. Challenging these controlling images has long been a core theme in Black feminist thought.

As part of a generalized ideology of domination, stereotypical images of Black womanhood take on special meaning. Because the authority to define societal values is a major instrument of power, elite groups, in exercising power, manipulate ideas about Black womanhood. They do so by exploiting already existing symbols, or creating new ones. Hazel Carby suggests that the objective of stereotypes is "not to reflect or represent a reality but to function as a disguise, or mystification, of objective social relations" (1987, 22). These controlling images are designed to make racism, sexism, poverty, and other forms of social injustice appear to be natural, normal, and inevitable parts of everyday life.

Even when the initial conditions that foster controlling images disappear, such images prove remarkably tenacious because they not only subjugate U.S. Black women but are key in maintaining intersecting oppressions (Mullings 1997, 109–30). African-American women's status as outsiders becomes the point from which other groups define their normality. Ruth Shays, a Black inner-city resident, describes how the standpoint of a subordinate group is discredited: "It will not kill people to hear the truth, but they don't like it and they would much rather hear it from one of their own than from a stranger. Now, to white people your colored person is always a stranger. Not only that, we are supposed to be dumb strangers, so we can't tell them anything!" (Gwaltney 1980, 29). As the "Others" of society who can never really belong, strangers threaten the moral and social order. But they are simultaneously essential for its survival because those individuals who stand at the margins of society clarify its boundaries. African-American women, by not belonging, emphasize the significance of belonging.

U.S. Black Feminism in Transnational Context

Shifting to a global analysis not only reveals new dimensions of U.S. Black women's experiences in the particular matrix of domination that characterizes U.S. society, but it also illuminates how a transnational matrix of domination presents certain challenges for women of African descent. Intersecting oppressions do not stop at U.S. borders. Intersecting oppressions of race, class, gender, sexuality, and nation constitute global phenomena that have a particular organization in the United States. Nested within this U.S. version are distinctive group histories characterized by a unique combination of factors. U.S. Black women's experiences constitute one such group history that can be seen in the context of the particular social movements within the United States, the domestic policies of varying levels of U.S. government, and a global matrix of domination affecting women of African descent in general. Black women in Nigeria, Trinidad and Tobago, the United Kingdom, Botswana, Brazil, and other nation-states are similarly located. They encounter the contours of local social movements, the policies of their nation-states, and the same global matrix of domination in which U.S. Black women are situated. All of these groups of women thus are positioned with situations of domination that are characterized by intersecting oppressions, yet their angle of vision on domination will vary greatly.

Shifting to a transnational context also brings women's rights activities to the forefront of discussion (Lindsay 1980). In a transnational context, women in African, Latin American, and Asian nations have not sat idly by, waiting for middle-class, White women from North American and Western European nation-states to tell them what to do. Instead, using the United Nations as a vehicle, women from quite diverse backgrounds have identified gender oppression as a major theme affecting women transnationally (see, e.g., *Rights of Women* 1998). These women are not just "theorizing" about oppression; their theory emerges from within the practical terrain of activism.

Within this broad transnational context, women of African descent have a distinctive, shared legacy that in turn is part of a global women's movement. At the same time, due to the peculiar combination of the legacy of African cultures, a history of racial oppressions organized via slavery, colonialism, and imperialism, and an emerging global racism that, assisted by modern technology, moves across national borders with dizzying speed, women of African descent encounter particular issues. For example, just as African-American women constitute one of the poorest groups within the United States, so do Black women in Brazil. Similarly, in the context of global women's poverty, women in Africa remain among the poorest. In this sense, women of African descent share much with women's rights struggles globally, but do so through particular Black diasporic experiences characterized by substantial heterogeneity.

Despite the national barriers that separate women of African descent, Black women's experiences demonstrate marked similarities that "illustrate how the persistence of the legacy of colonialism with its racial/ethnic, sexist and class biases has resulted in a system of 'global gendered apartheid'—a global economic system characterized by the exploitation of the labour of women of colour everywhere" (Antrobus 1995, 55). In this context, as social theorist Obioma Nnaemeka points out, "as people of African descent, our attention should not be solely on how blacks in Africa and those in the African Diaspora are *related with* each another, but also on how they *relate to* each other" (1998, 377). One task, then, lies in stimulating dialogue across the very real limitations of national boundaries, to develop new ways of relating to one another, in order to unpack the interconnectedness of Black women's experiences.

Black Women in Transnational Context

Placing African-American women's experiences in a transnational context simultaneously provides a new angle of vision on U.S. Black feminism as a social justice project and decenters the White/Black binary that has long plagued U.S. feminism. Within the U.S. White/Black framework, U.S. Black feminism can be seen only as a derivative movement. African-American women who self-define as Black feminists can be accused of being "White" identified, as if no independent Black feminist consciousness is possible. Refracted through the lens of U.S. race relations that sees Blacks as sidekicks, followers, and dependent beings, this interpretation has surface validity. Within assumptions that one need not consider anything outside U.S. national borders, these Black/White dialogues become intensified and can work to drown out other issues. When these debates are taken to their logical extreme, U.S. feminism can become one huge discussion about identity—as Black and White women, why can't we get along?

Placing U.S. Black women's experiences in a transnational context shifts this understanding of U.S. Black feminism. Instead of being White feminism in blackface, the core themes of U.S. Black feminism resemble similar issues raised by women of African descent elsewhere. Issues that are of great concern to U.S. Black women—work and family, negative controlling images, struggles for self-definition in cultural contexts that deny Black women agency, sexual politics that make Black women vulnerable to sex work, rape, and media objectification, and understandings of motherwork within Black women's politics—find different meanings in a transnational context. As Andree Nicola McLaughlin points out, "The proliferation of Black women's organizations in the last decade signals a global phenomenon. Such organized political activity on the part of self-identified 'Black women' reflects a burgeoning, intercontinental Black women's consciousness movement" (1995, 73). Rather than being a White-identified anomaly within U.S. Black community development efforts, U.S. Black feminism can better be seen as part of an "intercontinental Black women's consciousness movement" that addresses the common concerns of women of African descent.

If common concerns link women of African descent transnationally, why don't more U.S. Black women see them? Certainly U.S. school curricula dedicated to glorifying American history and culture as well as a U.S. media that substitute news entertainment for serious coverage of global issues leave all U.S. citizens, including African-American women, ignorant of major world issues. But another important factor concerns U.S. Black women's relationships with two groups most closely aligned with African-American women's interests. Via their control over U.S. feminism and Black intellectual discourse, respectively, White American women and Black American men constitute two groups with which and through which African-American women construct U.S. Black feminism. Both groups may be well meaning, and in fact may express deep-seated concern for Black women's issues. But both groups find it difficult to get out of the way and encourage a fully articulated, Black feminist agenda where Black women are in charge.

Some strands of White Western feminism have been tireless in raising women's issues in defense of women who remain suppressed and therefore unable to speak for themselves. This is important work and often leads to valuable coalitions among First and Third World women. Yet the kinds of coalitions among groups such as these can become problematic. Because the groups remain so unequal in power, this inequality can foster a pseudo-maternalism among White women reminiscent of how U.S. middle-class social workers approached working-class, immigrant women in prior eras. The much-bandied-about accusation of racism in the women's movement may be much less about the racial attitudes of individual White women than it is about the unwillingness or inability of some Western White feminists to share power. These conflicts remain muted when the power differences among women are vast—the case when the interests of poor, rural, non-American Black women are championed by Western feminists. Yet when the power differentials shrink—the case of Black American and White American women who are seemingly equal under U.S. law—relationships become much more contentious.

U.S. Black men exercise a different kind of control. Here discourses of Black Nationalism with their implicit counsel of a racial solidarity built on unquestioned support of African-American men stifles dialogue. Whereas the majority of African-Americans would most likely not identify themselves as "Black nationalists," most do ascribe to many of the basic tenets of Black Nationalist-influenced ideologies that counsel Black self-determination (Franklin 1992). The historical viciousness and deeply entrenched nature of White supremacy in the United States makes this a rational response. Blacks may be the ones who are accused of "holding" onto race, but it is White Americans who move out of neighborhoods when Blacks move in. White Americans are the ones who want affirmative action programs in higher education dismantled, even if such efforts effectively bar African-American access to elite colleges. It is White Americans whose failure to vote for Black candidates forces civil rights organizations to remain embroiled in legal battles to find ways of ensuring Black representation under the rubric of American democracy. In this context, Black Nationalism is not irrational—it has been essential for Black progress. However, despite their contributions, not all Black nationalisms are the same. But they do seem to share one common feature, namely, a norm of racial solidarity based on Black women's unquestioned support of Black men without extracting a similar commitment on the part of Black men to Black women. In contrast to White women's maternalism, U.S. Black women are encouraged to embrace a Black paternalism, one where Black men reclaim their manhood because Black women "let them be men."

Not only are both of these political responses unacceptable, the energy required to deal with both White women and Black men leaves little left over to engage in dialogue with other groups, both within the United States and transnationally. But a U.S. Black feminism that does not do so runs the risk of quickly running out of steam. It is important to remember that just as African-American women are neither African nor American, neither is U.S. Black feminism. Instead, it occupies its own space that reflects the privileges of U.S. citizenship juxtaposed to the second-class nature of that citizenship. However, while U.S. Black feminism occupies this location between Americanness—the struggles with White feminists and with Black men—and women of African descent globally, the lion's share of its attention has been directed at American groups. As a result, U.S. Black feminism has been preoccupied with responding to the issues raised by American groups. The task now lies in fleshing out dialogues and coalitions with Black women who live elsewhere in the Black diaspora, keeping in mind that intersecting oppressions have left a path of common challenges that are differently organized and resisted.

Common Differences

Positioning African-American women within a transnational context suggests that U.S. Black women occupy a both/and status regarding U.S. feminism, Black diasporic feminisms, and transnational women's rights activism. On some dimensions, U.S. Black feminism resembles that of women within and from Black diasporic societies, while on other dimensions, it remains distinctively American. Collectively, these common areas of concern link the feminisms of women of African descent within a broader transnational context. They also provide a useful starting point for examining the common differences that characterize an intercontinental Black women's consciousness movement, one responding to intersecting oppressions that are differently organized via a global matrix of domination.

On the one hand, intersections of race and gender that frame the category "Black women" generate a shared set of challenges for all women of African descent, however differentially placed in other social hierarchies we may be. For example, not all Black women are poor, but Black women as a collectivity remain disproportionately poor. On the other hand, differences among Black women reflecting our diverse histories suggest that experiences with poverty will be far more complex than currently imagined. African-American women may be disproportionately poor, but Black women's poverty in the United States is organized differently from that confronting women of African descent transnationally. Despite the similarity of concerns, Black women in Africa, the Caribbean, South America, Canada,

and other places experience these concerns differently and, as a result, organize in response to them differently.

Groups, Coalitions, and Transversal Politics

The complexities of African-American women's group experiences challenge simple hierarchies that routinely label affluent White men as global oppressors, poor Black women as powerless victims, with other groups arrayed in between. Instead, race, gender, class, citizenship status, sexuality, and age shape any group's social location in the transnational matrix of domination. These locations in turn frame group participation in a wide range of activities. Because groups occupying different positions display varying expressions of power, they have distinctive patterns of participation in shaping domination and resistance. Coming to terms with these diverse group histories provides a new foundation for developing a transversal politics.

Originally coined by Italian feminists, transversal politics emphasizes coalition building that takes into account the specific positions of "political actors." As Nira Yuval-Davis describes it, "Transversal dialogue should be based on the principles of rooting and shifting—that is, being centered in one's own experience while being empathetic to the differential positioning of the partners in the dialogue ... the boundaries of the dialogue would be determined by the message rather than its messengers" (1997, 88).Within this framework, African-American women and other comparable groups constitute "political actors" or "messengers" aiming to craft a Black feminist "message." Within the assumptions of transversalism, participants bring with them a "rooting" in their own particular group histories, but at the same time realize that in order to engage in dialogue across multiple markers of difference, they must "shift" from their own centers.[2]

This recognition of how the experiences of Black women in Africa, the Caribbean, the United States, Europe, and Latin America demonstrate common differences generates several important issues concerning the contours and potential effectiveness of transversal politics. First, transversal politics requires a basic rethinking of cognitive frameworks used to understand the world and to change it. Transversal politics requires rejecting the binary thinking that has been so central to oppressions of race, class, gender, sexuality, and nation. Under such models, one must be one thing or the other—Black women are poor *either* because they are Black or because they are women. One is either a racist or an antiracist individual, a sexist person or not, an oppressor group or oppressed one. In contrast, transversal politics requires *both/and* thinking. In such frameworks, all individuals and groups possess varying amounts of penalty and privilege in one historically created system. Within U.S. history, for example, White women have been penalized by their gender but privileged by their race and citizenship status. Similarly, Black heterosexual women have been penalized by both race and gender yet privileged by their sexuality and citizenship status. In a transnational context, U.S. Black women are privileged by their citizenship yet disadvantaged by their gender. Depending on the context, individuals and groups may be alternately oppressors in some settings, oppressed in others, or simultaneously oppressing and oppressed in still others.

A second and related issue associated with transversal politics concerns definitions of how social groups are organized and maintained. Long-standing views of group organization see groups as fixed, unchanging, and with clear-cut boundaries. In contrast, the view advanced here retains historically constructed groups, but perceives these groups as being much more fluid. U.S. Black women's experiences illustrate this fluidity. Just as each individual African-American woman has a unique biography that reflects her experiences within intersecting oppressions, the experiences of U.S. Black women as a collectivity reflect a similar process.[3] Group boundaries are not fixed. Within the U.S. context, this more fluid notion of groups suggests that African-American women as a collectivity encounter a particular configuration of race, class, and gender politics that, while overlapping with those of some groups, resembling those of others, and differing from still others, remains distinctive to Black women. U.S. Black women's placement in a transnational context suggests a similar set of relationships. Thus, as an historically identifiable population, U.S. Black women are simultaneously privileged and penalized within a matrix of domination. Within any matrix of domination characterized by intersecting oppressions, any specific social location where such systems meet or intersect generates distinctive group histories.

A third requirement of transversal politics concerns the internal dynamics of groups. For U.S. Black women, engaging in processes of group self-definition requires confronting the entire constellation of our history, not just a selective reading of it. Via these internal dialogues, African-American women potentially take one important step toward transversal politics. These private conversations required for group self-definitions can be affirming. For example, the safe spaces that African-American women carve out for self-definitions have been designed to protect Black women from external assaults. The mirrors that Black women hold up to one another in such spaces can be affirming. But the existence of these spaces does not mean that ugliness does not occur in safe spaces. As Black lesbians point out, safe spaces are safer for some than for others.

Moreover, what quickly becomes apparent is that these internal processes of self-definition cannot continue indefinitely without engaging in relationships with other groups. Since groups are not hermetically sealed entities, coming to terms with a particular group history leads to the realization that groups can neither define themselves in isolation nor resist social injustice on their own. At best, each group possesses a partial perspective on its own experiences and on those of other groups. The critical self-reflection and community organizing accomplished via coming to terms with one's own group history builds the foundation for effective coalition. For example, it's not enough to see that "Nigerian and U.S. Black women have been victimized" and to build an alliance solely on the foundation of shared victimization. The reality is that while Black women's victimization in these two settings may be similar, it is not the same. Instead, coalitions are built via recognition of one's own group position and seeing how the social location of groups has been constructed in conjunction with one another. Empathy, not sympathy, becomes the basis of coalition.

This recognition stimulates a fourth issue associated with transversal politics, namely, recognizing that group histories are relational. It is important to remember that U.S. Black women's group history remains interdependent with those of other groups—patterns characterizing one group's experiences are intimately linked to those of other groups. For example, in the U.S. context, the social construction of U.S. White womanhood as pure, fragile, and in need of protection from the assaults of "violent" African-American men required the use of differential patterns of institutionalized sexual violence against both African-American women and men. The transnational context reveals similar contradictions. U.S. Black women may encounter state violence within the United States, but U.S. nation-state foreign policies inflict comparable violence upon women outside U.S. borders. Both domestically and transnationally,

through threats of violence or actual violence, groups actively police each other to ensure that domination is maintained.

Examining these interdependent group histories often reveals painful contradictions. It becomes more difficult, for example, for U.S. White women to retain moral credibility as survivors of sexual violence without simultaneously condemning the benefits that accompany racial violence enacted on their behalf. Similarly, claims by some African-American men that racial oppression is more fundamental than gender oppression sound hollow in a context of shirked responsibility for their violence against African-American women. Both cases reflect how White women and African-American men *both* experience the victimization that can serve as a foundation for building empathy with other groups, *and* bear some responsibility for systemic violence targeted to other groups. These examples suggest that moral positions as survivors of one expression of systemic violence become eroded in the absence of accepting responsibility for other expressions of systemic violence.

This recognition of relational group histories leads to a fifth issue associated with transversal politics, namely, the acknowledgment that coalitions with some groups are not possible. This is because while group experiences are interdependent, they are not equivalent. Even though, for example, U.S. White men and African-American women both have group histories that reflect patterns of privilege and oppression, these groups are far from equal in the transnational matrix of domination. Instead, each group reflects a distinctive constellation of victimization, access to positions of authority, unearned benefits, and traditions of resistance. While the histories of both groups reflect all dimensions, the patterns within each group will differ based on the overall placement of the group in relation to other race/gender groups, as well as variations within the group stemming from class, citizenship status, sexuality, and age.

This non-equivalency fosters a final important dimension of transversal politics—the dynamic nature of coalitions. Coalitions ebb and flow based on the perceived saliency of issues to group members. This non-equivalency of group experience means that groups find some oppressions more salient than others. Patterns of common differences among U.S. Black women and women within and from Black diasporic societies speak to the saliency of one form of oppression over another across different social settings. Race, class, and gender represent the three axes of oppression that African-American women routinely identify as being most important to them. But these systems and the economic, political, and ideological conditions that support them may not be seen as the most fundamental oppressions by women of African descent transnationally. This is one important feature of the matrix of domination—whereas all systems operate in framing the experiences of Black women transnationally, different configurations of such systems have saliency for Black women differently placed within them.

Overall, Black feminist knowledge and the transversal politics that might guide Black women's activism share important features. Both rely on paradigms of intersectionality to conceptualize intersecting oppressions and group behavior in resisting them. Both are collaboratively constructed, making it virtually impossible to extract either from actual power relations. Both exhibit moments of collaboration and confrontation necessary for constructing knowledge and building coalitions. Despite the tensions between sameness (race/gender inter-sections) and difference (class, citizenship, sexuality, and age) that distinguish the experiences of Black women in the Caribbean, the United States, Africa, Latin America, and Europe, it is important to recognize that women of African descent remain differentially placed within an overarching transnational context characterized by a global gendered apartheid. As a result, dialogues among African-American women and other historically identifiable oppressed groups should benefit from the multiple angles of vision that accompany multiple group standpoints. These dialogues not only promise to shed light on current issues within U.S. Black feminism, they potentially inform new directions for transversal politics.

BLACK FEMINIST EPISTEMOLOGY

Because U.S. Black women have access to the experiences that accrue to being both Black and female, an alternative epistemology used to rearticulate a Black women's standpoint should reflect the convergence of both sets of experiences. Race and gender may be analytically distinct, but in Black women's everyday lives, they work together. The search for the distinguishing features of an alternative epistemology used by African-American women reveals that some ideas that Africanist scholars identify as characteristically "Black" often bear remarkable resemblance to similar ideas claimed by feminist scholars as characteristically "female." This similarity suggests that the actual contours of intersecting oppressions can vary dramatically and yet generate some uniformity in the epistemologies used by subordinate groups. Just as U.S. Black women and African women encountered diverse patterns of intersecting oppressions yet generated similar agendas concerning what mattered in their feminisms, a similar process may be at work regarding the epistemologies of oppressed groups. Thus the significance of a Black feminist epistemology may lie in its ability to enrich our understanding of how subordinate groups create knowledge that fosters both their empowerment and social justice.

This approach to Black feminist thought allows African-American women to explore the epistemological implications of transversal politics. Eventually this approach may get us to a point at which, claims Elsa Barkley Brown, "all people can learn to center in another experience, validate it, and judge it by its own standards without need of comparison or need to adopt that framework as their own" (1989, 922). In such politics, "one has no need to 'decenter' anyone in order to center someone else; one has only to constantly, appropriately, 'pivot the center'" (p. 922).

Rather than emphasizing how a Black women's standpoint and its accompanying epistemology differ from those of White women, Black men, and other collectivities, Black women's experiences serve as one specific social location for examining points of connection among multiple epistemologies. Viewing Black feminist epistemology in this way challenges additive analyses of oppression claiming that Black women have a more accurate view of oppression than do other groups. Such approaches suggest that oppression can be quantified and compared and that adding layers of oppression produces a potentially clearer standpoint (Spelman 1988). One implication of some uses of standpoint theory is that the more subordinated the group, the purer the vision available to them. This is an outcome of the origins of standpoint approaches in Marxist social theory, itself reflecting the binary thinking of its Western origins. Although it is tempting to claim that Black women are more oppressed than everyone else and therefore have the best standpoint from which to understand the mechanisms, processes, and effects of oppression, this is not the case.

Instead, those ideas that are validated as true by African-American women, African-American men, Latina lesbians, Asian-American women, Puerto Rican men, and other groups with distinctive standpoints, with each group using the epistemological approaches growing from its unique standpoint, become the most "objective" truths. Each group speaks from its own standpoint and shares its own

partial, situated knowledge. But because each group perceives its own truth as partial, its knowledge is unfinished. Each group becomes better able to consider other groups' standpoints without relinquishing the uniqueness of its own standpoint or suppressing other groups' partial perspectives. "What is always needed in the appreciation of art, or life," maintains Alice Walker, "is the larger perspective. Connections made, or at least attempted, where none existed before, the straining to encompass in one's glance at the varied world the common thread, the unifying theme through immense diversity" (1983, 5). Partiality, and not universality, is the condition of being heard; individuals and groups forwarding knowledge claims without owning their position are deemed less credible than those who do.

Alternative knowledge claims in and of themselves are rarely threatening to conventional knowledge. Such claims are routinely ignored, discredited, or simply absorbed and marginalized in existing paradigms. Much more threatening is the challenge that alternative epistemologies offer to the basic process used by the powerful to legitimate knowledge claims that in turn justify their right to rule. If the epistemology used to validate knowledge comes into question, then all prior knowledge claims validated under the dominant model become suspect. Alternative epistemologies challenge all certified knowledge and open up the question of whether what has been taken to be true can stand the test of alternative ways of validating truth. The existence of a self-defined Black women's standpoint using Black feminist epistemology calls into question the content of what currently passes as truth and simultaneously challenges the process of arriving at that truth.

Toward a Politics of Empowerment

One way of approaching power concerns the dialectical relationship linking oppression and activism, where groups with greater power oppress those with lesser amounts. Rather than seeing social change or lack of it as preordained and outside the realm of human action, the notion of a dialectical relationship suggests that change results from human agency. Because African-American women remain relegated to the bottom of the social hierarchy from one generation to the next, U.S. Black women have a vested interest in opposing oppression. This is not an intellectual issue for most African-American women—it is a lived reality. As long as Black women's oppression persists, so will the need for Black women's activism. Moreover, dialectical analyses of power point out that when it comes to social injustice, groups have competing interests that often generate conflict. Even when groups understand the need for the type of transversal politics, they often find themselves on opposite sides of social issues. Oppression and resistance remain intricately linked such that the shape of one influences that of the other. At the same time, this relationship is far more complex than a simple model of permanent oppressors and perpetual victims.

Another way of approaching power views it not as something that groups possess, but as an intangible entity that circulates within a particular matrix of domination and to which individuals stand in varying relationships. These approaches emphasize how individual subjectivity frames human actions within a matrix of domination. U.S. Black women's efforts to grapple with the effects of domination in everyday life are evident in our creation of safe spaces that enable us to resist oppression, and in our struggles to form fully human love relations with one another, and with children, fathers, and brothers, as well as with individuals who do not see Black women as worthwhile. Oppression is not simply understood in the mind—it is felt in the body in myriad ways. Moreover, because oppression is constantly changing, different aspects of an individual U.S. Black woman's self-definitions intermingle and become more salient: Her gender may be more prominent when she becomes a mother, her race when she searches for housing, her social class when she applies for credit, her sexual orientation when she is walking with her lover, and her citizenship status when she applies for a job. In all of these contexts, her position in relation to and within intersecting oppressions shifts.

As each individual African-American woman changes her ideas and actions, so does the overall shape of power itself change. In the absence of Black feminist thought and other comparable oppositional knowledges, these micro-changes may remain invisible to individual women. Yet collectively, they can have a profound impact. When my mother taught me to read, took me to the public library when I was five, and told me that if I learned to read, I could experience a form of freedom, neither she nor I saw the magnitude of that one action in my life and the lives that my work has subsequently touched. As people push against, step away from, and shift the terms of their participation in power relations, the shape of power relations changes for everyone. Like individual subjectivity, resistance strategies and power are always multiple and in constant states of change.

Together, these two approaches to power point to two important uses of knowledge for African-American women and other social groups engaged in social justice projects. Dialectical approaches emphasize the significance of knowledge in developing self-defined, group-based standpoints that, in turn, can foster the type of group solidarity necessary for resisting oppressions. In contrast, subjectivity approaches emphasize how domination and resistance shape and are shaped by individual agency. Issues of consciousness link the two. In the former, group-based consciousness emerges through developing oppositional knowledges such as Black feminist thought. In the latter, individual self-definitions and behaviors shift in tandem with a changed consciousness concerning everyday lived experience. Black feminist thought encompasses both meanings of consciousness—neither is sufficient without the other. Together, both approaches to power also highlight the significance of multiplicity in shaping consciousness. For example, viewing domination itself as encompassing intersecting oppressions of race, class, gender, sexuality, and nation points to the significance of these oppressions in shaping the overall organization of a particular matrix of domination. Similarly, personal identities constructed around individual understandings of race, class, gender, sexuality, and nation define each individual's unique biography.

Both of these approaches remain theoretically useful because they each provide partial and different perspectives on empowerment. Unfortunately, these two views are often presented as *competing* rather than potentially *complementary* approaches. As a result, each provides a useful starting point for thinking through African-American women's empowerment in the context of constantly changing power relations, but neither is sufficient. Black feminism and other social justice projects require a language of power that is grounded within yet transcends these approaches. Social justice projects need a common, functional vocabulary that furthers their understanding of the politics of empowerment.

Thus far, using African-American women's experiences as a lens, this text has examined race, gender, class, sexuality, and nation as forms of oppression that work together in distinctive ways to produce a distinctive U.S. matrix of domination. Whether viewed through the lens of a single system of power, or through that of intersecting oppressions, any particular matrix of domination is organized via four

interrelated domains of power, namely, the structural, disciplinary, hegemonic, and interpersonal domains. Each domain serves a particular purpose. The structural domain organizes oppression, whereas the disciplinary domain manages it. The hegemonic domain justifies oppression, and the interpersonal domain influences everyday lived experience and the individual consciousness that ensues.

When it comes to power, the challenges raised by the synergistic relationship among domains of power generate new opportunities and constraints for African-American women who now desegregate schools and workplaces, as well as those who do not. On the one hand, entering places that denied access to our mothers provides new opportunities for fostering social justice. Depending on the setting, using the insights gained via outsider-within status can be a stimulus to creativity that helps both African-American women and our new organizational homes. On the other hand, the commodification of outsider-within status whereby African-American women's value to an organization lies solely in our ability to market a seemingly permanent marginal status can suppress Black women's empowerment. Being a permanent outsider-within can never lead to power because the category, by definition, requires marginality. Each individual must find her own way, recognizing that her personal biography, while unique, is never as unique as she thinks.

When it comes to knowledge, Black women's empowerment involves rejecting the dimensions of knowledge that perpetuate objectification, commodification, and exploitation. African-American women and others like us become empowered when we understand and use those dimensions of our individual, group, and formal educational ways of knowing that foster our humanity. When Black women value our self-definitions, participate in Black women's domestic and transnational activist traditions, view the skills gained in schools as part of a focused education for Black community development, and invoke Black feminist epistemologies as central to our worldviews, we empower ourselves. C. Wright Mills's (1959) concept of the "sociological imagination" identifies its task and its promise as a way of knowing that enables individuals to grasp the relations between history and biography within society. Resembling the holistic epistemology required by Black feminism, using one's point of view to engage the sociological imagination can empower the individual. "My fullest concentration of energy is available to me," Audre Lorde maintains, "only when I integrate all the parts of who I am, openly, allowing power from particular sources of my living to flow back and forth freely through all my different selves, without the restriction of externally imposed definition" (1984, 120–21). Developing a Black women's standpoint to engage a collective Black feminist imagination can empower the group.

Black women's empowerment involves revitalizing U.S. Black feminism as a social justice project organized around the dual goals of empowering African-American women and fostering social justice in a transnational context. Black feminist thought's emphasis on the ongoing interplay between Black women's oppression and Black women's activism presents the matrix of domination and its interrelated domains of power as responsive to human agency. Such thought views the world as a dynamic place where the goal is not merely to survive or to fit in or to cope; rather, it becomes a place where we feel ownership and accountability. The existence of Black feminist thought suggests that there is always choice, and power to act, no matter how bleak the situation may appear to be. Viewing the world as one in the making raises the issue of individual responsibility for bringing about change. It also shows that while individual empowerment is key, only collective action can effectively generate the lasting institutional transformation required for social justice.

NOTES

1. My use of the term *subjugated knowledge* differs somewhat from Michel Foucault's (1980) definition. According to Foucault, subjugated knowledges are "those blocs of historical knowledge which were present but disguised," namely, "a whole set of knowledges that have been disqualified as inadequate to their task or insufficiently elaborated: naive knowledges, located low down on the hierarchy, beneath the required level of cognition or scientificity" (p. 82). I suggest that Black feminist thought is not a "naive knowledge" but has been made to appear so by those controlling knowledge validation procedures. Moreover, Foucault argues that subjugated knowledge is "a particular, local, regional knowledge, a differential knowledge incapable of unanimity and which owes its force only to the harshness with which it is opposed by everything surrounding it" (p. 82). The component of Black feminist thought that analyzes Black women's oppression partially fits this definition, but the long-standing, independent, African-derived influences within Black women's thought are omitted from Foucault's analysis.

2. I apply this concept of transversal politics to groups organized around historically constructed identities, in this case the identity of "Black woman." Groups, however, need not be formed around identity categories. The local group history can just as easily be constructed around an issue or an "affinity." Thus, the model of transversal politics advanced here concerns coalitions of all sorts, and can accommodate the contradictions that seemingly distinguish identity politics and affinity politics.

3. For a discussion of the similarities and differences of using the individual and the group as levels of analysis, see Collins (1998), especially pages 203–11.

REFERENCES

Antrobus, Peggy. 1995. "Women in the Caribbean: The Quadruple Burden of Gender, Race, Class and Imperialism." In *Connecting Across Cultures and Continent: Black Women Speak Out on Identity, Race and Development,* ed. Achola O. Pala, 53–60. New York: United Nations Development Fund for Women.

Brown, Elsa Barkley. 1989. "African-American Women's Quilting: A Framework for Conceptualizing and Teaching African-American Women's History." *Signs* 14 (4): 921–29.

Carby, Hazel. 1987. *Reconstructing Womanhood: The Emergence of the Afro-American Woman Novelist.* New York: Oxford University Press.

Childress, Alice. [1956] 1986. *Like One of the Family: Conversations from a Domestic's Life.* Boston: Beacon.

Christian, Barbara. 1989. "But Who Do You Really Belong to—Black Studies or Women's Studies?" *Women's Studies* 17 (1–2): 17–23.

Collins, Patricia Hill. 1986. "Learning from the Outsider Within: The Sociological Significance of Black Feminist Thought." *Social Problems* 33 (6): 14–32.

———. 1998. *Fighting Words: Black Women and the Search for Justice.* Minneapolis: University of Minnesota Press.

Foucault, Michel. 1980. *Power/Knowledge: Selected Interviews and Other Writings 1972–1977,* ed. Colin Gordon. New York: Pantheon.

Franklin, V.P. 1992. *Black Self-Determination: A Cultural History of African-American Resistance.* Chicago: Lawrence Hill books.

Gilkes, Cheryl Townsend. 1983. "From Slavery to Social Welfare: Racism and the Control of Black Women." In *Class, Race, and Sex: The Dynamics of Control*, ed. Amy Swerdlow and Hanna Lessinger, 288–300. Boston: G.K. Hall.

Gwaltney, John Langston. 1980. *Drylongso, A Self-Portrait of Black America*. New York: Vintage.

Hull, Gloria T., Patricia Bell Scott, and Barbara Smith, eds. 1982. *But Some of Us Are Brave*. Old Westbury, NY: Feminist Press.

Lindsay, Beverly, ed. 1980. *Comparative Perspectives of Third World Women: The Impact of Race, Sex, and Class*. New York: Praeger.

Lorde, Audre. 1984. *Sister Outsider*. Trumansberg, NY: Crossing Press.

McLaughlin, Andree Nicola. 1995. "The Impact of the Black Consciousness and Women's Movements on Black Women's Identity: Intercontinental Empowerment." In *Connecting Across Cultures and Continents: Black Women Speak Out on Identity, Race and Development*, ed. Achola O. Pala, 71–84. New York: United Nations Development Fund for Women.

Mills, C. Wright. 1959. *The Sociological Imagination*. New York: Oxford University Press.

Mullings, Leith. 1997. *On Our Own Terms: Race, Class, and Gender in the Lives of African American Women*. New York: Routledge.

Nnaemeka, Obioma. 1998. "This Women's Studies Business: Beyond Politics and History." In *Sisterhood, Feminisms, and Power: From Africa to the Diaspora*, ed. Obioma Nnaemeka, 351–86. Trenton, NJ: Africa World Press.

Rights of Women: A Guide to the Most Important United Nations Treaties on Women's Human Rights. 1998. New York: International Women's Tribune Centre.

Spelman, Elizabeth V. 1988. *Inessential Woman: Problems of Exclusion in Feminist Thought*. Boston: Beacon.

Squires, Gregory D. 1994. *Capital and Communities in Black and White: The Intersections of Race, Class, and Uneven Development*. Albany: State University of New York Press.

Walker, Alice. 1983. *In Search of Our Mother's Gardens*. New York: Harcourt Brace Jovanovich.

Yuval-Davis, Nira. 1997. *Gender and Nation*. Thousand Oaks, CA: Sage.

THE COSBY SHOW

THE VIEW FROM THE BLACK MIDDLE CLASS

By Leslie B. Inniss and Joe R. Feagin

Now that we have seen the final April 30, 1992, episode the television series *The Cosby Show*, "And So We Commence," we can examine the social and historical impact on its audiences. Commentators in the mass media have asserted that one of the show's greatest consequences was its help in improving race relations by projecting universal values that both Whites and Blacks could identify with, using the tried-and-true situation comedy format (Ehrenstein 1988; Gray 1989; Johnson 1986; Norment 1985; Stevens 1987). Believing that television mirrors society and articulates its values, proponents of this perspective point to the overwhelming popularity of the show among White viewers as well as its almost entirely positive assessment by White analysts and the White media. For many seasons, the show was highly rated and has been credited, among other consequences, with reviving the genre of the sitcom and saving the ailing NBC network (Curry 1986; Frank and Zweig 1988; Poussaint 1988; Taylor 1989).

However, a few recent researchers have suggested that, to the contrary, the show's popularity has set back race relations because its view of Black assimilation fails to take into account the context of the world outside of the four walls of the Huxtable household (Teachout, 1986), and because it allows Whites to excuse institutional discrimination and to become desensitized to racial inequality (Gates 1992). They do this by asserting that if Black people fail, they only have themselves to blame because any White person can point out the successful, affluent Black family on *The Cosby Show* and confirm their belief that affirmative action is no longer needed because Blacks now enjoy the same opportunities as Whites (Gates 1992).

In a recent book, *Enlightened Racism* (1992), Lewis and Jhally report on White focus groups that watched *The Cosby Show* as part of the recent research project. They found a contradiction in White responses to the show. On the one hand, the show was taken by Whites as proving that anyone can make it in the United States and that Black Americans should stop complaining about discrimination. On the other, the Whites articulated the view that the Cosbys were not like most Black Americans. This contradiction is rationalized by Whites in the study by the failure and laziness of other Blacks. "The Huxtables proved that black people can succeed; yet in so doing they also prove the inferiority of black people in general (who have, in comparison with whites, failed)" (Lewis and Jhally 1992, 95).

Lewis and Jhally (1992, 113–17) also deal briefly with some Black reactions to *The Cosby Show* and other comedy shows starring Black comedians. They used a general group of mixed-status Black Americans in Springfield, Massachusetts. In the data that follow, we go beyond their brief analysis to examine the reactions to *The Cosby Show* in greater depth. And we examine the reactions of middle-class and upper-middle-class Black Americans whose class position is close to that of the Huxtables in *The Cosby Show*. How do middle-class and upper-middle-class Black Americans view the show? Is their reaction positive? Do middle-class Blacks *accept The Cosby Show* version of Black assimilation and integration into America: the color-blind society where African Americans, European Americans, Asian Americans, and Hispanic Americans can all interact as human beings without any mention of or even a hint of racial differences being problematic? Can this Black middle-class audience relate to a Black middle-class lifestyle in which neither the doctor-father nor the lawyer-mother nor any of the school-age children ever experience racism or discrimination in their everyday lives?

Or do middle-class Blacks perceive *The Cosby Show* in a more negative manner? Do they believe that the show depicts a false image of assimilation and helps to foster the backlash against affirmative action? Or perhaps, rather than totally positive or totally negative reactions, there is more of an ambivalence among middle-class Blacks. Perhaps they feel that it is good to see any Blacks on television who are shown in a positive light instead of as the usual pimps, prostitutes, and maids reflecting the "Sambo syndrome" (Fife 1974). On the other hand, they might suggest that *The Cosby Show* is an exceptionally positive portrayal in the same vein as the "*Shaft* syndrome" (referring to a popular, well-made motion picture from the 1970s with a Black cast). As such, the Cosby portrayal would be as distorting as the previously excessively negative ones, in the sense that Blacks are still being shown in an exaggerated fashion rather than as ordinary, everyday human beings, some good, some bad, with others all along the good-bad spectrum. Given the pervasive impact of the mass media, particularly television (Asante 1976; Case and Greeley 1990; Goodlet 1974; Holz and Wright 1979; Leckenby and Surlin 1976; Stroman 1986), and especially the fact that Blacks watch more television than Whites and place more confidence in it (Bales 1986; Comstock and Cobbey 1979; Kassarjian 1973; Stroman and Becker 1978), it is important to examine the way in which Blacks have been portrayed. Television research has documented that the portrayal of Blacks in that and other mass media has always been inadequate and stereotypical, and generally has portrayed Black Americans as comedic characters (Carter 1988; Fife 1974; Gates 1992; O'Kelly and Bloomquist 1976; Seggar 1977). Moreover, research has shown the extent to which Blacks are underrepresented in all positions in the television industry. These data patterns underscore the need for a careful examination of Black middle-class responses to *The Cosby Show*.

THE DEBATE OVER *THE COSBY SHOW*

The Cosby Show began on September 20, 1984. The TV public was introduced to Dr. Heathcliff Huxtable, an obstetrician married to an attorney, played by Phylicia Rashad. The couple and their five children lived in a New York City brownstone and were clearly "Black middle class" at a time when that group was beginning to be recognized in the mass media. Indeed, they were upper middle class. The curtain-closing show, "And So We Commence," was on April 30, 1992, and had the extended Huxtable family prepare to celebrate the only son's graduation from New York University. During its eight-year, 198-episode run, *The Cosby Show* was lauded as a major milestone in popular entertainment: the first all-Black program that avoided racial stereotyping. Records reveal that the show was the top-rated show of the 1980s and the most-watched sitcom in television history. Bill Cosby, one of the show's creators, said he was returning to TV to save viewers from a "vast wasteland." He went on to explain his reasons for creating the show in an interview with Robert Johnson (1992, 57), editor of *Jet magazine*. Cosby told Johnson that he was tired of what he was seeing on television—tired of the car chases, the hookers with the Black pimps. Cosby believed that he could send vital messages along with the positive images of a Black family: Children are the same all over (Johnson 1986, 29).

Bill Cosby has responded to most criticisms lodged against his show during its eight-year run. For example, in answer to critics who urged him to deal with more racial issues, Cosby's response was that he would not let critics write his show and would not allow neoliberals to affect the image that the *Cosby* cast projects as a family (Johnson 1992, 60). Further, Cosby asserts that this criticism is unfair and holds him up to a different standard because other situation comedies are not expected to address pressing social problems such as racism. He stated that other shows, such as *Threes Company*, are not asked to deal with racism. Moreover, he feels that the show has addressed some tough social issues. For example, Cosby stated that the show consistently has addressed sexism as an issue, showing in a creative and humorous way how it should be resisted and debunked; at the same time, the show confronted the issue of machismo and promoted a richer understanding of fatherhood and a fuller meaning of manhood (Dyson 1989, 28). Additionally, whether through Cosby's wearing of collegiate sweatshirts or in the form of his spin-off program, *A Different World,* the show consistently sent out messages about the importance of Black academic institutions and the importance of Blacks supporting these institutions. This reflects Cosby's deep commitment to Black colleges surviving as an American institution (Cheers 1987, 28).

Other criticisms lodged against the show were that it was not "Black" enough because the family life being portrayed is not realistic, and that the show minimizes Black issues because it is a comedy rather than a dramatic series. In answer to critics who assert that the family being portrayed is not realistic enough, Cosby said, "I am not an expert on blackness" (Stevens 1987, 80), and that the show is about parents loving their children and giving them understanding. It is about people respecting each other (Johnson 1992, 60). He goes on to proclaim that although the show uses a new gimmick of centering on the parents rather than the children, without the children in the cast the show just would not work (Davidson 1986, 32). In support of the show, one writer has argued that a useful aspect of Cosby's dismantling of stereotyping and racial mythology is that it permits America to view Blacks as human beings, and it has shown that many concerns human beings have transcend race (Dyson 1989, 29). Alvin Poussaint (1988, 72), a Harvard psychiatrist and the show's psychological consultant, asserts that the Huxtables helped to dispel old stereotypes and to move the show's audience toward a more realistic perception of Blacks. Like Whites, Blacks should be portrayed on television in a full spectrum of roles and cultural styles and such an array of styles should not be challenged. Moreover, according to Poussaint, the Black culture of the characters comes through in their speech, intonations, and nuances; Black music, art, and dance are frequently displayed and Black roots and authors are often mentioned (74).

Finally, in response to those who complain that the show is a comedy rather than being more dramatic, Cosby maintains that each episode educates and informs even though the show's format is a situation comedy that entertains. He states that the shows are funny, with a caring, loving, feeling story line, and that the audience sitting at home will recognize themselves in the characters (Johnson 1986, 30). Moreover, one author admonishes Blacks to stop looking to TV for social liberation because "the revolution will not be televised" (Gates 1992, 317).

Our Research Study

To examine the Black middle-class response to *The Cosby Show*, we draw primarily on one hundred in-depth interviews from a larger study of 210 middle-class Black Americans in sixteen cities across the United States. The interviewing was done from 1988 to 1990. Black interviewers were used. We began with respondents known as members of the Black middle class to knowledgeable consultants in key cities. Snowball sampling from these multiple starting points was used to maximize diversity.

The questions in the research instrument were primarily designed to elicit detailed information on the general situations of the respondents and on the barriers encountered and managed in employment, education, and housing. The specific question used for this study asked about the portrayal of Blacks in the media. There were no specific questions about *The Cosby Show*—the discussion of that particular television program was volunteered in response to the general question about the media's portrayal of Black Americans. These volunteered responses signal the importance of this show. Although below we report mainly on the responses of the one hundred respondents who detailed specific reactions to *The Cosby Show*, in interpreting the Black middle-class response to *The Cosby Show* we also draw on some discussion in a larger sample of 117 interviews in which *The Cosby Show* was mentioned.

"Middle class" was defined broadly as those holding a white-collar job (including those in professional, managerial, and clerical jobs), college students preparing for white-collar jobs, and owners of successful businesses. This definition is consistent with recent analyses of the Black middle class (Landry 1987). The subsample of one hundred middle-class Blacks reporting a response to *The Cosby Show* is fairly representative of the demographic characteristics of the larger sample. The subsample's occupational distribution is broadly similar to the larger sample and includes university professors, college administrators, elementary and secondary teachers, physicians, attorneys, dentists, entrepreneurs, business managers and executives, doctoral students, and three retirees. There are roughly equal numbers of males (forty-eight) and females (fifty-two). The subsample has 23 percent younger than the age of thirty-five, 63 percent between thirty-five and fifty, and 14 percent older than fifty. All the respondents have at least a high school diploma, and 96 percent have some college, including 46 percent with advanced degrees. The modal income level is $56,000 or more, with 51 percent reporting this income. Seventeen percent report incomes between $36,000 and $55,000; 27 percent have incomes less than $35,000; and 5 percent refuse to disclose their income levels.

Viewing the Show as Unrealistic

The Black middle-class responses to *The Cosby Show* were ambivalent, reflecting both negative and positive aspects. Even the negative comments were often mixed with a positive preface, such as "I really like *The Cosby Show*, but …" or "I'm happy to see some positive images of Blacks on TV, but …" In many of the answers, there clearly is a dialectical tension, with a recognition of both the positive and the negative features of the program. For example, many negative responses centered on the show not providing a realistic portrayal of a Black family, or of a Black middle-class family. Yet many also felt that the show accurately reflected their own lifestyle and that of their friends.

Among our respondents, one common criticism of *The Cosby Show* was its lack of realism. As the following set of negative responses illustrate, the problem lies with the stereotypical nature of an upper-middle-class Black family that never experiences problems, especially racial problems. One respondent commented on the lack of tragedy this way: "And then *The Cosby Show,* well, they just got too love-happy for me, it's just too good. They used to have real problems that they were faced with, and now, what's the problem? Someone wears someone else's dress, what is that?"

The absence of serious tragedy like that faced by Black Americans in the real world caused many to speak of the lack of realism in the program: "*Cosby* is not real. One of the things that disturbs me is this house is always immaculate, there's no maid, the mother's an attorney who works all day, the father's a doctor who works all day, the children are out of the house all day. Who does the laundry? Who cleans up the house? Who prepares the meals? You see them cook a specialty dish from time to time, that's not for real."

One aspect of the unreality is the casting of the father and mother as upper-middle-class professionals. One middle-class respondent focused on the family context, including the likelihood of doctor-lawyer heads of household: "My issue with *Cosby* is how real is it? I mean, how many Black families do you know where the father's a doctor and the mother's a lawyer, and all the kids are wonderfully well-behaved, and they all deal at a psychological and emotional level of understanding? And so while I personally love *The Cosby Show,* I do question how real it is."

This questioning of the doctor-lawyer team came up a number of times and was connected to other issues. Another respondent noted the lack of attention to the racial trials: "I think if children, if people, if anybody looked at *The Cosby Show,* they'd think that everybody in the Black community has arrived like that, and it's just not true. I think it's wonderful that they portray a doctor and lawyer together working, and they live in a brownstone on a regular street, and they have children and everybody's hunky-dory. They never portray the trials and tribulations that families have. Or, if they do portray them, they portray them in a humorous light. But I think that it could be more realistic."

Another respondent wondered about the stereotyped character of a Black family like the Huxtables, who do not grapple with barriers like discrimination: "I think he's a doctor and she's a lawyer, so I think it's an upper-middle-class family. And it's just stereotyped. Nothing like that goes on in the family life every day. No family life runs smooth like that. You know, why not portray a family life story on television if you're going to use Blacks, and make it show the hard times that Blacks do run into? Why give it like it's all peaches and cream when it's not?"

Rather than viewing the Huxtables as role models, one father lamented the difficulty of explaining to his children why they don't live like the Cosbys: "I do know that this is just entertainment. But my kids think it's the way we should live. That is unfair. It is unfair for me to explain to my son that, no, mom is not a lawyer, dad is not a doctor, and these things don't work that way I think that's really sad."

Blacks in Whiteface?

The unreality of the show has other dimensions, including a too-White image of Black culture. For example, one male respondent criticized the false image of assimilation to White culture as presented by *The Cosby Show.* "A false image. Again, it seems like something out of a fantasy, of people living the good life, acting assimilated, the so-called new-generation type people that really don't exist. If you walk the streets of America, you see something totally different. ... The type of Blacks who have made it, everybody's happy, the don't-worry-be-happy type of Black people, again, it's a total farce, and they don't represent what the Black masses in this country are really like."

Another respondent accused the Huxtables of being "White people in blackface" and not a true representation of Black America: "From one extreme, you have the family on *The Cosby Show*. The happy-go-lucky Negro family that's made it. To me, all you're looking at are White people in blackface performing on television. That may be true to a certain extent, which may be going on, but it's not a true representation of the Black experience in America."

One female critic suggested that the show could be a "little less White," particularly in the area of problem-solving techniques: "Then you have the other extreme with Bill Cosby, that everybody is professional. And that's true, we have a lot of that. But the way problems are treated, I think is a little off the wall. I think it could be a little less White. I think that we just treat problems a little bit differently because, let's face it, whether we're professional or not, we all come from nothing. And we still don't have that totally White mentality about problem solving."

This commentary adds another dimension to our understanding of the fear fostered by assimilation. This respondent may be suggesting that the history of today's Blacks would not allow them to work out problems in the same manner that Whites would. The decline of segregation has allowed Black Americans to deal with their children in ways different from the days of segregation, indeed in ways similar to those of Whites. Under segregation, Black youngsters were usually taught to be deferential and self-effacing, often through harsh child-rearing practices admonishing a child not to speak unless spoken to and not to stare anyone in the eye. Because conditions have improved somewhat, many Black parents now encourage children in the same ways that White parents do, to be assertive, independent, and curious. There may also be a suggestion here that the Black approach to problem solving in some matters is still different in unspecified ways from that of White Americans, perhaps that there is a Black culture or African background to be considered.

These examples provide insight into the character of the criticisms that see the show as unreal. The general complaint is not that the show is an unreal portrait of a family, but of a Black family Cosby has argued that he is trying to show what true assimilation would be like, not what it already is—all racial and ethnic groups interacting as neighbors and friends without regard for physical differences.

There is a clear suggestion in our interviews that the Huxtables do not reflect most Black Americans. For many of our middle-class respondents this is problematic. Some had problems with the illusion of perfect integration whereby Black middle-class families no longer experience any racial problems and would in effect "live happily ever after." It seems that an underlying wish of these Black critics is that television shows featuring Blacks should be harder hitting and more realistic. There is a call here for greater seriousness in dealing with the Black experience, and a rejection of a happy-go-lucky stereotype of Black America. They have difficulty with a fantasy portrait of Black characters. None mentioned that if Black life as a whole is biting and difficult, then a show that is an escapist medium is useful. Only recently does there seem to be a push for seriousness and documentaries depicting only real-life dramas.

The Positive View: TV as Fantasy

In our interviews the negative responses are more than equaled by positive responses. Sometimes, particular individuals seem to be in a dialogue with themselves or their friends and relatives on these matters, for there is often an ambivalence about *The Cosby Show*.

A number of our middle-class respondents echoed Bill Cosby's response to some of his critics in regard to demanding too much in the way of realism from a show on television. "The problem I have with Cosby is the comments people make, in particular our own people, like what Black family has a doctor and a lawyer for a mom and dad and three or four well-behaved kids? They can't believe that could happen. And some White people too. And I sit and think, well, that's just as real as the Bionic Man, or Superman, or Batman and Robin. I mean, you don't see us walking around in tights with big Ss on our shirts."

"The *Cosby* sort of thing … isn't like most Black families. But then I'm not sure that you ought to expect television to portray anything realistically. I don't think they portray any family realistically, so why would they ever portray the Black family realistically, either?"

"It's not honest? Well, so what? So is almost everything else that you see on television. So why can't we be on television being fake? Or from that perspective, yeah, let us get somebody being fake, just like everybody else. It's an entertainment medium."

These positive assessments underscore the complexity of Black responses to Black-oriented shows. Explicit in these positive quotes is the idea that *The Cosby Show* is indeed unrealistic but so is most of television. The public does not ask other TV shows to be accurate representations of real life. In their view, because the public enjoys other shows that are just as fantasy oriented as *The Cosby Show* (for example, *The Bionic Woman* or *The Six Million Dollar Man*), it is not fair to expect that when Blacks are involved that the shows provide both entertainment and great realism.

Everyday Life and Role Models

Some of the positive comments took the form of acknowledging that the experiences on the show paralleled their own; "I think that … *Cosby* is an excellent example of our life and family." "*Cosby* parallels quite significantly my family life and that of my friends, particularly those who have teenagers or children of a wide variety of age ranges. And that's particularly a family joke with several of our friends, because we look at *Cosby* to see what's going to happen in our lives that week." These respondents are selecting out of the show's account of the Black experience common family problems. Others who had a positive views of the show were happy with the portrayal of Blacks in a positive light in order to counteract the many negative portrayals of Black Americans in the mass media, and thus in the White mind. "I think that it's about time that White America sees Black America in a positive, natural environment." "I wish we had more shows like … *Cosby* on TV, where you have a Black doctor, and the wife is a lawyer, because they do exist. I mean they're on a small scale, percentage-wise, but they do exist.

And I think we take too many negatives and blow them up." "I thought it was good that Black people, and Whites, could see that we all don't live in ghettos and projects and kill each other." "There are a lot of Black families that have doctors and lawyers and stuff like that, you just don't ever hear about them, people don't write stories about them." Clearly, these middle-class Black Americans are concerned about the tendency of the media, and White Americans, to exaggerate the image of Black Americans as criminal and deviant.

Those who affirm the show's merits see *Cosby*'s portrayal of Black men and Black families very positively: "*Cosby* is probably the only show, I think, that portrays Black men in a positive role." "I think that no question Bill Cosby has done a tremendous amount. And I think he portrays and projects a very,

very positive image, what we need to see more." "Because I think it is a family together, and it shows that Black men can be leaders in their families, yet at the same time be responsible." One respondent emphasized the importance of stressing the commonality of the values of all Americans, regardless of racial and ethnic background: "I think that I am glad to see them portraying Blacks in middle-class roles, and realizing that Black people, Black middle-class people, have some of the same values as White middle class, Hispanic middle class, or Oriental middle class. It's not necessarily a race that determines it, it's just middle-class people sometimes have similar values. So I'm glad to see they are now portraying Blacks okay. *The Cosby Show* and these other shows that are coming on TV, you know, we both have some of the same values." This means that the general image of Black Americans as being like other Americans is an important contribution of *The Cosby Show*.

The Black Community

Other respondents noted the importance of *The Cosby Show* within the Black community. They enjoyed the Huxtable family portrayal because it offered Black people role models, positive values, and important messages for Black Americans. "I'm pleased with the Cosby portrayal because I think it sets a good example for younger Black children, not so much in the stereotypical 'when I grow up I'm going to be a doctor' kind of thing, but just in the overall quality of life and the values." "But I didn't see that being unrealistic, the type of family, a doctor and a lawyer. I didn't see that as being unrealistic. There's quite a few Black doctors and lawyers, so I thought that was a good image builder for the kids." "I think you could look around this great country of America for the next 708 years, and I don't think you're ever going to find a Huxtable family. But hey, you know, to me it creates a dream. I've always believed that if you can see it in your mind, it's possible. And like the Cos, he plays a doctor. Hey, a little five-year-old Black kid, I want to be a doctor just like Heathcliff. That's cool. I like that." To be able to see a Black female lawyer, a Black doctor, and Black youngsters going to college is a very positive incentive for inner-city Black children who may not see those same types in their own neighborhoods. Here the accent is on positive role models for Black children. Others commented in a general vein. "It's ideal. It's family structured. It's something basic. It has good moral … everything you want to look for is in that show." "I do like *The Cosby Show because* [it] delivers a whole bunch of messages, to African Americans in particular. You know if you watch it, there's always a message." "Bill Cosby, I love Bill Cosby. It's not a put-on, it's a true family setting. You've got a doctor and a lawyer, but you do have that. But they deal with down-to-earth issues, realistic issues. So, I think that's a pretty good image." The importance of positive role models for all Black Americans, not just for children, is a significant theme here and in the rest of the interviews.

THE FAILURE TO ADDRESS SOCIAL ISSUES

Another major category of criticism is related to those just discussed, that *The Cosby Show* does not address any important racial or other social issues, particularly those facing Black Americans today. The following quote illustrates this criticism:

> They're not fully representative, that's for sure. Yes, we see the successful Cosby family, but that's only a slice of the average American Black family. The family is completely advantaged. They have both parents, they're together. They're both fully employed. And they have a happy

environment. That family appears to be insulated from racism. Everything's always so wonderful on their block. Well, shoot, that doesn't happen. … So it's misleading. It leaves you with a flicker of hope that's not realistic and doesn't give us enough information about what to do if your family isn't like that, isn't ideal, isn't two-parent, or isn't really healthy. No one ever gets sick on *The Cosby Show*. No one has a debilitating illness. Cosby has not chosen to address sexual abuse. He's minimally addressed substance abuse on there, and he's rarely talked about sex. That's not reality at all. None of those daughters have had unwanted pregnancies.

This respondent suggests that the show has not dealt with any of the major problems facing Black Americans, including questions of racism or unwed pregnancies. There is a tough call for the program to be more than a situation comedy. Other respondents expanded on the theme of the failure to deal with racial discrimination. "I have a problem with the fact that *The Cosby Show* will build a thirty-minute episode around Heathcliff Huxtable building a hero sandwich. Why aren't we dealing with, and I'm not saying do this every week, but every now and then why aren't we dealing with some real issues that are confronting the Black middle class. Yeah, there are some people who live like that … what happened to me in the courtroom, if I'm an attorney, or what racist thing happened to me in the hospital, if I'm a surgeon. That's what they come home talking about, and yes their kids go to NYU and other great universities like that, but what they come home talking about is what this racist professor said and did. And I don't see that occurring on *The Cosby Show?* "It is not indicative of what Black life is really like. You would think that when Theo goes out he never has problems except in dealing with his buddies. Or that when his mother goes about her legal duties as a lawyer that she never confronts discrimination." On the air, the Huxtable family never faces or copes with discrimination. Although asking a comedy show to deal seriously with such issues as sexual abuse may be asking too much, these respondents do point to the serious issue of racial discrimination at the middle-class level. Upper middle-class Black Americans experience much discrimination, and it is overt, recognizable, and everyday. Because this discrimination is common and daily, it does not seem unreasonable to expect that a Black lawyer or doctor, and certainly a Black college student, would experience it and deal with it in daily life.

A Subtle Treatment of Racism

None of our respondents explicitly disagreed with the criticisms just noted. On the overt level, they agreed that *The Cosby Show* does not deal with racism and discrimination. However, at another level there is a battle going on against racism. One respondent noted that Cosby tends to approach the problem of racism in a subtle way, by allusion and indirection: "But at another level they deal with a lot of issues in a rather subtle way. There was an episode where Martin Luther King's 'I Have a Dream' speech was being watched by the family at the very end of the show, after I think there had been different family squabbles." This subtle treatment was examined eloquently by a professor: "In the show you can see a kind of intervention against racism, by the depiction of a family that is not totally constructed by racism. They have a life that speaks to Black art, Black music, including a traditionally Black college. But having said all that, the very scarcity of representations of racism means that one can look at *The Cosby Show* and decide on the basis of just that representation that everything is OK, when everything is very much not OK. So what might be itself harmless under one set of circumstances, ends up being hideously harmful under another set of circumstances."

What comes out as positive from a Black point of view—the ability to live outside of racism for a time—becomes a negative when Whites take the absence of racism to mean that things are fine for Black Americans. This problem is underscored in the study by Lewis and Jhally (1992, 110), where they conclude that for many of their White respondents "the Huxtables' achievement for the American dream leads them to a world where race no longer matters. This enables white viewers to combine an impeccable liberal attitude toward race with a deep-rooted suspicion of black people." In this way, *The Cosby Show* functions for Whites in a way much different from the way it functions for Blacks. It panders to the limits of White acceptance of Black Americans in the late twentieth century.

Black Life Only As Comedy

We have seen in the previous analyses some tendency to negatively or positively judge the show's content. The following responses are directed at the genre of the show. Similar to earlier comments, these critics feel that always seeing Blacks in situation comedies indicates that Black life and Black issues are not taken seriously. "True, *Cosby* has a great Black image, but basically, it's still a situation comedy. It's still comic. It's still laughter. It's still entertainment. It's not real, intense drama." "In terms of Black portrayals in television, it's a rather sad commentary that Blacks as clowns, or Blacks as those who laugh, continues to be the main image that's portrayed. ... It's still clear that Blacks as humans that have to deal with a variety of serious issues doesn't seem to get across ... it hasn't dealt seriously enough with topics that Blacks in general have to face." "*The Cosby Show* shows a set of affluent Blacks, but still it's a situation comedy. There are no shows that can deal with the Black person seriously, as a serious person. It seems like in order to discuss Black issues, you have to laugh." One respondent took a more positive approach to Cosby's achievements in his comedy show: "I'm a firm believer that the strength of the Black community is always in the family, and they're starting to show Blacks in a strong family situation. I think *The Cosby Show* started that instead of the slapstick comedy type. I think we're still not taken seriously because all of those are still in the sitcom type situation. I think it's difficult for most people to accept that Blacks have normal family problems, and they deal with them similarly as they do." A clear advantage is that *Cosby* has moved the situation comedy to a level beyond that of the more typical Sambo-type Black comedy. This puts the earlier comments into greater perspective. These last two responses seem to be arguing the case for the importance of class position over racial identity. These comments raise the important question as to why White Americans have a "comfort zone," which means that Whites will only watch those Black shows with which they feel comfortable. Because White viewers have the numbers to make or break a show and influence its sponsors, they are the ones whose interests are usually met. Why is the White comfort zone only able to encompass Blacks as comedians? One might say that to Whites, Black life and problems are not seen as serious. Or it may be something unconscious and less devious. It is doubtless linked to the old stereotypes where Blacks are seen as buffoons and Stepin Fetchits.

Conclusion

We have examined the Black middle-class response to *The Cosby Show* and found a mixed view of the show and its impact. The responses are both positive and negative in tone. Yet the interviews indicate a reluctance to be totally negative about one of the few positive portrayals of Blacks on TV. Middle-class Blacks want positive depictions of their lives. Many also want more realistic portrayals. Some feel that these realistic depictions can only be accomplished through a genre other than comedy. For them, to always portray Blacks as comedians makes light of the Black situation and indicates that Black life with all its inherent problems is not taken seriously. Our interviews highlight two significant aspects of their responses: (a) the fear that the show will render Black problems as irrelevant, and (b) the hope and optimism that with continued work the Black condition can improve.

The negative responses highlight both the ambivalence of the respondents and the fear that the show fosters the false assumption that Black problems have been solved and are no longer relevant. By showing a Black family that for all intents and purposes has fully assimilated, we are led to believe that we are indeed living in an equal-opportunity society and with a little hard work and lots of perseverance, anyone can make it. When we meet the Huxtable grandparents, we are shown that they had a difficult life. The grandfather lived in a time of segregated armed forces and segregated music clubs where he was accepted as a musician but not as a person. But he worked hard, and now he has a doctor son, a lawyer daughter-in-law, and grandchildren in college. The overall impression is that the American dream is real for anyone who is willing to play by the rules. We are shown substantial upward mobility in only one generation and led to believe that mobility will be even more pronounced for the Huxtable children because they too are playing by the rules. We are left with the impression that they will not face any barriers or obstacles in their quest for the good life. They are decidedly upper middle class and can only go up—no discrimination or downward mobility for the Huxtables or by extension for Blacks as a group. The positive interviews highlight another significant aspect of the Black middle-class response to *The Cosby Show*: hope or optimism. Although it is true that not all Blacks are living the good life, with prestigious jobs, decent housing and living conditions, and college-bound children, one can always hope for and work toward these things. Just seeing what life like this could be like may be a tremendous motivator. It may inspire hard work and ward off discouragement. One middle-aged Black female was articulate on this point:

Like the average woman in society is not blonde and blue-eyed, the average Black family by no means comes close to the Cosby family But I think what it does, on the other hand, is suggest that there are some Black people and families out there that display those characteristics and qualities. ... I think that it displays the fact that there is hope, and even if that's not a predominant condition in society, I think that just by the mere fact that it's on television says to people in this country that you can get there.

Generally, then, the opportunity cost of having positive Black television characters seems to be a lessening of the concern with the Black condition and a fostering of hope that things can get better. This is perhaps the dilemma that fosters the ambivalence in Black middle-class responses to *The Cosby Show*.

REFERENCES

Asante, M. K. [A. L. Smith]. (1976). Television and Black consciousness. *Journal of Communication 26* (4); 137–41.

Bales, E. (1986). Television use and confidence in television by Blacks and Whites in four selected years. *Journal of Black Studies* 16: 283–91.

Carter, R. G. (1988). TV's Black comfort zone for Whites. *Television (Quarterly* 23 (4): 29–34.

Case, C. E., and A. M. Greeley. (1990). Attitudes toward racial equality. *Humboldt Journal of Social Relations* 16 (1): 67–94.

Cheers, D. M. (1987). The Cosby Show goes to Spelman College for the season finale. *Jet 72* (2): 28–30.

Comstock, G., and R. E. Cobbey. (1979). Television and the children of ethnic minorities. *Journal of Communication* 29 (1): 104–15.

Curry, J. (1986). The cloning of "Cosby." *American Film* 12 (1): 49–52.

Davidson, B. (1986). How Bill Cosby turned 4 kids into stars. *McCall,* September.

Dyson, M. (1989). Bill Cosby and the politics of race. *Z Magazine* 2(3):26–30.

Ehrenstein, D. (1988). The color of laughter. *American Film,* September, pp. 8–11.

Fife, M. D. (1974). Black image in American TV: The first two decades. *Black Scholar,* November, pp. 7–15.

Frank, A. D., and J. Zweig. (1988). Who's making the big bucks? *Reader's Digest,* January, pp. 118–22.

Gates, H. L. Jr. (1992). TV's Black world turns—but stays unreal. In M. L. Andersen and P. H. Collins, eds., *Race, class, and gender: An anthology* (pp. 310–17). Belmont, Calif.: Wadsworth.

Goodlet, C. B. (1974). Mass Communications USA: His feet of clay. *Black Scholar* 6 (3): 2–6.

Gray, H. (1989). Television. Black Americans, and the American dream. *Critical Studies in Mass Communication* 6: 376–86.

Holz, J. R., and C. R. Wright. (1979). Sociology of mass communications. *Annual Review of Sociology* 5: 193–217.

Johnson, R. E. (1986). TV's top mom and dad. *Ebony* 41 (4): 29–34.

———. (1992). The Cosby Show ends after 8 years with a vital message to all young Blacks. *Jet 82* (2): 56–61.

Kassarjian, W. (1973). Blacks as communicators and interpreters of mass communication. *Journalism Quarterly* 50: 285–91.

Landry, B. (1987). *The new Black middle class.* Berkeley: University of California Press.

Leckenby, J. D., and S. H. Surlin. (1976). Incidental social learning and viewer race: "All in the Family" and "Sanford and Son." *Journal of Broadcasting* 20: 481–94.

Lewis, J., and S. Jhally. (1992). *Enlightened racism.* Boulder, Colo.: Westview Press.

Norment, L (1985). *The Cosby Show. Ebony* 40 (6): 27–34.

O'Kelly, C., and L. E. Bloomquist. (1976). Women and Blacks on TV. *Journal of Communication* 26 (4): 179–84.

Poussaint, A. E. (1988). The Huxtables: Fact or fantasy? *Ebony* 43 (12): 72–74.

Seggar, J. F. (1977). Television's portrayal of minorities and women: 1971–75. *Journal of Broadcasting 21:* 435–46.

Stevens, R. (1987). Blacks and Whites, days and nights. *Television Quarterly* 22 (4): 77–87.

Stroman, C. A. (1986). Television viewing and self-concept among Black children. *Journal of Broadcasting and Electronic Media* 30 (1): 87–93.

Stroman, C. A., and L. B. Becker. (1978). Racial differences in gratification. *Journalism Quarterly* 55: 767–71.

Taylor, E. (1989). From the Nelsons to the Huxtables: Genre and family imagery in American network television. *Qualitative Sociology* 12 (1): 13–28.

Teachout, T. (1986). Black, brown and beige. *National Review,* July, pp. 59–60.

Walsh, M. A. (1992). *Cosby* lauded by church officials as series ends. *Florida Catholic,* April 24, p. 14.

Williams, D. A. (1992). The prime time teachings of Dr. Cos. *Emerge* 3 (7): 22–26.

IT'S A RACE WAR

RACE AND LEISURE EXPERIENCES IN CALIFORNIA STATE PRISON

By Laurel P. Richmond and Corey W. Johnson

The purpose of this research study was to use critical race theory to guide the exploration of leisure experiences of men in prison. Ten men reflected upon the time they spent in various California State Prisons, in specific reference to their perceptions of race and power behind bars. The analysis revealed that every decision in prison is made with survival in mind and race is central to determining survival strategies and who has access to power. The system of Racially Organized Prison Politics (ROPP) influenced each and every decision behind bars, including leisure decisions. The supportive themes of indoctrination, maintenance, and structural support were found to reinforce and regulate ROPP. Further research is needed to learn more about the influence of race on institutional support systems.

... it could go down at any time and usually when it does it's racial. It's not really whites on whites, Mexicans on Mexicans, blacks on blacks. You know what I'm saying? It's basically a race war. Once something goes down, it's a race war. (Mark)

Upon incarceration, prisoners are shoved, haphazardly, into an unfamiliar, highly controlled environment with little support to navigate this experience. They no longer make daily personal decisions and must rely on the prison system to feed, clothe, and protect them from other prisoners (Lee, 1996). Surprisingly, they still have exceptional amounts of free time that they must fill with chosen sanctioned activities, in addition to navigating their new identities within the prison setting. Instead of floundering and willingly accepting the regulations imposed by the prison staff, the participants in this study described a peer-imposed system of power that guided daily behavior. The prison setting provides the much-needed opportunity to explore the intertwining topics of race, power, and leisure in an institutional setting. Studying leisure experiences in a controlled environment provides an opportunity to learn more about why leisure decisions are made (Frey & Delaney, 1996) and the role of race in decision-making.

Using prison as a setting, critical race theory as a framework, and the tool of semi-structured interviews, we asked former prisoners to reflect upon their time spent in prison in an effort to generate greater understanding of their experiences. Constant comparative analysis resulted in the identification of patterns of data connected to a core dimension (Corbin & Strauss, 1990) we labeled Racially Organized Prison Politics or ROPP. The sub-categories of indoctrination, maintenance, and structural support all work together to maintain power and position as well as dictate leisure decisions, and are completely intertwined with the core dimension of ROPP (Corbin & Strauss, 1990). And though leisure was experienced differently within prison walls, rather than on the outside—free from the scrutiny of the prison staff and other prisoners; participants remembered the power and privilege derived from or afforded to whiteness on the outside and it had a lingering impact. We found the interconnected system of power and race, created and maintained by the prisoners, existed to promote, protect, and control themselves and others.

Within leisure scholarship, there is a lack of attention paid to institutionalized, structural and hegemonic power associated with both race and leisure. The complex relationship between ROPP and leisure provides researchers unique insight into the relationship between race and the prison experience.

RACE, LEISURE, AND PRISON

Race is a socially constructed term and the definition is constantly under theoretical scrutiny. The scrutiny exists based on new research developments, or the context in which the term is being applied. Researchers have discovered that differences do exist between white and non-white groups as related to leisure experiences. These differences reflect power structures that are not neutral and are not inclusive (Killian, 2001). Phillip (2000) found that places of leisure have become identified as racial locations. Groups and individuals chose activities or leisure spaces based on who has historically participated in these activities or spaces and what groups they may encounter when they leave the comfort of their homes in order to participate.

Leisure provides researchers with space to learn more about our fluid personal identities, based upon the subjectivity of the self (Jackson, 2004). The self we present to the world shifts from moment to moment depending on the context and the power of the persons involved. Race plays a large role in the development and maintenance of our personal identity. Depending on the situation, race can be used to generate more power for oneself, such as when employing the privileges attached to whiteness (McDonald, 2008). Yet, race is fundamentally a social construct used to describe people even as it plays a large role in the creation of identity and the maintenance of power. As leisure scholarship continues to develop, reflection on the past indicates that research surrounding race has evolved. Kivel, Johnson, Scraton (this issue) indicate that leisure scholars have avoided investigating institutional racism as related to leisure in the past, focusing instead on individual differences. The political manner in which leisure operates, often around discourses of race, allows researchers the opportunity to explore the influence that race and leisure may have in perpetuating oppression in society. Glover (2007) reminded us to reflect on the seemingly neutral policies associated with leisure programs that may in fact work to reinforce racial inequity. As leisure operates to oppress people, it can also work to provide opportunities for change and growth in society. In addition, Floyd, Bocarro, and Thompson (2008) noted that leisure researchers must use theories of race and ethnicity in reference to their studies to address the increasing diversity in North America. Addressing the limited understandings of non-dominant people requires the use of more research focused on race within the leisure field.

Leisure researchers are beginning to focus on marginalized prison populations (cf. Pedlar, Yuen, & Fortune, 2008), but the focus is on rehabilitative efforts of the individual and the normalization of behaviors. Rehabilitation is not the focus of American prisons, especially with the continued privatization of prison. The work done by Canadian researchers has brought to light the needs of women prisoners re-entering mainstream society and the role that community plays in this process (Pedlar, Arai, Yuen, & Fortune, 2008). Yet, there is a lack of research on prison systems in the United States and the prison experience itself as an institution that impacts groups. The values held by a nation are reflected in their treatment of prisoners. We can learn much about how a marginalized group is viewed by learning more about prison experiences in different countries.

CRITICAL RACE THEORY & PRISON

In an attempt to bring race, history, and context to a center position and to understand the hegemony prevalent in American society, legal scholars turned to critical race theory (CRT). CRT theorists operate with the understanding that only overt racism, primarily the exclusion of people, was addressed by the civil rights movement. Consequently, the subtle racism that encompasses American society is allowed to continue, supported by the legal system. CRT allows us to investigate race and power, especially in arenas that insist they are devoid of overt, formal racism. Striving for the seemingly simple idea of fair and equal treatment of all without investigating how power is distributed only results in a false sense of equality that CRT is dedicated to addressing within the legal system (Crenshaw, Gotanda, Pellar, & Thomas, 1995).

CRT allows us to explore the social systems at work on a deeper level rather than merely addressing discrimination based on skin color. Racial identity is not cloaked entirely in skin color, but also in culture, community, and politics (Crenshaw et al., 1995). The labeling and subsequent placement of people in undefined and unexplained social categories by researchers perpetuates hegemonic power structures as the reader must use stereotypes to assume what it means to be placed in each category (Kivel, 2000). CRT strives to bring race consciousness to the forefront in contrast to the accepted model of color-blindness, in an effort to combat the limited understanding of how racism exists within hegemonic power structures in American society. As legal studies and the law reinforce white privilege, CRT challenges the construction of race in both legal studies and American culture to understand how white privilege is maintained and how the subordination of minorities continues. Not only must understanding and knowledge be generated by CRT, change must also be supported (Crenshaw et al., 1995).

In an attempt to combat the unequal distribution of power surrounding race and the social construction of race, Hylton (2005) identified five main tenants utilized by CRT. First, race and racism cannot be isolated from power structures and are always impacted by outside influences. Second, CRT calls into question the use of color-blind policies, meritocracy, and so-called objective, race neutral policies. Third, CRT uses techniques of social justice to position the oppressed at the center of the discussion or research and not at the periphery. Fourth, topics examined by white researchers are viewed as truth in relation to race and results in a biased political viewpoint. Therefore, it becomes necessary to perform research from the viewpoint of the other. Fifth, it is useful to use CRT across disciplines, applying information learned to other forms of social sciences, resulting in a transdisciplinary way of exploring race. CRT belief holds that we live in an unequal society, with unequal distributions of power and resources. This distribution of power marginalizes minorities and their position in society (Hylton, 2005).

The greatest impact the legal system has is on those who have been or who currently are incarcerated. Prisoners are tried, convicted, and sentenced by judges and juries intent on following the letter of the law. Not only does the legal system determine the amount of time prisoners must spend behind bars, it also determines how the body is treated and managed while incarcerated. The legal management of the body in prison is not concerned with the exclusion of certain races. In fact, the opposite is true. In California, 28.8% of state prisoners are black, 38.6% are Hispanic, 5.9% are other, and 26.7% are white (California Department of Corrections and Rehabilitation (CDCR), 2007). The racial classification system utilized forces prisoners into one of four classification categories, effectively labeling a person as black, white, Hispanic, or other. As evidenced by the CDCR statistics, the legal system punishes minorities to a greater extent than the privileged whites. In addition, recidivism rates and the high occurrence of extended punishments for crimes committed while in prison contributes to lengthier and more frequent prison sentences. Conviction rates and the subsequent banishment of a now invisible population of minorities behind bars results in a forgotten segment of society. CRT's attempts to address race in the legal system has the potential to reveal the hidden populations of people deemed deviant by society and essentially thrown away and forgotten.

Important cultural differences exist that should not be erased by assimilation into "mainstream" American society. Courts and justice systems punish the body, according to Foucault (1975), but they are also erasing the culture and traditions of entire groups. It is necessary to question why the rate of incarcerated minorities is growing disproportionately to the overall population. What systemic disadvantages take place that result in a higher rate of crimes committed and the subsequent greater numbers incarcerated?

In addition, CRT is a strategy used by scholars to reveal hidden racism in American legal and social systems, as well as in the education system (Lynn, 2004; Parker & Lynn, 2002). Understanding the influence that race has on behavior and recreation choices can be extended to choices made while in prison. Prisoners are expected to behave appropriately behind bars and yet are given no choice as to who they must see and interact with on a daily basis. CRT provides researchers with a tool to analyze systemic disadvantages and offers greater understanding of the impacts race has on leisure choices.

Racial Characteristics of Prison

Prisons are tools used by both the federal and state governments to hold and punish those who have been found guilty of disobeying the laws of society. Sentenced to a specific period of time, prisoners are treated as isolated bodies, sent to prison to be punished. The prisoner is not incarcerated for his crime, but as Foucault (1994) said, for having a "criminal personality" (p. 387). On occasion, prisoners are allowed to work, or attend school or drug programs within the prison walls; however, most often, prisoners are simply held by the government until they have completed their sentence. In California, for example, 53.6% of prisoners are employed and the remaining prisoners are either ineligible or on a waiting list for employment (CDCR, 2007). Researchers found that income impacted incarceration on some levels; however, race did not prove to be a predictor (Arvanites & Asher, 1998). The idea that race has less of an influence upon incarceration rates than income gives further insight into the characteristics of the prison population. Generally, regardless of race, a prisoner may have a greater chance of coming from a low income background.

The CDCR (2007) is responsible for 33 state prisons, which are currently holding 158,437 prison inmates, 93.3% of whom are male. At this time, California does not utilize other racial categories beyond black, white, Hispanic, or other when describing their population. The average reading level is seventh grade and the average age is 37. Per 100,000 residents of California, 461.5 people are incarcerated. This large and growing transitional population of men behind bars has added to the growth of a prison sub-culture. The behavior that the prison sub-culture teaches is then brought to the general population by the release of prisoners back into society. Racial experiences in prison reach outside of the prison walls and into society once each prisoner is released.

Prison Sub-Culture

Prisoners develop their own rules and values to cope with their time behind bars. Hie dominant ideology is that of survival at all cost. Values held by the prison subculture are often at odds with society's values as a whole (Santos, 2004). A prisoner is expected to act one way while in prison, and another when entrenched in mainstream society. Switching from one set of expected behaviors to another is difficult for some and frequently results in a return to prison. Prisoners are more influenced by other prisoners than by correctional officers and have developed a prison code to manage behavior (Schwaebe, 2005). The prison code is defined as "... inmates demonstrated solidarity and loyalty to fellow inmates by sharply distinguishing themselves from prison staff through a set of prescribed behaviors and attitudes" (Schwaebe, 2005, p. 615). The prison code, with its strict behavioral tenets, offers guidelines and orientation to prison life, and guidelines to dealing with correctional staff. Following the prison code also "...involves taking care of one's own problems and never cooperating with the law" (Santos, 2004, p. 100). In this case, the law includes correctional officers who staff the prisons. Once a prisoner learns and follows the prison code, he often is able to stay out of trouble and soon finds himself labeled as a "straight con."

METHODOLOGY

Acknowledging that race is socially constructed, and in an effort to discuss race directly, this study was created along CRT guidelines (Parker & Lynn, 2002). Although by definition a prisoner is not "free," he is still at liberty to choose from a limited amount of daily activities and with whom he associates. The time spent while incarcerated is not all scheduled time; prisoners are able to make personal decisions surrounding how they will fill their free time. These free-choices can reveal cultural attitudes towards race and leisure and thus warrants further exploration.

Study participants responded to ads placed in local newspapers seeking men who had spent at least six months in a California State Prison. We then conducted semi-structured University Institutional Review Board mandated phone interviews with 10 men of various racial identities (five white, two Black, two Hispanic, and one Asian). Each participant was interviewed once, for approximately one hour. With the exception of two interviews, in which the participants requested that they not be recorded, the interviews were recorded and then transcribed. During the two interviews that were not recorded, copious notes were taken by the first researcher, including the use of key phrases and terms. Often, the participants were asked to verify a statement or the meaning of their words during the note taking process. As more phone interviews were conducted, information provided by each participant verified the trustworthiness of previous interviews. In fact, 12 interviews in total were conducted, but two of the original participant's information did not corroborate with the experiences of the other ten men. It soon became clear that these two participants did not meet the requirements of this study and had spent time in a different type of setting. As such, their data were removed.

We asked participants to think back to their time spent in prison and to reflect on both their race and leisure experiences. Participants were asked specific questions about race in the prison environment. They were asked to describe a typical day in prison and to talk about the people with whom they associated. They were also asked if they chose to overtly "display" their race while in prison and how their race influenced their daily decision making. Stories were then elicited and/or probed from these questions. Participants discussed prison sentences that ranged from nine months to ten years and the majority of participants had been released from prison within the 2 years prior to data collection. Several of the participants had been incarcerated more than once and were able to describe numerous descriptive events in which they believed race played a large role.

Interviews were conducted following grounded theory techniques (Corbin & Strauss, 1990), which allowed the researcher to begin data analysis immediately. This data analysis resulted in the development of richer data as the interviews progressed and as the interview questions were adapted to elicit more information concerning race and the prison experience. Once the interviews were transcribed, the first author coded the transcriptions using open and axial coding. During our focused coding, we were able to identify a central theme or core dimension, which interconnected all of the smaller themes that were identified from the data. These themes, also called categories, are comprised of related data that "stand in relationship to the core" and support the main phenomenon described by the core dimension (Corbin & Strauss, 1990, p. 14). The relation of these categories grew together to create the core dimension of Racially Organized Prison Politics, which illustrates the impact of race in the prison system.

FINDINGS

Our findings demonstrated that the core dimension of Racially Organized Prison Politics were impossible to avoid while incarcerated. Participants described a system of prisoner enforced rules that guided daily behavior and decision making solely along racial lines. ROPP was supported by three other main themes including indoctrination, maintenance, and structural support. This section outlines and describes these themes to expose the extent to which race was utilized as a mechanism of social control by the prisoners over other prisoners.

Keeping Race Central: ROPP

Within the California prison system, prisoners exist in an environment that places great emphasis on skin color and racial identity. In fact, the prison that a prisoner is incarcerated in is determined by the time to be served, the type of crime, and the racial identity of the prisoner, as categorized by the State of California. Participants in this study often referred to "politics" when discussing the culture and management of the prison. This language was always used in conjunction with racial terms and therefore we expanded the term "politics" into the new dimension of ROPP. It is impossible to exist independent of the system of ROPP while incarcerated in the California prison system. Therefore, the findings of this study are organized around the major themes of indoctrination, maintenance, and structural support, which work together to inform leisure decisions, under the system of Racially Organized Prison Politics. Hie complex relationships between these themes demonstrated and reinforced the hegemonic power structures at work in the prison setting.

Racially Organized Prison Politics had an influence upon every decision, regardless how seemingly minute, while in prison. Mark, a white man, described ROPP as, "All kind of rules, all types of rules. Couldn't walk in certain areas. Couldn't say certain things. You know, you couldn't really associate with other races like that." ROPP was a tool used by the prisoners to maintain and control daily behavior of the other prisoners based on the visual indicator of skin color. As Lance, a black man, described:

> They call it respect. And they would say something out of anger, just a moment of anger, say something they shouldn't and get people mad about it. And what would happen is if one race said it against another then it involved everybody. This is the way politics are in prison.

Since ROPP was guided solely by race, each participant was categorized upon entering prison, not only by the prison, but also by the other prisoners. This created clearly identifiable group memberships and allegiances.

Indoctrination

Clemmer (1958) stated that prisoners' social relationships are often determined by their experiences on the outside. Participants in this study refuted this assertion and instead described being classified entirely based upon race. They were not able to draw on friendships or other such experiences from the outside in order to maintain a day-to-day existence in prison.

Several of the participants were not aware of how they would be expected to negotiate the prison system. These participants had to learn from other prisoners. Timothy, a white man, learned about ROPP his first day in the system. He said:

> They kinda like give you the rules. Most everybody gets to know what you can do and what you can't do after a few hours of going through the process. They just tell you stuff like you'll have your own sinks; every race will have their own sinks. Or they'll have their own telephones. Like you get in a lot of trouble if you are a white guy and you use a black phone. Or a Mexican phone, I mean you'll get in a fight over something like that.

He quickly became aware of acceptable and unacceptable behavior. The rules had already been created; it was up to the participant to decide to follow them in order to have the most uneventful time in prison as possible. Ken, an Asian man, also learned of ROPP his first day in prison. Ken was immediately labeled as Asian by his looks and was approached by another Asian. He was never asked his race. It was simply assumed by his skin color and appearance that he was Asian. As Ken described, "The leader of the Asian group or whatever, came up to me and introduced himself and said let me tell you where you're gonna sleep, where we eat, what we do, and how it works here."

Mark, a black man, learned about ROPP by listening to others. He further explained how people are grouped and how he learned of the rules he would have to abide by during his time in prison.

> Basically, people talk all day. All they do is talk. So you just listen, be silent. Listen to all the stories, war stories people tell. I'm always just hearing stories, talking about this and that, this and that. Plus, there's always a rep, there's a rep for each race, each race will pretty much inform you when you get to your new house basically. Where you're gonna be staying, there's a rep who will come and get you and pretty much tell you the house rules.

Mark was prepared and knew that he would have to find the dorm representative when he arrived at prison. He knew that he would only be allowed to use certain facilities and was ready to learn the dorm rules. He was labeled immediately upon entering the prison as a black man and was approached by other blacks. Listening provided Mark the opportunity to learn the rules and made his transition into prison life easier.

The indoctrination into ROPP that each participant experienced upon entering the prison system was extremely important in determining his day to day activities and associates. Without learning and abiding by the rules of the prison, violence and mayhem would rule their individual prison experiences. Once the rules were learned, it was necessary to become educated about how the rules were interwoven into daily life.

Maintenance

Once each participant was indoctrinated into the system of ROPP, he would then have to learn how the system was maintained. It was not only necessary for the rules of ROPP to exist; the rules had to be reinforced and upheld. To that end, ROPP itself was a system of self and peer-imposed segregation. As ROPP was a system created by prisoners, it also created an atmosphere of segregation within the prison system. Ken explained the experience he had while in prison. "In the California prison system, I mean, everything, absolutely everything is decided upon and based upon your ethnicity. For instance, myself being Asian, I only associated basically with the other Asians."

Ken also believed that the racial politics and self-segregation were "ridiculous," yet he and the other participants did not try to exist outside of the rules of ROPP. Upon entering the system, they learned that they would have to follow the predetermined rules previously created and maintained by the prisoners. To exist as peacefully and as inconspicuously as possible within the prison system, regardless of agreement or not with ROPP, one still followed the rules. Mark, a black man, stated, "You couldn't mix with others... That's one thing I hated about incarceration. That's how they keep you like, it's like the 1800s or something. It's all segregated." Mark expressed great disgust for the existence and rules of ROPP. Yet, he had no choice but to live within these rules, as the violent consequences were too great. Hassine (1999) experienced this as well and noted that whites and blacks segregate themselves while in prison.

The exception to this was that of the white participants, who carried the privilege of whiteness from the outside into the prison system. They were still expected to know and to enforce the rules of ROPP for other groups, but white men experienced more flexibility when navigating through the prison system. Historically, prisons were racially segregated by state law and this carried over into job assignments as well (Jacobs,

1979). White participants were more likely to hold a job and were able to enjoy the benefits of working while in prison. For example, Dante, a white man, worked in the prison library. He was able to work in an air-conditioned environment that brought relief from the heat of the desert. He would not have experienced that relief without the privilege of working. White participants were also able to navigate among the racial groups with less fear of the consequences. For instance, Dante talked about his ability to associate with the Hispanics who controlled the prison. Dante's whiteness and the privilege attached to it provided him with the freedom to interact with members of the racial group that enforced the racial rules of prison.

Structural Support

ROPP was a system created and maintained by the prisoners to monitor the behavior of other prisoners. All decisions, leisure or otherwise, were influenced almost entirely by ROPP. However, the prison bureaucracy also influenced leisure decisions in prison by maintaining a neutral position on this matter. As McDonald (2008) described, white privilege is allowed to flourish by the appearance of normalcy. All of the participants agreed that ROPP was accepted as part of the prison culture and in fact was endorsed by prison staff by either ignoring the rules or ensuring that white participants navigated the system more easily. Adopting neutral strategies as described by Glover (2007), the staff reproduced racial inequality.

The prison staff, in the opinion of the participants, supported the use of race as a method for controlling prisoners and supporting white privilege. Timothy, a white man, experienced this first hand. He felt that the white prison staff would ensure that white prisoners were treated differently.

> … everyone had to work out. You know push ups, jumping jacks and it was actually a pretty intense, military style work out. And some of the correctional officers would actually walk around and make sure the white guys were doing their exercises.

To maintain white privilege, prison staff ensured the white groups conducted their workouts so that if there were an altercation between races, the whites would be able to dominate.

The prison bureaucracy played a role in the maintenance of the system of ROPP. However, Schwaebe (2005) found that prisoners were more influenced by other prisoners than by prison staff. Prisoners changed their behavior to survive, often in reaction to a system such as ROPP. Yet, order in prison was also maintained by "subtle interplay of relationships" between the prison staff and the prisoners (Bottoms, 1999, p. 210). The balance of rules and power between differing groups within the prison and the prison bureaucracy resulted in a power structure highly influenced by race. Participants had no choice but to live within the system and to decide which rules they would follow and which, if any, they would ignore. Alex found that when one race had more members than another, power shifted into the majority's favor. Yet, Dante's experience of being allowed to keep to himself, as only a white man would be allowed, demonstrated that whites were still able to benefit from their privilege even if they were in the racial minority.

Leisure Decisions

Once each participant became familiar with the basic system-imposed rules of ROPP, they would begin to navigate the prison system and make decisions related to their leisure time. Each prisoner had free time during each day that was his alone to fill. Other than work responsibilities or a drug or education program that required attendance, there were many hours of free time to manage. However, decisions made had to fall within the system of ROPP. As such, the participants believed that race did influence their free time decisions.

Several leisure decisions made while in prison revolved around leisure as a service. Lance spent a great deal of his free time drawing on white handkerchiefs. He would sell his artwork to other prisoners. It was acceptable for Lance to associate with people from other races because he was performing a service and he possessed white privilege. As long as money or goods exchanged hands, he was allowed by ROPP to speak with those of other races to determine what they wanted drawn and how much they would pay for his service. Lance used his leisure time to provide a service that was desirable to other prisoners. Money made the difference in the interaction and it became acceptable for Lance to associate with different races to conduct his business.

Lance's experience as a white man selling a product was extremely different from the situation Timothy described about a Hispanic man who earned money tattooing. This man was able to tattoo other Hispanics and whites, but Timothy observed this man tattooing a black man. Once the Hispanics learned of this, they beat the tattoo artist. It was unacceptable for him to tattoo blacks. ROPP dictated that it was acceptable for Hispanics and whites to interact for the purpose of tattooing, but Hispanics were expressly forbidden from interacting with blacks and this man was punished, regardless of whether or not money was changing hands. Several other instances of this type existed in the larger data set supporting Phillip (2000) who found that places of leisure could be identified as racial locations. There is a degree of welcomeness associated with these leisure places. For example, in this study, it was mentioned that black prisoners were not welcome to watch a Hispanic television. This welcomeness is only one tactic prisoners use to control each other through leisure decision-making. The result is a continued marginalization of certain groups as they are prevented from exercising choice when making decisions.

In Paul's experience as a white man, he found that whites could give something to a person of another race, but he could never take anything from another race. This runs contrary to the experience of Mark, a black man, who was not able to give or receive goods from any person other than another black. White privilege allowed Paul to speak to people who were from other races to give something away, but determined that it was not acceptable for him to take something from someone of another race.

DISCUSSION

The use of ROPP by the prisoners, and the prison's staff support of this system by maintaining neutrality, created a sanctioned use of racial marginalization within prison walls. The classification of others based solely on skin color forces people into visual identification categories. They then must follow the rules of ROPP or face violent consequences. This study provided us with much information in relation to the management of the physical body while in prison and the nature of punishment in relation to race. Finally, implications of this research are presented, along with opportunities for future research.

Privilege and Punishment

Prison exists to hold and punish individuals, based on legal requirements and court sentences. The prison's responsibility is to hold and punish the body, in an effort to prevent and reduce crime. The mind is addressed through rehabilitation; however, rehabilitation is often a low priority as prisons become overcrowded. The management of the body takes precedence over rehabilitation when there is limited space and resources. ROPP allows for the discipline and control of others by groups within the prison setting. ROPP reinforces the prison (and punishment) experience and does not require anything from prison staff. A willingness to look the other way as these men are being punished, and the control of individuals by a group mentality contributes to the greater punishment of incarceration and reinforces tenets of white privilege.

Punishment is political and often in judgment, the legal system is punishing the body for far more than the actual crime (Foucault, 1975). Morality, considerations of future behavior, and speculations as to why the crime was committed all impact punishments. Punishment is only physical in the sense that prisoners are locked up; courts go to great lengths to ensure that the physical body is not harmed or tortured. Prisoners disciplining one another physically may be seen as an extension of the punishment for crimes committed. Continued marginalization based on race, and additional punishment of prisoners outside the guidelines of the court, as supported by ROPP has implications both inside and outside of the prison walls.

Power produces knowledge (Foucault, 1975), reminding us that those holding power within the prison and are also the ones with knowledge of how best to navigate the system. Power and knowledge go hand in hand; one informs the other. Therefore, white participants in this study, holding the privilege and power of whiteness, had more knowledge than other participants about navigating ROPP and how to benefit from the system. However, whiteness is not equal or uniform and is an elastic concept (McDonald, 2008). The power gained from whiteness does not automatically result in the best prison experience possible. The interactions of other social factors (e.g., age, ability, and sexual orientation) work together to determine the privilege attached to whiteness. Yet, the overall impact of whiteness on the prison institution cannot be denied.

The prison system itself produces and reinforces the undesired behavior that initially caused prisoners to be imprisoned (Foucault, 1975). Prisons also do not positively impact the crime rate or prevent recidivism, and the prison experience has lingering effects on the family of the imprisoned. These consequences of the prison system that is meant to punish and then release a reformed man back into society are greater than the system can address.

Social Justice Implications

This study provided a look at how ten men viewed race in prison in relation to their leisure experiences. Participants were required to exist within a racially charged environment and their interviews provided a glimpse into the structural and interpersonal constraints impacting their leisure time decisions. This information detailed a unique social system where race was highlighted, in accordance with the guidelines surrounding critical race theory. Regardless of the fact that whites are only 26.7% of prisoners, they enjoyed greater freedoms, power, and benefits from both the other prisoners and the staff. The prison situation described by participants in this study was one where race was always a concern, as illustrated by the existence of ROPP. Participants discussed and emphasized race in a frank and descriptive manner. This facilitated the engagement of critical race theory and its use as a tool to question power in society and the prison system. In turn, the research also presents opportunities for social justice that works towards change.

We can no longer deny that race exists (Glover, 2007) and impacts the daily experiences of prisoners. The prison itself is a racialized location, but the laws that govern the facility are professed as race neutral. Yet, CRT calls the neutrality of these laws into question. Discrepancies between policies and reality have resulted in a system that allowed ROPP to develop and flourish. CRT requires that for change to occur the laws must directly address race and not continue to reinforce white privilege. The court system must critically evaluate its sentencing policies and investigate the role that whiteness plays in the life situations which results in a prisoner standing before the court. Participants in this study generated information that revealed a prison experience colored by race. Race-neutral policies of the State of California prisoner classification system results in a racially biased system where whiteness benefits.

Social justice requires both liberation and transformation (Hylton, 2005). Use of a critical lens to examine social markers which lead to varied treatment within a system that professes to value neutral policies is required if social justice is to be achieved. To achieve both social justice goals and CRT goals, evaluations of color-blindness should occur. We know that "Color-blind policy initiatives subsequently expunge race while preserving the social, political, economic and cultural status quo" (Glover, 2007, p. 196). Also, Hylton (2005) believed that color-blindness encourages racial disadvantages. This is true in many environments, including the CDCR, where the promotion of color-blind polices has proven to be problematic. Transformation of the legal system is only possible if color-blind policies are abolished.

We now know that race is used as a tool for survival within prison walls. ROPP exists to generate power and maintain privilege and the State of California must critically evaluate the prison system and its basic structure if transformation is to occur. Prisoners themselves may have created the system of prison politics, but the CDCR allows prisoners to enforce these rules by ignoring the system of ROPP and allowing it to become a normal part of prison sub-culture. Looking the other way while ROPP flourishes provides prisoners the opportunity to use race as a tool to generate more power for themselves. Within the current structure, social justice is not possible.

The privilege of whiteness does not begin and end inside the prison system. In keeping with the tenants of CRT, it is important to begin with the color-blind legal system. These color-blind policies actually encompass two groups: one comprised of those who are absent of color and the other of those who are marked by color. Until the privilege of whiteness is eliminated at the stage of arrest and punishment within the court system, it will not be reduced within the prison system. The systemic problem of raced individuals disproportionately experiencing lower incomes, less education, being arrested more often, and sentenced to prison at greater rates than whites is not a problem that can be treated from within prison walls. Liberation from these systemic problems is necessary if change is to be achieved.

Information we learned from the participants tells us about the impacts of whiteness as demonstrated through leisure experiences. We must work backwards from prison to the court system to the home to completely address white privilege in prison. The prison system is working to normalize behavior through punishment (Foucault, 1975); however, the message sent is the standard of white behavior for all prisoners, even though this goal is unreachable as the visual markers of whiteness cannot be achieved.

In addition, ROPP feeds into Foucault's concept of surveillance. Prisoners themselves are observing and monitoring the behavior of others and imposing control through this surveillance. The monitoring of leisure decisions is used as one form of social control and works to reinforce the theory of surveillance.

Aspects of racial identity are constantly expressed simply by staying within one's designated racial group. Prisoners need prison supported programs to help them adjust and develop coping mechanisms (Adams, 1992). In addition, the use of three static categories when describing race does not allow for growth and diversity when thinking about race. The CDCR reduces identity construction into a tight space, only offering the option of "other" to those who cannot be forced into categories of black, white, or Hispanic.

As Frey and Delaney (1996) advised, greater understanding around prisoners and their leisure time will help prison officials better monitor the prison. To prevent violence, understanding that leisure decisions are made based upon race and noticing a shift away from race-based decisions may indicate a potential problem or situation requiring prison officials to respond. In prisons, problems of under-stimulation are likely to be more serious in overcrowded facilities where many prisoners are idle. A boring, monotonous, prison routine not only deprives prisoners from activities to distract from personal concerns and difficulties, but also creates additional stress by reinforcing negative feelings such as emptiness, despondency, and despair (Adams, 1992). The recent removal of recreation equipment and programming from California prisons only adds to the stress of prison life. To transform the institution, social justice changes for prisoners require that quality of life issues, such as recreation, be addressed and not eliminated.

Future Research

Leisure researchers investigating the prison experience have focused on the rehabilitation of individual prisoners (Williams, 2005), the normalizing effects of leisure on rehabilitative efforts (Pedlar, Yuen, & Fortune, 2008), and social inclusion back into local communities after prison (Pedlar, Arai, & Yuen, 2007). The focus on rehabilitation, the post-prison experience, and the individual all result in a lack of attention to the institutional structure that governs behavior. This study only begins to look at institutions as racialized entities. Continued research into prisons, in addition to groups that exist within and influence the structure, reveals the racialized society that exists, and the role leisure plays in maintaining this system. Further, investigation of prison policies in the United States explores alternative ways to sentence and house prisoners, while at the same time, allowing racial freedom. Abolishing ROPP polices is the first step in creating an atmosphere of equality within California's prisons.

McDonald (2008) called for researchers to look at "the various ways whiteness is asserted and resisted via leisure practices and contexts" (p. 26). In addition, white value systems are imposed through recreation (Glover, 2007). Therefore, a critical exploration of the life experiences of both men and women who become incarceration must be undertaken, including the role of leisure. Researchers have looked at women's prison experiences in Canada (Pedlar, Arai, Yuen, 2007; Pedlar, Yuen, Fortune, 2008) but the American focus on punishment rather than rehabilitation creates starkly different prison environments. The daily occurrence of institutional oppressions that result in a large discrepancy in the racial demographics within incarcerated populations must be addressed. Greater understanding of the role that leisure does (or does not) play prior to incarceration may

reveal inadequacies in social support of all citizens. Any future research must employ the idea of change. Change within the system is reinforced by critical race theory and is necessary for a de-marginalization of society.

REFERENCES

Adams, K. (1992). Adjusting to prison life. *Crime and Justice, 16,* 275–359.

Arvanites, T. M., & Asher, M. A. (1998). State and county incarceration rates: The direct and indirect effects of race and inequality. *The American Journal of Economics and Sociology, 57*(2), 207–221.

Bottoms, A. E. (1999). Interpersonal violence and social order in prisons. *Crime and Justice, 26,* 205–281.

California Department of Corrections and Rehabilitation. (2007) Fourth Quarter 2007 Facts and Figures. Retrieved May 22, 2008, from www.corrxa.gov/DivisionsBoards/AOAP/FactsFigures.html.

Clemmer, D. (1958). *The prison community.* New York: Holt, Rinehart and Winston.

Corbin, J., & Strauss, A. (1990). Grounded theory research: Procedures, canons, and evaluative criteria. *Qualitative Sociology, 13*(1), 3–21.

Crenshaw, K., Gotanda, N., Pellar, K., & Thomas, K. (Eds.). (1995). *Critical Race Theory: The Key Writings That Formed the Movement.* New York: The New Press.

Floyd, M. F. (1998). Getting beyond marginality and ethnicity: The challenge for race and ethnic studies in leisure research. *Journal of Leisure Research, 30*(1), 3–22.

Floyd, M. F., Bocarro, J. N., & Thompson, T. D. (2008). Research on race and ethnicity in leisure studies: A review of 5 major journals. *Journal of Leisure Research, 40*(1), 1–22.

Foucault, M. (1975) *Discipline & punish: The birth of the prison.* New York: Vintage Books.

Foucault, M. (1994). Hie subject and power. In J. D. Faubion (Ed.), *Power* (pp. 326–348). New York: New Press.

Frey, J. H., & Delaney, T. (1996). The role of leisure participation in prison: A report from consumers. *Journal of Offender Rehabilitation, 23*(1/2), 79–89.

Glover, T. D. (2007). Ugly on the diamonds: An examination of white privilege in youth baseball. *Leisure Sciences, 29*(2), 199–130.

Hassine, V. (1999) *Life without parole: Living in prison today* (2nd ed.). Los Angeles: Roxbury.

Hylton, K. (2005). 'Race', sport and leisure: lessons from critical race theory. *Leisure Studies, 24*(1), 81–98.

Jackson, A. Y. (2004). Performativity identified. *Qualitative Inquiry, 10*(5), 673–690.

Jacobs, J. B. (1979). Race relations and the prison subculture. *Crime and Justice, 1,* 1–27.

Killian, K. D. (2001). Crossing borders: Race, gender, and their intersections in interracial couples. *Journal of Feminist Family Therapy, 13*(1), 1–31.

Kivel, B. D. (2000). Leisure experience and identity: What difference does difference make? *Journal of Leisure Research, 32*(l), 79–81.

Kivel, B. D., Johnson, C. W., & Scraton, S. J. (2009). (Re)Theorizing leisure experiences and race: Using collective memory work and critical ethnography. *Journal of Leisure Research, 41,* (4), 473–493.

Lee, R. D. (1996). Prisoners' rights to recreation: Quantity, quality, and other aspects. *Journal of Criminal Justice, 24*(2), 167–178.

Lynn, M. (2004). Inserting the 'race' into critical pedagogy: An analysis of 'race-based epistemologies'. *Educational Philosophy and Theory, 36*(2), 153–165.

McDonald, M. G. (2008). Dialogues on whiteness, leisure, and (anti)racism. *Presented at the George Butler Lecture, Leisure Research Symposium, National Recreation and Parks Association Conference, Baltimore, MD.*

Parker, L., & Lynn, M. (2002). What's race got to do with it? Critical race theory's conflict with and connections to qualitative research methodology and epistemology. *Qualitative Inquiry, 8,* 7–22.

Pedlar, A. M., Arai, S. M., & Yuen, F. (2007). Media representation of federally sentenced women and leisure opportunities: Ramifications for social inclusion. *Leisure/Loisir, 31,* 255–276.

Pedlar, A. M., Arai, S. M., Yuen, F., & Fortune, D. (2008). Uncertain futures: Women leaving prison and re-entering community. *Research Report.* Retrieved from http://www.ahs.uwaterloo.ca/uncertainfutures. Waterloo, ON: University of Waterloo.

Pedlar, A. M., Yuen, F., & Fortune, D. (2008). Incarcerated women and leisure: Making good girls out of bad? *Therapeutic Recreation Journal, 42*(1), 24–36.

Phillip, S. (2000). Race and the pursuit of happiness. *Journal of Leisure Research, 32*(1), 121–124.

Santos, M. G. (2004). *About prison.* Belmont, CA: Thomson Wadsworth.

Schwaebe, C. (2005). Learning to pass: Sex offenders' strategies for establishing a viable identity in the prison general population. *International Journal of Offender Therapy and Comparative Criminology, 49*(6), 614–625.

Williams, D. J. (2005). Functions of leisure and recreational activities within a sexual assault cycle: A case study. *Sexual Addiction and Compulsivity, 12,* 295–309.

Afterword

By Robin Dearmon Muhammad

The story of black struggles is still being written. While the persistence of white privilege is evident, so is the triumph of ordinary black citizens over rampant employment discrimination, cultural marginalization, and modern-day disenfranchisement through the prison industrial complex.

Through these readings we have engaged in rigorous thinking, research, analysis, and synthesis of matters pertaining to the African American experience in the United States. While many courses on African American history are available in various formats, the use of this text allows students to discuss, intelligently and with respect for the opinions of others, present-day controversies surrounding race and ethnicity in the United States. Whether this is your first course in African American Studies or this one of many, you can see how your role as a student is critical to situating these texts in real-life experiences. It has been the intent of this textbook to allow each student an opportunity to develop essential 21st-century skills based on (a) having examined the legal, political, economic, cultural, and historical antecedents of such issues and (b) having learned how these matters are interconnected.

This textbook also attempts to reflect the variety of careers students of African American Studies enter: education, public service and the arts. Among the many worthwhile disciplines to study, African American Studies has a unique place among other interdisciplinary efforts: emerging from the human rights struggles of the late twentieth century, African American Studies has always been explicitly engaged in questioning the status quo, recovering the past Africana people and empowering all students of the black experience to fulfill their quest for a representative mosaic of experiences.

CPSIA information can be obtained
at www.ICGtesting.com
Printed in the USA
LVHW060822200122
708844LV00004B/105